HAZLE BUCK EWING

These pages are dedicated to
my beloved husband, Chuck,
who has so selflessly supported the
writing of this book in all ways. It truly
would not have come to be without him.

HAZLE BUCK EWING

*Promoter of Peace on Earth
and Good Will toward Men*

By
Karen Griep Heilbrun

Shimmering Swan Creations: Aurora, Oregon

Hazle Buck Ewing:
Promoter of Peace on Earth and Goodwill toward Men

First Edition
Copyright © 2010 by Karen Griep Heilbrun
Published by Shimmering Swan Creations, Aurora, Oregon.

Printed in the United States of America.

The research and writing were done by Karen Griep Heilbrun.
Photographs are used by permission of Lucinda (Cindy) Buck Ewing
and The Principia.

Cover photograph of Hazle Buck Ewing is used by permission
of Lucinda Buck Ewing.

The writings by Mary Baker Eddy and hymns from the *Christian Science
Hymnal* are used by permission of The Mary Baker Eddy Collection a
division of The First Church of Christ, Scientist in
Boston, Massachusetts.

ISBN 978-0-9830618-4-7

Library of Congress Cataloging Number 2010917719

TABLE OF CONTENTS

FOREWORD

$\mathcal{I}$ am a great believer in stories, especially when they help one see and feel in new ways. This biography of my Grandmother Ewing certainly does meet those criteria. The account of her life demonstrates how one's situation and resources, together with large measures of persistence and grace, can serve the greater good.

Hazle (she and all of the family have spent time and ink making sure the l precedes the e) Buck Ewing was ahead of her times in many ways; actively involved in a variety of causes. I knew she was a suffragette, a founder of a boys' home, a staunch advocate for the League of Nations and United Nations, protector of the environment, and proponent of cross cultural understanding and education. I knew also that she cared deeply about her family, church, and community.

What I did not know was the depth and breadth of her active engagement in all the above. It is remarkable what comes to light through intentional and thorough research such as Karen Griep Heilbrun has done. Myriad correspondence provided a wealth of information and nuance that added dimensions I have not encountered before. Until now I have been content with accounts and recollections read or heard. For instance, "Hazle picketed the White House for women's right to vote." She did not, but she was a major supporter of the suffrage movement financially and strategically.

I am but one of many whose life and values were shaped by her presence, however brief or longstanding. I do not remember many extended conversations with Grandmother, but my love of travel, global and local work with women's and human rights, peace and justice mirror hers. My hope that my photography helps people see across cultural divides is a visual echo of her School of Nations. I do remember her teaching me how to ride horses and to love, respect, and care for all in the natural world.

Hazle Buck Ewing's vision, integrity, and determination come through the author's rich narrative of her purposeful and purpose filled life. May we all take note.

Lucinda (Cindy) Buck Ewing
Carmel, California
October 2010

AUTHOR'S PREFACE

*T*he journey to recording Hazle Buck Ewing's life-story began before I even knew anything about her. The summer following my junior year at Principia College in Elsah, Illinois, I had the opportunity to participate in an internship that involved writing biographical sketches about women who had established lodges and/or related businesses in Estes Park, Colorado. What I learned about researching and writing while working on the Estes Park project gave me the skills I would need to write Hazle's biography.

During my senior year at Principia, I began an independent study course focused on writing the biography of one individual. It was in April 2005 that I first learned of Hazle Buck Ewing in the basement of the School of Nations building, the location of the College archives. Majoring in English, I spent much time in classrooms in the School of Nations building, but I knew nothing about the School of Nations program, the woman who founded it, or the history of the building. The drama of Hazle's accomplishment unfolded as I daily pored over letters to her and from her and other information available in the archives. I soon became Hazle's ardent admirer.

I discovered that Hazle had a deep interest in education and for many years supported The Principia. She gave generously to the College on the Elsah campus and the Upper and Lower Schools located on the St. Louis campus. She made donations of land for the expansion of the school, as well as substantial financial contributions. Hazle founded the School of Nations program and Museum, provided funds for students to attend the school, promoted the school on her travels around the United States and abroad, and served as a member of The Principia Board of

Trustees for thirty years. She actively participated in the Principia community—attending talks, conferences and commencement exercises, in addition to Board meetings.

Hazle lived most of her adult life in Bloomington-Normal, Illinois, where she and her husband Davis built the home they had designed, known as Sunset Hill. The first time I visited Hazle's home, I was quite taken with the elegant winding staircase and highly polished wooden floors. A tour of the house and grounds revealed her attention to decorative details, furnishings and landscaping. I also learned that she took a deep interest in her Sunset Hill neighbors and the community of Bloomington at large, donating land for two public parks. She supported Illinois State University in Normal, Illinois, which was not far from her home. Currently Sunset Hill is the Ewing Cultural Center and is owned by Illinois State University—a gift from Hazle.

In the Milner Library Archives at Illinois State University in Bloomington, I found an abundance of material pertaining to Hazle's involvement in woman's suffrage and her interest in politics. The McLean County Historical Museum provided much information about Hazle's activities in the community and her correspondence with Adlai E. Stevenson II. At the Children's Foundation, I was generously supplied with information about Hazle's active participation in establishing Victory Hall, a home for boys, shortly after the end of World War I.

Through my research, Hazle's lifelong involvement with nature emerged. It intrigued me to discover that at an early age she disciplined herself to learn how to identify flowers, trees, and birds any season of the year. As an adult, she actively supported conservation efforts in her home state and around the country. Hazle also maintained and enjoyed domestic animals and had a special affinity with horses. She owned horses during her residence in Bloomington and went horseback riding nearly every day. She even transported her horses to the family ranch in Wisconsin every summer where she vacationed.

The privilege of interviewing individuals who knew Hazle reaffirmed and expanded upon what I had already discovered of Hazle's deep concern for and helpfulness toward her fellow man. A few of those interviewed had known Hazle when they were youngsters in Bloomington, while others had been at Principia when Hazle was a member of the Board of Trustees and were there when the School of Nations building was erected in Elsah. I also had the opportunity to talk with a few relatives of Hazle. The personal interviews revealed that Hazle had a positive influence on the lives of those around her, not only by what she said, but by what she did. She took a deep interest in others and encouraged them to pursue their dreams.

To those nearest and dearest to her, Hazle expressed her strong belief that the right kind of education could resolve international difficulties caused by cultural differences and would ultimately result in world peace. She provided a good example by acting on her desire to promote peace—a desire that was never far from her thoughts—by establishing the School of Nations at Principia College.

I returned to my home in Oregon after graduating from college and continued to research and write about Hazle's life. During that time, I had two phone interviews with Hazle's granddaughter, Lucinda (Cindy) Buck Ewing. In our second telephone conversation we decided that it would be helpful for me to visit her at her home in Santa Fe, New Mexico. Cindy had saved boxes filled with articles, letters, journals, photographs, and other information pertaining to her grandmother. One of the items was the journal Hazle started writing at the beginning of the ten-month world trip she took with her husband, Davis, and their son, Ralph in 1924. Although Hazle discontinued making any entries in her journal after only a few weeks, she did write many letters home to her good friend, Julia Fairfield Hodge, who had saved them. In order to learn more about their trip, a pivotal point in Hazle's experience, I spent most of my ten-day stay at Cindy's immersed in the bound journals comprised of letters Davis wrote home to his family during that time. In addition to the information Cindy had stored in boxes, she openly shared with me her memories of her grandmother. I had learned a great deal about Hazle by the end of my stay, but there were many letters I did not have time to read. Thankfully, Cindy allowed me to take the letters as well as some photographs home with me. These family treasures proved to be invaluable in gaining some understanding of Hazle's relationships with her family members and friends.

From the beginning of this journey, I have been led to the right individual at the right time to assist me with what I needed to know or do, making the whole process of researching and writing about Hazle's life a most interesting as well as enriching experience. I have been deeply impressed by Hazle's exceptional depth and breadth of patience and persistence, exemplary compassion and care for others, extraordinary philanthropy, and her variety of interests. What moved me most, however, was the remarkable foresight and determination required of Hazle in order to accomplish her dream of establishing the School of Nations at Principia College. My deep desire is that all who read the pages of this book will also find Hazle's well lived life a source of inspiration and hope.

Karen Griep Heilbrun
July 25, 2010

ACKNOWLEDGMENTS

aterials for this book came from a variety of sources, including historical societies, college and university archives, libraries, and newspapers in the state of Illinois, as well as personal interviews. A debt of gratitude is owed to each one involved. I wish to express my sincere thanks to the following past and present members of the Principia College community: Jonathan W. Palmer, President of Principia College; Jane Pfeifer, Principia College Archivist; Lynn Horth, English Department Head; Dinah Ryan, English Professor; Carolyn G. Burns, staff member; Ruth and Warren Clinton, of Estes Park, Colorado; and John Glen, History Professor; also to those who provided assistance in Bloomington-Normal, Illinois: Rebecca Ann Landau, Executive Director of Ewing Properties for Illinois State University; Jo Ann Rayfield, Archivist at Milner Library, Illinois State University, Normal; Bill Steinbacher-Kemp, Librarian/Archivist, and Preston Hawks Assistant Librarian/Archivist, of McLean County Museum of History; Patricia O'Dell, former Regional Development Manager, and Lisa Pieper, current Regional Development Manager, of the Children's Foundation; and Sally Ulrich of The Mary Baker Eddy Collection, a department of The First Church of Christ, Scientist, in Boston, Massachusetts; the staff of the Bloomington Public Library; Eden Juron Pearlman, Curator of Collections at Evanston Historical Society; the staff of the University of Chicago Archives; the staff of the Wesleyan University Archives, Bloomington, Illinois.

Also, to those individuals who provided information through personal interviews, I wish to express my deep appreciation: Lucinda (Cindy) Buck Ewing, granddaughter of Hazle; Nancy Ranson, niece of Hazle; Alice Taylor Reed, former resident of Bloomington and student of Principia College; Cecily Quantinilla, niece of Alice Taylor Reed; Helen Andrews, wife of David Andrews, former President of Principia College; Jeff and Beth Carey, former students of Principia; Ned Bradley, former French Professor at Principia College; Jennifer Bunting Dyck, former Spanish teacher at Principia Upper School; Art Eiff, former resident of the Sunset Road community; Gwen Edwards and Jeanne Wroan, co-authors of *Sunset Road: History and Memories*.

Without the assistance of Lucinda (Cindy) Buck Ewing, Hazle's granddaughter, information about Hazle's personal life would not have come to light. Cindy has carefully collected and saved journals, letters, photographs, and her memories, all of which she freely shared with me. She has been a great supporter and encourager of this work since she first learned of it, for which I am truly grateful.

Jane Pfeifer, Principia College Archivist, supplied the answer to the all-important question of who would be a good subject for my first biography, for which I am profoundly thankful. Jane firmly believed Hazle Buck Ewing, as the founder of the School of Nations at Principia, to be a most interesting and worthy woman. She could not have been more right. Jane has been an invaluable source of information and encouragement through the entire process of researching and writing this book.

Lynn Horth, my academic advisor and the head of the English Department at Principia College, encouraged me to apply for a writing internship in the summer of 2004 in Estes Park, Colorado and suggested that we develop an independent study course focused on writing a biography about one individual. For her wise counsel, I am most grateful.

To Ruth and Warren Clinton, who gave me the opportunity to write biographical sketches of Estes Park women and enabled me to learn the skills needed for future writing projects, I wish to express my heartfelt gratitude.

Dinah Ryan guided me through the Estes Park internship experience and enabled me to complete it successfully, for which I am deeply thankful.

Rebecca Ann Landau, Executive Director of Ewing Properties allowed me to spend hours doing research at the Ewing Cultural Center, Hazle's former home, and to take more than one tour of the house and grounds. I wish to express my gratitude for her assistance.

To Jo Ann Rayfield, Archivist of the Milner Library at Illinois State University, I want to express my appreciation for providing materials pertaining to Hazle's involvement with the woman's suffrage movement.

Bill Steinbacher-Kemp, Librarian/Archivist, and Preston Hawks, Assistant Librarian/Archivist at the McLean County Museum of History in Bloomington, gave me access to invaluable information about Hazle's community activities and answered my many questions for which I want to express my gratitude.

Art Eiff generously told me about his experiences growing up on Sunset Road and his friendship with Hazle, for which I am deeply appreciative. It was fortunate that Art happened to be visiting in Bloomington from Europe when I was there doing research about Hazle.

Gwen Edwards and Jeanne Wroan also provided information about the Sunset Road community, for which I am most thankful.

I wish to thank Patricia O'Dell, former Regional Development Manager of the Children's Foundation, for permitting me to read and use information taken from the early Board minutes for Victory Hall; I also extend my gratitude to her successor, Lisa Pieper, for her willingness to support this project.

To those individuals who assisted in editing, designing and printing this book, I wish to express my grateful appreciation: Carolyn G. Burns, my good friend and staff member of Principia College, faithfully read through each chapter and offered many helpful suggestions for improvement and helped me to keep moving forward; Serena Sinclair Lesley assisted me to clarify my writing through her journalistic experience and expertise; Chris Nordquist ably edited the manuscript for publication and expressed sincere interest in and enthusiasm for Hazle's story; Gail Watson, owner of Creative Print Services, LLC, who provided the book layout and jacket design; and Madge Walls, of All Sky Indexing, who prepared the index.

The support of my family has always meant a great deal to me, and I wish to express my gratitude to each one of them.

This book is dedicated to my dear husband, Chuck, to whom I owe the greatest gratitude and appreciation. In keeping with his thoughtful nature, he has never failed to provide whatever has been needed. He is my champion.

Thanks be unto God.

Karen Griep Heilbrun
Aurora, Oregon

THE DREAM

CHAPTER 1

THE LETTER

*H*azle breathed in the crisp, cool, early morning air and settled down in her favorite place in the garden where she could feel the warmth of the sun on her back. Removed from the demands of daily life, she prayed with a heart yearning for a practical way to promote world peace. Even as a child in grade school, discovering that the history of the world seemed to be almost entirely about war, she desperately wanted the peoples of the world to live in peace. She had protested against war and international discord through the only avenue available to her at that time: writing school papers on that topic. Today, seeking a more tangible way to fulfill her heart's desire, she turned to the Bible and *Science and Health with Key to the Scriptures* by Mary Baker Eddy and began reading the "Daily Bible Lesson." As she read, the answer that she had been seeking suddenly came to her, and she knew what she needed to do.

On November 7, 1925, after discussing the idea with her husband, Davis, she wrote a letter to Frederic Morgan, the President of The Principia, a school for Christian Science children located in St. Louis, Missouri. With Davis's approval, she told Morgan, "Mr. Ewing and I should like to see at the new Principia University . . . as fine a School of International Relations as there is in this country."[1] She had confidence in Morgan's ability to recognize the importance of what they were proposing, and she believed he would be willing to implement the idea if she and Davis offered to support it financially.

3

Shortly after she wrote the letter to Morgan, she went to Chicago to visit her mother, Lillian Brewer Buck. Desiring to discuss her idea with him as soon as possible, however, she informed him that he could reach her at her mother's home. Hazle and her mother shared a mutual interest in (and dedication to) Christian Science. It was through an experience of her mother's that Hazle had been introduced to Christian Science. Some years earlier, Lillian came down with a serious illness. She had sought help from doctors and specialists of all types, but none could offer her a cure. One day, a friend of hers jokingly suggested that she try Christian Science. She decided she had nothing to lose and contacted a Christian Science practitioner to pray for her. Healed by the prayer of the practitioner, she became a devout Christian Scientist. Following her mother's healing, Hazle became a serious student of the religion.[2]

As a Christian Scientist living in the mid-West, Hazle knew the history of The Principia and agreed with and supported its educational philosophy. Frederic Morgan's mother, Mary Kimball Morgan, had founded the school, after investigating the public schools in St. Louis, Missouri, in 1897. What Mrs. Morgan learned about the education of children in the public schools did not agree with her understanding and application of Christian Science in regard to raising and educating her two sons. As a result, she searched for and discovered what she considered to be acceptable textbooks and began teaching her own sons, Frederic and William, in the fall of 1897. A friend of the boys soon joined them.[3] By the fall of 1898, Mrs. Morgan had 15 students and had hired another teacher.

At that point, she named the school "The Principia" and founded it on her educational philosophy, which included not only the intellectual, physical, and social development of children, but the moral and spiritual aspects as well. *Principia* is a Latin word for principle, which means governing rules and dominion. Morgan based her school on the governing rules of Spirit, which, when obeyed, gives one dominion. She founded her educational system on the "concept of man" that she found on page 475 of the Christian Science textbook, *Science and Health with Key to the Scriptures* by Mary Baker Eddy. Mrs. Morgan endeavored to live, and to teach her students to live, this concept of man both in and outside the classroom.

Upon this educational foundation, The Principia grew and prospered, and, in the spring of 1906, the school had its first high school graduation.[4] It became an accredited Junior College in 1917.[5] Mrs. Morgan appointed her son, Frederic Morgan, to be the Executive Director of The Principia in 1919, providing him with guidance, as needed, in the administration of the school.[6] On May 30, 1922, it was announced that The Principia would build a four-year college.[7] Prior to this announcement, Clarence H. Howard had purchased and held a suitable tract of land in St. Louis, known as Loch Lin, for just such an expansion. When Hazle learned of the possibility of Principia having a four-year college, her fifteen-year-old son, Ralph, was attending the school. As tangible evidence of her support of this project, she donated 15 acres of woodland in 1923, which bordered the tract of land purchased by Howard.[8]

Although the school now had the land on which to build a college, it needed funding for the construction and an architect to design it. During their search for an architect, the administrators contacted Bernard R. Maybeck, who was well-known for his work in San Francisco. Maybeck had studied at several European schools, including the Sorbonne, and also at the University of California, and he had substantial experience in designing college and university buildings. He had worked for the University of California and on the planning of the Mills College campus in Oakland, California. Maybeck accepted Principia's offer to work on the project, and he visited the campus in April of 1923, staying for several weeks.[9]

In the meantime, the lack of funds to build and establish the four-year college remained unresolved. Although the Junior College at Principia had been accredited in 1917, administrators had not been able to secure the $200,000 needed in its endowment fund as required by the North Central Association in order to maintain accreditation. This fact added to the challenge of obtaining at least $2 million to build the college. Despite these difficulties, Hazle remained enthusiastic about the idea of a four-year college. She felt completely confident that Mrs. Morgan and The Principia would meet this challenge as they had met others in the past. It was her confidence in the administrators of the school and their educational philosophy that prompted her to propose to Morgan that an International School of Relations should be part of the new college.

Frederic Morgan responded promptly to Hazle's letter, sending a telegram to her mother's home on November 10, 1925, telling her, "Your wonderful letter received."[10] He added that Mr. Clarence Howard, Vice President of the Board of the Trustees of The Principia and Mr. Thomas E. Blackwell, business manager for the college, planned to arrive in Chicago at 2:30 on the afternoon of November 11. They would meet with her any time or place she named, and Morgan would join them.

Hazle met with Morgan, Howard, and Blackwell on November 11, as Morgan had proposed. Two days later, Blackwell telegraphed her that Morgan was leaving for the east with Maybeck to gather more ideas for designing the new college campus buildings. Morgan had requested him "to express our deepest appreciation of your desire to see at the new Principia University 'as fine a School of International Relations as there is in this country.'"[11]

A few days later, on November 17, 1925, Davis and Hazle received a letter from Arthur T. Morey, President of the Board of Trustees of The Principia, expressing the board's interest in their proposal of a School of International Relations. He admitted "it is becoming increasingly apparent that only the Truth can pour oil on the troubled waters and save the world."[12] He further pointed out:

> India is in fermentation; the Mohammedan world is in
> motion; China is awakening with Bolshevism next door;
> Russia is doing things that appear to us as inconceivable;
> and they say conditions in England are pretty bad. I see
> in the morning paper that a movement has started in
> France to have a dictator instead of a republic.[13]

Morey recognized the importance of their proposal, and told them,
"Our young people need to have a world vision and full reason for
the faith that is in them and have confidence in the Truth." [14] He
believed that a School of International Relations would have a
profound influence on the lives of many Principia students in the
years to come.

   Although the idea of a School of International Relations was
being broadly discussed by the board of trustee members and the
administration, it took them some months to formulate a plan
of action. Consequently, through the winter months, Hazle did
not receive any news regarding a plan to establish a School for
International Relations at Principia. She patiently waited to see how
her proposal would unfold, and in late April of 1926, she received
a letter from Morgan informing her of the discussions of her idea,
which had included Gardner Chase Anthony, the department
head of the Engineering School at Tufts University.[15]

   It pleased Hazle to know that her idea had received so much
attention and that some important steps had been taken to make
the School of International Relations a reality. The board and
administration had chosen George A. Andrews, who currently
headed the History department, to study the proposal and determine
how to implement it. He had been given a leave of absence in order
to devote his full attention to this project. Andrews planned to
interview men and women all over the country in search of ideas
that would assist them in fulfilling Hazle's vision.[16]

A 1907 high school graduate from Principia, Andrews had a sincere interest in the success of the College. He had given up his job with the Navy to work at Principia for one-third his naval pay, and he and his wife, Frances, had enrolled their four boys in the school. Andrews had graduated from the United States Naval Academy at Annapolis and had attended Boston Tech from which he had graduated among the top three in his class. But what especially qualified Andrews for this assignment was his life-long study of history and international relations.

Morgan wanted to arrange a meeting between Hazle and Andrews before Andrews's summer activities at the Institute of Politics in Williamstown, Virginia, consumed all of his time. In the fall, Andrews intended to explore the possibilities of implementing Hazle's idea for a School of International Relations. Morgan told Hazle, "It seems to all of us that a most wonderful idea has been unfolded," and he added, "To undertake the study of international relations as a basis for friendship, and according to the teachings of Christian Science, certainly opens up an entirely new field of thought."[17]

Hazle responded to Morgan's letter on May 3, 1926, telling him, "Rather interestingly your plan is about exactly the one that has gradually taken form in my own thought—and I have been planning to write to you of it."[18] She suggested that she meet him or Andrews at the Bloomington, Illinois, train station on May 4, because she would be leaving that day for three weeks. In case that date did not work for them, she added, May 25 was another possibility—if that wasn't too late to meet.

The meeting was set for May 4, but Andrews apparently did not arrive on time, and Hazle's train pulled out of the station before the meeting could take place. Andrews wrote to her the next day, "Last evening, I was very much chagrined to think that my arrangements for meeting you at the station were so ineffective." Although disappointed that he had bungled their meeting plans, Andrews expressed his enthusiasm for her idea: "It seems to me to give a field of the finest kind of constructive endeavor, and to provide a new channel for introducing the leaven into the lump of the world thought and international understanding."[19] He recognized that courses of this nature would require "specialization in foreign languages to obtain a speaking knowledge of them, rather than merely literary acquaintance."[20] He also thought that history, political science, and international law would be needed. He suggested that economics and commercial law could be substituted for international law and political science to prepare students for employment in international trade and banking. He believed that this program would draw students to Principia from foreign countries where Christian Science was growing.[21]

Morgan also wrote a letter of apology to Hazle for not being able to meet her at the train station. He reaffirmed Principia's desire to be in close contact with her regarding the work they were doing on the School of International Relations. He believed that this work should be kept confidential until their plans had been firmly established. Then, they would make an announcement to the faculty and staff regarding the work that had been done.

On June 8, Hazle had time to catch up on her correspondence. She wrote a post card to Andrews telling him that she had received his letter of May 5 and had found it "thoroughly interesting."[22] Since she would be leaving again in two weeks, she wondered if he could come up from St. Louis to Bloomington to meet with her early the next week. She also wrote to Morgan agreeing that the plans for the School of International Relations should be kept quiet until they were completed. She assured Morgan that the only people who knew about the plans on her end were Davis, Ralph, and her mother, Lillian.[23]

A three-page letter Hazle received from Andrews on September 17, 1926, made it apparent that Andrews's activities had revolved around their joint project since their last meeting, and he had given it a lot of thought over the summer. He believed that he could give her a more detailed report in person, and suggested that he come see her as soon as possible. He had gone to Chicago to attend the last week of lectures given at the Harrison Foundation and talked with Professor Quincy Wright. His talk with Wright had convinced him that their main focus should be on studying cultures of other countries, rather than on politics.[24]

While at Williamstown, he had the opportunity to interview several men, including Dr. McLaren, secretary of the Institute of Politics, who expressed great interest in the project and offered his assistance in securing lecturers on the subject. Another lecturer at Williamstown, William Abbott, editor of *The Christian Science Monitor*, invited Andrews to visit him in Boston, which he did a week later. But Andrews assured Hazle he had not mentioned any names. Abbott expressed an interest in the program and a willingness to cooperate in whatever way he could. He also told Andrews that the *Monitor* would be interested in hiring Principia students who could speak foreign languages as correspondents.

Andrews also had a long talk with Stephen Pierce Duggan, Director of The Institute for International Education that is financed by Carnegie. Duggan seemed quite interested in the project, and he promised to introduce Andrews to others who might be of assistance. Andrews told Hazle, "It is so apparent that the practical application of the Golden Rule in daily living is the means of bringing an end to strife, that it seemed astonishing that many of the members of the Institute who are people of wide experience and who are devoting their lives to the promotion of peace, should neglect, often in their own daily contacts, such an obvious remedy."[25]

Hazle responded to Andrews's lengthy letter on December 19, 1926, assuring him that it was not because of a lack of interest she had not written sooner, but she had been out of town. She explained that she would have more time in January when they could meet to discuss his ideas on how to implement her proposal for the School of International Relations.[26]

On December 27, Andrews reassured Hazle that he understood she had other commitments to fulfill, and he had not been concerned about her lack of immediate response. But he did have more information to share with her since his last letter. He had made a trip to the congress of The World Alliance for International Friendship held in Pittsburgh. While there, he had the opportunity to talk to Albert F. Gilmore, editor of the Christian Science publications, who represented The Mother Church at the meeting. In addition, he had an interview with Professor James T. Shotwell of New York. He had also gone to Washington, D.C., with Anthony, who had been the Dean of Engineering at Tufts University, but "is now devoting himself to Principia." Andrews and Anthony met with James Brown Scott of the Carnegie Foundation and others "who would be helpful to us."[27] Andrews told her that Morgan proposed a meeting in the latter part of January when Anthony would be back from Boston. Hazle looked forward to meeting with Andrews, Morgan, and Anthony in January of 1927.

Her idea for a School of International Relations originated during a trip around the world that she and her family took from August 1924 to September 1925. It now seemed the idea could become a reality. In her memory, vivid scenes remained of children and adults living in poverty, filth, ugliness, fear, and war—yet expressing beauty, faith, and the resiliency of the human spirit. These experiences had prompted her to write that initial letter to Morgan, thus instigating this new School of International Relations.

THE TRIP

CHAPTER 2

WORLDS AND WORLDS OF PEOPLE

*H*azle had long cherished the desire to take a trip around the world, which would be extensive and thorough enough to give her a deeper understanding of the cultures and customs of peoples in other lands. She had kept a copy of the book, *The Art of Travel: the Laboratory Study of Civilization*, written by Harry Huntington Powers, since girlhood, believing that she would one day be able to apply the ideas it contained. And now her desire would be fulfilled. In 1923, her husband, Davis, reorganized the well-established concrete business he had started in the early 1900s, initially to lay concrete sidewalks. It had grown to include the 100-year fence posts, concrete building blocks, and concrete silos, for which he held patents in the United States and Canada. During the reorganization of his company, Davis renamed it "The Permanent Productions Company" and established another office in Chicago to accommodate the need for a large sales organization. He wisely located his main office in Bloomington, on East Emerson Street, not far from the Illinois Central Railroad, making it convenient to ship his products around the country.[28]

By 1924, Davis found that it would be possible for him to be away from his business for an extended period of time, thus enabling the Ewings to go on a long awaited ten-month trip around the world with their seventeen year-old son, Ralph. Hazle and Davis departed from Bloomington on August 1 to meet Ralph, who had gone ahead of his parents to visit some friends in Colorado Springs, Colorado.

While in Colorado, the family enjoyed a few days together in the
Rocky Mountain National Park before going on to San Francisco
and boarding the SS Siberia Maru.

Their world trip officially began on August 15, at noon, as the
ship they had boarded sailed through the Golden Gate and headed
for Honolulu. A cold west wind chilled them to the bone, but the
next morning they awakened to the comforting warmth of a bright,
sunny day on the open sea. On August 19, Diamond Head rose up
before them on the horizon. After several hours of waiting, they
landed on Waikiki Beach, Hawaii, and enjoyed dinner at the Moana
Hotel. They spent their short time on the islands being tourists in
the mornings and students in the afternoons, listening to lectures
on Buddhism and Brahmanism to prepare them for the first stop on
their world tour—Japan.[29]

Arriving in Tokyo on the first of September, they were greeted
by the sight of devastation and destruction left by an earthquake
that had occurred nearly a year earlier. As they disembarked from
the ship, the sobering scene of the ruins momentarily dampened
their enthusiasm. But, upon entering the city, their initial shock
subsided, and the tourists regained their sense of adventure.

The Imperial Hotel in Tokyo, designed by Frank Lloyd Wright
and built to withstand the shock of earthquakes, became their first
home away from home.[30] Their tour guide and instructor during this
portion of the trip was Dr. A. K. Coomaraswamy, an East Indian
born in Ceylon and educated in England, who currently held the
position of Curator at the Eastern Art Museums. He took them to
visit many of the Buddhist temples and shrines in the city, which
Davis thoroughly enjoyed.

Hazle thought the people, landscape, and animals to be much
more interesting. The village of Nikko reminded her of Switzerland
with its lovely wooded mountains. And the sight of "an old white-
robed priest using all his strength to pull a great log that sounds
the bell" remained etched in her memory.[31] At the train station

in Nikko on September 7, Hazle waited for Davis, who had gone out early to take some pictures of a temple. She watched a "little old woman street cleaner" who "was hardly taller than [her] arm-pits" with her "tightly wrapped black legs and double leather-soled 'toed' socks." The woman wore a "short black and white kimono bunched up around [her] waist," and her "neck and head bundled to keep out the dust," and "a 'roof-hat' on top of all!" The little old woman swiftly and effectively swept the street clean with a broom that looked like a "loose bunch of brush." And "not a scrap of anything escaped her sharp little black eyes and capable hands."[32] In a nearby shop, Hazle observed a young woman with a baby on her back looking up to the mountain and repeating a prayer aloud, oblivious to everything going on around her.[33]

When they boarded the train bound for Tokyo, she noticed that the best dressed women carried blankets to spread on the train seats before sitting down, and many of the people sat on their feet, "some with their backs to the aisles, heads against the side of [the] car to sleep." Others ate the "neat little lunches to be had at the stations: daintily put up in divided wooden boxes—(chopsticks furnished) four or five different kinds of food—meat, fish, vegetable, pickle, and a sweet."[34]

They left the earthquake zone around Tokyo and traveled toward Nara and Kyoto. Looking out the window of the moving train, Hazle watched men in the open country carrying baskets and pails on long poles slung over their shoulders, some of them watering their crops with dippers. Others appeared to be harvesting small delicious water-melons. Everyone seemed to be working, except the very small children.[35]

When they arrived at the Imperial Hotel in Nara, Hazle thought the door girls "cute enough for watch charms" with their "sweet complacent expressions." She also found one of the two boys who served their table to be so charming that she wanted to take him home with them. The wildlife in Nara also interested her. One afternoon they took a rickshaw ride through the deer-filled 1,300 acre Nara Park. It amused and amazed her to see the deer reach out to anyone passing by in a rickshaw or an automobile for the cakes that could be purchased on every corner in the park.[36]

Early one morning, a few days after their ride in the park, Hazle saw "a big brown-eyed young buck lying under a good sized tree not ten feet" from their windows. She called to the deer, and he stood up and came over to the window. She raised the screen and held out some rice-wafers, which she had saved from the previous day. The deer gently ate the offering out of her hand and stood waiting for more. Davis realized what was going on and "hunted up some [rice-wafers] he had saved for (picture taking) and our pretty spotted friend had a good breakfast." She wondered if the deer "told his family about it."[37]

Hazle enjoyed watching the Japanese children as they played games, and it especially delighted her when the children would romp behind the rickshaw, chasing them and calling out "to other children to come and see." Riding in a rickshaw also provided her the opportunity to see the "endless variety and curious combinations of garments" that the Japanese wore.[38]

They arrived at Osaka on September 21, the newest and most commercial city in Japan, which contrasted strikingly with Kyoto, the oldest city. One day, they visited the remains of the Osaka castle, which had been turned into a barracks. Hazle noticed a soldier's horse hitched facing outward in its stall, and she stopped to pet him. He was a pretty sorrel, with a velvet nose and he loved the petting she gave him as well as nibbling from her hand. He nickered to them when they came back from touring the castle. Later she confessed in her journal, "I should have never spoken to or petted or fed him if his heels had been toward me, well as I love and understand horses. I'd not be sure that he would understand my language!"[39]

But the experience that made the deepest impression on her

occurred the day before they left Osaka. A friend of one in their group, Mr. Araki, had secured an invitation for the tour group to have tea at the summer home of Mr. Nayamaka, a wealthy business-man who had given a talk that Ralph had attended. His house looked quite European, and Hazle appreciated the excellent Continental meal Nayamaka served them. But the "feast of reason, and flow of brotherliness and comradeship" had meant infinitely more to her.

Although they had to communicate through an interpreter, Hazle recognized in Nayamaka a kindred spirit. She thought, "He feels the utter uselessness and extravagance of war as keenly as I do." She told him, "The world could much better use war-money in building schools than in keeping armaments." He agreed with her and asked her to write in his guest book. She wrote, "You are building well in the structure of brotherhood for which the world is striving."[40] Meeting and talking with Nayamaka seemed to spark within Hazle the idea that ultimately led her to proposing the educational program at Principia to promote world peace.

When they arrived in Korea on September 23, she had no doubt that they were no longer in Japan. Her attention was immediately caught by men wearing light pineapple colored apparel, consisting of wide kimonos, loose coats, and baggy trousers gathered at the ankles, low pump-like shoes with turned-up toes, and the black mosquito netting caps that the men wore over their uncut hair, topped with "little square-edge" towers and brims of netting, and held on their heads with black chin straps. By her own admission, she could have spent an hour or more at the station writing about the men squatting about with "huge wood back-yokes that look like enormous antlers hung over their shoulders." Leaving the dock, she saw adults wearing long, flowing white garments, and children dressed in bright solid colors: "vivid blue and brilliant cerise." Women carried large pails and buckets on their heads, "with the same stolid walk of French peasant women," and some of the men had huge loads of brush piled three to five feet high on their back-yokes.[41]

From the beginning of their travels, Hazle kept in touch with her friend, Julia Fairfax Hodge, describing their adventures and confiding to Julia her thoughts about what she saw. In turn, Julia wrote to Hazle of how Emma Foster and her husband were managing at the Ewings' home in Bloomington, shared the local news, and sent an occasional package of goodies. Julia had been a resident of Bloomington most of her life, since her family had moved there shortly after her birth in 1878 from Danvers, Illinois. Hazle and Julia shared common interests in the Art Association, which Julia had helped to start; the League of Women Voters, in which both were members; the theatre, of which Julia had been a promoter and an early worker; and the Chicago branch of The American Association for the United Nations.[42]

The Ewings all appreciated the large quantity of mixed nuts that Julia had sent them, to fill in the "hungers of an unsatisfying Japanese meal."[43] And Hazle was grateful that she could ask Julia the question closest to her heart—"how is Sonny doing?" She deeply missed her six-year-old son, Sonny, who they had to leave behind in the care of her friends, Graham Bartow and Dorothy Knight, while he attended school at The Principia. She and Davis had felt he was too young to take such a long trip. She asked Julia, many times, to "Please give Sonny several hugs and kisses for me" the next time she went to St. Louis. Hazle confided to her friend, "My! How I'd like to have him here this minute. And you. What a talk-fest we could have!"[44]

Hazle wrote to Julia about the deep disappointment she felt when she learned they could not go to China because of the impending war. But she confessed that she was glad to have a chance to visit Korea, for she had "already seen enough to make it worthwhile." She was especially impressed by how the land owners cut every little tuft of grass to take home to their stock. They were "Real conservationists." The Koreans, like the Japanese, made use of every foot of ground.[45]

"All Korean women [wore] their hair slicked back and tight and smooth as possible—full ear showing—and coiled loosely (held by a short ornament thrust thro) low down on the neck. No variation," Hazle observed. And the young girls wore their hair in braids with a ribbon on the end, but not tied in a bow. She admired the "most vivid colours" that the young children wore.[46] She saw some "fine-looking" schools in the Korean cities, but the children in villages did not seem to have any schools. It amazed her that in both Japan and Korea "everybody" reads, even young children read the newspapers. But she found a striking difference between Japan and Korea—the way they treated their animals. The horses and dogs in Korea seemed to be "poorly fed and unhappy looking," whereas in Japan she had seen "only kindness, love and good care" given to animals.[47]

It delighted Hazle when the tour group learned they *would* be going to China; they were "going to see something of it after all the 'wars and rumors of war!'" Passengers boarding the SS Hokurei Maru bound for China included people of Slovak, Russian, and Dutch, as well as Korean, Japanese, and Chinese descent. That evening on board the ship, they stood on the deck watching lighthouses blinking and winking all around them, and the next morning dawned "gorgeous" with the colors changing on the mountains: "rose and mauve and a deep purple and soft shadowy blue."[48] The ship had been crowded but comfortable, and they enjoyed excellent food during their three-day trip to Peking.[49]

The last night on the ship before arriving in China, Hazle could not sleep for excitement. She rose at dawn on September 30 on the chance they might reach Taku Port of Tientsin at the estimated time of arrival: 6:00 a.m. She poked her head out of the porthole several times, looking for signs of land and being careful to avoid bumping her head on the prickly cross-beam. At 5:50 a.m., she noticed a fleet of boats anchored idly not far from them, and she knew there must be land somewhere nearby. "Almost at the moment of six" there appeared a pilot-boat right at their portal. It seemed impossible that they were so near land because all they could see was open ocean surrounding them. The pilot of the ship they were on received instructions from the pilot-boat on how to enter the Yellow River safely.[50]

It surprised Hazle to see that the Yellow River really was yellow. Entering at its mouth, they could see low mounds on either side, which they learned were Taku forts with good-sized guns in back of them: Peking's first line of defense. The "Chinese villages entirely of adobe," made of mud and reeds, "fairly hung to the sides of the river." These adobe homes fascinated Hazle. She could see "here and there parts of walls had been washed away, showing the inside arrangement" of the huts. The homes appeared to be wretched and shabby, but a fellow traveler informed her that the huts were "exceedingly comfortable" and the better ones "roomy and pleasant," cool in the summer and warm in the winter. Every inch of the land appeared to be tilled, and the Chinese grew a variety of crops. The ship made its way down the river, creating quite a disturbance. Hazle watched as the nude children, boys and girls, rushed to the shore of the river to watch them pass by, playing and shouting in the sucking waves.

She noticed some small barges loaded with reeds that looked like "adventuring straw-stacks starting down river." She could not see the rowers and wondered how they could ever reach port. Boats of every description sailed on the river and had many varieties of sails, some of them "like patchwork quilts from mending."[51]

A swarm of activity greeted them when docking at Tientsin. Hazle saw "more hard labor by humans, and by animals," as they carried heavy loads to and from ships than she had ever seen in her life back home. Her heart ached for these people. "It must be a bitter struggle for existence that spurs them on to make such enormous physical effort," she thought. In spite of the scene at the dock, Tientsin had the appearance of a cosmopolitan city. The stars and stripes waved a welcome from the American consulate. As they entered the city, there were many banks and businesses built in the European style, and the dusty streets thronged with a constant parade of humanity.[52]

When they boarded a train to Peking, Hazle instantly became aware that there was a war going on in China. Their first class train compartments had been taken over by a young general headed for Peking, accompanied by his family, his aides, and their families. At first she wondered what they should do if these men should get troublesome. One of the men "looked rather ferocious," and three of the men began drinking something out of a thermos. Then one of them stripped off his clothes to the embarrassment of the rest of the passengers and the young conductor, who felt helpless to do anything about it. "Quite unconsciously," a young woman in their group, a teacher, began teaching one of the small Chinese boys English, and one by one the others joined in, including the fathers. The tension eased and "soon the whole car-full were fraternizing like old friends!" The Chinese mothers tried to join in, "balancing difficultly on their poor little mutilated stubs of feet!" Hazle would "never get over the feeling of horror that those poor tortured legs and feet" gave her![53]

The Chinese expressed a great deal of interest in the Americans' clothing and belongings. The young general tried on Ralph's hat and attempted to buy an expensive pair of binoculars from him. Some of the Chinese shared pears and buns with them, and the Ewings shared some of their nuts with the Chinese. Then everyone began to quiet down.

They had hoped to reach Peking by 6:00 p.m., "Troop trains not preventing. . . . But troop trains did decidedly prevent, and it was 8:30 before [they] drew into the little lighted final Station at P[eking]."[54] Hazle felt greatly relieved when they finally reached Peking and settled comfortably into the large Grand Hotel, which was under French management and served delicious food.[55] From

the window in their room, Hazle had an excellent view of the
"never-ending stream" of little horses, mules, and men exerting
every ounce of strength to drag their heavy loads through the mud
and deep ruts. Only a few Chinese lived in comfort and luxury; the
common man lived a mere existence.

The condition of abject poverty of most of the Chinese became
undeniably apparent one day when the tour group took a drive
out into the country on the Imperial Highway. Garbage had been
dumped along the side of the road, and both animals and humans
desperately scavenged it for food. That all-too-common occurrence
in China was depressing to Hazle.[56] Indeed, many of the things
she saw in China deeply troubled her. It was heartbreaking to see
so many young boys serving as soldiers, and evidence of poverty
seemed everywhere, as well as the common practice of mistreating
animals. She confided to Julia, it is "just hopeless to write it all.
Everything is so completely different that there is nothing to start
with—no standard of comparisons."[57]

Amidst the dismal conditions surrounding them, Davis's cousin,
the young and good-looking Ewing Scott, who lived in Peking,
provided some cheerful entertainment. He had "a pleasant and
attractive establishment of his own and three devoted Chinese to
minister to his slightest need." Hazle confessed to Julia: "I could get
really fond of these devoted Chinese helpers." Visiting with Ewing
in his home gave Hazle, Davis, and Ralph a temporary escape from
the reality of the war that raged not far away.[58]

But the war in China caught up with them on October 10, 1924.
Davis had just returned to their room from the American Express
office with money that had been wired to them when the business
manager of the Bureau, Mr. Braden, informed them that they must
prepare to leave that afternoon. Hazle had to cancel her shopping
trip and tea date with a local woman, as well as their plans to share
a moonlight picnic with Ewing Scott that evening.

Because of the dire situation, they arrived at the train station early. While waiting three hours for the train, Hazle wrote to Julia, "We have just been plunged into the greatest excitement by the word that we are to leave this afternoon at three instead of tomorrow morning."[59] At last the train arrived and everyone rushed madly to get on, blocking those trying to get off. The men in their tour group tried unsuccessfully to hold back the crowd so the ladies could board the train. It seemed an eternity before they got on, and then they found that their seats had been taken and they could barely find room to stand. The train conductor, an Englishman, quickly took charge of the situation and regained their reserved seats for them. But then they dared not leave their seats for fear of losing them. It took them 15 hours to travel 48 miles. However, they later learned that they narrowly escaped, for theirs was the last passenger train to leave China![60]

After a day of rest at Tientsin, they took a twenty-six hour train trip through the prosperous Shanhung Province to Nanking and boarded a steamer the next afternoon for Shanghai. While they were settling into their quarters, the ship suddenly stopped. Wondering what could be wrong, they went on deck. There they found an unexpected and chaotic scene. Frightened people, trying desperately to escape the war and despairing of being left behind were clambering onto the ship from rafts. Hazle witnessed women being thrown on board who were barely caught by their fellow travelers and narrowly escaped falling into the churning water. Hazle could not bear to watch the heartbreaking sight. She returned to their stateroom to quiet her thoughts and pray. Although the presence of English and American warships provided some reassurance, they were now acutely aware that fighting was taking place only ten miles from Shanghai.[61]

When they reached the city of Hong Kong, they were grateful and relieved to have escaped China's war zone. The lights of that beautiful city glimmered in the water, giving Hazle a sense of comfort and safety. The gaiety of Hong Kong provided her a short reprieve from the depressing and sobering memories of what they had seen and experienced in China. The atmosphere of the city revitalized them. Hazle and Davis went dancing and attended parties and began to feel too young to have a nearly grown son. One evening, before leaving Hong Kong, they attended an event involving "fourteen nationalities represented by people of all ages, from 16-50." They all seemed to be having a good time together, and it occurred to her that "Nations could do the same, if they just <u>would</u>."[62]

Although Hazle enjoyed Hong Kong and the sense of peace she felt there, her experiences in China had made a lasting impression on her. A letter she wrote to Julia at that time reveals her evolving thought: "I am so overwhelmed by what we are seeing and learning that I feel that a trip around the world ought to be a compulsory part of any education that deserves the name education." She tried to write up her notes, but she confessed to Julia, "I am so swamped with things I'd like to put into words, that I hardly dare begin!" She thought she had gained a "pretty broad conception of people and ideas" between her travels throughout the United States and what she knew of Europe and South America. But "only two months on our way in this round the world trip I find there are worlds and worlds of people and ideas that will be untouched when the trip is finished!"[63]

Her experiences in Asia served to solidify and strengthen her conviction that education played a key role in world peace. She thought that "<u>no</u> senator or representative should ever be allowed to go to Wash[ington] to represent his home state without first taking a comprehensive world trip with both eyes and mind open!" She fervently believed that such a requirement would prevent "many mistakes in international matters."[64]

CHAPTER 3

PLACES OF MYSTERY AND MAJESTY

While the Ewings were en route from Hong Kong to Angkor, Cambodia, Hazle realized that some changes had been taking place in Ralph. He seemed to be "having a very good time—seeing and developing a lot." She felt certain that their friends and family would see "a decided difference in him" when they returned home. The trip had given her the opportunity to spend some time with him every day, reading the Christian Science Bible Lesson, writing, and having some nice talks. These quiet times together were helping Hazle and Ralph get to know and understand each other better.[65]

Arriving in Angkor, Davis was fascinated with the bas-relief-covered walls portraying the legends of Angkor carved by Khmer artists. Hazle enjoyed the beauty of the place, and she found the native people's apparel and homes most interesting. Both men and women wore a length of cloth wrapped around their bodies, making it difficult to tell them apart. The native homes of palm leaves and poles that rose up on stilts, even when not constructed near water, intrigued her.[66] Ralph learned about the economics of the area and the lifestyles of both the wealthy and the poor.

While in that part of the world, they also visited Siam, which is now known as Thailand. Hazle was encouraged to learn that King Rama VI of Siam had made some improvements in the status of women in his country, allowing them to have some education. She hoped that trend would continue. From there they traveled to

27

Malaysia, and she noticed that the native people there had darker
skin and wore brighter colored clothing than those of Siam. The
East Indian tribesmen of Tamil, who also lived there, were easily
recognized by their long, black, curly hair. [67]

Then they boarded a train that took them to Singapore, an
island at the tip of the Malay Peninsula connected by a bridge to
the mainland. There they had accommodations at the Raffles Hotel,
named for Stamford Raffles of the East India Bay Company. Hazle's
brother, Ellsworth Buck, had a representative of his company, James
Graham, living in Singapore. Graham assisted them with mailing
packages and took them to his home for tea. While in Singapore,
they also visited the Christian Science Reading Room. They were
surprised to find the newspapers and magazines nailed down to the
tables so they could not be stolen. The night before leaving for Java,
the Ewings stayed aboard the ship since it was to leave at 6 a.m.,
which prevented them from seeing the Grahams one last time. They
felt especially bad about missing the Thanksgiving dinner that the
hotel would be serving. But, to their surprise and delight, the ship's
chef provided for them a turkey dinner with all the trimmings.[68]

In Java, they visited the city of Bandung, where they enjoyed a
modern room with a bathtub, and the village of Lemahabang where
they sampled authentic native life at the market place. Traveling
around the country, they saw rice paddies at different stages of
growth. Java has no specific growing season because of the country's
mild weather, where crops can be grown all year long. The Javanese
seemed to be a most industrious people, always working in their
fields of rice, tobacco, and sugar cane, or in their homes. They also
visited a women's prison there and watched the entire process of
the inmates producing brightly colored batik, including the making
of the dyes. Members of their group purchased several pieces of the
cloth, including some silk batik, which they had not seen anywhere
else during their travels.[69]

When they returned to Singapore, they visited the Grahams

again, and then on December 11, 1924, they boarded a ship bound
for the city of Rangoon in Burma. Hazle was entranced by the East
Indians who served their dinner in the ship's dining room wearing
"long, flowing, white robes, tied at the waist with black and white
belts; their white turbans trimmed in black that contrasted strikingly
with their dark skin."[70]

Entering the mouth of the Rangoon River, they could see
sunlight shimmering on the gold-leaf roof of the Shwe Dagon
Pagoda, the center of religious life in Burma. The city of Rangoon,
one of the most important seaports of the British Empire, was
twenty miles up the river.[71] It thrived as a center for exporting
rice, petroleum, hides, cotton, and teak wood, as well as importing
cotton goods, machinery, coal, silk, and sugar. When they arrived in
Rangoon, it appeared to be quite a modern city with European style
buildings and paved streets. The Hindus, Moslems, Chinese, and
Burmese who made up the population of Burma seemed to live in
comparative peace and quiet. The Burmese natives appeared to be
clean and honest, but not as industrious or numerous as the Chinese
living in Burma. Hazle thought it interesting and commendable
that the government of Burma provided village schools throughout
the country. She also noted that there was no caste system in Burma
as there was in India.

After a cold, twenty-four hour train ride from Rangoon, they
arrived in Mandalay populated mainly by Burmese. The roads
in the town were unpaved and everything appeared dusty and
unkempt. Here they boarded a ship on the Irrawaddy River, and
enjoyed warmer weather.[72] They anchored each night and traveled
only during the day, making at least ten stops along the way to take
on cargo. Hazle took advantage of the opportunity to observe the
natives who crowded along the shore to watch the ship when they
were docked. She enjoyed a never-ending picture of diversity, which
satisfied her much more than visiting temples and ruins.

The people along the river seemed to be dressed in heavier and darker clothing than in other places they had visited. The drivers of ox carts wore ear and nose rings, plus turbans of all sizes and colors. Both men and women wore a one-piece silk garment, called lungyi, in various shades. On the river, she noticed families living in wooden shacks on rafts transporting teak wood to one of the larger cities to be exported. She learned that the families lived on the rafts for the 6 to 8 months it took to reach their destinations. Hazle thought it looked like a pleasant and easy life, until the boat they were on ran into one of the rafts, cutting it in half. The family on the raft quickly and deftly tied it back together, as though this was a regular occurrence. She thought it fortunate that their shack had not been disturbed by the accident. [73]

On December 22, 1924, Hazle, Davis, Ralph, and the rest of the tour group boarded the SS Aronda and arrived in Calcutta, India, on Christmas afternoon. They planned to leave that evening for the mountains of north India, where they hoped to see some snow since the weather in India was so similar to that of the United States. Having been in climates unlike her home, especially in China and Japan, Hazle had experienced bouts of illness. But after arriving in Calcutta, she realized that these bouts had no longer occurred. Thankfully, she had been healed. She could now eat or drink anything and sleep anywhere.[74]

On Christmas Day in Calcutta, they enjoyed a traditional Christmas dinner at a crowded hotel and then took a train to a hotel in Darjeeling. They changed trains in Siliguri, at the base of the Himalayas, 300 feet above sea level. Then, Hazle watched from her window as the train climbed 7,100 feet to the snow-capped mountains glimmering in the sunlight and then dropped 1,000 feet into Darjeeling. It did not snow in Darjeeling because of its location, but the cold air seemed to cling to them and soak into their clothing during their ride in an open car to Hotel Mt. Everest. They looked forward to warming up when they reached the hotel, but instead found that the heating system consisted of electric bulbs and a fireplace fed by coal. The only place where they could find some warmth was under the bed covers![75]

They arose at 2:00 a.m. the next morning. Hazle, Davis, and Ralph dressed warmly and joined some of their fellow travelers to take a trip to Tiger Hill to view the sunrise over the Himalayas. The two-hour pony ride in the dark seemed to go on forever. At last they reached their destination—the top floor of a concrete tower. There they stood in the crisp cool morning air and watched the sun rise over the mountain peaks in a pink glow, changing into red, orange, and scarlet. They could barely see the 29,000-foot Mt. Everest in the distance. Then it vanished from their sight as the sun rose higher in the sky with its golden-white rays reflecting off the pure white snow. But they could still see the closer 28,150-foot Mt. Kinchinjunga. Descending Tiger Hill in the morning light, the Swiss-like snow-covered mountains surrounding them sparkled with almost blinding brilliancy.[76]

Before returning to Calcutta, they visited a market near Darjeeling on Sunday morning and found a diversity of people, including a few from Nepal and Tibet. When Davis tried to take a picture of some women merchants, they turned away from the camera. But several young men willingly posed for him. They also encountered an abundance of sacred cows roaming about. One cow stood in the doorway of the Golden Temple eating visitors' flower garlands and preventing them from entering. At the Holy of Holies, the Ewings found themselves in the presence of a large white cow, the Holy Cow, which the Indians believed could impart virtue to anyone touching her.[77]

Although their experiences with the sacred cows had been interesting, and they enjoyed many other sights in India, nothing compared with their trip to Agra, where they saw "the most exquisite piece of architecture in the world, the Taj Mahal." It had been built by Shah Jahan in honor of his beloved Empress. They had seen pictures of it, but the actual structure of red sandstone with inlaid black and white marble far exceeded their expectations. They spent only two days in Agra, but the Ewings managed to visit the monument five times. At midnight, the last night of their stay, the Taj Mahal shimmered in the moonlight and seemed quite ethereal, stirring their emotions and awakening their imaginations.[78]

Reluctantly, they left Agra to visit the modern-looking city of Gwalior, where they glimpsed native life at a fair thronged with people dressed in holiday attire. The fair seemed much like any they had attended at home, with booths, tents, and machinery, but the people surrounding them were quite different. Hazle found herself entranced with the women in their gaily-colored dresses and bright shawls, and the men dressed in their turbans and flowing trousers.

That night in the flickering gas light of the dining room at the Grand Hotel in Gwalior, Sir Edwin John, an Englishman, entertained them with stories of his friendship with the Maharajah. His stories reminded them of their childhood and the *Tales of the Arabian Nights*—and, seemed equally as fantastic. The next day, to their surprise, the Maharajah provided elephants for them to ride to visit a nearby fort. It was their first time riding on elephants. While mahots, or attendants, commanded the elephants to kneel, Hazle, Davis, Ralph and the other tourists climbed the ladders and took their seats atop the giant backs. As the elephant on which Hazle was seated rose, she felt a lurching sensation back and forth, but then it moved smoothly and gently forward and proved to be a pleasant ride.[79] Although the elephants and sacred cows seemed to be well cared for, she had seen some disturbing mistreatment of other animals in India.

Visiting a rug factory one day, however, they discovered something even more troubling than the abuse of animals. In a dark back room of the factory, a dozen small children, none over the age of ten, sat in front of a large loom, and behind the loom stood a lad of about fifteen giving them instructions. All the children appeared thin and pallid from malnutrition and lack of sunlight and air. No one in their group could bring themselves to purchase a rug from that factory.[80] The memory of those children would haunt Hazle for some time.

She also learned of the serious plight of the Indian farmers, who depended on rainfall to produce crops. If the rain did not come, they faced drought conditions. Only a quarter of the land received water through irrigation—half from wells and half from canals built by the English. Some of the land remained unfertilized, greatly reducing the production of crops.[81] The common Indian farmer's main concern was survival.

Leaving Gwalior, the Ewings and their fellow travelers arrived at Bombay, the Gateway of India and center of England's East India trade—a "magnificent harbor and splendid dockage" defended by heavy artillery. Bombay's large population, representing many races and religions, provided a fascinating scene of diversity. The most interesting people seemed to be the fair-skinned, dark-eyed, prominent-nosed Parsees, who stood out among the other sects and who had influence in the city out of proportion to their numbers.

Passing through Bombay, they arrived at The Rajputana Hotel in Madras at Mount Abu. The letter and package Julia had sent them for Christmas finally caught up with them there. Hazle eagerly opened the letter and package. She unfolded the dainty hankie Julia had sent and admired it. She also found a fruitcake in the package, which she and her family enjoyed immensely. She wrote to Julia, "No fruitcake ever tasted half so good anywhere before! . . . It was just as moist and luscious as if it had not traveled half-way round the world to us." The Ewings set up the little tree Julia had thoughtfully included with their gifts, unpacked their candles, and "had a real Christmas feeling just as if it were December 25, instead of January 19."[82]

They left Madras for Madura (now known as Madurai), and Hazle wrote Julia: "I wish I could draw a picture that could give you even a faint idea of the sort of things we are seeing and living among these days." She explained that she, Davis, and Dr.

Coomaraswamy started for Madura a day before Ralph and the rest of the tour group "in order to have some extra time for the two men picture-takers—and so here we are in the station hotel." The station hotel had been the only alternative to staying at the Government Rest house, where they could have slept on cots if they had their own bedding. She thought Madura to be the most thoroughly native city they had visited, having few foreigners living among them and maintaining their Indian customs, clothing, and architecture.[83]

At the hotel, Hazle had been surprised to see how the "little black-skinned dwarf of an Indian woman," who managed the hotel, ordered around the "even blacker-skinned long-legged South Indian men."[84] The woman had offered to prepare her a bath, which she gratefully accepted. And in a few moments, "a grey-headed & bearded old man, with bare black legs—and seemingly barer black body above a narrow loin cloth about his hips—tufts of wiry grey hair straggling over chest and trunk," appeared at her door with "a large red earthen jar balanced on his head" and made his way to the bathroom. She indicated to the man that she must have a second jar of water, but she was not sure he understood. In a few minutes, however, he returned with another jar of water, leaving the "dirty prints of his calloused feet all around the large modern enameled tub," which was large enough for a sleeping room.[85]

She confessed to Julia: "The combination of Indian and European things never ceases to seem almost unbelievably incongruous to me, some way or other." They had been provided many comforts, "but at such cost of laborious effort." The travel group had come to Madura to see the Dravidian Temple of India, but "the streets and people" interested Hazle far more. She "never supposed that anywhere, except among savage hill tribes, should we still see ear-lobes stretched out until they look like rubber bands." But they had seen them here.[86] Her own ignorance of customs and cultures of other countries strengthened her conviction that education could play a major role in attaining world understanding and peace.

Leaving Madura, they traveled to Ceylon (currently Sri Lanka), located off the most southern tip of India. The lush, green, tropical countryside seemed especially appealing to Hazle after seeing so much parched land in other parts of Asia. Nor did Ceylon appear to be plagued with the problem of poverty that seemed so prevalent in some of the other places they had visited. The rest of the tour group took a train to the capital city of Colombo, but the Ewings hired a car to drive there so they could see more of the countryside where rubber and cocoa trees and tea grew in abundance.[87]

On February 4, 1925, while in Ceylon, Hazle received some mail from her friends, Graham Bartow and Dorothy Knight in St. Louis, who were taking care of Sonny during their trip. They reported that he seemed to be doing well. But it troubled Hazle that she had not heard from her mother about Sonny's Christmas in Evanston. She missed their family and friends, but she especially missed their little boy. As Hazle traveled in a world far different from her own, Julia's faithfully-written newsy letters provided her some comfort and often included news about Sonny.[88]

From Ceylon they sailed for Egypt on the SS Lotus for a four-week stay.[89] The Shepherd Hotel in Cairo became their address while they traveled up and down the Nile River. Cairo seemed to be a fairly modern city and full of tourists that time of the year. The Arabs, in their clean turbans and long flowing robes of soft tans and blues, served as their guides in Egypt. Since they had to wait a few days for another group of tourists and their new manager to arrive from New York, they decided to visit the Pyramids. But when they stepped outside the hotel, local entrepreneurs crowded around them, all having something to sell or offering services.[90]

They finally managed to break free and drove to the Pyramids, enjoying the sights along the way. They saw men in turbans and gaily-colored robes; women in black, with only their eyes showing above black veils; and donkeys, camels, and water buffalo laboring to carry or pull their burdens of people and packages. When they reached the Pyramids, they did not look at all like the pictures that the Ewings had seen. These Pyramids were not towering over the great Nile River—they were not even near the river. They did not realize that they had come during the dry season and the river had receded, leaving the Pyramids on the dry sand. Taking a closer look, however, the Ewings were amazed by the soft sandstone blocks measuring from three to five feet high from which the massive Pyramids had been constructed. They wondered how they could ever have been built. The mystery and majesty of the Pyramids drew the Ewings and the other tourists back time and time again. The Pyramids glowing in the moonlight seemed especially picturesque to Hazle.[91]

When their new manager, Mr. Allan, and the group from New York arrived, their journey up the Nile began. Hazle watched farmers in the fertile Nile valley tending to their crops of cotton, sugar cane, and rice. She observed the natives on the river banks and in small boats on the river going about their daily lives. The ship docked at several points along the river, giving the Ewings and their fellow tourists the opportunity to take short carriage rides inland where they discovered that the land was nothing but desert: "dry and unproductive as a bone."

As a part of their tour of Egypt, the Ewings visited the burial ground at Necropolis and some of the tombs. They enjoyed listening to Dr. Allan, an archeologist and Egyptologist, who read the hieroglyphs on the temple walls bringing them to life. The scenes on the walls told them how the Egyptians made boats, slaughtered oxen, served dinner, snared birds, sowed, reaped, threshed, winnowed, collected taxes, kept accounts, and transported giant statues.[92]

They also stopped at the city of Luxor, across from the Thebes River and the Valley of the Kings, where they toured the tombs of King Amenhotep II and the famous King Tut-Ankh-Amen.[93] They saw the Temple of the Lions at EsSebua, but Hazle thought the Nubians who lived in the area more fascinating than the ancient ruins. The women dressed in black garb, wore their hair plaited in tiny long braids, and had brass rings in their noses.

As they headed back down-stream, the boat became stuck on a sand bar, but none of them thought anything about it since that happened at least once or twice a day. The crew had the boat free within an hour, and they resumed their trip. At lunch time, they heard a loud noise and the boat lurched, startling them all. The ship had become lodged between two hidden rocks, which made a hole in the ship's bow.[94] This time the crew removed all the passengers to land, and Hazle, feeling no concern about the situation, settled down to write in her journal "to have it on the spot," and to catch up on some of her correspondence.[95]

She wrote to Julia that she thought the situation was "rather a picnic."[96] After writing all the news she had to share, she put away the letter and stood up with the intention of visiting with her fellow passengers. At that moment, Farajalla, the ship's captain, motioned to them to come back aboard the ship. Although the crew had worked on the ship all afternoon, they had hot tea awaiting the tourists when they boarded, and, a short time later, served them a delicious dinner.[97] That night the ship remained on the sand bar; the crew completed the necessary repairs the next morning, and they set sail at 10:00 a.m.[98]

The mysterious and majestic places visited on this portion of their trip provided the Ewings with several interesting experiences to relate to their family and friends back home. They would not soon forget the breath-taking view from Tiger Hill, or the Taj Mahal glimmering in the moonlight, or the majestic pyramids. Davis found the architecture especially interesting, while Hazle collected memories of and information from the diversity of the people she saw; Ralph learned much about Egyptian entrepreneurs and the difficult lives of the Indian farmers. They would also long remember the pleasure of being unexpectedly shipwrecked on the Nile River. Arriving in Cairo, the Ewings looked forward to the next part of their journey, wondering what unexpected adventures lay ahead.

CHAPTER 4

MEMORIES FROM AN ANCIENT LAND

*A*t Cairo, the Ewing family and the tour group boarded a train that took them to the Suez Canal, on which they ferried across to catch the smallest train Hazle had ever seen. The miniature train pulled out of the station, heading for Jerusalem, and she settled into her seat. She watched an endless tapestry of cultivated fields, fruit trees in full bloom, soft-colored rocks on hills, sage green olive trees, bright green fig trees, plots of grass, and the clear blue sky pass by her window. The scene outside seemed to be constantly changing, and Hazle wondered what interesting experiences awaited them in the Holy Land.

At the outskirts of Jerusalem, they stepped off the train and climbed into cars that took them to the Grand Hotel, which was just inside the Jaffa Gate.[99] Arriving at the hotel, Hazle soon learned that no cars could enter Jerusalem. From their hotel door, she saw the breach in the city wall that had been made in honor of William II of Germany when he and his entourage of nearly 200 arrived in the city on October 29, 1898 for a six-day visit. The breach was made to enable his horsemen to enter the city with a full display of their flags without dismounting. Although William II and his wife, Augusta Viktoria, visited many of the sites around the city, his main objective was to strengthen the ties between the German and Ottoman Empires.[100] On the day of the Ewings' arrival, men, women, and children dressed in all kinds of costumes, and all sorts of animals carrying or pulling a variety of loads, flowed like a living stream into the city through the breach in the wall and the Jaffa Gate.

Eager to explore the city, Hazle, Davis, and Ralph left their hotel soon after arriving and followed the nearby Street of David into Jerusalem. They soon encountered a camel train in a street so narrow they had to step aside to allow it past. On both sides of the street, shop windows filled with fascinating merchandise drew their attention. And before they realized it, they had arrived at the market place in the center of the city.[101] Looking about them, it seemed almost as if they had been transported many centuries back in time.

Portions of the ancient wall and gateways surrounding the city were still standing. The narrow streets, which looked like they had been laid down in steps, swarmed with beggars, blind men, women dressed in black with veils over their faces, and Bedouins with flowing robes and colored scarf bands on their heads. The vast variety of individuals and costumes intrigued Hazle; Davis and Ralph thought the Bedouins' nomadic Arab clothing the most appealing, and they immediately decided to obtain their own. With that intent, they made their way to the native quarter of the city, and after much bartering, bought the articles they needed to create their own Bedouin costumes.[102]

Entranced by the sights and sounds of Jerusalem, they wandered through the city until they found themselves on a narrow and winding street—Via Dolorosa. It was down this street that Jesus was supposed to have borne his cross to the Crucifixion. They observed the houses that over shadowed the street and tried to imagine what the street might have looked like in the time of Jesus.[103]

The following day, they went with their tour group beyond the wall of Jerusalem, and Hazle especially enjoyed their excursion to Palestine with its rolling hills and valleys stretching out for miles in all directions from the Mount of Olives. She could see the Dead Sea in the distance, the mountains of Moab beyond, and behind them—Jerusalem, sitting on a hill, surrounded by sections of the ancient wall. On the Mount of Olives stood a large group of buildings, including a mosque and a Greek convent.

As they descended the Mount by way of the Garden of Gethsemane, located in a narrow valley between the Mount of Olives and the city, their guide led them to an enormous old olive tree. He told them that this tree was where Jesus may have prayed just before Judas betrayed him to the Romans.[104] Hazle had read the story of the betrayal of Jesus many times, as had many others in their tour group. The thought that they could be standing where Jesus prayed in the face of the severest challenge of his life inspired them with awe.

The next morning, they walked through the streets to the Temple Area, and then entered a large enclosure containing the 'Holy of Holies' of the Jew, Moslem, and Christian—the Mosque of Omar. The present building, the 'Dome of the Rock,' is believed to be standing over the rock on which Abraham attempted to sacrifice Isaac; and was later used by David as a place of prayer; where Solomon built his temple; and the site from which Jesus drove away the money changers.

Their tour that day also included the Church of the Holy Sepulcher, which is supposed to be standing over the site of the Crucifixion and the tomb of the Saviour. The Greeks had unearthed the ruins many years ago, and built a church there, which strengthened their claim that the Church of the Holy Sepulcher stood on the site of Calvary. The ancient church had been outside the city gates, according to the Bible.[105] Hazle realized that much of the Biblical lore and tradition surrounding Jerusalem was probably more tradition than fact. Although the sites they visited may not have been the exact places where the history of Jesus had taken place, Hazle still found it deeply moving to think they were seeing places where the Master might have actually been.[106]

As part of their experience in Jerusalem, some of the group spent a few days living in Arabian tents lined with patchwork

patterns in an olive grove just outside the city, while the rest of
the tour group stayed at the hotel. Both groups traveled together
to Solomon's quarries from which stone had been procured to
build Solomon's Temple. Here they followed a long tunnel and
entered a large room supposed to be under the Dome of the Rock
where the early Christians held their secret meetings. Next, going
down a flight of stairs, they visited the Tomb of the Kings deep
underground. Here they learned about the rolling stone that is used
to seal a tomb and is shaped somewhat like a drum, or a millstone,
four or five feet in diameter and twelve inches thick. The stone is
set into a groove cut into the rock. Then a small stone is set behind
the rolling stone on the outside of the tomb. This made the rolling
stone immoveable from inside the tomb. Only someone outside the
tomb could remove the small stone and make it possible to roll
away the rolling stone.[107] This fact seemed especially interesting in
relation to the feat of Jesus escaping from the sepulcher in which he
had been entombed after the Crucifixion.

Another day, the tour group took a trip to Bethlehem and
Hebron driving over the plains where David fought the Philistines.
They also passed the Well of the Magi where the Wise Men saw
the star reflected in the well water when they stooped to drink,
and the place where the angels had appeared to the shepherds.
They stopped to visit the tomb of Rachel, the only monument
about which there is no doubt. When they reached Bethlehem,
they toured the Church of Nativity and looked at the altar built
on the site, which is claimed to be over the manger that had been
used as a bed for Jesus. Arriving in Hebron, one of the oldest
cities in the world, Hazle thought it interesting that the locals
still dressed in the garb worn in Biblical days. Hebron is the place
where Abraham parted from Lot; and where David lived as a young
man and established his seat of government before he captured
Jerusalem.[108] They also visited Bethany, where Mary and Martha,
the sisters of Lazarus, whom Jesus raised from the dead, had their

home, and toured the Apostle's Wall where they observed women filling Standard Oil cans with water.

Near the end of their eight days in Jerusalem, the tour group traveled to the Dead Sea. Located in an arid valley between the mountains of Judea and the Moabite Plateau, the supposed site of Sodom and Gomorrah, mists of evaporating water obscured the sea from their view. They soon understood the reason for its name. The Dead Sea has no outlet, and the brackish water kills any fish that flow into it from the Jordan River, the river where John the Baptist baptized Jesus. From the Dead Sea, they drove on to look at the fallen Wall of Jericho, from which they could also see the Mountain of Temptation in the distance where Jesus had been tempted by the Devil. They had lunch in New Jericho and it surprised Hazle to find the inhabitants of the city to be almost entirely English and Arabian.[109]

When the time came to leave Jerusalem, they traveled to Nazareth, the boyhood home of Jesus, stopping at Nablus, the ancient city of Sachem, for lunch. Here Hazle found lots of local color. Passing through Samaria, she discovered that only a few Samaritans remained in the ancient town now populated mainly by Arabs. Reaching the top of the Mount of Transfiguration, they could see Nazareth ahead, stretching across the hills.

Arriving in Nazareth, they witnessed worshippers sitting on the pavement listening to a chanting Arab. Then they walked about the city visiting the shops. In one of the shops, they met a woman selling lace and learned that she was struggling to support her four children with her meager earnings. A natural rapport developed between the Americans and the woman, and she invited them to her home, the home of her deceased husband's family, and they accepted the invitation. When visiting the woman at her home, it became apparent to Hazle that the woman and her four children occupied only one room of the house. The woman provided cake and coffee for her American guests, and they talked quietly while

her children slept in various places about the room. The generosity
of this woman, struggling to support her four children, deeply
impressed Hazle.[110]

After visiting many sites of religious tradition in and around
Nazareth, the travelers drove on to Damascus, which seemed to be an
especially interesting place for students of Biblical history. Through
a friend of their guide, a visit to the home of a wealthy landowner
had been arranged in that city. On the appointed evening, they
drove to a three-story house surrounded by a divided courtyard.
Entering the home, they found their host dressed in European style
clothing and learned that he spoke only French. The women of
the house did not join them. They sat on comfortable divans and
cushions drinking Turkish coffee and conversing in French with
their host.[111] That evening in Damascus contrasted strikingly with
the visit they had in Nazareth with the widow woman surrounded
by her sleeping children.

Leaving Damascus, they drove over a mountain pass into a fertile
valley filled with vineyards to the town of Baalbeck, nestled in the
Lebanon Mountains. Here they spent a few days visiting sites of
interest. The April morning they were supposed to drive to Beirut to
board a ship to Constantinople, they awakened to snow. It continued
to snow until noon and then stopped, so after lunch they climbed into
cars and drove to Beirut. Their visit to the Holy Land had now come
to an end, but they had many vivid memories of their experiences.[112]

Arriving in Beirut, the chief seaport of Lebanon, they had time
to visit only a few of the institutions in the city before boarding the
Italian SS Semaramis bound for Constantinople.[113] They stopped
along the way to visit Tripoli in Lebanon, the Turkish cities of
Mersin and Adana (the largest seaport on the southern coast of Asia
Minor), and the city of Rhodes. The city had high walls between
towers and a moat surrounding it, which gave it a mediaeval
aspect. Rhodes is known for its legends of the Order of Knights
Templar, and while there, they visited a museum that had originally

been a Hospice of the Order, where knights had stayed when ill. It was a fascinating place with flying stairs, dungeons and chains, instruments of torture, a banquet hall with vaulted ceilings, deep casement windows, and small gardens in unexpected corners.[114]

Before continuing to Constantinople, they returned to Turkey and docked at Smyrna, the most important city in Asia Minor at that time, and the principal port of the Turkish Republic, trading tobacco, silk, figs, and raisins with Great Britain. The evidence of the fire of 1922, which had blazed through the Armenian sector covering half the city, could still be seen. As they drove through the ruins, it troubled Hazle that little had been done to restore the area. But the port seemed to be filled with ships, indicating that the trading business had not suffered.[115] After the depressing drive through the ruins, Hazle gladly returned to the ship to resume their journey to Constantinople.[116]

Approaching Constantinople, they could see the heavily fortified walls built by Constantine, which nearly isolated the city from the rest of the world. It seemed to be fortified even against their visit; they had to wait until afternoon before they received permission to go ashore. When allowed to enter the city, they went first to visit the Walls of Theodosius, including gates, towers, fortresses, and castles which encircled the old part of the city.[117] From this vantage point, they could see the homes of the poorer inhabitants of the city constructed of various flammable materials, and it became apparent to them why Constantinople had been destroyed by fire so many times. They also visited Robert's College, located on a high bluff overlooking the water. Hazle thought it encouraging that the school appeared to be prospering with the attendance of many Turkish students. The school was founded in 1866 by Christopher Rhinelander Robert, an American industrialist, and Cyrus Hamlin, a New Englander, who started a boys' seminary in the city in 1839.[118] They also toured the Woman's College, erected at a later date with the financial support of American philanthropists, including Miss

Helen Miller Gould, daughter of Jay Gould, American financier and speculator. They celebrated their last evening in Constantinople with dinner at a Russian café run by Russian refugees.[119]

When they arrived at Athens, they discovered that the shops, museums, and ruins had closed for the Orthodox Holy week, but they had the opportunity to attend the midnight ceremonies on Easter eve. Before the ceremonies began, Hazle observed a company of soldiers dressed in old Albanian costumes resembling ballet skirts and tights. When midnight struck, a procession of priests came into the church shouting "Christ is risen" and performed a ceremony on the platform. At the conclusion of the ceremony, all the attendees left the square with their candles burning, illuming the dark streets.[120]

Dr. Powers, head of the tour company, joined them in Athens, where they visited the Parthenon. At Mars Hill, Powers discussed Apostle Paul's sermons and why they failed to impress the Greeks. During a lecture by Dr. Allen on Greek plays, they sat on the cool marble seats in the Theatre Dionysius and could almost imagine attending a play there. Then they enjoyed a walk through the ruins of the Temple of Zeus. On their last day in Athens, they visited the Temple of Poseidon, constructed of lovely white marble, and the nearby Temple of Athena, where they enjoyed a picnic lunch.[121] Leaving Athens, they toured Greece in Cadillac automobiles.

Early in the morning as they prepared to leave Greece, Hazle heard the sweet song of a nightingale. Readily recognizing the source of the song, she later thought it a fitting prelude when they arrived in Patras that May Day in 1925 and observed the celebrations of the locals. Driving by the train station on their way to board a ship, they noticed a colorful wreath of flowers hanging over the doorway of the train station, and garlands of flowers adorning the school children. It provided a pleasant farewell to the travelers as they started out on the final portion of their journey. Patras, a commercial hub and point of trade and communication with Italy, soon disappeared from their sight as the small, comfortable steamer they had boarded sailed for Brindisi, Italy.[122]

CHAPTER 5

CLOSER AND CLOSER TO HOME

*A*fter arriving in Brindisi, the Ewings and their tour group took an excursion into Pompeii. There they watched workmen making plaster casts to capture the details of the city, which had been destroyed in 79 A.D. when Mount Vesuvius erupted burying the city in molten ash and rock.[123] That night, the Ewings could see the steam-spouting Mount Vesuvius and the Bay of Naples from their hotel room window in Sorrento. The next day they visited the prosperous city of Naples where an unpleasant and disturbing incident occurred. While they were having lunch at a café, it appalled Hazle and Davis to see a man striking his horse nearby. Unwilling to tolerate any abuse to animals, Davis leaped up from their table and ran over to the man and stopped him. The man and his friends urged Davis to forget about the incident and not report it to the authorities. Unmoved by their pleas, Davis followed his conscience and reported the abuse to the Humane Society.[124]

Leaving Naples and the unfortunate incident behind, they traveled with the tour group to Rome where they spent the next week studying some of the master painters under the instruction of Dr. Powers. When visiting the Sistine Chapel, Powers explained to them how Donato Bramante had proposed to construct a scaffold of flat board suspended from the ceiling from which Michelangelo could paint. Michelangelo, however, believed this method would leave holes in the ceiling. Instead of following Bramante's proposal, he designed his own scaffolding, from which he stood painting with his neck craned back for long hours. The technique he used of painting on wet plaster which dried in twelve hours, required that the work be done quickly and accurately. If he had not finished a section or needed to make major changes to it, the plaster had to be chipped off and he had start all over on that section. Working under such conditions, it is little wonder why it took him from May 10, 1508, to October 31, 1512, to complete the paintings in the Sistine Chapel.[125] Realizing the difficulty Michelangelo had in accomplishing this great work made a deep impression on all the members of the tour group.

The tour group spent a week in Florence visiting the picture galleries and listening to talks by Dr. Powers on such subjects such as the Medici family and the life of Savonarola.[126] The Ewings learned that the Medici family acquired their wealth through their banking enterprise, the Medici Bank, in which they were the first to use the bookkeeping method of double entry. They used their wealth to exercise a powerful influence in the Catholic Church and in the government of the city. The Medicis dominated the government of Florence for most of the fifteenth century, during which time the Italian Renaissance began and flourished through their strong support. Girolamo Savonarola, on the other hand, was a Dominican priest and leader who did not support the rule of the Medici and preached against what he saw as moral corruption in the Church. Because he openly expressed his strong opposition to the activities of the Church, he was put to death in 1498.[127] The Ewings and the rest of the tour group learned much about Italian history in addition to Italian art in Florence.

On the morning of June 8, 1925, the Ewings awakened to the roaring engine of an airplane flying over the hotel in Venice where they were staying. Hazle wrote to Julia of the experience and added, "Otherwise the island city is delightfully quiet—with only gondolas slopping thro small canals—[and] the occasional slow-moving steamer going up and down the main highway of the

'Grand Canal,'" that runs in an S-shape through the central part of the city. One of Hazle's favorite pastimes in Venice was riding in a gondola along the Grand Canal and gliding beneath the graceful stone structure of the Rialto Bridge, which enabled the inhabitants of the city who lived on the west bank of the river to shop at the Rialto Market on the east bank. From the gondola, she also saw many fine buildings. She also told Julia that she had heard rumors that, within a few years the gondolas would be replaced by gasoline launches. Hazle believed this change would negatively impact the peaceful and pleasant atmosphere of the city.[128]

At that point she put aside her letter, for Ralph had come in for his weekly settling up of finances. They also read half of the weekly Bible Lesson together, as they did each day, before preparing to leave Venice for a two-day stay in Milan. Following their stay in Milan, they traveled to the Hotel du Louvre in Paris, arriving in time for breakfast. Immediately after breakfast, Davis bought a week's supply of opera tickets, including tickets to see *Faust*. On the morning of June 17, 1925, Hazle accompanied a member of their tour group, Miss Edith Spaulding, a young woman from Worcester, Massachusetts, to do some clothes shopping in Paris. Edith found some items of clothing that she liked, but Hazle did not see anything she wanted to buy.[129]

That afternoon, Miss Spaulding joined the Ewings for sightseeing around Paris. That night they all attended the opera to hear *The Magic Flute*, a two-act opera by Mozart. Hazle declared that she had "heard almost as much grand opera [that] winter and spring" as she had in her whole life. "If not that, at least more in a short time than ever before."[130] While in Paris, they attended many musical programs and saw the works of several artists, including: Murillo, Velasquez, Rubens, Rembrandt, Van Dyck, and Holbein. In addition, they visited the Art Department of the Sorbonne, which is a part of the University of Paris.

Paris provided many attractions and activities for the Ewings, but they also encountered people they knew who were not part of their tour group. Hazle wrote to Julia one day, "To our delighted surprise, we <u>bumped</u>, literally, into Mrs. Soper this morning,— seeing pictures with Dudley Crafts Watson if you please." Mrs. Soper promptly introduced them to Mr. Watson. Seeing someone they knew made them feel a little closer to home, and Hazle thought it would be "even nicer" to see a member of her own family. She was especially looking forward to visiting with her cousin, Mildred Dilling, a well-known harpist who lived in England.[131]

When their tour of Paris came to a close in late June, their world trip and association with the Bureau of University Travel also ended. But the Ewings planned to stay in Europe until the end of the summer. After Paris, they visited Brussels, Belgium, where Davis had spent time as a boy during his father's appointment as Minister to Belgium under President Grover Cleveland. The first day in Brussels, the Ewings went to see the house on 43 Rue Belliard, where Davis and his family had lived. They also visited the fencing school he had attended. After Davis dismissed their driver, they walked for a few blocks and then stood by the statue of Godfrey de Bolliard while Davis looked for the familiar street, Mantangne de la Coeur, where he had spent many happy hours as a boy when he lived there. But he could not seem to find it until he realized it was where it had always been, but it had changed so much he did not recognize it. Then he located the Tartine Flammande at Von Hille and indulged in cups of delicious hot chocolate, which reminded him of his boyhood days in Brussels and it seemed almost like home again.[132]

After three days in Brussels, the Ewings boarded an airplane to England where Hazle's cousin, Mildred Dilling, would meet them. They had never flown before, nor had they seen any commercial airplanes. Awakening the morning of their flight to pouring rain and gusting winds, the Ewings anticipated that they would be flying in the open air and dressed appropriately, putting on several layers of clothing. Arriving at the air field, they were surprised to find that the airplane was enclosed and their seats were much like easy chairs. They settled into their seats, and the airplane taxied down the runway, but it took several attempts before it rose successfully off the ground. When the plane finally succeeded in taking off, the Ewings removed some layers of their clothing and attempted to relax and enjoy the flight. When they arrived in England and once again planted their feet on solid ground, they admitted that the flight had not been too bad.[133]

Mildred met them and took them directly to her home in Kent where they stayed for two days and then moved into a cottage in Beaconfield, a suburb of London. The cottage provided a place for them to rest and relax for three weeks, before starting on their month-long motor trip around the United Kingdom. Mildred came to visit them at the cottage before they left on their trip, and, since she was an avid horsewoman, Davis found some horses so they could all go riding. They celebrated July 4 with Mildred by attending the finals of the Oxford-Cambridge boat races at Henley. A few days later, they took a tour of Windsor Castle and had time to watch a cricket game at Lord's Field. To their surprise, at 4:15 p.m., in the midst of the game, all the cricket players dropped their bats and went into the club house for tea while the spectators wandered about waiting for the game to resume.[134]

On July 23, 1925, Edith Spaulding joined the Ewings as they began their motor trip around the island in a limousine. They stopped first at the small town of Buckingham to see the home of Hazle's father's forebears. Then they visited Sulgrave Manor, which had been the home of George Washington's ancestors.[135] Arriving at the Shakespeare Hotel at Stratford-on-Avon, where each room bore the name of a Shakespearean play, they stayed for several days, visiting sites of historic interest and attending the festival plays. The first night, they saw *Macbeth*, and the next day, *Twelfth Night* at the Shakespeare Memorial Theatre. They had planned this part of the trip "so that Ralph could have the part of the motor trip most interesting to him—Stratford-on-Avon and the Lake country."[136]

After leaving Stratford-on-Avon, they visited the home of Shakespeare's father, in Snitterfield, and then stopped at the Forest of Arden, Warwick Castle, Guy's Cliff, the Kenilworth Castle of Sir Walter Scott fame, and passed Tumble Down Stile.[137] A letter from Julia reached them at "Grasmere—in the heart of the charming English Lake country—that so many poets (Wordsworth, esp.) have immortalized." Answering Julia's letter from the Grosvenor Hotel in Chester, Hazle told her, "Old Chester is a fascinating place. One of the few remaining English walled towns, where the walls are intact." They had walked half way around the town on top of the walls the previous day.

After leaving Chester, they drove along the north coast of Wales, visiting the island of Anglesey, where they saw fertile, prosperous, cultivated fields (even more fertile than on the mainland), and herds of milk cows. After crossing many interesting bridges, and visiting some abbeys, they reached the hot sulphur springs of Bath. At Minehead, the Ewings put Miss Spaulding on a train for London. Then they continued their tour, going southwest and driving along the western coast, arriving for a five-day stay at St. Ives, an important fishing village known for its herring and mackerel, at that time, and later for its artist colony.[138]

When leaving the Tregenna Castle Hotel at St. Ives on August 13, 1925, Hazle attempted to write another letter to Julia while Davis oversaw the loading of their luggage on top of the car. She had used her portfolio as her desk all the months they had been traveling and it was quite full, as her desks always were. It bothered her that she did not seem to have time to answer the letters she received as promptly as she thought she should.[139] That morning she wrote to Julia regarding Julia's business success in selling silk items saying, "I am delighted it is going so well. I may be able to give you a good-sized order. I have had to buy a little, but I need much more." She added, "I hope you will not be disappointed. I did not buy anything in Paris. The styles were not at all my kind."[140]

Knowing they would soon be returning home, Hazle found herself thinking often about their need to hire some domestic workers, so she enlisted Julia's help. She had hired young girls in the past, but she told Julia she was "not going to be satisfied with young girls this time." She wanted reliable and settled help; for she expected that, after they returned from this trip, they would want to stay around home "for many, many, moons." She explained to Julia that their hired help would have to live in the garage, which had been converted into living quarters, and the workers would need to be "willing to stay in the house in the evening," when they went out and had to leave Sonny at home.[141]

Hazle's concerns about finding domestic workers did not dampen her enthusiasm for sightseeing, however. She told Julia, "We are all enjoying it hugely—yesterday we went through Lorna Doone country—and saw King Arthur's birthplace and castle—with all the backgrounds for the 'Round Table' legends." The five-day stay at St. Ives concluded their tour of the United Kingdom.[142]

They returned to London and spent their last week at the Rembrandt Hotel, sailing for home on the SS Minnewaska, an Atlantic Transport, from the Royal Albert Dock in London, on August 29, 1925. They expected to arrive in the United States on September 7 and to be in Bloomington on September 15. Before leaving London, Hazle learned that Julia would be away when they returned, and she lamented, "I'll miss you a lot, Dear, I'm plumb full of things I've been wishing to tell you—but of course they will keep a month or two longer—after all the weeks that I have been bottling them in so far." She added, "And, perhaps, by the time you are home again—I'll have found the right helpers, and will have things running smoothly enough so that we can really have some time together."[143]

On September 1, 1925, she wrote to Julia from the SS Minnewaska, "We are on our way home! And not one of you can possibly be one hundredth part as glad as we are."[144] On September 7, 1925, Hazle wrote again to Julia, "[We are] anchored in the harbor of NY!! Waiting for our medical inspection. It is a misty moisty morning, and Labor Day." Hazle could see Staten Island where her brother, Ellsworth, and his family lived, and she wondered if they could see the SS Minnewaska docked in the harbor. It seemed to take a long time for them to receive permission to come ashore, but in spite of that she was happy to be "so near home." Looking around her, it amazed Hazle that she hardly recognized people they had been traveling with for months, they looked so different in their "landing clothes."[145]

When they made it ashore, the welcome they received overwhelmed them. In addition to those who met them in person, Hazle also found two letters from Julia waiting for her in New York. The next day, she found time to respond to Julia's letters and told her of the welcome that she and Davis had received: "I feel as I did when we were first married! We did not know we had so many devoted friends and how we do appreciate it!" But all Hazle really wanted was to go home, and she confided to Julia, "I have learned to be patient this year—but even so—I can hardly wait—for Tuesday."[146]

They arrived home on September 15, 1925, without Ralph, who had stayed in Marion, Massachusetts, to attend Tabor Academy. Their reunion with Sonny was a happy one, and it amazed Hazle to see how much he had grown while they were away. Their return made quite a stir in Bloomington, and it did not take long for a reporter from The Daily Bulletin to contact them for an interview. Hazle met with the reporter, and she enjoyed sharing some of their adventures for an article that appeared in the September 18, newspaper. The reporter wrote:

> It is an experience of utter charm to listen to Mrs. Ewing, in an informal 'Travelogue' of their experiences, which included so many that never fall to the lot of the swift tourists, for this tour of the Ewings' was utterly distinct from a 'cruise'; it was the genuine sharing of the life of the different countries visited.[147]

Hazle gave credit to The Bureau of University Travel, who "At all times . . . provided authoritative men, specialists in their various lines, who brought special values to the sights and peoples seen."[148]

Soon after they returned home, Davis began to develop a lecture on Angkor, Cambodia, from the pictures he had taken and some of the letters he had written home to his family. He later had all the letters he had written home compiled in chronological order and bound in several journals. The trip had given Hazle the opportunity to "renew and verify her early impressions" of other peoples and cultures which she had formed during a similar trip she took as a girl with her parents traveling as far as Constantinople. The seed of interest in other peoples and lands had been planted during that trip and had grown over the years. Her recent world-trip had also enlivened her desire to find a concrete way to help promote world peace.[149.]

THE SEED

CHAPTER 6

FROM A GIRL

*H*azle's father, Orlando J. Buck, came from an established New England family, the son of John and Abbie Morse Buck. He received his education in the public schools and Normal School in Paris, Maine. After he graduated from public school, Orlando became a teacher for a time, and then a clerk for the Quincy Street Market in Boston. He moved from Boston to New York to become an apprentice in a rubber paint manufacturing company. He hoped this change would lead to a promising career.[150]

He applied himself to this new venture and soon became a proficient chemist. His efforts brought him an offer of employment from the New York City branch of the Cleveland Ohio Rubber Paint Company, which he accepted. Through this new employment opportunity, he came to know Lillian Louise Brewer, the daughter of Caroline and Nelson Brewer, the owners of the rubber paint company. Orlando and Lillian were married on January 21, 1880, in Cleveland. Orlando continued to manage the New York branch of the factory until December 20, 1880. Their first child, Lillian Hazle Buck, was born that year on Christmas Day, in Cleveland, Ohio. Hazle seemed destined to live a life devoted to the promotion of peace on earth and good will toward men.[151]

On January 1, 1881, Orlando, Lillian, and their small daughter moved to Chicago where Orlando worked for his father-in-law as superintendent of that branch of the rubber paint company, and later became an officer and a large stock holder. After moving to

Chicago, Orlando and Lillian had a son, Nelson Leroy, born on December 2, 1882. During those years, Orlando learned a great deal about running the company and, in early 1890, he and A.G. Cox became partners and combined their resources to buy the Rubber Paint Company.[152]

Then one evening at the dinner table, Hazle remembered her father saying to her mother, "I think I am going to buy a chewing gum company." Her mother responded, "I would just as soon you buy a saloon as run a chewing gum company."[153] Orlando disregarded his wife's misgivings and pursued his interest in the gum business, and, in 1892, he became part owner of the Zeno Company, which produced gum-ball machines. That same year, Hazle's second brother, Ellsworth Brewer, was born on July 3.[154]

Orlando supervised the production of the brightly colored gum-balls to fill the gum-ball machines, and greatly increased his new company's revenue.[155] Following his instincts regarding the chewing gum company led to his connection with William Wrigley, Jr., some years later. In 1911, Orlando became the General Manager of factories and a director of the William Wrigley, Jr. Company. He retired as the General Manager in 1914, but he remained a director of the corporation until his death in 1919. Through his association with Wrigley, Orlando accrued a substantial amount of wealth that was passed on to his family.[156]

The success that Orlando experienced with the Zeno Company and, later, his association with William Wrigley, Jr. Company, enabled the family to live in the prestigious Auburn Park section of Chicago, where Hazle attended grammar school. As a child, Hazle developed a deep interest in nature and set a goal for herself of learning how to identify three trees, three flowers, and three birds a year. She learned how to identify the trees by their bark as well as their leaves so that she would be able to recognize them at different times of the year. Hazle watched for the flowers to bloom and committed to memory the names of each flowering plant, as well as what time of year it bloomed. She developed the ability to identify birds by their color, habitats, and songs.[157]

Hazle attended and graduated from Calumet High School and began her college career at the University of Chicago in the fall of 1898. She spent a quarter of the school year of 1899 at Stetson University in Deland, Florida, as an exchange student. She loved to travel, and the opportunity to live in another part of the country for a time gave her a great sense of satisfaction and pleasure. Hazle believed that being an exchange student broadened her college experience, and she maintained a life-long interest in Florida, visiting the state often during the cold Illinois winters.

After her quarter in Deland, Hazle returned to Chicago to continue her education at the University and took advantage of the opportunity to play sports. She especially enjoyed playing basketball, but she also became one of the first women to play golf at the University. Agile and slender, Hazle, at 5' 4 ½" tall, could move easily and quickly about the basketball court. As in all aspects of her life, Hazle played basketball and golf with intensity.

In 1900, while a junior at the college, Hazle played in the position of right guard on a team of talented women. That year "the interest in women's athletics"[158] was greater than in previous years. Over one hundred women tried out for the teams. In spite of the intense competition, Hazle won a place on one of the teams. On January 12 of that year, the team she played on defeated the Graduates with a score of 8 to 5. They succeeded in beating the Seniors in the two games they played in February. The first game on February 15, they won 8 to 4; but the second game, on February 23, had been more difficult to win, with a final score of 6 to 4.[159]

In addition to playing sports, Hazle took part in the drama club, enjoying the opportunity to act. During the school year of 1901 and 1902, the members of the club put their efforts into establishing, "a permanent and consistent place among student interest."[160] That year the students chose to put on the play, *All the Comforts of Home*, written by William Gillette. The club paid the royalties to put on the play and rehearsals began at once, but the faculty thought parts of the play were objectionable. The club quickly regrouped and chose to perform *The Secretary* by Von Moser instead, with *A Complicated Affair* as the curtain raiser, in which Hazle played the part of Stella Glynn, the sister of the main character, Frank Glynn. The opening performances on December 14 had the distinction of being the first opportunity for the club to appear in the downtown theater at the University of Fine Arts Building.[161]

The untimely death of the director and professional coach of the drama club, H. Stanley Davies, on January 25, 1902, greatly saddened the members. The students had been fond of Davies, a "talented, conscientious, and ambitious worker, who had the interests of the club deeply at heart." They believed that Davies' "personal magnetism, ready grasp of dramatic situations, and complications, and thorough knowledge of the [personnel] of the club won for him the respect and admiration of all the members."[162] In memory of Davies, the students continued to support the drama club and his replacement, Bartley Cushing. The membership of the club increased from twenty members to thirty members by the end of January.

In the spring of 1902, Hazle graduated from the University of Chicago with a degree in philosophy and the high hopes and aspirations of youth. As with many young women of her time who received a college degree, she wanted to accomplish something useful with her education. Sometime after her graduation from college, Hazle decided to take class instruction in Christian Science from Ruth Babcock Ewing in Chicago, the wife of Judge William Ewing, who had become a Christian Science Lecturer in 1899.[163]

It was at a Christian Science meeting in Chicago that Hazle met the interesting and attractive Davis Ewing. Davis lived in Bloomington, Illinois, and was the nephew of Judge William Ewing. Davis's father, James Stevenson Ewing, also of Bloomington, had been appointed as minister to Belgium during Grover Cleveland's presidential term in 1892. Davis had lived with his parents and siblings in Belgium during Cleveland's term in office, which gave him a base for traveling extensively in Europe. Both William and James Ewing were double cousins of Adlai Ewing Stevenson I, who had been Vice President to Grover Cleveland.

Among the interests that Hazle and Davis shared was their devotion to Christian Science and their enjoyment of world travel. One of Davis's more recent adventures had led him to Mexico where he had been in charge of a large rubber plant. By the time he met Hazle, he had successfully established the Davis Ewing Concrete Company in Bloomington. When he asked her to marry him, Hazle accepted his proposal, and prepared to move to Bloomington. The distance between Chicago and Bloomington did not present a barrier to Hazle visiting her family or attending events taking place in Chicago, since it was only a short train ride away.

The couple married quietly in Chicago on October 22, 1907, with Reverend R.A. White officiating at the home of Hazle's parents. Hazle and Davis wanted their wedding to be informal and cozy and had invited only close relatives and a few intimate friends to attend. Hazle and Davis said their wedding vows in front of the living room fireplace that had been decorated with autumn leaves. A basket of chrysanthemums had been placed on the dining room table, along with similax maiden-hair ferns, candles, and many gifts from their guests. Judge William Ewing and other relatives of Davis's from Bloomington came to wish the newlyweds well and to see them off on their honeymoon.[164]

Davis and Hazle spent their honeymoon in the western and southern parts of the United States before taking up residence in Bloomington on December 1, 1907. They settled down to married life in a small, but cozy cottage, which provided a comfortable home for them as Davis worked to enlarge his concrete company and increase their income. Davis had the foresight to realize that a concrete company would be needed as the town of Bloomington grew. He began by laying concrete sidewalks and then developed and constructed other concrete products.

The prosperity of Davis's company enabled the couple to move to a larger home, located at 1522 E. Olive Street. While Davis continued to work diligently on the development of his concrete business, Hazle put her efforts into the social reforms of her day, and took an interest in local, national, and international politics. As her interest in politics grew, Hazle became convinced that women should have a say in the government that ruled their lives.

$\mathscr{S}$TRUGGLE
FOR THE RIGHT TO VOTE

CHAPTER 7

THE RIGHTS OF WOMEN

$\mathscr{I}$n 1913, the state of Illinois gave women the right to vote in presidential and municipal elections. Hazle became actively involved in the Woman's Suffrage movement in 1915 because of her belief that women should have the right to help decide who would be elected to city, state, and federal government offices. When she joined the battle, the struggle for women to gain the right to vote had been going on for over sixty-five years.

The struggle really got its start in the summer of 1848. Lucretia Mott and Elizabeth Cady Stanton organized the First Woman's Rights Convention in Seneca Falls, New York, on July 18 and 19 that year. This convention served as the beginning of a movement to unite women in the United States in the cause for enfranchisement. Later, when Elizabeth Cady Stanton met Susan B. Anthony, the two women recognized that they had a common cause and began working together to form the American Rights National Convention.[165]

In 1869, two factions developed in the woman's suffrage group, and the convention was dissolved. Anthony and Stanton then formed the radical National Suffrage Woman Association (NSWA), and Lucy Stone organized the more conservative American Suffrage Woman Association (ASWA). The more radical group endeavored to gain the vote for all women through a federal Amendment, while the more conservative group of women worked to win the vote for women state by state. Unfortunately, this division of efforts toward their common

67

goal impaired the progress of the woman's movement. [166]

In 1875, endeavoring to make progress for suffrage, Susan B. Anthony drafted what became the 19th Amendment, which consisted of two parts. The first part gave all citizens of the United States the right to vote, which could not be denied or changed by the United States or any State because of sex. The second part, safeguarding the first, demanded that Congress would have the power to enforce the provision of the article through proper legislation. [167] But the amendment did not receive much attention until 1887, when the Senate showed some interest in it. The women of the NSWA clung to the hope that the Senate would pass the amendment. The Senate did not pass it, however, and it was soon forgotten.

In 1890, the NSWA and the ASWA decided to unite under the leadership of Anthony as the National American Woman Suffrage Association (NAWSA), taking on the more conservative aspects of the ASWA. [168] Anthony soon found it necessary to retire, however, and chose Carrie Chapman Catt over Anna Howard Shaw to succeed her. Although Shaw was a better orator, Catt had superior organizational skills. In 1904, however, Catt resigned from the position to care for her ill husband, and Shaw took over. As Anthony had foreseen, Shaw did not have the organizational skills to sustain the work of the association. Under Shaw's leadership, some of the younger women grew impatient and began seeking a more militant approach to securing the right for women to vote. [169]

In 1910, two young women, Alice Paul and Lucy Burns, who had become acquainted in England as members of the Women's Social and Political Union under the leadership of Emmeline Pankhurst, returned to America. The lethargic state of the American suffragists disappointed Paul and Burns. They saw that little progress had been made in the United States towards women acquiring the right to vote. So, despite their disappointment in the NAWSA, Paul and Burns became actively involved with the organization in 1912. That year the NAWSA gained some state support, but also suffered great losses in New Jersey, New York, Pennsylvania, and Massachusetts. The two young women became members of the Congressional Union Committee of the NAWSA, which focused attention on reviving the organization's interest in the federal amendment.

In 1913, the Congressional Union endeavored to push the resolution through the committee and the Senate. On March 13, the day before Woodrow Wilson's inauguration, Paul and Burns persuaded the Congressional Union Committee to organize a parade in front of the White House. The two women then implemented three important tactics they had learned from Pankhurst's organization in England: to hold the political party in power responsible for failing to support the suffrage amendment, to get publicity, and to organize protests that would focus attention on the demand for the amendment.[170] The parade successfully met those three criteria and encouraged the Congressional Union to launch another mass demonstration in front of the White House in support of the amendment on April 7, 1913.

In July of 1913, the Senate took up the discussion of the amendment for the first time since 1887. When the Senate voted on the amendment in early 1914, however, it failed once again to receive the two-thirds majority of votes required to pass it. Although the amendment failed, the Congressional Union did not give up. The women recognized that the amendment had received more attention that year than it had received over the past sixteen years. While the Senate had been discussing the amendment, the women had been actively seeking the attention of the President and the House of Representatives.

In 1915, Catt resumed the leadership of the NAWSA, after Shaw had been asked to resign. After resuming her leadership role, Catt became increasingly uncomfortable with the militant tactics of the Congressional Union, even though its efforts had resulted in the House of Representatives voting on the amendment in January

1915 for the first time. When the amendment did not pass in the House of the Representatives, the Congressional Union continued their militant tactics, causing Catt and the more conservative members of the association to be concerned for the success of the movement. But the members of the Congressional Union fervently believed that, in order for the movement to succeed in getting the amendment passed, they must continue lobbying and employing other militant tactics.

As a subscriber to the weekly paper promoted by Paul and Burns, *The Suffragist*, Hazle received a letter written on May 15, 1915, from one of the paper's staff members informing her of the need to increase the circulation of the paper. She was asked to send in two new subscriptions as soon as possible.[171] Because of the conflict with the conservative members of the NAWAS, the Congressional Union needed to attract more members and other sources of money to support their militant activities. The writer of the letter suggested that Hazle subscribe to the paper for the Senators and/ or Congressmen in her state, and to start a local organization to increase the circulation of the weekly. The letter concluded, *The Suffragist* is the most effective instrument in securing the Susan B. Anthony Amendment in this season of Congress."[172] Hazle wanted the amendment to pass, but the tone of the letter made her uneasy with the militant group's approach.

Consequently, she felt compelled to write a letter to the Congressional Union Committee, in which she expressed her concern regarding some of the things she had read in the weekly. In particular, Hazle did not believe it necessary to attack President Wilson, whose views on neutrality toward the war in Europe she supported. She hoped that the women were not "going to let any feeling of bitterness creep into the pages of *The Suffragist*"[173]

Lucy Burns quickly responded to the letter on June 5, 1915. Burns assured Hazle that they agreed with her that bitterness had "no place in so hopeful a movement as the woman suffrage movement."[174] Burns also explained that they did not intend that women should not support neutrality, but they "meant only to point out that the President's office was a representative one, deriving its dignity not from birth or rank but solely from its representative character, and the President does not represent women," because he had not been elected by them.[175] She further explained that it was not an attack on Wilson personally, but on the office of President, and she noted that Wilson, as President, had not supported woman's suffrage.

Although Hazle did not agree with some of the methods used by the Congressional Union, she continued to support the organization. On June 15, 1915, Gertrude Lynde Crocker of the Congressional Union wrote to her regarding suffrage work in Chicago, saying, "Membership is open to all women" who believe "that suffrage is fundamental to democratic progress."[176] She told Hazle that in the last Congress, which was the 63rd, the name of the Amendment had been changed to the Bristow-Mondell Amendment, since Senator Bristow of Kansas had introduced it in the Senate and Congressman Mondell of Wyoming had presented it to the House of Representatives.

Crocker urged Hazle to become a member of the Congressional Union, or contribute to the Susan B. Anthony Memorial Fund, or buy a year's subscription to The Suffragist for one dollar in order to secure the success of their mission. Hazle realized that the women of the United States needed to be united in order to convince the 64th Congress that they should be awarded the right to vote. She thoughtfully and prayerfully contemplated her own role in the suffrage movement.

As summer passed into late fall, the need for financial support of the Susan B. Anthony Amendment increased, and, on November 25, 1915, Alice Paul sent a letter to the workers in the suffrage field. The Amendment seemed close to passing in the Senate, having failed by only 11 votes. Paul pointed out that this near victory had come about mainly by the work and financial support of the women in the District of Columbia. Paul believed that, "If the women of the whole country will join with the District of Columbia, success is assured."[177] Already nearly 400,000 women had been given the vote in the West. One-fourth of the Senate, one-sixth of the House, and one-fifth of the electoral vote now came from suffrage states. Paul maintained that "nothing can prevent the success of the national amendment if we unite in its support."[178] She also suggested that the failure of the referendum campaigns in New Jersey, New York, Pennsylvania, and Massachusetts should make the suffrage supporters "realize the wisdom of concentrating our strength upon the national government rather than dissipating it in many state referendums."[179]

As the New Year began, the Congressional Union suffragists focused their attention on supporting the 19th Amendment, and Hazle heard from a co-worker in the suffrage movement, Dora Lewis, in early January. Lewis solicited Hazle's financial support of the Union's efforts to win over the government.[180] And Hazle's friend, Josephine K. Linton, the recently appointed chairman for *The Suffragist* in Chicago, also wrote her a letter. Linton asked Hazle to join her committee and help her secure subscriptions for the paper. Hazle responded positively to both of her friends' requests for help.

In early 1916, Mabel Sippy of the Congressional Union wrote to Hazle regarding a meeting of the disenfranchised states to be held at the Union's national headquarters in Washington. She told Hazle, "Our hope for success lies in convincing Congress that we have such support among voting women that we will be a real factor in the coming elections in case the amendment is not put through."[181] The suffragists needed to convince Congress that an organization of voting women existed and was ready to act. A party of thirty-six women would arrive from the east at Pennsylvania Station in Chicago on Monday, April 10, at 2 p.m. Sippy added, "You are urged to be a part of the two days' demonstration planned in honor of the Eastern visitors, to urge immediate action in favor

of the Susan B. Anthony Amendment."[182] Hazle hoped to attend
the meeting so she could learn first-hand about the activities of the
suffrage movement in Washington, D.C.

In March 1916, the Illinois Congressional Union moved to new
headquarters at Room 1004 Stevens Building, on 9 North State
Street. To celebrate the occasion, Mrs. Gilson Gardner and Mrs.
Edward Russell (both from Washington) and Florence Kelly of the
National Advisory Council spoke on March 22 to a gathering of
women, followed by refreshments. In addition to celebrating their
move, the women felt encouraged by the Judiciary Committee's
"unanimous consent to set March 28th as the day for reconsideration
of the Suffrage Amendment." The women thought "An explicit
demand for favorable action now from the women voters will be
certain to win."[183]

Recognizing the need to take action, Hazle wrote a letter to
Wm. Elza Williams of the Illinois House of Representatives, who
was on the Judiciary Committee. Williams responded to her letter
on March 23, 1916. Hazle felt disappointed as she read, "I beg to
say that . . . I do not believe it wise, in view of the present state
of public affairs, for Congress to take on any new legislation at
this session that is not immediately necessary." But he continued,
"out of consideration for the wishes of the good women who are
interested in woman's suffrage, I have consented to favor a report
at this session." [184] The Congressman's consent to support woman's
suffrage seemed to justify the hope of the suffrage women that the
amendment would soon pass.

In the meantime, in Washington, D.C., Wilson struggled with
the fear of American involvement in the war in Europe, especially
intensified since March 1916, when the French ship, the *Sussex*,
had been bombarded by the Germans. Matters of urgent national
and international affairs demanded his time and attention.
Although aware of the threat to American neutrality, the militant
suffragists refused to give up their fight for the right to vote as

previous suffragists had done during the Civil War. (At that time,
the women had put aside their desire to gain their right to vote to
fight for the freedom of the enslaved blacks, thinking this would
lead to women eventually being given the right to vote. When the
Civil War ended, however, black men were given the right to vote,
but not women, black *or* white.) Even if America joined the war in
Europe, the militant suffragists felt they could not afford to give up
the fight now.

While in Chicago in April, Hazle visited the new headquarters
of the Illinois Congressional Union and attended the organization's
banquet. The speeches had been inspiring, and Hazle continued
to entertain the hope that women all over the country would be
empowered to vote. The women expressed their unity of purpose
by wearing accessories of white and gold. Hazle had apparently
misplaced her "colors" and returned home without them. A few days
later, she received a letter from her friend, Mellie, who explained,
"Your gay colors came home safely in [my husband] Roy's pocket! I
am sending them back to you. Roy was very much surprised when
his pocket blossomed out this morning in white and gold." [185]

In early May, Hazle attended a suffragist meeting in Normal,
Illinois, and had the opportunity to hear a speech given by
Emmeline Pankhurst, the leader of England's Women's Social and
Political Union. Inspired by the speech, Hazle wrote a letter to the
City Editor of the Bloomington paper, the *Pantagraph*, on May 11,
1916, in defense of Pankhurst. She told the editor, "I have been
more deeply impressed with the marvelous change of attitude in
regard to [Pankhurst's] work and personality than has come to this
country in the last four or five years." Hazle admitted, "It is not much
longer ago than . . . I myself first began to be open-minded about
what [Pankhurst] and her colleagues were trying to do." Hazle had
realized "there was little authentic information to be had, and few
indeed were they who had anything but ridicule and condemnation
both for [Pankhurst] and her associates." She had learned that the

headlines regarding Pankhurst should not be taken at face value and had come to see Pankhurst and her group as "a body of intelligent women who are willing to endure not only insult and injury—but death and torture as well, for their cause."[186]

Hazle valued the commitment of these women to their country even though that country had denied them a voice in the decisions it made. She felt it significant that "there is hardly a substantial newspaper in this country that does not fully recognize the . . . importance of Mrs. Pankhurst's personality and work." From what Hazle had read about Pankhurst in the United States newspapers, she believed her to be "an international figure—and a maker of history."[187]

Being fully committed to the cause of suffrage, Hazle patronized *The Woman's Journal* and *Suffrage News*, a paper that promoted the work of the suffragists. In late May, she bought a ticket to attend the National Woman's Party Convention organized by the Congressional Union of the NAWSA to be held June 5 through 7 in Chicago, but it is uncertain if she actually attended the convention. The NAWSA and the Congressional Union officially split later in June. The more conservative members of the NAWSA disapproved of the militant tactics practiced by the Congressional Union members.[188]

In spite of the changes that were taking place within the movement, Hazle continued in her efforts to gain support for woman's suffrage. She contacted Mrs. Lillard, the owner of the Durley Building in Bloomington, to put up a banner for the Woman's Suffrage movement. Lillard refused when she learned that "the banner is intended to carry adverse direction or criticism against a candidate for President of the United States."[189] Although disappointed, Hazle had some of her own reservations regarding the display of a banner disparaging President Wilson, who was running for re-election that year.

In mid-September, Hazle received the official announcement

from Alva Belmont at the headquarters of the National Woman's
Party (NWP) in Washington D.C. that, "For the first time in all
history women have formed a political party."[190] The Woman's
Party would be campaigning in the states where women could vote,
encouraging them to vote against Wilson and all other Democratic
candidates; it was angered by both Wilson and the Democratic
Party's indifference to woman's suffrage, and it intended to make
its anger felt throughout the country. The hostility being expressed
toward the President troubled Hazle. But she understood that the
patience of the suffragists had worn thin. They had grown weary of
waiting for the President and the branches of the federal government
to acknowledge that women should have the right to vote.

Hazle received a handwritten invitation from Jessie Hardy
McKaye on September 14, 1916, to attend a demonstration on
September 19 in Chicago in honor of Charles Evans Hughes,
a Republican and former governor of New York, who was also
running for the Presidency. McKaye told her, "We need all hands!
It would be splendid if you could come over from Bloomington."[191]
The National Woman's Party (NWP) hoped that their support
of the Republicans would awaken the Democrats in office to take
action on behalf of woman's suffrage.[192] On September 19, 1916,
the NWP carried out its plan, meeting Hughes at the train and
forming a parade in which they carried a big amendment banner.
But Hazle did not want to support the Republican candidate if it
could be avoided.

CHAPTER 8

THE CONFLICT WITHIN

*H*azle earnestly supported woman's suffrage, but she also wanted to vote for President Wilson in the upcoming election. In spite of his apparent lack of interest in the franchise of women, she fervently hoped that the President would be moved to approve and actively back the Susan B. Anthony Amendment. In September 1916, prior to the NWP's parade for Hughes, Hazle attempted to encourage the local Democratic Party to consider the plight of women by writing to E.E. Donnelly, a lawyer and a member of the McLean County Democratic Central Committee. She included materials on the suffrage movement with her letter.

Responding to her letter on September 16, Donnelly began by telling Hazle that he did not want to "agrify" her. He realized she had given the materials "careful consideration," but reminded her, "There are many elements to be considered." Donnelly believed that the women of Illinois should be "either entitled to full rights or none." But he did not see an end to the current condition for years to come, and he was certain that "Wilson's attitude on the question is right." Hazle could see that the information she had sent Donnelly had not made the desired impression on him.[193]

Donnelly thought that women needed to be educated before they would be fit "to vote," for in the South, he informed Hazle, "disastrous results" had occurred when colored men received the franchise "years before they were ready for it." He questioned the wisdom of giving southern colored women the right to vote, and continued, "As far as the Republican women are concerned I believe party candidates and methods will advocate that the Democratic ladies remain quite neutral." [194] Hazle did not agree.

In answer to Donnelly's letter, she wrote, "As far as the great mass of women of this country are concerned, it seems to me personally that they are quite prepared right now to exercise the full rights of franchise as most men who have rigorously earned their rights by their twenty-first birthday." She continued, "I myself have never heard of groups of newly enfranchised young men getting together under a capable teacher for an earnest study of the law and [government] . . . before they are to vote." On the contrary, "I have known of thousands of intelligent and public-spirited women doing this even before they were enfranchised." [195]

Donnelly answered Hazle's response to his letter on September 23, 1916: "I will appreciate any efforts you may make in the future towards interesting our lady voters in Mr. Wilson ... and ... attending any political meetings we may have here this campaign." Donnelly told her that they hoped to have "a few first class political events here and shall be pleased if our audiences are at least fifty per cent ladies."[196] Donnelly's attitude did not deter Hazle, and in reply she sent him additional suffrage materials.

On September 26, Hazle received a telegram sent from Mrs. Gilson Gardner in response to Hazle's request for an effective speaker to give a rousing speech to the ladies of Bloomington. Gardner suggested Louisine Waldron Havemeyer of New York and asked Hazle's assistance in putting together a social function for the occasion.[197] Hazle agreed to give the needed assistance and used her influence in the Bloomington area to make the event a success.

Hazle also signed up to be on the Campaign Fund Committee for the National Woman's Party. Alva Belmont, of the NWP, wrote to her, "I am writing to express my appreciation for your willingness to become a member of my Committee for the raising of a $500,000 fund, and thank you for your personal contribution of $10 toward the fund." Belmont added, "I need to tell you how deeply appreciative I am of this prompt offer of cooperation on your part."[198] Belmont encouraged Hazle to secure other Committee members among her friends who would be willing to take on the task of raising the money for their cause.

On October 10, 1916, Hazle received another letter from Donnelly, but she did not find it any more encouraging or satisfying than his previous response. He told her, "As to how, when, and thru whom general suffrage will come does not at this time concern me. We are about to elect a president and I am principally interested in getting as many votes, men and women, for Mr. Wilson as possible." In her previous letter, Hazle had told Donnelly she was considering voting for the Republican candidate, Hughes, to which Donnelly responded, "I am sorry to believe that you propose to vote for Mr. Hughes." He continued, "You would make a splendid supporter of our President," and he added, "Please do not understand that I am trying to start an argument, far be it from me thus to err."[199]

That same day, Sara Feltman, who was a fellow worker in the NWP in Colorado, wrote to Hazle, telling her, "I was arrested here last night giving out literature at a Democratic meeting and taken to the station in a patrol wagon." She continued, "Of course, I was discharged at once but it was very interesting to know what the Democrats will do when you are opposing their party."[200] That a woman could be arrested for trying to exercise her right to freely express her beliefs seemed amazing to Hazle. It also saddened and disappointed her. She had been a supporter of the Democratic Party for some time, and her friend's experience did not indicate that the Democratic Party was going to change its position regarding the enfranchisement of women, as Hazle had hoped.

After receiving Feltman's letter, Hazle wrote to Donnelly, "The women of this country have waited for sixty years . . . hoping this country would furnish the one case in history in which a body of disfranchised citizens might be able to secure its right of franchise without a united fight for it." She added, "The failure of this hope—after so many years of patient waiting has been a bitter disappointment." Saddened over the lack of attention Wilson had given to woman's suffrage, and her knowledge of the plight of some of her single women friends, Hazle insisted, "Taxation without representation is no less tyrannical today than when we fought our revolution." She told Donnelly, "the spirit actuating this new and peaceable revolution is no less high-principled and determined. I wish the great Democratic Party might recognize this before the end of the present campaign."[201] Hazle admired President Wilson's stand for peace and wanted to vote for him, but she was determined to support the rights of women, even if that meant disregarding her partisan devotion.

Hazle also wrote letters to the White House in September and October. She received confirmation that her letters had been received both months, but she had no other indication that the message they carried was given any attention. Although disheartened by this seeming lack of interest by the Democratic Party in the plight of women, Hazle continued to support the NWP, confident that right must win.

A letter written on November 14, 1916, by Mabel Sippy, State Chairman of the NWP, gave Hazle encouragement to continue in her efforts. Sippy wrote, "The next work for the Woman's Party is to strengthen its committee in each congressional district and to put the committees to work on organizing a deputation to the congressman of each district." She explained, "Deputations are a distinctive form of work used by the Congressional Union and the Woman's Party. By going in a group before your congressman you demonstrate to him that there is a real interest in the action he takes on the federal suffrage amendment." She added, "At such hearings there usually are one or two speeches made and the response from the congressman completes the event."[202] Hazle and her committee arranged for a deputation meeting with Congressman John Sterling and informed Sippy of the date. She replied, urging Hazle to "personally conduct the deputation and introduce the speakers." Hazle accepted responsibility for conducting the meeting.[203]

Only days before the scheduled deputation, an editorial appeared in the *Pantagraph* regarding Elihu Root's address before the Anti-Suffrage Association Convention. Hazle responded to the editorial, taking advantage of the opportunity to clarify why the Woman's Party had chosen to pursue a federal amendment over the state-by-state provision for women to vote. She wrote to the editor, "Since the disadvantage of the federal amendment has been put forth . . . would you not be glad to give the readers . . . the benefit of the arguments on the other side." She wanted it to be understood that she and some of her co-workers in the suffrage movement "would still prefer the 'state-by-state' method, if victory for our just cause were thus humanly possible within the next decade."[204]

Hazle pointed out that Harriet Stanton Blatch, the daughter of Elizabeth Cady Stanton, had told a crowd of suffrage supporters in June that she could no longer support the state-by-state tactic. Blatch and many other devoted women had "Labored for months and years in the emigrant-flooded eastern states, and often sending their plea for freedom through half a dozen interpreters on one platform—only to find their cause defeated when the ballots were counted." Hazle reiterated that Susan B. Anthony's amendment declares that no one in the United Stated should be denied the right to vote "on account of sex."[205]

Hazle thought that there were "few indeed among the rank and file who have stopped to consider either the difficulties of amending state constitutions, or the advantages of the federal amendment." Hazle conceded that "[s]eldom are reforms brought about thru ideally perfect methods." She was certain the end result providing the right to vote for both men and women—justified the need for a federal amendment, although it would "require some compromise of the essential principle of state sovereignty."[206] Hazle believed that any thinking citizen should consider the compromise worth making.

Hazle's response to the anti-suffrage editorial appeared in the *Pantagraph* on November 27, the day of the deputation with Congressman Sterling. Sippy had come to give her support to Hazle and her committee and to participate in the meeting. As the deputation began in the Supervisor's room in the Bloomington Court House, Hazle, as the master of ceremonies, kept her speech brief so that the other speakers would have ample time for their talks. She introduced the first speaker at the session, Mrs. Anna B. Lewis, a successful business woman and a single parent, who made a strong argument for women's right to vote when she told the group, "A woman thrown upon her own resources finds that she is in the midst of a man's world with all laws made by man. She is taxed for her properties the same as men, but has no voice in the laws by which this tax is administered."[207] Speaking for women's rights as business and property owners, Lewis urged Congressman Sterling to support the federal amendment.

Following Lewis's talk, Hazle introduced Mrs. Abbie Bowman, who represented the WCTU (Women's Christian Temperance Union). After forty years of struggle, Bowman thought that women could find some encouragement in the fact that some public men had come to the support of woman's suffrage. Then a former resident of Pennsylvania, Mrs. R. B. McCarroll, spoke of the struggle to obtain the vote that was going on in Pennsylvania. Next, Mrs. Jessie Lummis, of Normal, who had been a resident of Wyoming where women had the right to vote, lamented losing part of her voting privileges since moving to Illinois. The last speaker Hazle introduced was Sippy, who gave a brief history of the organization of the National Woman's Suffrage Party. She informed the group that twelve states had given women the right to vote. Hazle thoroughly agreed with Sippy's summation that, "In asking for a federal suffrage law, [women] are simply asking for a measure of pure justice."[208]

After Sippy concluded her talk, Hazle asked Congressman

Sterling if he would like to make any comments. Sterling promptly took the floor and talked for twenty minutes. He stated that he "appreciated the opportunity of hearing this company of women plead for the success of their cause." If they had come to convince him to support their cause, however, they had wasted their time. Sterling had already made his support of woman's suffrage known. But he gladly gave the reasons for his support, which included the fact that he had heard Susan B. Anthony and her co-workers speak on the subject many years earlier. Sterling confessed he had never understood why women had not been given the right to vote, and any argument he had ever heard against it had not made sense to him. "As Mrs. Ewing has already said it is no longer a method of principle, but a method as to how this government should be cured," Sterling told the group. During his campaign, Sterling had found that women voters were "good listeners and intelligent attendants at all political meetings." They composed half of his audiences, and he appreciated the different perspective that women brought to the discussions.[209]

When Sterling concluded his comments, Hazle and the other women thanked him for his address, his support, and his encouragement. The meeting was adjourned and the women gathered at the Woman's Exchange for tea. Although they had been encouraged by the deputation, the women knew that a long and hard fight to achieve their goal still lay ahead of them, for not all the Congressmen in the country had the same attitude as Sterling.

The following day, November 28, 1916, an article on the deputation with Congressman John Sterling appeared in the Bloomington paper. Impressed with the accurate and fair article that the reporter had written, Hazle wrote to him, "Please accept my deep appreciation of your being with us in person during our meeting with Mr. Sterling yesterday; and also of your broad-mindedness, accuracy, and generosity in the report of it in this morning's *Pantagraph*." And, she added, "Just recognition of our efforts gives us more hope and courage to go on—and moreover, earns the lasting gratitude of everyone who is working in this great cause of <u>equal</u> <u>suffrage</u>."[210]

Reading about the success of Woman's Suffrage in the West inspired Hazle to write a poem, which she sent to *The Woman's Journal and Suffrage News*. Near mid-December, she received a reply from the paper written by Agnes E. Ryan, who told her, "We are glad to accept your poem, 'Out West,' . . . and we expect to print it in an early issue of the *Journal*." Ryan added, "We would be glad to see other material you may care to send us. We will send you a copy of the *Journal* in which your poem appears."[211] The *Journal's* acceptance of Hazle's poem gave her another avenue through which to contribute to the woman's suffrage movement. It was clear to Hazle that women must be granted the right to vote in the near future. But she had not completely resolved the conflict over her support of woman's suffrage and her desire to vote for President Wilson, who did not seem inclined to support the Nineteenth Amendment.

CHAPTER 9

SWEET VICTORY

$\mathcal{W}$ hile other women picketed the White House on January 10, 1917, Hazle devoted her efforts to collecting subscriptions for *The Suffragist* magazine. But the subscriptions she sent did not reach their destination or had been misplaced. On February 9, 1917, Elizabeth L. Kind wrote to Hazle regarding the missing subscriptions, "I have spoken to Miss Paul and others in authority at Suffrage Headquarters and I hope the matter has been satisfactorily cleared up in regard to *The Suffragist* subscribers whose names you sent in." Kind apologized for the situation, assuring Hazle that this was most unusual. From Kind's lengthy hand-written letter, Hazle learned that although the suffragists expected the Amendment to pass in the Senate, the ratification of the bill by the states would take another two years to complete. Hazle agreed with Kind's sentiment, that "the joys of working for suffrage are the enduring friendships we form and the deep interest we take in the lives of those who have worked with us."[212]

On April 2, 1917, President Wilson called the War Session of the Sixty-fifth Congress to declare war on Germany. By that date, nineteen States had given women the right to vote. The women participating in the National Woman's Party faced a difficult decision. They could put all their efforts into supporting the war effort, or continue to work for their political freedom. The organization chose to continue working for the enfranchisement of women, but left it to the individual members to decide what their duties would be in the war effort.[213]

In spite of the declaration of war on Germany, the suffrage women continued to picket the White House. On June 22, 1917, a group of women picketing in front of the White House were arrested and charged with obstructing traffic. The women were released, however, without charges being brought against them. When the picketing continued, it became apparent to the government that merely arresting the women had not discouraged them. On June 26, six women were arrested, tried, found guilty, and fined. The women refused to pay the fines because they believed that doing so would be an admission of guilt.

Consequently, on July 14, sixteen women were arrested in front of the White House, and after an intense two-day trial, the women were sentenced to a twenty dollar fine and warned that, if the fines were not paid, they would be confined in the Occoquan workhouse for sixty days. The women refused to pay fines for a crime they had not committed and were transported from the District of Columbia to the Occoquan workhouse in Virginia.[214]

Allowed to visit the women the next day, a representative from the Woman's Party headquarters informed the women of protests made on their behalf to President Wilson. After hearing the women's sentences, Dudley Field Malone, the Collector of the Port of New York, went directly to the White House to protest to the President in person regarding the treatment of the women. Malone reported that President Wilson seemed shocked over the sixty-day sentence the women had received, and he denied any knowledge of it. J.A.H. Hopkins, who had been a member of the Democratic Campaign Committee of 1916, followed Malone's example. The wife of Hopkins was among the sixteen women who had been arrested and sentenced to sixty days in the work house. When asked by the President what should be done, Hopkins responded that the Susan B. Anthony Amendment should be passed immediately. The President chose not to take that course of action.[215]

Women around the country objected to the treatment of the women, even if they did not agree with them picketing, and sent telegrams to the White House to express their sentiments. The protests had the desired result, for on the third day of their imprisonment the women learned that President Wilson had pardoned them and they were released—but the President still gave no indication of his support of the Susan B. Anthony Amendment. Embroiled with events taking place in Europe, Wilson had little time or thought for the woman's suffrage movement.

Refusing to become discouraged over the lack of a positive response from the President, the women resumed picketing without arrests until August of 1917. Resenting the fact they could not vote but were expected to give their full support to the war, the women held up a banner addressing the President as "Kaiser" Wilson on August 14. The women did not expect so violent a reaction as this act produced. Young men attacked the women and a riot ensued as the police stood by and watched.

On August 17, 1917, Alice Paul received a warning at headquarters from the police that women carrying banners would be arrested. The threat became a reality at 4:00 that afternoon when six women were arrested, charged with "obstructing traffic," and found guilty. The women received a sentence of thirty days at Occoquan or a ten-dollar fine.[216] One of the women arrested was Lucy Ewing, a cousin of Hazle's husband, Davis.

As the White House picketing continued, Hazle supported the efforts of the picketers and sent a fifty-dollar contribution to the NWP. The treasurer acknowledged Hazle's donation on August 20: "We are . . . glad to hear of your sympathy with the picketing."[217] Learning of Lucy Ewing's arrest on August 17, Hazle questioned the wisdom of the picketers carrying a banner addressed to "Kaiser Wilson," and wondered if this action had led to the arrest of the women. She did not believe it would serve the suffragist cause to personally attack the President.

Again, Hazle struggled with the conflict between her desire to support the suffrage movement and her recognition of Wilson's responsibilities and concerns since America had entered World War I. The treasurer informed Hazle that, "When the pickets were arrested on Friday none of them were carrying the Kaiser banner and none of them had taken it out all day." That fact did not alleviate Hazle's concern for Lucy's welfare, however, or her uncertainty of the wisdom of some of the militant tactics now being employed. Nor did she find any comfort from the report that the Illinois Democratic Senator, J. Hamilton Lewis, brought back after his visit to the prison, which had been prompted by alarming reports he received from his constituent, Adlai Stevenson, Lucy's uncle.[218]

In September, the woman's suffrage movement did receive some encouragement, when Malone, who had been a long-time friend and supporter of President Wilson, resigned his post. Malone had supported Wilson during his 1916 campaign and had gained support for Wilson among women voters, believing that Wilson would support woman's suffrage in his next term and discontinue arresting women for picketing. When it became clear that Wilson did not intend to stop the arrests or publicly support the suffrage amendment, Malone saw no other recourse than to resign his position. Malone's resignation came as a shock to the Government, and awakened the general public to the seriousness of the controversy between the suffragists and the Administration in the White House. Following Malone's resignation, a Committee on Woman Suffrage that had been pending since 1913 was finally instituted. The suffragists understood and appreciated Malone's courage and the sacrifice he made of his position and income for their cause.[219]

Also appreciating the sacrifice that Malone had made for picketers, Hazle continued to support the suffrage movement financially and through the organization of meetings. On September 25, 1917, Margaret Whittemore, the National Organizer for the Woman's Party, contacted Hazle. Whittemore would be coming to

Bloomington in advance of the speaking tour of Miss Mabel Vernon and Mrs. Anna B. Lewis. She told Hazle, "I would like very much to have you call a group of women together so I could consult with them on Friday afternoon, at three o'clock of this week."[220]

Prior to the scheduled meeting, Hazle received a telegram and then a letter from Lucy Ewing, who wrote, "I have just sent you a telegram to the effect that I would come to Bloomington on Tuesday on the morning train with Mrs. Lewis and Miss Vernon." She continued, "I can't come earlier as we are having a Convention here on Monday and I must be present." And she concluded, "I'll stay a day or so after the meeting if you want me, but if you are coming up to Chicago yourself then that's something else." As Hazle prepared for the upcoming event, she looked forward to seeing Lucy and hearing from her the details of her twenty-five day imprisonment for picketing.[221]

Whittemore sent press bulletins to Hazle, who made certain that an announcement appeared in the local paper, *The Pantagraph*, on October 8, regarding the meeting to be held in the high school auditorium. The press release announced that the meeting "is free to the public and is to be held in the evening in order that both men and women may be present to hear why the National Woman's Party was formed." [222] The audience would also learn "why some of its members have picketed the congress and the White House and just what the Woman Suffrage situation is in Washington today."[223] On October 9, Whittemore wrote a "thank you" note in advance to Hazle for her help in preparing for the meetings and tea party, and for being willing to act as hostess to Lewis and Vernon, who are "looking forward to your meeting or meetings with a great deal of interest and enthusiasm."[224]

Hazle and the others invited to the meeting learned much about the experience of these women who had been imprisoned for picketing. After the meetings, Vernon, Lewis, and Lucy returned to Washington. On October 16, 1917, Paul sent a letter to the suffrage field stating, "Now that the special session of Congress has closed, we are working for action in the next session which opens the first week in December." She assured the suffragists, "We are planning to continue picketing of the White House," for picketing has "been our most effective method of voicing to the Administration the protest of women against the disfranchisement." But Paul warned the suffragists, "All who picket must be prepared for imprisonment."[225] Hazle recalled Lucy's description of her imprisonment, and she fervently hoped and prayed that the amendment would be passed in the next session of Congress, so that the picketers would not be subjected to endure such unpleasant experiences.

Although Hazle was not on the picket line, she desired to do her part for the suffrage cause and wrote to Herbert Hoover at the United States Food and Drug Administration Department in Washington, D.C. Hoover was the head of the program that provided food for war-ravaged Europe, a program in which Hazle had invested time and money. She hoped that Hoover would lend his support to the woman's suffrage movement, but, to her disappointment, she received only a short letter from Hoover's secretary, written on October 29, telling her, "Mr. Hoover has consistently refused to take part in any matters of public controversy."[226]

Clouds of discouragement seemed to be darkening as Hazle read a letter from Lucy Burns written on November 9, 1917, announcing that Paul "is being force fed in the District of Columbia Jail." Paul and six other women had been arrested and sentenced to serve seven months for holding a banner at the White House gates asking President Wilson to "grant women political liberty." Paul and Miss Rose Winslow had begun a hunger strike the previous Tuesday "to secure for their comrades treatment accorded to political prisoners in every civilized county but their own." The women's requests to receive papers, mail, and books, to see visitors at reasonable intervals, to buy food, and to wear their own clothes had been denied. Burns urged her readers to write immediately to President Wilson, to Commissioner Gardiner, of the District of Columbia, and to Mr. L. F. Zinkhan, Warden of the District Jail, to "protest against this barbarous treatment of a political offender."[227]

Although Paul had been arrested, the picketing did not stop. On November 10, the longest picket line ever organized by the women assembled in front of the White House. The police arrested forty-one women, found them guilty, but released them. A few days later, other women were arrested while picketing. Although they received a sentence to serve in the District Jail with Paul and the others, most of them were sent to Occoquan. In response to the cruel treatment received at Occoquan, the women began a hunger strike and attempted to obtain a writ of habeas corpus in order to be freed from Occoquan and Superintendent Whittaker's control.

The Occoquan prisoners' trial finally took place on November 23, 1917, at which Dudley Malone and Matthew O'Brien provided counsel for the women prisoners. Judge Edmund Waddil, seeing the state of the women, quickly ruled that the women be taken to the District Jail where they joined Paul and Winslow in their hunger strike. All the suffrage prisoners were released from jail on November 27 and 28.[228] Hazle hoped this would be the end of the arrests.

When the first week of the next session of Congress began on December 4, President Wilson delivered his message to Congress focusing on the war effort. In spite of the fact that the Administration had been forced to release suffrage prisoners only a few days before the session, Wilson did not mention the suffrage amendment, which sent the suffrage workers into immediate action.[229]

Hazle received a letter from Anne Martin, the Chairman of the Legislative Department of the Woman's Party, written on Christmas Eve, 1917. Martin asked her to "bring every possible pressure to bear upon" Congressman Sterling "to secure votes of other Republicans in Congress who are not favorable." Martin urged her to "secure his promise to be present to cast his vote at the time the vote is taken."

The suffragists had secured 260 votes, but they needed 290 for the necessary two-thirds majority.[230]

On December 27, Hazle received several petitions and resolution forms from Martin for the Congressional District Chairman. Martin told her, "We hope you will have these petitions signed by as many men and women of your district as possible, with their addresses." When Hazle had obtained the signatures, she sent them to Congressman Sterling and asked him to file the petitions in the House as soon as he received them. Martin had also advised Hazle to "have resolutions adopted by as many other men's and women's organizations" in her district as possible, "urging immediate and favorable action on the national suffrage amendment." These resolutions would be sent to the senators and representatives to be "read into the Congressional record before January 10," the date the vote would be taken. The resolutions were also to be sent to the President and other administration leaders.[231]

On January 8, 1918, President Wilson announced to Congress his American plan for peace, consisting of fourteen parts he hoped would lead to world peace. Hazle deeply desired world peace and fully supported the President's plan. But she would also continue to support the suffrage amendment until it passed. She was grateful to hear from Congressman Sterling that he had received the signed petitions in time, and he assured her, "I am pleased to advise you that I shall support the woman suffrage movement."[232]

On January 9, 1918, Wilson finally declared publicly his support of the 19th Amendment to a committee of Democratic Congressmen. The following day, forty years to the day that the amendment was first introduced into Congress, the amendment passed the House of Representatives—after an extensive debate and with just one vote over the two-thirds needed. Pressure was applied to those Senators who had not yet declared their support. Several men in public positions assisted the women by encouraging the Senators to support the suffrage amendment.[233]

Hazle wrote to Senator Lawrence Y. Sherman, of Illinois, requesting his support of the suffrage amendment and received his reply on May 13, 1918, "I had your message in due time. I have heretofore and shall continue to vote for the Susan B. Anthony amendment whenever it comes before the Senate."[234]

On May 19, 1918, the Administration tried to force a vote on the bill in the Senate, but those supporting the bill stopped it because they knew the bill did not have enough support to pass. The vote was set for June 27, but it was postponed. The suffragists, fearing that the bill might fail, organized a national protest in Washington on August 6, 1918. The women met at the base of the Lafayette Monument in the park located across the street from the White House. Dora Lewis, with whom Hazle had become acquainted through her suffrage work in Bloomington, began the talks and was immediately arrested, as were the forty-seven other women who attempted to speak about the suffrage amendment.[235]

The women waited ten days for their trial because it was uncertain what crime they had committed. At last the women were charged with having a meeting on public grounds and climbing on the statue. Those women who had climbed on the statue were sentenced to fifteen days in jail, while the women who had only attended the meeting were sentenced to ten days. The women were taken to the District Prison grounds to a building that had been condemned in 1909. Recognizing their deplorable situation, the women, out of self-protection, began a hunger strike immediately. The Administration released the women at the end of the fifth day of the hunger strike.[236]

When sending a check to suffrage headquarters after the arrests, Hazle expressed her concerns about the arrests and wondered if the women had been within their legal rights to hold the meeting in the park across from the White House. Ella J. Abeel responded, "I think the women in Washington made quite sure that they were within their legal rights before the meeting took place. All the Bulletins I have received show a resort to legal counsel before the act."[237]

Dora Lewis wrote to the suffragists on September 5, 1918, informing them that "The suffrage amendment is still blocked in the Senate. The Administration and Senate show no signs of acting on it." Lewis pointed out to her readers that Congress would soon end, and if the Senate did not act before that "all that has been gained by its passage in the House will be lost." She encouraged the women to protest against this delay in the Senate. She also informed them that "In Washington, on Monday September 16th, another protest meeting will be held at Lafayette Statue." Lewis assured them a permit had been issued to them, but she admitted they had been warned it "is no guarantee that there will not again be arrests and imprisonments." She concluded "every sacrifice we make now will bear its own fruit for the women of our nation in all time to come."[238]

When President Wilson learned that the women planned to hold another protest on September 16 at Lafayette Park if no action was taken, he called for a meeting with the leaders of the National Woman's Party at 2:00 PM the day of the protest. He told the women that he was doing everything possible to get the bill passed. Unconvinced of the President's sincerity, the women went forward with the protest. And, to their surprise, no arrests were made and the women received many generous donations to their cause.[239]

On September 26, 1918, the debate of the suffrage amendment opened in the Senate, and discussion continued for days. The President made an eloquent speech to the Senate in support of the bill, but when the vote was called on October 1, 1918, the amendment failed to pass by only two votes. Acting quickly, Senator Andrieus A. Jones, Chairman of the Suffrage Committee, changed his vote from a "yea" to a "nay," which enabled him to move for a reconsideration of the measure and to keep it on the Senate calendar.[240]

In the November elections, the Republicans gained control of

Congress. Shortly after the elections, the Allies won the war against Germany, and on November 11, 1918, the armistice took effect. On December 2, 1918, for the first time, President Wilson included suffrage in his message to Congress. The women hoped he would take up a plan of action, but two days later he sailed to France to attend the postwar peace conferences. The women's hopes sailed with him, for they believed that only the President could secure the last two votes needed to pass the amendment in the Senate.[241]

Hazle supported President Wilson's commitment to bringing about lasting peace for the United States and the world, but she also felt the disappointment of the suffragists. After the President's departure, the women held a somber demonstration on December 16, at the foot of Lafayette's statue. The eloquent but ineffective words of Wilson were burned. The demonstration proceeded quietly and without incident, and, although the women knew the White House was empty, they hoped that their actions and words would reach Wilson in France. The women repeated the ceremony several times during the first two months of 1919, and the pattern of arrests, imprisonment, hunger strikes, and release resumed.[242]

When the NWP learned that President Wilson would arrive in Boston from Europe in late February, Paul arranged a demonstration to greet him, hoping to apply some pressure on the President to secure the last votes needed to pass the amendment by March 3. The women who were to participate in the demonstration were arrested before the President even arrived.

On February 28, 1919, Mabel Vernon wrote a note to Hazle and included a newspaper clipping. She told Hazle of the "Prison Special" to be held in Chicago the next Thursday, March 6. The article pertained to meetings being held by women who had suffered imprisonment and were touring the country in a special train car to arouse public sentiment for their cause. Vernon urged her to "come up for the meetings which we hope to make a great success."[243]

The "Prison Special" kept the attention of the public on

the suffrage amendment, but the Sixty-fifth Congress, with a Democratic majority, closed on March 3 without passing the bill.[244] The Republican majority would not sit in Congress until December 1919, unless the President called for a special session. Paul quickly organized a demonstration for March 4 that she hoped would convince the President to call for a special session. The women were detained by New York City policemen and an angry mob, however, and did not even make it to the Opera House where they planned to hold their demonstration.

Although Wilson left for Paris again, the threatened demonstrations caused him great concern, because he believed they could adversely influence his efforts to establish the League of Nations. With encouragement from his fellow Democrats, Wilson secured the last vote needed for the amendment to pass in the Senate while he was still in Paris. He called a Special Session of Congress to begin on March 19, 1919. The amendment passed in the House on March 21, 1919, and it was passed in the Senate on June 4, 1919, but the right for women to vote would not be secured until three-fourths of the States in the United States had ratified the bill.[245]

Soon after the women had won their victory in Washington, the President concluded his mission in Europe. Wilson received support for the League of Nations from France and England, after making some compromises, and the Treaty of Versailles was signed on June 28, 1919. On August 26, 1920, the Secretary of State of the United States announced that the Nineteenth Amendment had become a law of the land. In November 1920, women in all states of the United States had the opportunity to vote in the national elections for the first time.

NEW BEGINNINGS

CHAPTER 10

A HOME FOR THE BOYS

*O*ne summer day in 1918, only a few months after the war had ended, and before the woman's suffrage movement had obtained the right for all women to vote, Hazle came face-to-face with the aftermath of World War I. She received a call from Lucy Orme Morgan, the President of the Industrial Home for Girls, founded in 1889. Morgan called Hazle regarding the need to organize and establish a home for twenty-three boys who were currently at the Home for Girls. The Home had always taken in boys as well as girls, but since the end of World War I, the numbers of boys under their care had increased beyond what the Girls' Home could provide. Morgan felt it was time to establish a separate Home for boys.[246]

Hazle and her mother, Lillian, had an interest in the Industrial Home for Girls and visited there on more than one occasion in addition to financially supporting it. Thus Morgan had some knowledge of Hazle and believed she could be counted on to give her full support to the work of founding a Boys' Home. As hoped, Hazle responded positively to Morgan's request to join two other friends, Mrs. Charles Burr and Miss Bertha Cowles, to meet with the Board of Directors of the Industrial Home for Girls. All three women had been recommended by Judge James C. Riley and were known to be civic-minded citizens who actively responded to the needs of the community.[247]

After meeting with the Board of the Industrial Home for Girls in 1918, Hazle and the other two women realized they had much work to do and many people to contact. The women met several

times before their first official meeting of the Board of the Boys'
Home of McLean County, which took place on the second Tuesday
in January, 1919. The Board was made up of five women: Mrs.
Charles Burr, Miss Bertha Cowles, Mrs. Oscar Mandel, Mrs. Kelly
R. Johnston, and Hazle Buck Ewing. Following their first official
gathering in January, several meetings followed in quick succession,
at one of which Miss Jewell of the State Visitor Department talked
with the women about the work that lay ahead of them. On February
5, Mrs. Fred B. Capen agreed to be the chairwoman of the Board.
The women who constituted the Board did not yet fully realize all
that would be required to establish a home for boys. But they did
know two things for certain: They needed money to support the
formation of the organization, and they had to find a suitable house
in a good location.[248]

At their meeting on February 26, the women formed six
committees which included: a site committee, a finance committee,
an education and recreation committee, a sewing committee, a house
committee, and a publicity committee. Hazle became a member of
the site committee which had the task of finding a suitable home
for the boys. She also agreed to chair the finance committee. She
had certainly gained some experience in raising money through her
work for woman's suffrage.[249]

On March 17, 1919, Mrs. Capen presided over the meeting
of the Board, which fourteen women attended. Hazle reported
to the group that the finance committee had concluded $2,500
would be enough to start the Home. After a lengthy discussion,
the women decided to attempt to raise the money through personal
solicitation. The site committee told the Board they had looked
at several properties but not found anything suitable. The women
also discussed names for the Home, but could not agree upon any.
Before closing the meeting, Mrs. Capen appointed Mrs. Marian
Smith Wallis as Vice Chairman and Hazle to serve as a temporary
Vice Chairman. Additional committees were also formed,

including—the committee on incorporation, the committee on constitution and bylaws, the committee to find a suitable matron, the grounds committee, and the committee on livestock.[250]

Hazle, as the temporary Vice Chairman, presided over the meeting held at the local library on April 4, 1919. During the meeting, it was decided that the publicity chair, Mrs. Kelly Johnston, should request suggestions for a name for the Home through the newspapers. She had already succeeded in having articles published in both the *Pantagraph* and the *Bulletin*, announcing plans for starting a Home for boys. In addition, she had written and mailed solicitation letters to 175 individuals, which cost the committee only the price of postage. Desiring even more media exposure, the Board decided that all future Board meetings should be covered by the newspapers. The women created a small fund for postage and publicity expenses, requiring each member to donate $1 to the fund. The site committee reported on three properties that had been offered to them for the Home, but no decision was made to accept or reject any of them. At the close of the meeting, Hazle stressed the urgent need to solicit funds, and the women decided to meet again on April 14 to compile a list of people to contact and to discuss other ways of raising money.[251]

In early May, the site committee looked at a large brick house known as the Brooks Property, located at 904 Hovey Avenue in Normal. The committee thought it would be an ideal house and property for the Home since it was near good schools and churches and could be made into a real home for the boys similar to what other children had. The women believed a homelike atmosphere essential to promote a desire in the boys to become "real, self-respecting citizens." All of the Board members agreed that the site committee had made a good choice.[252]

The owner of the property, E. R. Mikelberry, of Champaign, Illinois, had been a resident of Bloomington and offered to sell the house to the Board for $9,600. He required $600 down in cash,

$4,000 to be paid within six months, and the remaining $5,000 on a five-year mortgage at 6% interest. The women then took the next step necessary to establish the Home—the formation of a legal corporation.[253]

After establishing the corporation, the women began in earnest to think of a suitable name. Many names were discussed, but Hazle thought Capen's proposal of Victory Hall seemed the most appropriate. Capen stated that she thought the name of "Victory Hall" would commemorate the end of World War I, and represent their hope that each boy who came to live at the Home would be victorious in becoming a valuable citizen wherever he lived. At last, the Board had selected a name for the Home.[254]

The officers of the Board met with the State Investigator for the Board of Charities, Dr. Virden, at the office of Dr. Hanson, Mikelberry's attorney, for approval of their plan for the Boys' Home and property. After hearing the details of their plan and thoroughly inspecting the property, Virden assured the women they would have no problem securing a charter. The next week, on May 23, the Board and the site committee members met at the law office of Mr. Morrissey, signed the contract for the deed to the Brooks Property, and filed the contract and charter with the registrar of deeds for McLean County.[255]

The next day, an article appeared in the Bloomington newspaper, *The Daily Pantagraph*, regarding the purchase of the Brooks Property for the purpose of establishing a Home for orphaned and dependent boys. The article indicated that the low price Mikelberry had offered for the nine-bedroom house with a deep cellar had been prompted by his interest in the philanthropic work of the women, and that his generous offer had enabled the women to purchase the property instead of renting it. The spacious grounds and location of the house in a residential neighborhood made it the kind of home the women had hoped to find for the boys. The enthusiastic endorsement of Judge James Riley, of the county court, provided the women with additional assurance that they had made the right decision to purchase the Brooks house.[256]

After making the down payment on the house, the women began preparing diligently for the boys to be able to move into it. The sewing committee, under Burr's direction, produced twenty-two waistcoats from fifty yards of donated flannel. A building committee was formed and the grounds committee put the yard into shape. Johnston promoted the work through publicity in the newspapers, and she provided the Rotary Club with cards detailing the objectives of the Board of the Boys' Home. The women considered having an advisory board of men, but reached no definite conclusion.[257]

By mid-June, the women had a total of $1,941.40 in the bank. But Hazle and the other members of the finance committee soon realized it would take more money to run Victory Hall than previously anticipated. They decided to continue seeking general solicitations, however, since they had not developed other means of obtaining funds. The Rotary Club had secured $3,000 in pledges. In addition, the Rotary Club members believed they could collect more through their "connection with their Big Brother movement," and planned to canvas their members for funds. Following the meeting, Hazle prepared and mailed reminder cards to individuals who had pledged money but not yet made good on their pledges.[258]

Although the women faced financial challenges, they continued to make progress in their preparations for the opening of the Boys' Home. Dishes, a variety of kitchen equipment, and other items that had been used during the war were purchased from the Illinois Wesleyan Barracks at a reasonable price. As news of the women's efforts spread, contributions to help make Victory Hall a reality came from many sources. It seemed that people everywhere were inspired to give to the Home.[259]

The bylaws had been submitted to Judge Riley for his approval. The building committee received a bid from W.D. Andrews & Company in the amount of $705 to build a sleeping porch over the *porte-cochere*, with a roof opening from the third floor so bedding could be aired, and to replace the dormer windows with casement windows on the third floor. They also received a bid for thirteen dollars for some plumbing work. The building committee was given authority to have necessary work done without waiting for the approval of the entire Board. This would enable them to have the work completed more quickly so the Home could open sooner.[260]

The house committee had been given a gas stove that was almost new, but it was impractical in the Boys' Home. When they contacted the gas company, the committee found that the donated stove and the one in Victory Hall could be traded toward the cost of a stove that would be more practical for their use. The grounds committee reported they had borrowed a lawn mower to cut the grass, but they believed they should purchase one of their own. After discussing some of the other items that the Home could use, the women decided to publish their needs in the newspaper.[261]

On July 7, 1919, Hazle's father, Orlando J. Buck, passed away, and Hazle went to Chicago to be with her mother. That month was the first time Hazle had to miss a Victory Hall meeting. During her absence, the equipment committee bought a six-burner A. & B. Gas Range and a stove for the laundry room for an additional $51. The women purchased 120 sheets, and decided to buy beds from Ensenberger's for $14.50 each, which included mattresses and pillows. They selected fabric for the bedspreads and tablecloths, and chose to purchase dining tables and benches.[262]

While the women had been working to prepare the Home for its ultimate opening, the number of boys at the Girls' Home had increased to 30. The oldest boy was 11, the youngest was 2-1/2; five of the boys were under school age, representing a variety of needs. The Board hired Mrs. Keyes to fill the position of Matron, who would be responsible for the care of the boys when Victory Hall opened. The Board also discussed Judge Riley's recommendation that they increase their membership to 21, but no action was taken.

They concluded at the end of the July meeting that, since so many members would be gone during August, they would not meet again until September.[263]

Hazle returned to Bloomington in time to attend the first board meeting held at Victory Hall, on September 8, 1919, at 2:00 in the afternoon. They had a balance of $1,679.45 in the bank, and Hazle reported that $13,000 had been received from pledges, but some of the pledges remained unpaid. Hazle gladly accepted the decision of the Board to make the treasurer, Amy DeMange, responsible for mailing out reminders.[264]

It delighted Hazle to learn that many improvements had been made during the summer on the Home, including painting the inside and outside of the house, having the plumbing repaired, installing a heating plant, updating the electric lights, and restoring the yard, which was an expensive endeavor because it had been neglected for years. Hazle offered to donate some shrubs to the grounds committee when they were ready to replant the yard. Her brother-in-law, Spencer Ewing, had helped the grounds committee with the sign for the Home, and it would soon be in place.

Also during the summer, the sewing committee hemmed 144 napkins, 18 table cloths, 6 dozen Turkish bath towels, and 24 dozen face towels; had purchased 75 blankets but still needed pillow cases. Coal had been delivered for the furnace. The employment of Mrs. Keyes was confirmed at $50 a month, and Mrs. Taupe would fill the cook's position for $8 a week. Mr. Morrisey, who had donated his services when they purchased Victory Hall, agreed to be the attorney for the Home. But they still needed some major items, such as a porcelain-lined ice box and an electric clothes washer.[265]

On September 19, 1919, the long-awaited day arrived, when 36 boys moved into Victory Hall. The Board held a special meeting at the library, on September 25, to determine how things stood since the arrival of the boys. The bank balance had been reduced to $2,398.03, because the boys needed flannel pajamas, the sleeping porch had to have screens, and the dormitory door had to be repaired. Fortunately, the Normal Board of Education would be supplying textbooks for the boys.[266]

Marian Wallis, the Vice Chairman, agreed to help Hazle and the finance committee collect funds in Normal for Victory Hall. The women continued to have difficulty collecting money that had been pledged, though. Since they had not received enough funds to purchase the ice box, they decided they would have to use the cave in the yard that had been used by occupants of the house many years past—at least for the winter. In addition, they had not found a laundress or the proper equipment to launder the boys' clothes. But they had hired an Assistant Superintendent for a month, which gave the Board a little more time to find someone to take the position permanently. It also seemed desirable to have a separate house to care for boys who became ill, but the price for the cottage and seven lots adjoining the Victory Hall property seemed too high. Hazle offered $3,000 dollars that she would receive from her father's estate towards the purchase of the cottage and lots. Based on her offer, the Board decided to contact the owner and try to work out an agreement.[267]

In October, the Home still had $1,940 in outstanding pledges from the Rotary Club. They had $3,247.30 in cash for operating the Home, but they still needed to purchase a washer, and since winter was nearing, the grounds committee needed to replant the shrubbery and complete other yard work. Despite the challenges the Board faced, however, the boys seemed to be settling into their new home, and all of them had been registered in appropriate schools. The Secretary for the Boy Scouts, Mr. Myers, had been hired for $6 a week to provide physical training for the boys every Saturday morning between 10:00 and noon, so the boys had that outlet in addition to their school activities.[268]

Concerned about being able to financially maintain the Home, Hazle and the finance committee had a special meeting with Capen to discuss ways and means of raising money. As a result of the meeting, the committee decided that, in addition to the definite pledges of $5,978 that had been received, they required at least $2,000 more in cash or pledges to carry the Home through January 1, 1920. And they desperately needed to purchase an electric washing machine, which would cost them $140, and other necessary laundry equipment. The boys also required more winter clothing, and they did not have a sufficient supply of blankets, sheets, and bed spreads.[269]

While the Board endeavored to work out the difficulties they faced, the recreation committee hosted a picnic at Miller Park for the boys, and, as a memento of the day, individual board members paid for enlarging and framing a picture taken of all the boys at the park. They also entertained the boys with an inexpensive Halloween party using decorations from the Bloomington Country Club and purchasing party supplies with money donated by some of the board members.[270]

At the November 10, 1919, meeting, Hazle presented the challenging financial situation to the entire Board. She shared the ideas that resulted from the meeting with Capen, which included having a Minstrel Show and a ball to be hosted by Miss Winifred Elliot and friends in late November. The finance committee expected that the combined activities would bring in a least $1,000—half of the funds needed. At Hazle's suggestion, the Board also considered meeting with the County Supervisors to ask for an increase in their allotment, but did not make a decision.[271]

In addition to the financial difficulties of running the Home, other issues demanded the attention of the Board. The Deputy State Fire Marshal inspected the outside stairs leading to the basement and determined that, for safety reasons, it would be impossible for the women to make any of the changes they wanted to make to the outside stairs in order to enlarge the basement. Retaining reliable employees also seemed to be a problem, and currently they needed someone to fill the position of superintendent, since Mrs. Lloyd, who had taken the position on a temporary basis, had resigned. Their search for a suitable person to fill the position had been thus far unsuccessful.[272]

The women held their last Victory Hall Board meeting for 1919 on December 8. The Home had a bank balance of $3,129.03; however, $2,500 of that amount would be spent before the end of the month. The financial situation was relieved somewhat by $523 made in their fund-raising activities and a gift of $500. They also received $792 from the County Supervisors during December, even though they had not made a request for additional aid.[273]

Because of the uncertainty of the financial situation of the Home, they did not buy a dryer, but instead purchased a wire clothes line for $1.45. The Home had more pressing needs, such as a new bed for the recently hired Superintendent, Miss McGlossem, whom they would pay $75 a month to take care of the house. The Board also had the good fortune to employ another trained worker, Mrs. Margaret Darsham, who would take care of the boys for $65 a month. Mrs. Lloyd, the former Superintendent, offered to help work up a budget for food and to assist the new superintendent in keeping track of the consumption of coal to make sure they did not run out unexpectedly during cold weather.[274]

That winter, the Home received some assistance from outside sources, such as My Store, a local mercantile, that sold potatoes to the Home for $2.15 a bushel and stored them, delivering the potatoes only when they were needed. The ladies of the Christian Church in Normal provided Thanksgiving dinner for the boys. And individuals from the community took the boys to the movies on occasion.[275]

At their December meeting, each board member chose two boys to buy a gift for or to do something special with, but a ringworm epidemic changed their plans, and it seemed best for all the boys to stay at Victory Hall on Christmas Day. In order to provide the boys with some Christmas cheer, Amy DeMange brought the boys a Christmas tree, Hazle provided the lights to decorate it, Mrs. Capen contributed ice cream, and Mrs. Lain supplied chickens for the boys' dinner.[276]

The ringworm epidemic made the women determined to find a way to isolate the boys suffering with contagious illnesses from the rest of the Home. But the price of the nearby house and lots still seemed too high, so they declined to buy them. Hazle again offered the $3,000, which she would make immediately available to be kept in a fund for the Home to buy more property in the future. The Board gratefully accepted Hazle's offer, and decided to place the money in an interest-bearing account. With the promise of money available to purchase more property, and $1,323 in cash, the women were confident they could provide the daily needs of the Home, at least until January 1.

CHAPTER 11

A Promising Year

At the first meeting of the Board of Directors of Victory Hall in 1920, on January 12, Capen presided for the last time, having resigned in 1919. She announced that Hazle had given the Boys' Home a personal check for the promised $3,000, which would be invested in a mortgage. Several other donations had been made to the Home in December, including: $150 for Christmas presents for the boys. The Board of Supervisors had provided $16 for Christmas candies, and Johnston had collected $57, which had been used to buy more blankets and other miscellaneous items. Since the Home had received generous donations, the Board passed the benefits on to the capable and businesslike Superintendent McGlossem, raising her salary to $250. But they could not honor Darsham with a raise, because she had resigned. Hazle suggested that a committee be sent to Darsham immediately to express their appreciation for her work and to offer her more money to stay.[277]

Capen reported that 4,092 meals, at an average cost of 7 cents each, had been served in the Home in December. The Commercial Club had given sufficient food for two of the meals. An anonymous Christmas gift had been given to the Home, which the women decided should be used to start a fund for the much needed playground equipment. The Woman's Relief Corp had donated two quilts and a comforter. Many groups in the Bloomington-Normal community seemed to be interested in providing assistance in a variety of ways, for which the Board members were sincerely grateful.[278]

The women held their first Annual Meeting of the Board of

Directors of Victory Hall immediately following their regular meeting. Capen outlined all that had been accomplished during the first year of the Board's activities and pointed out what needed to be done in the coming year. The Home was triumphantly in the black at the end of the first year, with receipts of $12,500.14 and disbursements of $11,182.60. Reporting for the finance committee, Hazle reminded the group of the different methods that had been employed to raise $4,000 during the past year. She also recalled how they had innocently thought, in the beginning, that it would take only $2,500 to start the Home. But they soon realized it would take at least $10,000.[279]

In addition to the financial business, it was decided that the new Board officers would be Mrs. A.V. S. Lloyd, Chairman; Mrs. H. K. Hoblit, Vice Chairman; and Mrs. F. S. Chase, Secretary-Treasurer. When the women voted to fill the Board membership positions for one, two, and three-year terms, Hazle was elected for three years.[280]

On February 9, 1920, at their next meeting, the new chairman, Mrs. A. V. S. Lloyd, presided as the Board discussed the ringworm epidemic, for which twenty-seven boys had received treatment around Christmas time. Currently five boys were still receiving treatment, and two of them were in the hospital. The women knew they needed an isolation room, but there seemed to be no room in the house to provide for this need. They considered using the boys' playroom and allowing them to play in the basement, but it was currently being used to hang out the laundry to dry because they had no clothes dryer. Mrs. Lain presented plans for an addition to Victory Hall that would meet all these needs. Although the women discussed the plans thoroughly, they did not make a decision to accept them.[281]

The Board was grateful to receive the good news in February that Darsham had been persuaded to stay, and they increased her pay to $75 a month. But when Darsham agreed to stay, the Board believed she would be relieved of the care of some of the pre-school age boys during the day. However, they soon learned that because the boys had not turned six until that winter, according to school regulations, they could not begin school until the coming fall. After some discussion of the situation, the board members resolved that Victory Hall could only take boys between the ages of six and fourteen. Considering the difficulty of finding suitable employees for the Home, they felt unable to adequately meet the needs of younger or older boys at that time.[282]

In March 1920, the home had an extremely low bank account of $104. Some of the boys continued to have health issues, and some of the other boys had challenges in school. In addition, the effort to buy the land in back of Victory Hall had received no response, and plans for a garden were discussed, but no decisions made. In the midst of these challenges, the boys attended a symphony concert and enjoyed a talk on birds. And the County Supervisors gave the Home an unexpected increase in funds.[283]

The women believed there should be a way for the boys to earn an allowance and gain a sense of responsibility by helping out around the Home. Mrs. Lloyd came up with a plan that she wanted to try out for the next three months. She would pay the boys for chores done at the Home with money that her husband had agreed to provide. Her plan succeeded and was expanded so that each boy assisted in taking care of the house and grounds by helping in the kitchen, dining room, dormitory, or doing yard work.[284] In addition, the older boys were allowed to have part-time jobs outside the Home to earn some spending money.[285]

When April arrived, the Easter Day celebration which the boys planned to attend at the Normal College campus was postponed because of weather. Instead, the boys celebrated Easter at home with ice cream and cookies cut in the shape of chickens, and received Easter candies and new clothing. It was also in April that the Board learned that two of the boys would not pass to the next grade. But the ringworm problem had finally subsided.[286]

Later that month, they had a response regarding the property and cottage in back of Victory Hall, which they wanted to buy. They made a counter offer. The $3,000 that Hazle had provided would be part of the payment on the land, if they purchased it. Darsham resigned for the second time, and the Board felt it should accept her resignation since she seemed unwilling to stay. They also received the disappointing news that the expected adoption of two boys had not worked out, for reasons which were not recorded. It troubled Hazle that they had not yet been successful in securing permanent homes for any of the boys at Victory Hall.[287]

In early May, they purchased the cottage and property behind the Home; however, a family was living in the cottage. The Board decided to allow the family to stay until the end of the summer. They also began making preparations for planting a garden. They purchased seeds and found a student at the State Agriculture Department in Normal who was willing to supervise the boys in planting, weeding, and watering the garden. The Board hired Miss Williams to take Darsham's place, and hired Miss Pruitt as her assistant. In addition, the Board unanimously approved free swimming lessons at the Y.M.C.A. for the older boys. But the women did not know what to do with the boys who would not pass their academic classes. They had thought the solution would be to send the boys to summer school, but learned there was no room for them.[288]

In May, Hazle proposed a membership campaign to which members would pay not less than $5 a year. She received approval from the Board to work out the details of the campaign, and she lost no time in organizing a committee and making the necessary plans. Since some of the boys staying at the Home were not from McLean County, but had come from Ford, Woodford, Fayette, and DeWitt counties, Hazle's plan included the involvement of women connected to the Home Bureau in those counties. She organized a luncheon held on June 4, which the Victory Hall Board hosted at the Bloomington Country Club for women who had an interest in supporting the Home from Bloomington-Normal and the counties from which some of the boys had come. Leo Phillips, superintendent of the Glenwood Training Schools for Boys, and Judge Riley were the speakers. The women received encouragement through the speeches—especially the remark of Phillips' that, "There is a universal appeal about this kind of work that touches practically all the people you approach for money."[289]

Lloyd presided over the luncheon meeting while Hazle instructed the women on how to solicit members for the Victory Hall Association, passing out cards designed to help the women in their efforts. The Board planned to create a sustaining fund by finding 500 people willing to become members of the Association for a yearly membership fee of $5. Hazle and her committee urged each woman who attended the luncheon to return home and solicit members in her township. The eagerness of the women who attended the luncheon reassured Hazle that the campaign would bring in sufficient financial support to make the future of Victory Hall more secure.[290]

When the Board met on June 14, they enthusiastically discussed the luncheon held at the country club for the sustaining membership campaign. Hazle and her committee provided glowing reports of the meeting, and the Board determined that the luncheon had been quite successful. Hazle expressed gratitude for Phillips, who had kindly spoken at the luncheon free of charge and refused to be reimbursed for his travel expenses.[291]

That month, the older boys began taking swimming lessons at the Y. M. C. A. The music committee purchased a piano for $100 with the help of the Young Men's Business Club, the Philharmonic Society, and Capen, who each donated $25. But the gardening project had run into a snag. The student from the State department had left, and there was no one to help the boys with the garden.[292]

At their August 9 meeting, Hazle reported to an appreciative Board the good news that $278.20 had been received from the membership campaign so far. But the out-break of a mumps epidemic at Victory Hall demanded the immediate attention of the women. The boys affected had been moved to the cottage, but then the boys had to be moved back to Victory Hall because some of the workers had become ill, so both the cottage and the Home had to be quarantined.[293]

Mrs. Lloyd introduced for discussion the idea of moving some of the workers to the cottage, and using the basement of the cottage for the laundry facility. Then the basement in Victory Hall could be made into a playroom and there would be space available for an isolation room in the house. The Home would also be able to accommodate fifty boys instead of their present number of forty-three boys.[294]

When school started in September, forty of the boys living at Victory Hall attended school; the other three were too young to go. Many second-hand books and a large quantity of tablets and pencils had been purchased for the school-age boys. The Board decided to make the changes suggested by Lloyd in the August meeting that would enable them to take in more boys. This decision meant they needed another washer and more beds. They hoped that the beds and some other needed items, such as bedspreads, sheets, and tablecloths, would be donated. Also, some maintenance work had to be done on the house before winter, and the driveway and steps to the street needed to be fixed. Hazle told the Board that Davis would be willing to provide the cement to repair the driveway and steps. She then reported the good news: Another $255 had come in from the membership campaign, and a plan was in place to send out notices regarding delinquent payments. The women also decided that an open house at Victory Hall would help their cause, and planned the event for September 26.[295]

The open house proved to be a resounding success. The women also found they had the funds to purchase winter clothing for the boys. That fall, the boys once again went on a picnic, which became an annual event. As the membership campaign continued, Hazle had the pleasure of hearing reports from women telling of their successes in soliciting new members. Also that fall, during canning season, Williams canned so many bushels of fruits and vegetables that she nearly ran out of jars. The Board had to place an ad for canning jars in both local papers. Some of the fruits and vegetables had been donated, but much of the produce came from the additional property that the women had purchased in May. By October 11, Williams had canned 900 quarts of fruit and 200 quarts of tomatoes, and had received an abundance of Mason jars through the ads.[296]

When the Board met on November 9, the isolation room had been set up in the house and the new laundry facility had been installed in the basement of the cottage. A laundry marking system had been devised to ensure that the boys would receive their own clothing back from the laundry. With the laundry facility moved from the basement of Victory Hall, the basement became a playroom for the boys during the winter months. The membership campaign continued to bring in members. Hazle collected $847 from the county membership committee, and Mrs. Harry Hoblit received $1,165 from the city members.[297]

In mid-December of 1920, Hazle reported that the membership campaign had brought in a total of $1,151.40 from the county membership committee, and she suggested that at least $50 be appropriated for the boys' Christmas. While preparing for the holidays, the sewing committee received help finishing the boys' pajamas, and had been given some sweaters for the boys. The Board decided, in the spirit of Christmas, that a gift should be selected for Williams that would express their appreciation of her services.[298]

The New Year began with a bank balance of $1,102.35, which indicated that 1920, the first full year of the Home's operation, had been successful. Hazle received many encouraging reports from various county committees, and Hoblit shared the encouraging news of final receipts from the city committees amounting to $1,106. In addition, they had the good fortune of renting the unused portion of the cottage to a school teacher, who had offered part of her time to help the boys who were struggling with their school work.[299]

At 3:00 Monday afternoon, January 31, 1921, the second Annual Meeting of the Board of Directors of Victory Hall assembled, and Lloyd gave special recognition to Williams, who had canned nearly 2000 quarts of fruits and vegetables that fall. She also reported that eighty boys had been cared for in the Home since it opened on September 19, 1919. She noted that the annual audit found the books to be in good order, and that the purchase of the cottage, which Hazle had helped make possible, had been a big blessing. The New Year looked promising for the boys at Victory Hall.[300]

CHAPTER 12

BOYS OF HER OWN

lthough 1920 had been a successful year for Victory Hall
in many ways, it troubled Hazle that they had not found homes
for any of the boys. She believed it was important for children to
have a home and a family of their own. She understood the need
for Victory Hall. But, she believed that boys should be placed in
the Home only until a suitable home and family could be found
for each one of them. She had come to this conviction through
her own experience, which had given her a unique opportunity
for understanding the needs of children living in such a home as
Victory Hall.

In 1917, Hazle and her mother, Lillian Brewer Buck, visited the
Industrial Home for Girls, and, while there, learned about Ralph
Nelson and were deeply touched by the sad life-story of the ten-year-
old boy.[301] Ralph's mother had come to this country from Sweden as
a young girl and had ended up in Bloomington, Illinois. She worked
hard to support herself, faithfully attended church, and became a
member of the choir. As an attractive young woman alone in a strange
country, however, she had the misfortune of becoming involved with
a married man. When she informed him that she carried his child,
he refused to take any responsibility for her or the child. Having
no resources, the young woman accepted help from a kindly older
woman, Nora Hasslinger, who befriended her and provided a home
for her and baby, Ralph, who was born on April 5, 1907.[302]

Ralph's mother died when he was still a baby, leaving him in
Hasslinger's care. When he was seven years old, the woman found

119

she could no longer take care of him, and, on November 25, 1914, Ralph became a ward of the State. At that time, the Boys' Home did not exist, and Ralph was placed with a couple who owned a farm. But, being so young, Ralph could not do much farm work. The couple eventually returned him to the care of the State, where Hazle and her mother discovered him. Determined to find a way to help Ralph, Hazle went home from the visit and told Davis about him. They agreed to look into the possibility of having Ralph come live with them. Within a short time Ralph came to stay at their home.[303]

In 1921, four years later, when the Ewings were in the process of adopting Ralph, Nora Hasslinger wrote to Hazle explaining that she had tried unsuccessfully to reestablish a home for Ralph. Hazle responded to Hasslinger's letter telling her of their intention and efforts to adopt Ralph. On March 11, Hasslinger responded to Hazle's letter: "I prayed God is good that he would place the child in a good home some day, and I feel as though he is in a good home with you, Mrs. Ewing." Hasslinger had been concerned for Ralph, for she knew better than anyone else what he had been through. She assured Hazle, "I am not going to intrude & worry you nor Ralph. He stays as long with you as he wants to. The child is smart [and] he knows he has a good home with you. The best of it is he loves you people."[304] Hasslinger appreciated that Hazle had responded promptly to her letter and knew that Ralph had been and would be well cared for by the Ewings.

On August 19, 1921, Hazle, Davis, and Ralph went before the Judge to finalize the adoption. Although Ralph had given his consent to the adoption, the Judge asked him, at the hearing, if he wanted to be adopted by the Ewings. Ralph eagerly answered that he did. That day, Ralph became the Ewings' legally adopted son, but he had been part of their family from the first day they had taken him into their home.[305] Hazle learned much about orphaned and dependent boys from her experience with Ralph. She knew first-hand what it would mean for each one of those boys at Victory Hall to have a home and family of his own.

During the year of 1921, Hazle and the other board members worked to improve conditions at Victory Hall and diligently sought acceptable homes for the boys. In the meantime, Ralph attended the Principia School in St. Louis, Missouri, frequently writing home to Hazle and Davis. On May 6, 1921, he wrote: "Dear Mother, We have just thought that Sunday is Mother's Day and I wish to express my love and gratitude for all the things you have done for me, since I have lived under your care and protection." He added, "I kind of wish I was a Day Pupil. I'll sure be glad to be home." In another letter written on November 20, 1921, Ralph reminded Hazle, "School will be out on the 21st of December," and he asked her, "How are the horses getting along, have you had many rides?" Ralph looked forward to coming home to Bloomington and spending time with his family and riding the horses. The home that Davis and Hazle provided Ralph gave him financial security and opportunities to experience a life that he would not have had otherwise.[306]

In 1922, Hazle became president of the Board for Victory Hall, and continued her efforts to make the Boys' Home more financially secure.[307] As the new school year began that fall, it became increasingly apparent to her that Ralph lacked experience and knowledge in taking care of his own finances. He wrote to her on October 28, 1922, "I am getting worried about my money matters. Here I thought everything was going fine. And now I find that after paying my bills and all that, I have less than $10 left till Christmas. The bill is $26.50 but I think that after I see about it I can bring it down to $20." After telling his mother about their football game and a lecture by an American sculptor, Lorado Taft, he ended his letter asking for money, saying, "I need it very much."[308]

As Ralph worked to master his financial difficulties, Hazle attained some financial success for the Boys' Home. On December 9, 1922 a newspaper article announced that Victory Hall would receive $3,800 from the United Welfare Campaign, which was the amount the Home had received in the past through memberships and fund-raisers.[309] Under her direction that year, Victory Hall was included in the United Welfare Campaign that ran from December 12 through 20, 1922.

On January 22, 1923, Hazle began her second year as president of the Board. At the annual meeting, she recounted how 1922 had been a memorable year in many ways. A substantial amount of money had been received from two bequests that made it possible to build an addition on the main house, furnish the cottage with hospital beds and supplies to care for any boys who became ill, update the laundry equipment, and replenish the linen supplies. In addition, the placement committee had successfully found homes for three boys, and there had been interest shown in the adoption of a fourth.[310]

One of those boys, Emery E. Crabtree, had been adopted by Sterling Bennison who owned a ranch in Riverton, Utah. Emery had lived under the care of the State since he was four years old. He wrote to his friends at Victory Hall that he was "having a fine time." When he first arrived at the ranch, he had to ride to school on horseback, but then Mr. Bennison purchased a wagon in which Emery drove other students to school for a fee, and he had been "putting $40 a month in the bank."[311] Hazle and the other women rejoiced in the successful placement of this young man and the other two for whom they had been able to find homes.

The New Year of 1923 looked bright for Victory Hall, for which Hazle felt deeply grateful. But for Ralph it would be a year of learning and growing. He wrote to his mother on February 8, 1923: "I received your letter this morning and I know it must be pretty discouraging to you, to see that report." He assured Hazle, however, that "Ever since the new term and before I have kept my work up a whole lot better. And especially since the new term." He seemed to be making the effort to do better in school, but he still struggled with his finances, writing that he had an outstanding bill of $8.15

and asked if she would send him $10.[312]

After receiving Hazle's response to his letter, Ralph wrote to her again on February 11: "[L]ast night I started as a regular waiter for a while at least. So that will help. That is just about all there is to do but now that I have the job and can keep it, it will give me between $12 and $15 a month." Regarding his school-work, he said, "The only thing I can do now is to take summer school and come back with 11 ½ credits that is if I take 2 whole subjects or 1 and make up the English."[313]

At the Boys' Home, another year of success seemed assured when, in March, Miss Gallagher, the State Inspector, came to scrutinize Victory Hall. Hazle was pleased that the inspector thought their menus and sleeping arrangements for the boys more than adequate. But what impressed Gallagher most was that Victory Hall had formed a Boy Scout Troop within the institution, and that most of the boys had received good grades. Hazle and the other women had the satisfaction of knowing that Victory Hall was considered a "model" Boys' Home.[314]

It was not surprising that the Home received high praise from the inspector, because Hazle and the other women made a consecrated effort to insure that they provided the best care for the boys. As the president of the Victory Hall Board, Hazle had been involved with preparing for Gallagher's visit and had not written to Ralph as often as she usually did. Ralph, not fully aware of his mother's activities, wrote to her on March 18, 1923: "I haven't heard from you for a long time and am wondering what kind of time you are having." He told her that the weather had been cold in St. Louis, "but today is wonderful." He added, "I sure wish I had one of our horses here today it sure would be wonderful riding."[315] It is notable in this letter that Ralph did not mention any problems with his school-work or finances. Clearly, he had made some definite improvements.

Following the inspection of Victory Hall, Hazle and Davis made a trip to St. Louis to visit Ralph, assuring him that he had not been forgotten. After they returned home, Ralph wrote, "It surely was wonderful to have you all here for that short time and be able to see you and do so many nice things."[316]

During most of the summer of 1923, the sixteen-year-old Ralph stayed at the Mountain Lake cabin on the family ranch in Crivitz, Wisconsin. Hazle had gone to the ranch with him, but she found it necessary to return to Bloomington at the end of June. She left Ralph at the ranch knowing he would be well-supervised and kept busy. He also had ample opportunity to go horseback riding on the trails that Hazle had designed and that he was helping to clear. He wrote to her on July 2: "We haven't done any more work on the trails, but have hauled 19 loads of sand and have begun work on the garage." He had also helped with stacking the kindling and making some bridle gates for the paths. He and two other young men had gone for a ride the day before, and "rode to where the old blackberry picking cave used to be and then cut across country and circled around the cave in the steer pasture and home." Ralph seemed to enjoy being at the ranch even though his parents were not able to be there.[317]

At the end of the summer, Ralph returned to school in St. Louis. During the winter break, he went home to Bloomington and enjoyed Christmas with his family, which now included five-year old Nelson, whom Hazle and Davis had taken into their home and affectionately called "Sonny." Ralph enjoyed his vacation with the family. He wrote to Hazle from school in January 1924: "I want to tell you and Dad and Sonny what a happy Christmas I had. It was about the best that I have had. In fact it was great. Thank you all very much for the beautiful presents."[318]

Ralph had begun to mature. He seemed to enjoy having a younger brother, although he did not see much of him since he was away at school. During the winter quarter, Ralph looked forward to the world trip he would be taking in the fall with his parents, who had been planning it for months. While the rest of the family traveled, Sonny would stay with good friends of the family at

Principia, being too young to take such an extended trip.

Hazle had watched as Ralph visibly matured during their trip, and she knew that Sonny would be growing up while they were gone. She also thought about the boys at Victory Hall and the important work being done there. When she wrote home to her friends in Bloomington, especially to Julia, she always asked for news about Sonny and Victory Hall.

When Hazle returned to Bloomington, she realized how much Sonny had grown and changed while they had been traveling. She determined not to leave on another extensive trip without him. Resuming her work with Victory Hall, it pleased her to see that the Home had continued to prosper during the year she had been away. Her example as a civic-minded citizen through her work with and support of the Boys' Home was not lost on her sons, who became active citizens in their own communities as adults.

Through Hazle's experiences with Ralph and Nelson and the successful establishment of Victory Hall, she recognized what an individual could do on a local level to make a real difference. The trip she and her family took around the world strengthened her desire to promote peace through improved international relations. Her desire had prompted her to take the initial step of writing to Frederic Morgan at Principia College in 1925 about establishing a school of international relations. By the end of the next year, much research had been done by George Andrews to begin the development of an international relations program. Hazle looked forward to discussing some of her ideas for the program with him and Frederic Morgan.

MORE THAN A MERE DREAM

CHAPTER 13

THE MEETING

$\mathcal{H}$azle received an important letter written by Frederic Morgan on January 8, 1927. He proposed that they meet at the end of the month to discuss her ideas for the School of Nations program. Anthony, the educational advisor for Principia, who would facilitate the development of the School of Nations courses, would be available then. In response to Morgan's request for a date that would work best for her, Hazle wrote, "Won't you make it as early in the last week as possible?" She told him that she would be attending a talk on the 21st—and she and Davis planned to visit Ralph at Rollins College in Florida at the end of the month.[319] Knowing that this meeting could make her dream to have a School of Nations at Principia a reality, Hazle did not want to delay it any longer than necessary.

The week before the Ewings planned to go to Florida, they met with Morgan, Andrews, and Anthony at their home on Olive Street in Bloomington. A few days after the meeting, Hazle received an encouraging letter from Andrews, who wrote: "The entire visit with you was much enjoyed and it gave me much inspiration to continue in this work with increasing enthusiasm. . . . Please be sure that we are happy to consider any suggestions which you may send us, and we will endeavor to take each step in conformance with your ideas." And he confided, "I find that its importance and value [has] grown upon me constantly and I am happy to be associated with you in it."[320] Knowing of the genuine interest of Andrews in the project, Hazle felt certain the School of Nations program would soon be established as a part of the Principia College curriculum.

Hazle's confidence in Andrews's interest in the program was not unfounded. Acting on the inspiration he had gained from the meeting with her and Davis, Andrews wrote the "Proposal for Proceeding with International Education at Principia" to present to the Board of Trustees.[321] In his proposal, he expressed the need for the immediate organization of a development committee to plan work for the next summer and school year of 1927-1928. Following the establishment of the committee, he felt it important to make a general and confidential announcement explaining this opportunity to the Principia faculty and staff at their February meeting. He believed the faculty and staff could assist in cherishing and developing the idea, and he was eager to show them how they could use it in their current course work. He also proposed that the College sophomore class be given, in confidence, a general outline regarding the development of the program and specific information on how they could help with the work. And he suggested that the School of Nations provide one or two scholarships for students who had proved their sincere interest in the project.

In order to gain additional support beyond the faculty, staff and students, Andrews proposed making a brief statement at the Parents' Meeting in June of the basic elements of the project, and to print an announcement in the June *Progress*, a school magazine. He also thought that a definite plan for student participation in international education should be presented to all the College students in October 1927, which would include a competition for scholarships to participate in a senior college program or for summer travel in 1928. To launch the program, he suggested that they consider sending a representative student to study at Middlebury College of Modern Language Summer School in Vermont and one to study at the Institute of Politics in Williamstown, Virginia.

The first of February, Hazle received a letter from Morgan informing her of Andrews's presentation of her ideas to the Board of Trustees. Andrews had also informed the Board of her "desire to finance the beginning of the 'School of Nations.'"[322] However, Morgan expressed some concern about accomplishing what they had set out to do in regard to the program, because the School of Nations project depended on Principia being an accredited college, and this seemed to be a problem.

Morgan had recently gone before the Reviewing Committee in Chicago to insure that Principia would continue to be on the North Central Association list of accredited Junior Colleges. There he learned that, in order to remain on the list, Principia needed a $200,000 endowment. When the planned four-year college was completed, the endowment fund must be increased to $500,000. He confided to Hazle that they had collected only $7,000 and a member of the Board of Trustees had offered to contribute $75,000 if the school could secure the rest of the funds needed.[323]

Responding to Morgan's explanation of Principia's need, Hazle sent a gift to the endowment fund. On February 7, Morgan wrote, expressing deep appreciation for her gift. He also assured her that Andrews would continue developing a plan for the School of Nations program for the coming summer. He added that Blackwell had been working on "a simple and clear system for accounting to you the receipt and expenditures of money in connection with the School of Nations Fund."[324]

Also in early February, Andrews informed Hazle that his presentation of the proposal for an international relations program to the Board of Trustees had gone well. The administration and trustees wanted to inform the entire faculty and staff of Principia about the project. He assured her that no names would be mentioned, but they planned to describe the various activities through which each department of the school could participate in the project "and ask for their wholehearted" support.[325] The Board also suggested informing the students who would be graduating from Principia's Junior College this year, so that students wanting to specialize in international relations work had the opportunity to qualify for the scholarships Principia would provide.

Hazle wrote to Andrews, enthusiastically approving his plan to inform the Principia faculty and staff of the project. She told him that she preferred no public announcement be made until a comprehensive list of studies could be offered "in a distinctive school—such as might make up a 'School of Nations,' if we decide to call it that."[326] But they should make a public announcement as soon as they were ready. She believed that it might encourage other universities and colleges to follow their example.

In the meantime, Blackwell had set up the School of Nations Maintenance Fund, and Hazle made her first donation of $1,000 on March 10, 1927. Her financial support of the program had officially begun. Since they did not know how much money would be needed to maintain the program, Hazle told Morgan to let her know when he needed another check.

Taking the first step to launch the program, Andrews organized the School of Nations committee. At the end of May, Hazle received her first School of Nations committee report from Andrews. He explained that it had been delayed until the committee could make a recommendation for the next year's scholarship. He outlined the activities of the committee and reported that Anthony had met with them as a representative of the Board of Trustees, and Morgan as the Director of the Board. The committee members included Andrews, who was directing the program and representing the History department; William E. Morgan Jr., brother of Frederic Morgan, serving in the interest of the fine arts; Miss Elizabeth Jenkins, head of the English Department; and Miss E. Olive Davis, chair of the French Department.[327]

From Andrews's report, Hazle learned that the confidential announcement to the staff had been made, and the staff had already supplied the committee with many helpful suggestions. It pleased Hazle to read about Andrews's work with the modern language teacher to develop a method of teaching that would enable students to speak a foreign language and not just translate it, and that French and Spanish Clubs had been established. She had been especially interested in the news that two students, Mallory Browne and Harriett Kellond, had been recommended by the committee and enrolled in the Foreign Study Plan at the University of Delaware.

The University of Delaware program would enable the two students to spend a year in France, at the cost of $1,500 per student, and Principia would provide approximately $700 for each student.[328] The committee also recommended that James Penfield of San Francisco, William Karnes of Chicago, and William Moreland of Portland, Oregon, take the Foreign Service examinations, which would enable them to obtain positions in the Unites States government offices in foreign countries or as foreign correspondents. In addition to the activities of these five college students, two grade school children, who had lived in Java, shared what they had experienced in that country with the committee. The invaluable information provided by the two children would aid the committee in developing a program designed to promote understanding between nations for the grade school children. Hazle looked forward to hearing more about the development of this program.[329] Her vision for the School of International Relations was beginning to take form and already having an influence on the lives of these college students and grade school children.

Andrews diligently worked to develop additional contacts and activities outside of the school that would enrich their educational program. He went to Washington, D.C., to attend the American Society of International Law meetings in April. He talked with Mr. Norton of the personnel division at the State Department, who provided information regarding the requirements for students to enter the United States Foreign Service. He also visited George Washington University and the University of Maryland, where students of Principia could complete their Foreign Service preparations.[330]

Since two students were already enrolled in the Foreign Study Plan at the University of Delaware, he visited with President Hullihen at a branch of the University in Newark to learn about their Foreign Study Plan. While there, he talked with Mallory Browne, one of the Principia students enrolled in the program, who expressed his enthusiastic support for Principia's School of Nations. Stopping in New York, Andrews contacted Stephan Duggan of the Institute of International Education and presented an outline of Principia's plans. Duggan approved the plan and offered to give his personal endorsement to Principia students planning to attend the University of Delaware's program, which would aid their acceptance into the program. Duggan also suggested that Andrews encourage Principia students to compete for scholarships administered by his institution. Hazle appreciated Andrews's efforts to secure success for their joint venture. Hazle felt sure that all the work Andrews had done and the knowledge he had gained would be useful in establishing the program as a viable and valuable part of the college curriculum.[331]

In May, the English Department sponsored a contest based on the subject, 'International Friends,' and Andrews sent Hazle a copy of the winning essay at the end of the month. As she thoughtfully read what Iolani Ingalls, a student from Hawaii, had written, it confirmed for her the important role that the School of Nations could play in encouraging the right kind of thinking in students, and that students were interested in world peace. Ingalls wrote about how she thought she could develop international friendship from "the standpoint of the possibilities of a traveler, musician, artist, educator, and radio-operator." Although she was none of these, Ingalls concluded, "There remain several things, which I, as a school-girl can do to help cultivate a better international understanding. . . . I know that by the practice of the golden rule and by endeavoring to love mankind, I can in some small way help unify nations."[332]

Hazle felt immensely grateful to Andrews for his endeavors to keep their mutual project moving forward toward the goal of establishing the School of Nations as an official department of The Principia. In accord with this desire, Andrews made the initial effort to establish the School of Nations library and museum. He recommended that the books and other items, which Hazle's donations had enabled the faculty to purchase, be put on display. He also suggested that the School of Nations scholarships be announced at the commencement in June.[333]

CHAPTER 14

THE ANNOUNCEMENT

*A*s Andrews suggested, the School of Nations Scholarship program was announced at Principia's commencement exercises on June 3, 1927. Although Hazle had been unable to attend, she received a report from Andrews, with a copy of the announcement made by Clarence Howard, which began:

> [It] is a great privilege and pleasure to be able to announce the opening of a wider field of service for The Principia and Principians. Friends of The Principia who desire to remain anonymous have expressed a deep interest in aiding the development of a more thorough and better understanding among the nations of the world by entrusting to The Principia a fund for scholarships to help earnest young Christian Scientists,—Principians—to prepare themselves for careers which will be of direct service in the improvement of international relations.[334]

Following the announcement, Howard disclosed that Harriett Kellond and Mallory Browne, both 1926 graduates of Principia Junior College, had been awarded scholarships for continuing their education at a four-year college. And three other graduates, James Penfield, William Karnes, and William Moreland, had received scholarships to assist them in completing their university preparation for the United States Foreign Service examinations. Howard explained that "scholarships of this nature will be available to those Junior College students who desire to participate in this work and are found qualified to undertake it."[335]

Andrews told Hazle that he thought the entire commencement
emphasized the keynote of better international understanding, and
that "It seemed to be a spontaneous result of the work which has
been done during the past year, and was most gratifying to those
of us who have been engaged in the work." He affirmed that all
involved in the activities, whether adults or children, had been
influenced by her vision, and her courage to share it.[336]

Morgan wrote an encouraging letter to Hazle in early June
regarding the announcement of the scholarship program at the
graduation ceremonies. He said, "Remarks made, showed a very
definite awakening interest in matters of international brotherhood
. . . without any direct guidance on our part." He also noted that
the commencement at Washington University in St. Louis was
on the same topic. Morgan believed, "the announcement on
Commencement morning of the awarding of the School of Nations
Scholarship aroused very great interest, and I feel certain that
the seed has been sown and thus results will be, in time, truly
remarkable."[337]

The school year ended, but not Andrews's efforts to increase
his understanding of how the School of Nations program could be
developed to fulfill the promise announced at the commencement
to provide a School of Nations Scholarship. To begin this work, he
took classes in Boulder, Colorado, that would qualify him to manage
the courses that the School of Nations would require. He also
attended classes on the League of Nations and world government.[338]
Andrews's activities prevented him from attending the conferences
at Williamstown that summer, but Blackwell represented Principia
in his place. And William Morgan, Jr. attended the World Education
Alliance in Toronto, Canada, in August.

Also that summer, one of the students who received the
Foreign Preparation Scholarship, William Karnes, was present at
the Norman White Lectures given at the University of Chicago,
from which Hazle had graduated in 1902. Karnes's attendance of

the lectures enabled him to assist the School of Nations Committee in gathering information that would be useful to them in providing guidance for future recipients of the School of Nations Scholarships.

While Andrews spent the summer increasing his knowledge for the benefit of the School of Nations, Hazle spent time with her family at the ranch and received an interesting offer unrelated to the School of Nations' project. Her good friend, Mrs. Graham Bartow, offered to take Sonny (Nelson) into her home so that he could attend The Principia Lower School that fall. Hazle wrote to Morgan of this offer on August 17, 1927, and requested the necessary paperwork to enroll Sonny in the school.[339]

That fall, when she was in St. Louis to leave Sonny with Mrs. Bartow, Hazle discovered a model birch bark canoe at a shop. She purchased it, thinking that "placing the canoe in the hands of the children might vivify their work on Indian lore."[340] Hazle presented the model Native American canoe to one of the teachers at the school. The reaction of the children was immediate and enthusiastic, so much so that other teachers heard about it and started looking for similar items to bring into the classrooms. Learning of Hazle's donation and the children's reaction, Andrews wrote on October 19, telling her that the students would be using the canoe for the North American geography class, and a spinning wheel, which she had also donated, to enliven their study of Thanksgiving Day.[341]

In late October, Andrews informed Hazle that the School of Nations program was overdrawn on the funds available and needed an additional $2,000 to complete the year. Andrews felt that he, Morgan, or Blackwell should meet with her before proceeding any further with their plans. He concluded: "We are most enthusiastic over the work that is being accomplished through your generous aid, and we sincerely appreciate the opportunity to assist in it."[342]

In November, plans were being made to create a booklet describing the School of Nations. As part of this project, there had been a contest for creating a bookplate for the booklet. Andrews

sent Hazle three sketches chosen from the twelve submissions
received from Principia College art students who had entered the
contest. The students had designed the bookplates with only a
little assistance from the Art Department Director, Miss Cherry.
Andrews left the final selection up to Hazle, but added they would
be happy to extend the competition if she felt these were not
satisfactory, and any changes she desired could be incorporated.[343]
Hazle selected one of the three bookplates, which she returned to
Andrews. Responding, Andrews informed her that it would take
some time for the plate to be printed, but as soon as it was ready
they would send her a copy.[344]

While she awaited the arrival of the printed bookplate, she
received a report from Andrews, which included extracts from
letters written by the students who had received the School of
Nations scholarships. From the University of Nancy and the
Sorbonne in Paris, Harriett Kellond, wrote: "There couldn't be a
greater opportunity for proving what we know of Christian Science,
for really worthwhile study, friendly relations with foreigners of
several nations, and real enjoyment, than we are being offered
here." Kellond expressed her gratitude and stressed the importance
of students being able to speak the language. She believed that,
"Everything has combined to make this one of the happiest summers
I have ever had. It seems to me that I appreciate it enough now,
but I know that the real value will be more apparent later on."[345]
Kellond's letter confirmed for Hazle that the School of Nations
activities broadened the understanding of international relations
for the students who took part in the program.

Also participating in the University of Delaware Foreign Study
program in France, Mallory Browne found the group of American
students that he was with, made up of thirty girls and fourteen
boys from twenty-five colleges, to be as engaging as the French
students. He wrote, "There is hardly a member in the group who
does not do more than the average 'shining light' in almost any

American university." Since the students spent most of their time studying, however, their contact with the natives of France was limited. Most of their interactions were confined to the families with whom they were staying. Browne wrote of the couple who provided his housing: "The genuine love and consideration they have manifested toward me has been inspirational–the greatest thing of the whole experience so far." He also expressed his enjoyment of the few days that they spent in Geneva attending a session of the League of Nations. He added: "It has been, and continues to be, a wonderful experience: a wonderful opportunity to work and grow in [Christian] Science." And he concluded: "We appreciate what you are doing for us, and hope to show that appreciation in continued and increased right results."[346]

At George Washington University in Washington, D.C., William Karnes prepared to take the Foreign Service examination or to pursue a career in international journalism. He received encouragement from a special correspondent at *The Christian Science Monitor*, who told him that if he stayed in Washington, D.C. for the summer, he might be able to work for the paper. He also visited Mr. Norton in the Personnel Office of the State Department, who provided him with a list of books to study to prepare for the exam. Karnes wished to share his adventure and wrote: "If you could persuade some other Principians to come join me next year I'd like it even more."[347]

James Penfield and William Moreland were preparing for the Foreign Service exam at Stanford University. Penfield's father wrote a note of appreciation to the College, saying, "I wish to thank your officers in this matter as well as for the advice and encouragement you are giving James. I was down at Stanford about ten days ago and was pleased to see how nicely the boys are situated. . . ."[348]

In December, Morgan wrote to Hazle that $5,000 had been spent for the development of the School of Nations and its activities. He explained that they had received $3,000 dollars for

the Fund, but they still needed $2,000 to meet their bills. He added
that the expenditures for the coming year had been estimated to
be $5,000. Concluding his letter, he expressed gratitude for her
"generous, loving kindness to Principia which has indeed brought
great inspiration to every phase of our activity."[349] At the end of
1927, the School of Nations program became an established part
of The Principia curriculum, and the first students received the
benefits from the scholarships provided.

CHAPTER 15

BUILDING A FIRM FOUNDATION

*I*t was Davis Ewing who responded to Morgan's request for money to cover the overdraft for the end of 1927, sending a check for $2,000 to Principia on January 12, 1928.[350] Davis explained that Hazle had to leave town unexpectedly and did not have time to send the money herself. Then, on January 18, Davis sent another check to Morgan to be put in the School of Nations "special fund" to maintain the program.[351] With the second check, Davis wrote that he and Hazle intended to visit Principia on their way to Washington State in a few months. Now that the School of Nations seemed to be firmly established, they wanted to see how their ideas for the program had been implemented.

The Principia Committee on International Relations sent a report to Hazle in January that listed items which had been purchased through the School of Nations Fund, including books, pictures, and hand-made materials. The School of Nations had also received a collection of figurines and dolls dressed in costumes from Mrs. Kathryn Carter Davis, who continued to donate items to the museum over the years. The items had been cataloged and the list distributed to staff members, "with instructions regarding issue and care of the materials." The model birch bark canoe that Hazle donated in 1927 initiated the collection of artifacts from around the world, which created a foundation for the School of Nations Museum.[352]

In February, Hazle received a letter from Gertrude Foster Brown of the *Woman's Journal*, formerly known as the *Woman Citizen*, of which Carrie Chapman Catt was the Chief Contributions Editor.

143

Hazle continued to be interested in and supportive of women's rights and had become a guarantor of the magazine. Planning to feature their guarantors in the March issue, Hazle had been requested earlier in the year to send the magazine a picture of her and some personal information for a short biographical sketch. Hazle forwarded the requested photograph and information to Brown, who responded, "Your picture and letter came and have already gone to the printers. . . . The picture of you is quite lovely . . . We were able to make quite a nice story from the material you gave us." When the March issue came out, Hazle received a copy of the magazine in which her picture and biographical sketch appeared.[353]

Also in March 1928, the Ewings began laying the foundation of the new home they planned to build in a relatively undeveloped part of Bloomington. Hazle and Davis had originally purchased the property with another couple, Nan and Mark Evans, in 1923. The plot of land consisted of 66 acres previously known as Bosworth's Subdivision, later renamed after Ewing and Evans. In October 1928, Hazle and Davis purchased the Evans' interest in the land, planning to subdivide it into thirteen lots. They began building their home on the first lot and sold the other lots over a period of several years.[354]

Hazle and Davis had gathered ideas for their new home during their travels around the United States and abroad. Davis helped design the house, which included some of his and Hazle's specifications and innovations—such as a car wash and phone booth. The house plan they chose was only one room deep, with north and south exposures, and included garages, a carriage shed, and stables. The building materials consisted in part of sand-blasted cypress, to give it a weathered look, and old brick taken from the former Wochner Brewery in Bloomington. The kitchen, dining room, living room, and library made up the major portion of the first floor with a large entry hall and an elegant winding staircase leading to the second floor, which had five sleeping rooms. The basement consisted of a laundry room and a large room with a seating capacity of 100. Hazle and Davis planned to use the large room to show motion pictures of trips they had taken in the United States and around the world to large groups. They designed an inner courtyard hidden from the view of the outside world by two large castle-like doors, which opened out onto the driveway. From the inner courtyard they had access to the house, the garages, and the stables. Above the garages, the Ewings planned to build a two-bedroom apartment for their live-in employees.[355]

That spring, while their new Channel Norman style house was under construction, Hazle and Davis visited Principia. The Ewings found the School of Nations to be firmly established, and they approved of the program implemented and maintained by Andrews and the committee. In early April, Hazle wrote to Morgan from the Mission Inn at Riverside, California, expressing her gratitude for the "delightful" week they spent at Principia, which had confirmed her hope that the School of Nations would become a valuable part of the College. She told Morgan, "The many kindnesses of the Principia family have made happy memories."[356]

While the Ewings were traveling in the west, Hazle received a letter on April 24, 1928, from Gertrude Brown of the *Woman's Journal.* Brown wrote: "At the annual meeting on Friday, we increased our Board of Directors to fifteen, and you were elected to be one of us." Brown added: "The annual report is about ready and will be sent to you and to all the stockholders in about a week. As a director you will also receive the minutes of the directors' meeting."[357]

On May 29, 1928, Andrews sent Hazle a report on the School of Nations participants. Hazle was happy to learn that Mallory Browne had so impressed the administrators of the Delaware Foreign Study Group that they had recommended that the University of Delaware grant Browne a Bachelor of Arts degree when he completed his year's work in France. Harriett Kellond had done well academically, but her stay with a single woman had not been pleasant for her.

William Karnes did not pass the Foreign Service examination, but he had "made a credible showing." And Andrews believed Karnes to be worthy of encouragement.[358] Hazle could see from the reports that they still had some things to learn about implementing the School of Nations programs, but, she felt confident that the students' experiences would ultimately have a positive influence on their lives.

She also heard from Morgan, who wrote that the School of Nations reports "are bringing us encouragement and inspiration for the work, and we are very glad to share them with you." He also informed her that School of Nations Committee had selected another young woman, Esther Rice, to receive a scholarship to attend the Delaware Foreign Service Group to study in France the next year, which would be announced at commencement. Rice had also been awarded a scholarship from the Institute of International Education, which would cover her travel expenses. And Morgan told Hazle of the many expressions of gratitude he had heard from students and staff members for the books provided by the School of Nations Library and for the display of artistic materials. At the conclusion of his letter, Morgan added that the School of Nations Fund needed another $2,000 to cover expenses, which would bring the Fund into balance for the current year.[359]

In response to Morgan's request for more money, Davis sent a check for the School of Nations Fund in the amount of $2,000 on June 5, since Hazle was at the ranch in Wisconsin. Morgan promptly acknowledged receiving the money with gratitude, and confided:

> The new incentive and more vivid purpose which are creeping into our work through the channels this work is providing have been a surprise to us, for in a thoroughly practical and most valuable way the viewpoint of the institution as a whole is most certainly taking on an international color, not just a few courses and for specific purposes, but in practical, wider interest in world affairs.[360]

It pleased the Ewings that the recently established School of Nations seemed to be having a profound influence on the entire school.

When school resumed in the fall of 1928, Andrews had become Dean of the College, and he wrote to Hazle on October 20 to let her know he had arranged his schedule to give him a large portion of time to devote to the School of Nations. Hazle appreciated Andrews's dedication. It also pleased her to learn of the enrollment of their first international student in the School of Nations program, Ruth Luboke, a freshman from Hamburg, Germany. Miss Luboke's expenses had been paid in part by the School of Nations and by Miss Violet Ker Seymer, a Christian Science lecturer living in England, who had recommended the student. Miss Luboke had been well received by all the students, and especially by Miss Eugenie Bearns of France.[361]

Andrews also reported that Mallory Browne, who had returned to Princeton to continue his university work, had spoken to the first assembly at Principia College just before he left for school. The keynote of the assembly had been the "expansion and extension" of our work outside of America. Mallory had received a class "A" scholarship for his year's work at Princeton. His achievements, as one of the first School of Nations students, encouraged them all to believe that the School of Nations would fulfill its purpose of educating students to pursue careers in international relations, through which they could promote understanding and peace in the world.[362]

That fall seemed to be an especially busy one for Hazle, whose calendar was filled with teas, parties, dinners, entertaining guests, and a trip to Chicago. Because of her full schedule, she had fallen behind in her correspondence. Ralph wrote to his mother in mid-November 1928: "Received your letter last night and was glad to get it. Almost sent you a wire for not writing—you must not be so neglectful." Ralph teasingly added, "Seems to me that you have been having a pretty gay time—with all your tearing around." On a more serious note, Ralph expressed his concern that he would not be able to come home for Christmas." He seemed to be in a quandary about whether to come home, stay at the school and work, or go on a trip with the basketball team through Florida, Georgia, Tennessee, and the Carolinas. He told Hazle, "If it should work out that I don't see you this Christmas—remember that I will be with you in spirit anyway."[363]

In mid-December, Ralph wrote again telling Hazle that he definitely would not be coming home for Christmas.[364] It seemed necessary for Ralph to work through the holiday. After Christmas, he wrote: "I hope you all had a marvelous Christmas—I am sorry that I had to miss it." He thanked Hazle and Davis for paying part of his bills and for the gift of cash. He reported that he had used the cash for board and a new pair of shoes. He told them that the two bow ties they had sent "made it really seem like the holidays. . . . The green bow tie is one of the prettiest ties I have had and looks like a dream when on."[365] Ralph had been missed at Christmas, but Hazle knew he was learning valuable life-lessons that would help him build a firm foundation for his future.

At the beginning of 1929, Hazle received a book from Andrews with the intriguing title, *Between War and Peace*, written by Florence Brewer Boeckel, the Education Director for the National Council for the Prevention of War. Andrews directed her to look at pages 60 and 61. On the indicated pages, Hazle found that Boeckel had written a brief statement of the work Principia was doing through the School of Nations.[366] Andrews also told her of the talk that Frederick J. Libby, Secretary of the Council, had given to the students of Principia College in December, on the Kellogg Peace Pact, which had been signed on August 27, 1928, in Paris, with the hope of ending the use of war to settle international disputes.

Hazle thought it especially encouraging to learn from Andrews that donations to the School of Nations continued to grow. The School of Nations Museum had recently received and already had on display a gift of ceremonial dolls from the Matsukata family, who had been among the first Japanese to become Christian Scientists. Up to that time, the doll collection in the Museum contained only dolls from the United States. The Upper School students had written to the Matsukata family to express their "thanks" for the gift, and the Lower School planned to have a Doll Festival. Hazle was grateful to learn that Kathryn Carter Davis had supplied permanent exhibition cases for the Japanese dolls. Hazle hoped others would also be inclined to make such generous donations of money and items to the School of Nations Museum, or to the School of Nations Fund.

Hazle enjoyed reading Andrews's January report on the School of Nations students. She learned that Ruth Luboke, the student from Germany, seemed to be adjusting well to the Junior College, and that her family had sent letters expressing their gratitude. William Karnes was attending George Washington University and had taken the Foreign Service exam again, but he would not know if he passed until April. Mallory Browne, who continued his studies in France, received a scholarship from Princeton for $450 and a student loan for $250 in recognition of his excellent work. It seemed almost certain that he would be offered a position on the European staff of the *Christian Monitor*. Esther Rice had completed her courses at Nancy and would soon begin her studies at the Sorbonne in Paris.[367]

Andrews also sent Hazle pictures that he had taken of the doll festival at the Lower School. When writing to thank him for the pictures of the dolls, Hazle confided to him that Davis had put all of her donations under the title of Principia, beginning with her donations of the woodlands in 1923, so she could not tell where she stood in regard to the School of Nations Fund. "Couldn't we just decide on a fiscal year and have it understood that the $5,000 will be available in <u>one</u> or <u>two</u> regular payments, at stated intervals or dates?" she asked Andrews.[368]

His response helped her eliminate the confusion, reminding

her that they had begun the actual work on the School of Nations program the summer of 1926. In the two and a half years since the work had begun, she had donated $9,000 to the program. During that time, she had also made a contribution to The Principia College Endowment Fund. The $2,000 she sent in January of 1928 had been used to cover the $1,000 deficit in 1927. And there was a deficit of $2,600 for 1928.[369]

In the spirit of their developing friendship, Andrews also told Hazle that his son George had acquired a wire-haired terrier that he wanted to show Nelson (Sonny). He added that young George hoped that "Nelson would be in the 7th grade with him at Principia." Hazle thought Nelson would be glad to hear about young George's dog. She knew how much Nelson missed the Andrews boys, and how he wished that they lived closer.[370]

Responding to the financial information she received from Andrews, Hazle sent checks to cover the deficit for 1928 and the needs of the current year. And she informed Andrews of her decision to make a $5,000 donation every January to cover the entire year.[371] Andrews expressed his gratitude for the checks and graciously approved of her plan to make a single payment each year, enclosing a summarization of the many gifts she had made to Principia. She felt that her confusion over finances for the School of Nations program had been resolved, resulting in a more efficient way of keeping track of her donations. [372]

Writing to Hazle on January 15, Ralph expressed appreciation for the care package she sent him the first of the year, which contained a much needed pair of overshoes as well as candy and date-bars that he and his friends had been devouring. Knowing of Hazle's life-long interest in nature and wildlife, Ralph told her: "Am sending you the name and details of a book called *Sanctuary*. It is a bird book written by Percy MacKaye and I know you will enjoy it." Ralph had learned of the book when he attended talks and lectures by the author. Concluding his letter, Ralph asked if she could come down to Florida for a visit.[373]

Hazle realized that Ralph missed his family, and she wrote to him that she planned to visit him in a few weeks. Ralph responded, "Received your nice long letter yesterday noon and I am certainly glad to get it." He told her, "Am awfully glad to hear that you are coming down. Arrange it so you can stay longer than a few days. My play is the 21st, three weeks from yesterday." Since he last wrote to her, he had been busy with play rehearsals and other school-work, and he had "a personal talk or interview with W.S. Abbott, Editor of the *Monitor*."[374] Ralph thought Hazle would be especially interested in his talk with Abbott, since Abbott expressed an interest in the School of Nations.

Hazle's mother, Lillian Brewer Buck, and a friend, Miss Stoddard, accompanied her on the trip to Florida. The warm weather helped to make it an enjoyable time for all. Ralph seemed to be especially amiable during their visit. After her return home, it pleased Hazle to hear from Ralph that "It was great to have you here, even if only for a week. I really believe it was . . . the happiest visit we have had." He added: "It was great to have Miss Stoddard and Grandma here—everyone is crazy about them and I have heard a lot of nice things said about them."[375] He assured her that everything was going well, and he was even "picking up" in his studies.

An announcement in the *United States Daily* on March 5, 1929, of William Karnes's appointment to the Foreign Service gave Hazle a great sense of satisfaction. She thought it especially noteworthy that Karnes was the youngest candidate accepted. He would receive instruction from the State Department for a probationary period of one year and serve as a Junior Foreign Service Officer before being appointed to a foreign post. Hazle rejoiced with Andrews who wrote, "He will thus be the first of our School of Nations scholars to undertake service in international relations, although we feel that the students in France have done effective work of the type we wish to encourage." And Andrews firmly believed that

Karnes would "amply justify the investment which has been made in preparing him for his career."[376] The labor that Hazle, Andrews, and the School of Nations Committee had put into establishing a firm foundation for the program had begun to bear fruit.

In late April, Hazle learned from Andrews that Mallory Browne would graduate from Princeton in June and *The Christian Science Monitor* offered him a position upon his graduation. Browne would be spending part of his summer in New York, and then he would go to Boston to prepare for his position on the European staff. Andrews added that Ruth Luboke would be resuming her studies at the College in the fall with a scholarship provided by the School of Nations. Also, Principia had received inquiries from two Japanese girls about attending Principia College the next year.[377]

As the summer vacation began, Hazle learned from Andrews that the school yearbook, the *Sheaf*, had been dedicated to the School of Nations, and that the *Alumni Purpose* had featured articles about the program.[378] He also informed her that James Penfield planned to travel in Buenos Aries and South America; William Moreland was leaving for China; and Esther Rice would be finishing her year in France. [379] And he sent her the news that the American Association of Museums had inquired about the School of Nations Museum.

That summer, Hazle wrote frequently to Ralph, who had taken a job in Chicago. He responded to one of her letters on July 12, 1929, saying, "Thanks muchly for your cards and letters of the last few days. It was awfully nice to hear from you."[380] He especially appreciated her quick responses to his letters. They made him feel less lonely. Although Hazle had family in Chicago, Ralph did not want to impose on them too often. He wrote to Hazle in detail about what he did at work and during his off hours. He asked her to "Tell Sonny good-bye for me—I'm awfully sorry I won't see him again before he goes [to camp]." She kept in touch with both boys through letter-writing that summer.[381]

When school resumed in the fall, both boys returned to their schools, and Andrews wrote to Hazle on September 13, 1929, telling her that the two Japanese girls would be attending Principia for the next two or three years. One of the girls was Yuri Yajima, a cousin of the Matsukata family who had donated the Japanese ceremonial dolls. The other girl was Emi Takaki, the daughter of a lady-in-waiting to the Empress of Japan. He also updated her on the activities of the School of Nations students. Miss Rice had returned from France, Miss Bearns was in Nancy taking classes, and Karnes had been assigned to a post in San Luis Potosi, Mexico. He enclosed letters from Penfield and Moreland, who had returned from their summer travels. What great pleasure it gave Hazle to hear about the accomplishments of the students participating in the School of Nations program.[382]

The Ewings also rejoiced that fall over the completion of their home, "Sunset Hill." Moving into and furnishing their new home in September consumed much of Hazle's time and attention. Her mother had given them two jade, coral, and ivory Chinese panels as a house-warming gift, which they placed on the dining room walls opposite of each other. It took Hazle some time to find a rug that matched the panels. She chose salmon and sea foam as the color scheme for many of the rooms in the house and carefully selected drapes and rugs that corresponded to those colors. The Ewings also took great interest in the care of the grounds around their home. They hired Jens Jensen to landscape it for them, and Hazle selected only native vegetation, including rosebud, hawthorn, maple, crabapple trees, and bluebells to be planted along the curving driveway. Jensen also designed the Compass Garden to the south of the house, which many years later would be redesigned and renamed the Shakespeare Garden.[383]

By the fall of 1929, Davis and Hazle had moved into their new home, which stood firmly on the foundation that had been started over a year earlier. Hazle realized that during that year Ralph had gained a stronger sense of responsibility for his own life. She had also witnessed the success of the first graduates from the School of Nations program, and recognized that the experiences of those students provided a foundation on which future students could build.

CHAPTER 16

THE UNEXPECTED

$\mathcal{A}$t the end of October 1929, Hazle received an unexpected telegram from Frederic Morgan, who told her that Principia planned to open a four-year college in October 1932. He added, "I know that you will rejoice with us."[384] The decision to set a definite date for opening the four-year college had been made because the school had received two large, unanticipated donations for that purpose, one in the amount of $335 thousand and the other in the amount of $1 million. The prospect of Principia beginning construction on the four-year college in the near future was indeed exciting news to Hazle, and she certainly was rejoicing with them.[385]

In mid-November, Morgan wrote requesting an appointment to talk with Hazle and Davis regarding "some matters of great importance to the School of Nations."[386] Hazle believed that the meeting would present some interesting opportunities for the School of Nations program. She carefully read over the two pamphlets Morgan had included with his letter to prepare for their meeting.[387] The one pamphlet provided a record of what the School of Nations had accomplished so far and included a general plan for broadening the work. The other pamphlet contained a statement regarding the future plans for the School of Nations prepared for the upcoming Board of Trustees meeting that would soon take place in Chicago. Morgan had also sent the pamphlet regarding the history of the School of Nations and the plans for expansion to W. S. Abbott at the *Monitor*.[388]

When Morgan met with Hazle and Davis on Wednesday,

November 20, he read a letter to them he had received from Abbott
suggesting some changes in the School of Nations program. The
Ewings and Morgan discussed Abbott's letter and talked over the
general plan for expanding the program. The plan included the
opportunity to have a School of Nations building. Inspired by
this possibility, the Ewings reaffirmed their intention to continue
financially supporting the activities of the School of Nations,
however, because of the stock market crash of October 1929, they
were not financially prepared to set up an endowment fund for
maintaining the program at that time. They did promise to provide
$150 thousand, which was half the amount needed to construct
the building. The expansion plan allowed them a year to amass the
funds needed for construction.[389] Anticipating that the country's
financial situation would improve, Hazle and Davis thought they
could sell some of the lots in the subdivision they owned.

On November 26, 1929, Morgan wrote to the Ewings saying
that their promised contribution to the School of Nations building
had been an inspiration, and he hoped to announce their gift and
its source in the *Monitor*. He added:

> It is difficult for me to express, on the behalf of Principia,
> any proper measure of gratitude for what you have been
> doing and what you have agreed to do in the future. Your
> thought with regard to the right unfoldment of this inter-
> national work has brought us here the most stimulating
> activity and our horizon with regard to the four year
> college and the present School of Nations units, has
> broadened very greatly.[390]

Morgan believed that announcing the Ewings' contribution would
encourage others to make donations for the construction of the
four-year college.

A few days later, Hazle received a letter from an unexpected
source: A.J. Hanna, the assistant to President Hamilton Holt

of the Statesmanship Institution at Rollins College in Winter Park, Florida. He wrote to Hazle of his interest in the School of Nations. He had learned of the program when having lunch with Abbott. Hanna urged Hazle to share any announcements with the Statesmanship Institution regarding "its development, particularly the part of which pertains to international relations."[391] Hanna's interest encouraged Hazle to believe that other educational institutions would soon begin to support and teach the subject of international relations.

In addition to Hanna's interest in the program, reports from the School of Nations students in March 1930 seemed particularly encouraging to Hazle. She wrote to Andrews on March 24, "I was especially glad to see Mallory Browne's account of his experience in the *Monitor* offices. It is fine to know that the work goes on each day."[392] She also rejoiced in the success of Penfield and Moreland, who had done well on their Foreign Service exams and planned to visit colleges and share their experiences while on their way to the Pacific Coast to fill their appointed Foreign Service positions. In the fall, Penfield and Moreland would return to Washington, D.C. for special instruction at the State Department.

Although Hazle's official correspondence with Andrews ended at the close of school in June, she wrote to the Andrews family on August 17, 1930, to tell them about Nelson's summer at the ranch in Wisconsin and about her experiences at the Eaton's Ranch in Wolf, Wyoming.[393] Andrews responded to Hazle after school began in the fall with a lengthy letter expressing his pleasure in having Nelson back at Principia. He reported that Nelson had been over to play with his son George, and he added that they hoped to see more of her now that Nelson was there.[394]

Andrews also reported to Hazle that the College students seemed to have a greater interest in the School of Nations that fall, and he had received letters from other Schools of Nations at other institutions. Hazle enjoyed reading about his experiences in

England that summer where he had been preparing for the School
of Nations work. He had also made a trip to France to visit the
students studying with the University of Delaware Group. She
looked forward to receiving the students' reports, which Andrews
promised to send.[395]

The newspaper clippings that Andrews sent her in mid-
November, 1930, regarding how schools around the country were
beginning to implement the idea of a school of international
studies greatly encouraged Hazle. She also received support from
her mother, Lillian, who had been so inspired by The School of
Nations program at Principia that she provided a year's scholarship
for a School of Nations student. And Andrews assured her: "The
increasing number of students coming from abroad is direct evidence
of the far reaching influence of the School of Nations work."[396]

It surprised Hazle to receive a letter from Morgan in December,
since she thought he was in San Francisco with the architect,
Bernard Maybeck, working on the plans for the college campus.
He shared with her the startling news that it had been discovered
in October that the Loch Lin property on which Principia planned
to build their college had been slated by the city of St. Louis as the
site for a new highway. The highway would cut right through the
middle of the campus, which would make the woodland property
Hazle had donated to Principia as part of the college in 1923
unusable.[397] Morgan assured her, however, he had found a suitable
piece of property on the bluffs above Elsah, Illinois, on the bank of
the Mississippi River. He told her that there would be a new Ewing
Wood on the new campus, and "The new property is beautiful
beyond belief. The fact that it has been held intact all these years
is certainly wonderful evidence of God's protecting love for this
institution." He added that Maybeck is "quite beside himself with
joy over the opportunities which this property presents."[398]

Morgan explained the "immense" potential for the main piece
of property, which was "practically three miles long along the bluffs,

extending into the back country to depths of one-half mile to one mile." The area seemed ideal for horseback riding, and he told Hazle, "When the time comes, we are going to ask you if you won't help lay out 'our bridle paths' on this new property." He added, "I am more anxious to have you see it and rejoice with us over the progress this new campus represents." He also told her that the purchase price of the new property is less than the sewer tax on the old property would be for the next three or four years. He concluded, "It is hoped that actual work can be begun early next spring."[399]

Morgan's description of the Elsah property ignited Hazle's imagination and she looked forward to seeing the new campus site and where the School of Nations building would one day be erected. She and Davis had been able to sell four of the twelve lots in the subdivision they owned. She anticipated they would soon have the $150,000 to begin construction of the School of Nations building on the new campus.

Inspired by Morgan's news, Hazle wrote to Andrews that she planned to be in St. Louis on January 27. She wanted to see the new property and plans, if possible. She added, "I am enthusiastic about the possibilities of the new site." Responding to the recent School of Nations report, she told him, "It is a deep satisfaction to me to see practical results from our School of Nations." Prompted by A. J. Hanna's letter, Hazle asked Andrews to send a comprehensive statement of Principia's School of Nations work to Hanna at Rollins College in Florida. She also requested some materials that she could send to her local paper, *The Daily Pantagraph*, to promote interest in the program.[400]

In mid-January, Hazle received a package from Morgan, which contained *The Great River*, a book of poems by Frederick Oakes Sylvester. His enclosed note explained that Sylvester had taught art at The Principia and that "He had a summer home and studio at Elsah, Illinois, the site selected for the four-year college. Many of [Sylvester's] paintings dealt with the property which the school now owns." He sent her the book as a token of his appreciation for her interest in Principia, adding, "May it also serve as your introduction to that beautiful property upon which the college is to be erected."[401] The contents of the book intensified Hazle's desire to see the property in person.

While anticipating a visit to the new college site in Elsah, she received confirmation from Andrews that he had sent a packet of information on the School of Nations to Hanna at Rollins College. And she looked forward to receiving the half dozen folders describing the School of Nations that Andrews promised to send her, one of which she planned to share with the editor of the *Pantagraph*.

On January 21, Andrews reported that Karnes, Browne, and Penfield had each received more financial support than the amount of their scholarships, but that the young men had repaid it. The School of Nations Committee had decided that, in the future, "scholarships should cover only part of the student's expense," relying on the students and their families to pay the remainder of the financial requirements. In worthy cases, however, a loan could be made to help supplement a scholarship. Hazle fully agreed with the Committee's decision.[402]

After Hazle visited the new college site on January 27, she went south to Florida to escape the cold winter months in Illinois. Writing to Andrews in early May, she was eager to learn what had been done on the college site at Elsah while she had been away. She planned to be in St. Louis on May 20 and wanted to stop at the Elsah campus. She anticipated that work on the new campus had begun in earnest with the warmer weather, and she told Andrews, "It will be hard to keep away with so much happening."[403] Arriving in St. Louis on the expected day, Hazle and her friends thoroughly enjoyed their stay. She wrote a note of appreciation to Mrs. William E. (Dorinda) Morgan, Jr., for her thoughtfulness and hospitality, and added, "The Principia family grows constantly dearer to me each visit."[404]

In September 1931, the celebration of Principia's 33rd year in operation honored the establishment of the School of Nations. The activities opened with a flag ceremony in which twenty-three students from eleven foreign countries participated. As living witnesses to the value of the School of Nations, each of the foreign students shared information about themselves and their various countries. The school administration believed that the coming of the foreign students to Principia was "closely related to the School of Nations" program, a unique undertaking "in the educational world."[405]

During the ceremony, it was stated: "The purpose of the School of Nations is to educate students to a proper international point of view conducive to peace and friendship around the world." In order to achieve those goals, the School of Nations offered scholarships to assist foreign students to attend Principia and enabled graduates to continue their studies for careers in international service. In addition, the School of Nations Library provided books that gave students a better understanding of other nations, and the Museum exhibited and stored a variety of artifacts and items that could be borrowed by instructors for use in their classrooms.[406]

Hazle did not attend the ceremony, but Andrews sent her copies of the *Alumni Purpose* and *Progress at Principia*, both of which included accounts of the flag ceremonies. He suggested that the information in the two magazines would make good newspaper material since it had also been prepared for the *Monitor*. He also shared with Hazle the news that the American Consul in Mexico planned to send his son to Principia to take advantage of the "training we are providing in preparation for the Foreign Services."[407] It gratified Hazle to know that the influence of the School of Nations was spreading.

In the fall of 1931, no students were preparing for Foreign Service, but the School of Nations had assisted three students from abroad with scholarships. Four other students were also receiving financial assistance: Miss Elfriede Kaiser and Miss Rita Julien from Germany; and Douglas Foreman and Leon Nahapiet of England. And Andrews believed the international relations class to be better than ever.

Miss Frances Thurber Seal sent a copy of her recently published book, *Christian Science in Germany*, to each one of the School of Nations' committee members. In turn, Andrews sent a copy of the book to Hazle with an enclosed note from the committee, telling her: "We are most grateful to you for originating the School of Nations work and for the support and encouragement you have given us and it. It has broadened our vision of the scope of Principia's mission and has brought us many blessings in the interest of friendship of Christian Scientists around the world."[408]

Andrews also mentioned in his letter the need for more funds, which caused Hazle some concern. She thought she had paid the amount she had agreed to pay for the year. Since she was not at home, she called her secretary, who confirmed that she was right. She believed there must be some misunderstanding and felt certain it could be corrected. She wrote to Andrews on October 12 with the information she had received from her secretary.[409] He responded on October 16, including a memorandum of contributions she had made and an explanation of what may have caused the confusion.[410] Hazle did not agree with his understanding of the situation.[411]

Morgan wrote to Hazle, suggesting she meet with Andrews and Blackwell saying, "I am sure that their conference with you will set at rest any seeming confusion which may have existed." He also told Hazle about Blackwell working on various plans, "which might be suggested to you which would enable you to spread your payments" for the construction of the "School of Nations over a period of years." He assured her, "I do not want to bring any unwelcome pressure. I nevertheless want you to know that we are hoping most earnestly that the School of Nations Building can be erected as planned." He added that her promise to provide half the money for the building had been an important factor in computing funds available for the college. Although they had interrupted the work on the plans for her building because they "felt it essential to get the two-story dormitories under construction," he assured her that he and Maybeck would soon resume their work on the plans for the School of Nations building.[412]

On November 2, when Blackwell and Andrews arrived at her home to discuss the finances, Hazle received her guests with her usual gracious manner, and in "a very friendly spirit." Blackwell and Andrews reaffirmed Principia's desire to carry on the School of Nations work "in any way which will best suit [your] financial plans" and assured Hazle that Principia is "ready to support it during the interim which may be necessary until [you are] ready to again contribute." Hazle explained that she thought the confusion had come when her finances were in transition between Davis giving up control of her accounts, and her brother, Nelson Buck, taking them over. Hazle also told them that she was not sure that she would be able to provide the full $5,000 for next year. She assured Blackwell and Andrews that her questioning of Andrews about the finances had not in any way been intended to express dissatisfaction with the work they had accomplished for the School of Nations.[413]

Hazle felt the meeting had gone well and the confusion over the School of Nations Fund had been cleared up. She was also glad for the opportunity to assure Andrews of her confidence in the work he had done and continued to do for the School of Nations. What troubled her was her inability to give Principia any definite confirmation of the amount she would be able to contribute to the construction of the School of Nations building. She knew that her upcoming meeting with her brother, Nelson, would give her a better idea of what she could donate to the School of Nations maintenance and building funds.[414]

Unanticipated events of the recent past had brought about her present financial situation. When she and Davis had taken separate vacations, she had not known that it would turn out as it did. Their son, Nelson, had been left at their home in the care of Julia Hodge. Unexpectedly, Davis came home early from his trip. Julia soon discerned Davis's intent to move out of the house. When she tried to reason with him, to convince him that he should stay until Hazle returned so that they could talk things over, he responded, "There is nothing more to talk about." When Hazle reached home, Davis was already gone. Their divorce followed his departure. Hazle felt a keen sense of disappointment over their failed marriage, but she wanted to remain at Sunset Hill. Since it seemed unwise for her to live at the house alone, she invited Julia to be her paid companion. Julia accepted the position and moved into one of the bedroom suites, which consisted of a sleeping room, sitting room, and bathroom. To work out the details of maintaining her home, she relied on her brother, Nelson, for assistance.[415]

On November 5, Hazle received a supportive letter from Andrews, who wrote, "Your assurance of satisfaction with the progress of the School of Nations work is most heartening."[416] He affirmed his willingness to work with her on the financial element of the program to suit her needs, and that the committee would be open to other resources. He understood that her divorce from Davis had made it necessary for her to re-evaluate her financial situation.

Despite the uncertainty of Hazle's finances, Morgan and Maybeck resumed their work on the plans for the School of Nations building. On December 7, Andrews forwarded blueprints of the proposed School of Nations building to Hazle. She learned from Andrews that Morgan wanted to begin the construction of the School of Nations building in the near future. Looking over the blueprints, Hazle saw that the first floor of the School of Nations included three museum style classrooms: the German, French, and Spanish. Kathryn Carter Davis had already promised to provide $15 thousand for the interior of the French room. Also on the first floor, there would be three medium sized classrooms, one small conference room with a bay window, and, at the "gallery" end of the building, two small class-rooms in front of the museum storage space. The museum would take up the entire second floor. It had been estimated that the School of Nations proper, and the museum, could be built for $150 thousand.[417]

Not long after receiving the blueprints, Hazle met with her brother to discuss her finances. During their discussion, she realized it would be impossible to begin the construction of the School of Nations building as hoped. She could not make any substantial contribution to the fund for the School of Nations building during the coming spring or summer. Converting her assets into cash would seriously cripple her estate. She did begin the process of checking her accounts to see what she could safely give, however, and she safeguarded the amount that she had promised for the building in her will. Hazle's heart ached as she wrote to Morgan on December 19, 1931, "Please know that this situation is a very great disappointment to me."[418] This discouraging turn of events made the construction the School of Nations building seem a distant dream.

Starting Over

CHAPTER 17

RISING ABOVE DISAPPOINTMENT

*R*eceiving Hazle's letter of disappointment, Morgan responded on December 22, "We know with you that God will provide. . . . We know, therefore, that if divine Love alone guides and directs, and we are alert to hear only His Word, we shall not be troubled nor concerned whatever the leading may come to us through the action of infinite Wisdom." He told her that the Trustees and Administration of Principia had been surprised by this unexpected change, but "Every step in the history of the unfoldment and progress of Principia, has seemed to be taken in the face of what mortal mind would call an 'impossible' situation." As in all other 'impossible' situations they had met, this obstacle would be overcome. He assured her, "We want you to feel free to work out your own personal problem in connection with your desire to participate with this work in full and complete justice to yourself and to every other responsibility which you have assumed."[419] In Morgan's letter, Hazle found comfort and support.

Although unable to donate the full amount of money needed for the School of Nations building, Hazle found another way to contribute. She intensified her efforts to promote the educational program. She wrote to Andrews in January 1932 to request twelve to twenty School of Nations folders since she had given away all that she had. She told him that she planned to "spread the gospel" on her trip south. Sending the folders she had requested, Andrews assured her that the building would come about "at the right time when it will not be a source of difficulty for you" and will be a "real cause for rejoicing on the part of all concerned."[420]

She also found encouragement in Andrews's report on the
School of Nations students, which included the news that the
Christian Science Publishing Society had hired Eugenie Bearns as a
translator. Hazle read with interest the article Andrews had clipped
from the *Monitor*, dated January 23, 1932, announcing that Robert
Peary's North Pole flag had been presented to Principia by Frank A.
Miller. The newspaper story indicated that interest in the School of
Nations continued to grow and prosper.[421]

Attending the 1932 Winter Olympic Games held at Lake
Placid, New York, Hazle found the gathering of athletes from around
the world especially inspiring. It confirmed for her that "Each one
of such League of Nations gatherings does its part in the bringing
of the final [establishment of] world peace that must come." The
experience enlivened her desire for the School of Nations to play
its part toward that effort.[422]

While still in New York one cold February day, she sat at her
desk writing a letter to Andrews and watching the boys from the
Northwood School playing a game of ice hockey. She imagined
Nelson and young George Andrews among those boys below her
window, racing about on the ice and brandishing their hockey sticks.
What she would not give to hear Nelson's laughter and see his smile
at that moment. She derived some comfort, however, knowing that
the Andrews family often invited Nelson to their home and included
him in their activities. Thinking of their kindness toward her son,
Hazle wrote to Andrews, "I thank you for helping my Nelson."[423]

Although her affairs were now "in better running order," she
requested Andrews and the School of Nations committee to reduce
expenses as much as possible, so that she could focus on increasing
the building fund. When she had first spoken of supplying the
money for the building, she "had no idea there could be so many
complications." Despite the complications, she was grateful for each
donation that brought them closer to beginning the construction

on the building. The check her mother had given her for $300 was added to the fund, and she felt that it had been "an answer to prayer." It enabled her to send $600 in the letter to Andrews for the School of Nations building fund in late February. The School of Nations committee had already reduced the operating expenses of the program, but understanding Hazle's desire to increase her donations to the building fund, they decided not to sponsor any scholarships the next year.[424]

Hazle had taken full advantage of the opportunity to 'preach the gospel' at the Olympic Games. She requested another dozen booklets from Andrews, explaining that she had given away the ones he had sent her in January. She told him that she found many people, who were not Christian Scientists, interested in the School of Nations, and she wished more schools would promote similar programs.[425] Responding to Hazle's request for more booklets, Andrews wrote that he empathized with her desire to see a program such as theirs at other schools. He also expressed gratitude for her initiation of the School of Nations program. It "had been the largest single factor in making Principia known to a larger circle of friends both in America and throughout the world. . . . It is a center of interest as well as a source of inspiration for the growth and extension of the college," he told her.[426]

At the end of May 1932, Hazle found it possible to make a contribution of $10 thousand to Principia for a bird sanctuary on the Elsah campus, thus fulfilling a long-cherished desire to provide Principia College students with the opportunity to discover wildlife in its natural habitat. She thoughtfully and intentionally chose a section of land that contained a densely wooded ravine that would not be suitable for building. It covered approximately sixty acres of land, and the Board of Trustees officially designated it the Ewing Wood Bird Sanctuary.[427]

Having initiated the establishment of the bird sanctuary, Hazle again turned her attention to supporting the growth of the School of Nations in particular and providing some publicity for Principia in general. She requested and received from Andrews some pictures of the progress being made on the new college campus, which she made available for publication in her local newspaper. On June 12, 1932, an extensive article about the Principia College campus in Elsah appeared in the *Pantagraph* making use of the pictures Hazle had provided. The article was titled "School of Nations is a Unique Educational Project at Principia College for Fostering of World Peace" written by Mrs. E.B. Brindley.[428]

In her article, Brindley reported that a Bloomington woman "who had traveled widely," sent a letter to Principia in 1925 because she believed that the college should "eventually have a school of international relations," and that she would provide the financial assistance to make the project possible. At the time of the newspaper article, Hazle chose not to have her name publicized, but preferred "to remain anonymous."[429] The article outlined the current activities of the School of Nations, which included scholarships for students who wished to prepare for some form of international work; a special library, including approximately a thousand books, many of which had been purchased in Europe and encouraged an appreciation of other countries and cultures; and a museum containing various items from foreign lands.

Brindley gave the School of Nations much of the credit for the enrollment of two Japanese girls in Principia College in 1929, and two more Japanese students who attended the school in the fall of 1930. And "during the current year the largest number of students from foreign countries ever" were attending the College. The students originated from Canada, Ireland, England, Alaska, the Philippines, Hawaii, China, Peru, and Belgium. The article also mentioned that Ralph Ewing had attended Principia for five years, and that Nelson Ewing was currently a freshman at Principia High School.[430] Pleased with the publicity the article gave to the School of Nations and Principia, Hazle purchased several copies, some of which she sent to Andrews, who shared them with the Publications Office at the school.[431]

By late June, Hazle's financial situation had so improved that she sent a $5,000 check to cover the expenses of the School of Nations for the next year. Andrews assured her that the committee would continue to restrict their program, and they would transfer any balance left over from the $5,000 at the end of the year to the building fund. She looked forward to receiving from Andrews the accounting figures for the program for the past year and the estimated budget for the following year.[432]

That summer Hazle and Nelson made the trip to the ranch in Wisconsin where other members of their family gathered. Nelson had been disappointed that young George Andrews could not join them for a few weeks, but it did not take him long to find other young people near his age and entertaining activities in which to participate. For Hazel, their time at the ranch provided her an opportunity to renew acquaintances with rarely seen members of her family. She especially relished the cool evenings when she could sit by the fire and catch up on her reading. A few hours each day she enjoyed riding in the woods, drinking in the simple beauty and wonder of nature, and finding solitude and quietness.[433]

When Nelson returned to school in St. Louis in September, Hazle resumed her responsibilities in Bloomington. The October mail brought news from Andrews about activities taking place on the campus relating to the School of Nations work. He told her of the successes of two of their former School of Nations scholars: Mallory Browne, who had been appointed as the manager of *The Monitor* office in Paris; and James Moreland, who had been transferred from England to Holland. In addition, several students had enrolled to prepare for Foreign Service work, and Sam Baker, an enthusiastic Spanish instructor, had been added to the School of Nations committee.[434]

In late October, Hazle received from William Morgan a map of

Ewing Wood, which delighted her eyes and stirred her imagination. She told him, "All through the summer, I had hoped something would call me back . . . so that I could see it. . . . I had no idea it would be so beautiful . . . I feel now, that I could delve into Ewing Wood at any moment." She confided to William that the alluring map would induce them to start off "to Elsah at every possible opportunity."[435] She looked forward to hiking in the wooded ravine of Ewing Wood, where she could catch glimpses of the wildlife hidden there. She hoped that by spring Principia would have a lodge where she could stay and have easy access to the woods.

In January 1933, Hazle learned from Andrews that individuals interested in supporting the new campus had begun to seek enrollees for the College. Hazle soon became one of those individuals and actively participated in the effort to fill the new dormitories. She wrote to Frederic Morgan in mid-January of three students that she had met who were interested in attending Principia and assured him that she would "keep her ears open for more."[436]

Having moved beyond the sorrow of her divorce and her financial trouble, it surprised Hazle to receive a letter one day from Frederic Morgan's office addressed to "Mrs. Davis Ewing." Responding to the letter, she reminded him, "Since receiving the divorce from Davis a little more than a year ago, I have been using my name only. There is a Mrs. Davis Ewing who lives in Chicago."[437] Her letter received an immediate explanation and apology from Morgan's secretary, Virginia Ruf. She assured Hazle that it would not happen again.[438]

One warm day in late winter, Hazle retired to her garden to read the latest report from Andrews about the School of Nations students. The report contained the good news that Vice-Consul Penfield, one of their first students, was en route to his new position at Mukden, Manchuria in "recognition of his good work and an opportunity for greater usefulness." Also, Fredrika Morehouse, since returning from France, had been elected Phi Beta Kappa after only one year at the University of Rochester.

Fluent in Spanish and French, she had been recommended for a teaching position with the United Fruit Company in Cuba. At Hazle's alma mater, the University of Chicago, Katherine Hunter was engaged in earning her Master's degree and giving talks for the League of Nations Association.[439]

In the spring, when Andrews reported on some of the former School of Nations students, he told Hazle of the dilemma that two of the young women faced—marriage or career. He knew that both young women had worked hard to prepare for their careers and now were confronted with a difficult choice. He asked Hazle the rhetorical question, "What shall we do about these young women who must choose between a career and a husband?" In the end, one chose a husband and the other chose a career.[440]

One day, in late September, Hazle opened a letter written to her by Arthur T. Morey, the Secretary for the Board of Trustees of Principia, requesting her to attend the Board of Trustees meetings on October 8 and 9. The letter did not fully explain the purpose of the meeting, but the focus seemed to be the projected date for opening the four-year college—which had been postponed until the fall of 1935. The mystery of the letter intrigued her, and she replied that she would be happy to come to the meetings, but she had to attend her Christian Science Association that Saturday, October 8. She told Morey that she could come on Sunday, if that would be helpful. In response, Morey assured her that they would appreciate her presence at the meeting on Sunday.[441]

When she attended the meeting that Sunday, she discovered that she was one of six individuals who had been invited, as friends of the school, to discuss the opening date of the Elsah college campus. During the meeting, Hazle sensed there was some concern about Principia having funds to complete the work on the campus by the fall of 1935. Believing they should establish a goal, however, Hazle made a motion that the school should determine to go forward with the construction of the college campus and expect to open it on the projected date. The motion passed. The decision made by the board and the guests at that October meeting seemed to give an added impetus to the work on the campus; following that meeting, many generous donations were received.[442]

The additional income enabled Principia to complete the Chapel before Christmas that same year, and Morgan wrote to Hazle on December 21, 1933, suggesting that they start on the School of Nations building. He believed that what they had on hand and the portion of the $150,000 that she had accumulated for the building would be enough for them to begin the construction. He concluded: "The courage and vision shown by the Trustees and special guests at our October meeting have certainly borne fruit."[443]

CHAPTER 18

THE TRUSTEE

$\mathcal{A}$nticipating that construction would soon begin on the new College campus, Hazle met with Frederic Morgan in January 1934 to discuss her plans for the School of Nations building, which included a Museum. She envisioned a tower at the center, joined on one side by the Museum and on another by the foreign language building. Her ideas seemed somewhat elaborate, but she maintained that she could not provide more than her original offer of $150,000 for the construction. At the time of their meeting, the School of Nations Building Fund amounted to $26,000. Hazle believed that she would be able to add another $15,000 thousand in June. Thereafter, she thought she should be able to donate between $2,000 and $3,000 a month.[444]

Morgan requested Maybeck to begin designing the tower immediately, and, a few weeks later, he reported to Hazle that "it was developing beautifully." In addition, Dr. Charles Kelly, a parent of a Principia student and the Director of the Chicago Art Institute, had been hired to assist Maybeck with the design of the Museum building to insure there would be proper lighting for the display cabinets. Hazle looked forward to seeing the revisions that Maybeck was making to the sketches of the foreign language building, which she and Morgan had discussed at their recent meeting. She hoped that the plans would be ready in February.[445]

While waiting for the completion of the sketches, Hazle sought warmer weather in Mexico, leaving behind a wintry Bloomington. Near the end of February, she wired Morgan, asking if the preliminary plans had been completed. It must have been a disappointment to her to learn that the plans were not ready. They would not be finished for at least two or three months, maybe longer. Morgan assured her, however, "We are making progress but far from completion."[446]

After Hazle returned from Mexico, she received an invitation from Principia to become a member of the Board of Trustees. As a trustee, she would be more involved with the development of the new College campus and have the opportunity to help make the decisions that would influence the growth and prosperity of the school. With the anticipated opening of the new College in January 1935, Hazle thought it an especially exciting time to be a member of the Board of Trustees, and she accepted the invitation without hesitation.

Following her first board meeting, Morgan wrote to her on June 16, 1934, that he believed she would "bring to the deliberations of the Board an impersonal wisdom that the work requires." He also teasingly chided her for not charging her meals to Principia, saying, "We hate to think that our Trustees are starving only a few blocks away."[447]

Hazle responded, "You forgot that you gave us delightful luncheons and suppers each day, and then, besides, you put me for one, at least, under the pleasant wing of none other than Mr. Hamlin—who would not allow me to even sign my own breakfast check. So there!" A bantering tone had entered into Morgan's correspondence, and Hazle seemed comfortable responding in like manner. Although Hazle had been acquainted with Morgan for nearly ten years because of her association with Principia, through her work as a trustee she would come to know him better.[448]

Despite the bantering tone at the beginning of her letter, Hazle took her membership on the Board quite seriously, and she told Morgan, "Even now, when it is time for another Trustee meeting, I am feeling most humble about taking up the responsibility of being one of you." In her new role as trustee, Hazle had access to

information regarding the financial needs of the school, and as a
devout Christian Scientist, she began earnestly praying about those
needs. She deeply cherished one idea that had come to her as the
result of her prayers. She shared the idea with Morgan: "Supply for
right activity is adequate and infinite and we can prove it." She
looked forward to the next Trustee meetings, eager to be in the
midst of so much activity and to see how much progress had been
made on the construction of the buildings at the College campus.
She confessed to Morgan that she almost considered going back to
college so she could "have the joy of working and living in Elsah."[449]

The October Board of Trustees meetings inspired Hazle to work
out a way to make available the money needed to erect the School of
Nations building as soon as possible. In November 1934, she solidified
her plan. She then contacted Morgan, who informed the rest of the
Trustees. She felt certain that she would have the needed funds when
Principia could begin the construction on the building.[450]

Hazle did not feel as sure about her ability to fulfill a request
from a local group of young Christian Scientists to give a talk about
Principia on November 20. She wrote to Morgan asking him what
information she should present, and if he wanted to send someone
else to give the talk.[451] In addition, she wanted to know if the recent
news she had received about the College not moving to Elsah as
planned in January was true. According to her calculations, the
$400,000 needed for the move seemed to be practically in hand
without the school having to sell its securities.[452]

Morgan responded that he believed her to be qualified to give
the talk about Principia on November 20, especially since she was
both a parent and a trustee—although he offered to send someone
to help her if she did not feel comfortable about doing it. He also
promised to send a dozen College View Books and some College
catalogues. Regarding students interested in the Upper School,
she could send him their names and addresses and he would have
catalogues sent directly to them from the school. Fortified with this

information from Morgan and the assurance that her first-hand knowledge of Principia was sufficient, she felt more confident about giving the talk.[453]

Morgan also told her that the news she had heard about the College not making the move to Elsah in January was correct. He explained that Principia did not have as much money as she had thought. She had mistakenly included the depreciation account in her calculations, of which a large portion had already been spent. Morgan added, however, that his mother, Mary Kimball Morgan, "feels very strongly that it would be a great mistake not to make the move and she feels convinced that the move can and will be made."[454] Hazle agreed with Mrs. Morgan, but she also understood Frederic's concerns and reservations.

On November 20, Hazle talked to the group of young Christian Scientists, using the information about Principia College that Morgan had provided and enlisting the help of her friends, Dorothy Knight and Dave Rydin. The meeting went so well that she wrote to Morgan requesting three more copies of the College View Book. She also told him that while she was in New York at the home of her brother, Ellsworth, for Thanksgiving, he gave her permission to add the $500 he had contributed to the School of Nations Fund to help with the move to Elsah. She assured Morgan, it is "a rare privilege to have part in such constructive and inspiring work."[455]

In January, Hazle visited her mother. After Hazle left, Lillian felt inspired to send a check for $1,000 to Principia that could be used for "whatever is immediately needed." Lillian wanted it to be understood, however, that this was a loan. She expected the school to in turn contribute that amount to the School of Nations Building Fund. Hazle was thankful for the generosity of her family, and she fervently hoped that the move to Elsah would be accomplished before she and her mother planned to leave on a long vacation. Hazle wanted to be there to help with the move, but she had promised to travel with her mother that winter "anywhere and everywhere" she wanted to go.[456]

Morgan gratefully received the donation and assured Hazle that they would use the money only in an emergency, and that it would be credited to the School of Nations Fund, "under the same plan in which that portion of your building fund is now operating in our possession." When the weather turned bitterly cold in the latter part of January, Hazle asked Morgan how they could possibly make the move under such conditions. He admitted that they had not made much progress, and had postponed the move until February 21.[457]

In mid-February, Hazle received a financial report on the School of Nations from Andrews in which he had recorded the regular business of the School of Nations committee separately from the building fund. In addition to his financial report, Andrews wrote that "the *Monitor's* Paris correspondence has been positively brilliant," reminding her that Mallory Browne was in charge of the Paris office, and he frequently contributed articles.[458] It pleased Hazle to realize how successful some of the former School of Nations students had become in their Foreign Service careers.

But Hazle had some concerns that winter about the success of her own son, Nelson, who seemed to be struggling with most of his school work at Principia. After much prayer and thought, she believed that a change might do him some good. She decided to enroll him in the Cranbrook School, located in Bloomfield Hills, Michigan. She made the necessary arrangements for his transfer in February. Andrews supported her decision and told her, "We are sorry to have Nelson leave, but we join with you in wanting him to have any experience that means progress." Andrews's sister, Louise, would especially miss Nelson. She had become quite fond of him when he had taken one of her art classes, and she thought him to be quite talented.[459]

Shortly after the arrangements for Nelson to transfer to Cranbrook were made, Hazle received news that Principia College had been successfully moved to the Elsah campus on February 28,

1935. Mary Kimball Morgan wrote, "To any Principian who has
contributed in some measure to this happy achievement we extend
our heartfelt gratitude." Hazle had contributed substantially to
the move. She had taken over $30,000 dollars from the School
of Nations Building Fund to assist in paying for the installation
of the kitchen equipment. In addition, she had been able to loan
the College $120,000 and willingly accepted the only security the
school had to offer—the old college property in St. Louis. The move
had been made through the selfless generosity of many individuals
who contributed money and/or physical labor.[460]

While on vacation with her mother in May 1935, Hazle
received a note from Morgan, in which he told her, "We feel the
work undertaken for the School of Nations had been one of the
most significant . . . for Principia . . . This work . . . inspires the
outlook and very definitely widens the mental horizons of all our
group." When learning from Hazle that she would be unable to
attend the June Trustee meetings since she was still away with
her mother, he responded, "your vigorous enthusiasm" and "alert
outlook" will be missed.[461]

Following the Trustee meetings held in June, Hazle received
a report from Arthur Morey, who told her that the meetings had
been "remarkable" and that they had all felt the presence of divine
guidance regarding the decisions they had to make. He informed
her that $60,000 had come in during the meeting and they had
also received $50,000 from an anonymous donor who had never
even seen the College campus. He added that they had two new
members, Archibald Carey of Detroit and Hugh Prather of Dallas.[462]

Although she was still traveling in late June, Hazle donated
$2,500 to the School of Nations Building Fund through her
secretary. Andrews mistakenly added the donation to the School of
Nations Maintenance Fund. When Hazle returned to Bloomington
in November, she discovered the mistake, but by then the money
had been spent. Realizing that Andrews had made an honest

mistake, Hazle replaced $1,300 of the funds herself and arranged to receive $1,200 from the Emergency Scholarship Fund.[463]

Now that she was home, Hazle resumed her commitment to her trustee work and endeavored to catch up on the School of Nations activities. She still entertained the hope that the School of Nations building would be under construction in the near future, but being a member of the Board of Trustees had broadened her understanding of what the College's immediate needs were. The move to Elsah was only the beginning of the development of the College. The future held for Hazle and Principia many unforeseen challenges, demands, and opportunities for growth.

Hazle and her mother, Lillian Brewer Buck.

Hazle and Davis Ewing.

Photograph used by permission of Lucinda Buck Ewing.

Hazle sitting with the family dog on the steps of her cabin at Thunder Mountain Ranch in Crivitz, Wisconsin.

**Portrait of Hazle
by Alfred Partridge Klotz, 1936.**

The front entrance of Hazle's home, Sunset Hill.

The back entrance and yard of Hazle's home, Sunset Hill.

**Ewing Park I in Bloomington, Illinois
near Hazle's home, Sunset Hill.**

Photograph by Karen Griep Heilbrun.

**June 12, 1950, commencement at
Principia College.**

From left to right: Dorinda Morgan (Mrs. William E. Morgan, Jr.);
Toni Morgan (Mrs. Frederic E. Morgan; Beulah May Booth
(Mrs. W. Stuart Booth) of Denver, Colorado, the commencement
speaker; Helen Streight Hamlin (Mrs. G. Eldredge Hamlin);
Hazle Buck Ewing, Trustee; Eula Gertsch (Mrs. Alfred Gertsch).

June 10, 1952, commencement at Principia College.

From left to right: Hugh Prather, Trustee;
William E. Morgan, Vice President and Headmaster of Upper School;
Hazle Buck Ewing, Trustee; Frederic E. Morgan,
President of The Principia; Archibald Carey, speaker
(also a Trustee, Christian Science teacher and lecturer).

Frederic Morgan escorting Hazle to the auditorium
to attend the 1956 commencement.

**At the 1956 commencement, Hazle received an
honorary Doctor of Laws degree from The Principia.**

Hazle speaking at the dedication
of the School of Nations building, April 19, 1959.

An early School of Nations pamphlet.

The School of Nations building in 1960.

The Holt Gallery in the School of Nations.

The completed Japanese Room in the
School of Nations building at Principia College.

THE PHILANTHROPIST

CHAPTER 19

MATTERS OF THE HEART

*I*n February 1936, Hazle accepted the invitation of George T. Nickerson, a representative of the Cranbrook School, to serve on the Parents' Committee. Nearly a year had passed since Nelson transferred to Cranbrook from Principia, and it was obvious to Hazle the change had been good for him. Appreciating the help Nelson had received from his experiences at Cranbrook, Hazle invited a representative of the school to share information about Cranbrook with other Bloomington parents. She listened carefully to what was said during the presentation and retained copies of their printed materials. She shared the ideas and information presented at the meeting with Morgan, believing that he would find some of it useful in promoting Principia.[464]

As a member of Principia's Board of Trustees and a parent of former students, Hazle always looked for ways to help promote the school. Both Nelson and Ralph had benefited from the education they had received there. It was at Principia that Nelson had been introduced to metal work, which he wanted to pursue as a career. And, Ralph had received a good foundation on which he continued to build at Rollins College and in his work. Now 29 years old, Ralph had been employed by the Stix, Baer, and Fuller Company, a department store in St. Louis, for nearly three years. On March 24, 1936, he wrote to Hazle that there had been some trouble at work. He had gone over his manager's head and talked with Leo Fuller, one of the store owners, about a troubling situation. He told his mother, "Regardless of the reaction, I think my talk did

187

some good." He confided that, as the result of his talk with Fuller, he would be managing the Mail Order, Telephone Order, and the Public and Personal Service Departments after Easter, and he would receive a slight increase in pay as well as the opportunity for future advancement.[465]

Not only had Ralph made an advance in his career at the department store, but he had also met a bright young woman named Kate Lee Culbertson from Russell, Kansas, who worked in the Training Department and enjoyed playing cards as much as he did. Shortly before Thanksgiving that year, Ralph took Kate Lee to Bloomington so that Hazle could meet her. On the day of their arrival, they had fried chicken for dinner, a favorite of Kate Lee's. The chicken was delicious and she wanted desperately to have a second piece, but when the platter was passed around no one else took any. She did not want to appear too forward or greedy to Ralph's mother and Julia, so she did not take a second serving. Later, when Ralph told his mother that Kate Lee had been afraid to take another piece of chicken and had left the table hungry, Hazle assured her that she should eat as much as she wanted. This was a great relief to Kate Lee, who fully enjoyed the well-prepared meals at Sunset Hill during the rest of their stay.[466]

Hazle expected that Ralph and Kate Lee would go horseback riding since Ralph always took advantage of the opportunity to go riding when he came home for a visit. But, he seemed uncertain about going for a ride because Kate Lee had never been on a horse. Hazle urged him to take her, and Kate Lee expressed a desire to try it, so Ralph gave in. After returning to St. Louis, he wrote to his mother that he had been surprised and delighted to learn that "Kate Lee got a real thrill out of her short horseback ride & would really like to take it up."[467]

It pleased Hazle to know that Ralph and Kate Lee had enjoyed their stay at Sunset Hill, and she looked forward to seeing them both again at her mother's for Christmas. Ralph had written to

Grandmother Buck to let her know that he would definitely be coming to Chicago for Christmas and that Kate Lee would probably come with him. Christmas was always a time when the family made a special effort to be together to share the joys of the season. This year was no exception.

When Ralph and Kate Lee arrived at his grandmother's house on Christmas Day, it was filled with members of the Buck family and tantalizing aromas wafting from the kitchen. When the table had been set, the guests seated themselves and feasted on sumptuous and tempting dishes of food. When the clanking of spoons and forks died down, and everyone seemed to be contentedly full, Ralph stood up. He cleared his throat and announced to the Buck family that he and Kate Lee were engaged to be married—but "[a] definite date has not been set for the wedding yet." Cheers and warm congratulations followed.[468]

Kate Lee and Ralph were married on February 20, 1937, at 4:30 p.m., with Dr. Harold Martin, pastor of Second Presbyterian church, officiating in the presence of their families and friends at Sunset Hill. Helen Davis, Kate Lee's sister, came from Detroit, Michigan, to be her matron of honor. Nelson traveled from Pasadena, California, where he was studying to become a silversmith, to be his brother's best man. The wedding took place in the living room, where a warm fire crackled in the fireplace as the happy couple said their vows. Pedestals wreathed in Oregon huckleberry and crowned with Picardy gladiolus and calla lilies gleamed in the flickering fire light. The bride wore a tailored suit of two-tone thistle with navy blue accessories and carried a purse of orchids. The whole house seemed to be blooming with spring flowers.[469]

Holding a colonial bouquet and wearing a reseda green satin dress and coat of henna and gold, Hazle looked on with pride and gratitude as the man, who had grown from the ten-year old boy she and Davis had taken into their home now stood beaming beside his bride. All the troubles and challenges of his childhood had been overcome, and

Ralph had grown up into a fine man and a responsible citizen.

Some months after Ralph and Kate Lee's wedding, Hazle had an opportunity to help another young man. On September 8, 1937, after the conclusion of a trustee meeting at Principia, she suddenly felt impelled to tell Morgan of a need she had, but he was unavailable and she had to leave to catch a train. She hastily wrote a note informing him that she was seeking a driver, "who would be willing to fit in where needed," and left it with his secretary.[470] Later that day, Morgan was given the note. He immediately wired her, recommending a graduate of Principia, the 24-year-old Paul Hargraves.[471]

When Hazle received the telegram, she wired Morgan: "Delighted to try Hargraves."[472] She sent another telegram the next day, telling Morgan that she would be at the Thunder Mountain Ranch in Crivitz, Wisconsin, until the end of the month. She thought it would be a good place for her and Paul to get acquainted. She had been without a driver for a month—"for the first time in years"—and was looking forward to having one again. She believed that Morgan had introduced her to Paul on some prior occasion, for his name seemed familiar.[473]

On Monday, September 13, the young man departed from Alaska to meet Hazle at the Ewing family ranch in Wisconsin, expecting to arrive there on Wednesday. In the meantime, Morgan wrote a confidential letter to Hazle, giving her "some further word in regard to Paul." The letter explained that Paul's father had been an excellent student who had graduated from the Massachusetts Institute of Technology and seemed to have a bright future. He moved to northwestern Canada where he began his career as a mining engineer, married a Canadian woman having a fine moral character, and started a family. However, he fell victim to alcoholism and seemed unable to support his wife and children. When Paul became old enough, he helped his mother care for his younger brother and two younger sisters.[474]

Paul had received a four-year scholarship and arrived at Principia to attend his first year of high school with only one suit, which had been his father's. Morgan had come to know Paul quite well, since his wife, Madeline, had taken a liking to him and he had lived with them during his two years at Principia's Junior College. After completing college, Paul went to work in St. Louis. His mother and the other children came to live with him so that the younger children could attend school at Principia. They lived economically, almost "hand to mouth." But, during the winter, Paul's father's situation became acute, and his mother believed it necessary for all of them to return home. Feeling a sense of responsibility for his family, Paul went with them to Canada, where he could earn a higher wage than he could in St. Louis.[475]

The trip to Canada was grueling. Because of a severe snow storm, they could not fly home, but instead bought an old farm wagon and tied it behind their truck. They plowed their way through the snow, often staying in trappers' cabins at night in order to reach their home in northwestern Canada. His father's situation was so severe that Paul took on the responsibility of supporting the family and became the main wage-earner for four years.[476]

Morgan confided to Hazle: "I think Paul has never known a time when abject poverty, or a condition closely bordering that, did not face them." Recently, because one of his sisters married, the other sister and brother found jobs, and his mother had gotten a job as a cook at a mining camp, Paul felt free to strike out on his own. Through some of the young men he had kept in contact with from school, he found a job drilling oil in Alaska, but the company he worked for had shut down. When he contacted Morgan, he seemed to be "pretty much in a panic in his own quiet way," because of his financial situation and not having a car to enable him to find other work. Morgan told Hazle that her telegram had been "a god-send."[477] Hazle believed that God had brought them together and that this situation would be of mutual benefit.

Morgan assured Hazle that, "The boy is very loveable, gentle, absolutely honest, and fearless, at least in the usual sense of the term. He is loyal to the core." But Morgan confessed that Paul seemed to be introspective and suffered from periods of depression, which he attributed to Paul's difficult childhood and his working alone in the Alaskan oil fields. He expressed confidence in Hazle's ability to help Paul, saying, "In the happy, wonderfully loving environment which you create in your home, he will learn to break through the seeming problems facing him." He encouraged her to "have some good, quiet talks with" Paul, because he believed that she had an uncommon understanding of boys and young men.[478]

Morgan knew that if he could count on anyone to give Paul a chance for a better life, it was Hazle. How long Paul remained in her employ and what career he later pursued is unknown. It is certain, however, that Hazle's success in helping Ralph and Nelson enabled her to aid Paul in his time of need and that he received some benefit from being in her home and working for her.

CHAPTER 20

VARIED INTERESTS

*I*n December 1937, well aware of Principia's need to complete the new dormitory buildings, Hazle encouraged her mother, Lillian Buck, to make a contribution. Lillian responded by donating the entire amount of money needed for one of the buildings. Immediately after Mrs. Buck's generous contribution was announced, Mrs. Rackham provided the funds for the construction of one of the other dormitories. Morgan recognized the part Hazle had played in securing the needed funds and told her, "Your wise and demonstrated interpretation of Principia's work and its needs has resulted not only in the gift of the Lillian Brewer Buck House, but also has been instrumental in bringing in this second gift of Rackham Court." He added, "May I say most earnestly that we are deeply conscious of the extent to which your own generous, loving thought of Principia has been instrumental in lifting the work of this institution at many points."[479]

In addition to her interest in the construction of the dormitories, Hazle had some other projects in mind. She wanted to create foot paths and horse trails that would enable and encourage students to discover nature on their own. Having ridden horseback and hiked on such trails herself, Hazle felt certain that students would benefit from these activities. She recalled that when Morgan had first told her of the purchase of the property in Elsah, he indicated that they intended to invite her to plan bridle trails for the new College. She wrote him a letter reminding him of the invitation and returned two trustee expense checks, requesting that the money be used to establish a Foot and Bridle Paths Fund. She hoped that they could begin work on the paths in the spring and have them ready for use by the coming fall.

The idea of having bridle trails cleared on the College campus naturally led Hazle to entertain the possibility of having a stable on campus where students could board their own horses and where additional horses could be kept for others who wanted to ride. When Ralph was attending Principia, he had often told her how much he wished he had a horse to ride, and, through her contact with current students, she discovered that some of them had the same desire.

A disturbing experience she had when renting a horse from the stables at Pere Marquette, a few miles from Elsah, also contributed to her interest in having a riding stable at Principia. She had been given a fine-gaited mare, but the horse did not behave as she had expected. When she returned to the stable and the saddle was removed, she discovered why. The horse had "a bad open sore just where [her] weight pressed upon it!!" She believed that if horses were being stabled at the College, they would receive more thoughtful care.[480]

Morgan responded to Hazle's letter regarding the planning of the foot and bridle paths, suggesting that she come down in March. The grounds crew had already done the preliminary work of opening up a large riding area and clearing the unused old wagon road from Elsah.[481] It was not until June 1938, right after the commencement, however that Hazle and her friend, Julia, marked out two bridle trails and provided William Morgan, Jr., Frederic's brother, a detailed description of where they ran. Hazle also suggested that a third trail start at the Science building and stop at the river end of the Elsah village. She thought that all three trails "would make excellent and varied ways of getting back and forth to the village and could connect up with a number of circular routes on the campus."[482]

Hazle had gleaned much information about blazing horse trails from her visits to National Parks around the country and talking with forest rangers, and she had used what she learned to clear the trails on the family ranch in Wisconsin. She shared her knowledge and experience with William, encouraging him to use horses to help blaze the trails, for, "In a majority of our National Parks, the rangers have found that horse travel is a great help, not only in grading and firming the trails, but also, where there is sufficient use, in actually keeping the dust down." She believed this would save groundskeepers at the College from extensive maintenance of the trails the next season, for "all they [would have] to do for many miles of trail through comparatively level country, [is] to trim bushes, and . . . tree branches to give sufficient head room." William expressed his appreciation for the information she shared and assured her that the grounds crew would begin clearing the trails right away.[483]

In late June, Hazle received a letter from Frederic Morgan telling her that Mr. Bradley, who ran the horse stable at Pere Marquette, had paid him an unexpected visit. Morgan wrote that Bradley referred to a conversation he said he had with Mrs. Ewing about four or five students who wanted to keep horses on the campus. Also, Bradley indicated that Hazle had suggested he should check into operating a stable at the College, and that she thought the barn at Eliestoun could be refurbished. Apparently acting on Hazle's suggestion, Bradley offered to provide five horses—if he could be assured of boarding five more for $20 a month. Morgan, believing that Hazle had talked with Bradley about a stable at Principia, told her that he did not believe Eliestoun to be the right place to board horses, but that they could be stabled at the Lane farm located on the road leading from Elsah to Highway 109. He added that he did not object to students having horses available to ride, but he was curious to know the names of the students who wanted to board their horses on campus.[484]

Bradley's visit with Frederic surprised Hazle as much as it had him. She admitted that she and Dorothy Knight had gone on a ride with Bradley once, but it was he who thought it would be a good idea to fix up the barn at Eliestoun to board horses for students. She did not know the names of the students Bradley referred to, though she wished she did. In her contact with students, "any number [had] been enthusiastic about having horses and trails on campus." She suggested that an outline of the proposal be printed in the Principia Progress to see if there was any interest in it. If others were interested in the idea, she would be willing to make a small donation to establish a fund for the stable.[485]

Learning of the possibility of Principia having a stable, Hazle's son, Nelson, wrote to Morgan requesting an interview for the position of manager or riding instructor. But Morgan discouraged Nelson from pursuing the idea, and he wrote to Hazle of the inquiry, explaining that he felt that Bradley, because of his maturity and willingness to live meagerly, would be a better choice for the job. He believed that Nelson's talents could be better used in other endeavors, but he was, "delighted to know that Nelson's thoughts turn toward Principia."[486]

That summer, snakes overran the woods around the College making it dangerous to blaze the bridle trails, and the project had to be postponed until late October when the snakes would become dormant. While waiting for the work to resume on the trails, Hazle discovered some books about national park architecture, which she ordered for William Morgan from the Department of Interior. She thought he might find some useful ideas for constructing the bridle trails.[487]

Not only did Hazle have a deep interest in horseback riding, she also enjoyed taking motor trips and had become a member of the Motor Club based in Chicago. Inspired by her travels around the state of Illinois, she wrote an article that summer titled, "Scenic, Historic Illinois Calls," which appeared in the October 1938 edition of *Motor News*, the Chicago Motor Club's newspaper. She believed that the automobile and improved roads had opened up opportunities for Illinois residents to enjoy the natural wonders of their own state. Encouraging readers to do some sightseeing, she said, "Smooth ribbons of concrete and black-top, alluring side-roads of well-kept gravel now invite us to explore safely almost any nook or corner of our amazingly varied and richly scenic Illinois." She praised the White Pine Forest State Park, a few miles west of Oregon, Illinois, where "So tall are the magnificent trunks [of the native white pine] that reach up through the hardwoods to find the sunlight, that we have to tip our heads far back on our shoulders to follow the length of them." The park also offered hiking trails and places for those who wish to "stay on as shadows" lengthen and "coolness" entices. For "the enthusiastic botanist," of whom she was one, she suggested investigating Starved Rock or Giant City where lovely ferns grew that could be found nowhere else in the area. She also recommended Pere Marquette Park, for hikers seeking a more rugged terrain, and where a lodge would soon be built. "History lovers will revel in Lincoln country, and in Fort de Chartres and Kaskaskia, and all the lore that clings to them," she noted. Inviting readers to discover "charming" vacation spots in their own state, she concluded, "Scenic and historic Illinois beckons!"[488]

That fall there had been some interest shown in boarding horses at the College, but in late December 1938, Morgan wrote to Hazle, "my efforts to secure a stable of riding horses" have not worked out. He thanked her for her interest in the project and told her that he would talk to Bradley again in the spring and let her know the outcome. Although the prospect of having a horse stable at the College seemed stalled, Hazle remained hopeful that Morgan would meet with success in the spring.[489]

When the spring of 1939 arrived, Morgan was unable to come to an agreement with Bradley regarding the horse stable, and Hazle had become involved with another project. She frequently corresponded with William Morgan about the plans that he and Butler Sturtevant, Principia's landscaper, had been working on to make the Ewing Woods sanctuary ready for the College community to use and enjoy. In one of his letters, William enclosed a drawing of two octagonal pillars, on which would be attached the words "Ewing Woods," made of heavy iron letters, to mark the entrance of the sanctuary. He also described two bulletin boards that would be near the entrance: a glass-covered one to display pictures and descriptions of the types of wildlife living in the woods; and the other one, an engraved wood plank, stating the purpose of the area as a bird and animal sanctuary, and a preserve for native plant life.[490]

At the end of May, Hazle arrived at Principia to attend the Trustee meetings and took the opportunity to go with William to Ewing Woods. The lush green foliage growing on both sides of the road inspired Hazle to suggest to William the possibility of clearing hiking and riding paths that would be accessible from the road. She also thought it would be helpful if the paths had markers indicating the distance and length of time needed to hike them. William showed her where the bulletin boards were to be placed, and he explained how the glass-covered one would "help students to identify" the animals, birds, and plants, and "add to their interest in and understanding of nature." Wanting to maintain Ewing Woods in as natural a state as possible, Hazle left instructions with William that only native plants were to be allowed to grow there. In addition, the dead and dying trees, which provided homes for a variety of animals and birds, were not to be cut down or removed.[491]

Before leaving for home following the Trustee meetings, she induced her nephew Don Laughlin, who worked as the comptroller for the College, to accompany her on a walk around the campus. It surprised and delighted her to discover "the beauty of the ravine leading from the back of the fire house to the Field House and tennis courts." She told Don that she wanted to "provide the money for an inexpensive path along this ravine, with the hope that it would encourage students to enjoy the quietude of these out-of-the-way places." But later, she withdrew her suggestion, realizing that it would make more work for the grounds crew, who were already involved in several other projects.

Going over her finances in June, Hazle realized that she had acquired more than the $150,000 needed to begin the construction on the School of Nations building. Although she knew that Maybeck's health would not allow him to come to Elsah, she wrote to Frederic of her desire to have Maybeck design the building. He contacted Maybeck regarding the project, but, after some consideration, Maybeck declined the offer and recommended another architect, Henry S. Gutterson. A disappointed Hazle waited to hear if Gutterson accepted the offer.[492]

In the meantime, the shocking news that Adolph Hitler and the German Nazis had invaded and conquered Poland on September 1, 1939, overshadowed Hazle's thoughts about the School of Nations building. Her attention continued to be absorbed by matters abroad when, two days later, Britain, France, Australia, and New Zealand declared war on Germany. She recognized the seriousness of the situation and how vulnerable the European cities were when she learned that the British had evacuated their children to the country side, even before the mobilization of their troops began. Within a week, the newspapers disclosed that five more countries had declared war on Germany, including Canada and South Africa. It seemed that much of the world had quickly become engulfed in the war. Hazle's hope for world peace seemed far from actuality, and she could not help but wonder how long it would be before the United States would be drawn into the conflict.

Despite her concerns about the war, daily life demanded her attention, and Hazle began making travel plans for the October Board of Trustees' meetings. When notifying Frederic of the date and time of her arrival, she suddenly realized that the past summer had marked his twentieth year as president of the College. Acknowledging this milestone, she wrote, "Your foresight, resource, and tireless energy have been sources of inspiration to everyone connected with the work."[493]

The last month of 1939 was bitter-sweet for Hazle. The war in Europe raged on. When and if the United States would be drawn into the war seemed to be an ever-present concern. Her hope to have the plans for the School of Nations building completed had not been realized. She did receive an invitation to the Inter-American Relations in the Field of Education Conferences, however, which had been secured for her by James Penfield, as a token of his appreciation for the benefits he had gained from the School of Nations program. She also received recognition from Frederic of the many ways in which she had contributed to Principia. He wrote to her on December 21, 1939, "No friend of Principia has been more self-effacing or more positively helpful in this work than yourself."[494]

A WORLD AT WAR

CHAPTER 21

A SPIRIT OF HELPFULNESS

*H*azle's helpfulness in the work at Principia had a positive influence not only on members of her family, but also on their friends. In January 1940, Josephine Forsyth Myers of Cleveland, Ohio, established a trust fund for Principia students in the names of and in gratitude for Orlando J. and Lillian Brewer Buck. Myers specified that the trust fund of $10,000 be used to help worthy students in need of financial assistance, especially those interested in music. Myers appointed Hazle to be responsible for the distribution of the funds—a task she initially accepted. But, later in the year, Hazle turned over that responsibility to the administrators of Principia, believing they knew more about which students deserved and needed financial support than she did.[495]

Throughout that winter and spring, Hazle's thoughts turned often to war-ravaged Europe, and she felt an ever-greater need for the School of Nations program and its mission to help establish harmonious international relations and world peace. The annual check she sent in June for the maintenance of the program brought an especially meaningful response from Sam Baker, the chairman of the School of Nations committee. He wrote of his gratitude for: "the opportunity afforded both the faculty and students here for broader visions and closer bonds of international understanding made possible by the School of Nations Fund."[496] The world's need of the School of Nations program became even more apparent later that summer, when Hitler overwhelmed Norway, Belgium, Holland, and France.

He had not yet reached the United Kingdom, but the war intensified daily, and attaining world peace seemed like a distant possibility.

While staying at the ranch in September 1940, Hazle heard that the British had begun evacuating their children to other countries, including the United States. The battle at Dunkirk had influenced the decision of the British to take this drastic measure to safeguard their children, the future of their country. Britain and France had deployed troops to Dunkirk in an effort to aid the Belgians in fighting off the Germans. The Germans overwhelmed the British and French troops, however, and pushed them back to the sea, leaving them no way of escape by land. When the Germans discontinued their attack, the British saw that their only recourse was to form a fleet of ships to evacuate the troops. This bold move required vessels commandeered from commercial enterprises and individuals, in addition to all of the ships that belonged to the British navy. The evacuation took nine days, beginning on May 26.[497]

Hazle learned from Frederic Morgan that some British children, who were from Christian Science families, had been given refuge at Principia. She felt impelled to send $500 on September 3 to assist in paying for the children's care at the school. She told Frederic how grateful she was "that [the proposed] military training for Principia [students] has been postponed for the moment at least," and she added, "I hope with all my heart that the need will have disappeared before it can be established."[498] The arrival of the English children increased the ever-present concern that the United States could become drawn into the war.

In early October, Hazle received some good news from her son, Ralph, and his wife, Kate Lee, who had made their home in Russell, Kansas, where Kate Lee had lived as a girl. The couple had decided to try to adopt a child since they seemed unable to have one of their own. They had already filed the necessary paperwork, and it looked like they would be approved to adopt a child in the near future. Ralph and Kate Lee also shared with Hazle some of their activities. Kate Lee had been serving on the election board during voter registration and heading the tuberculosis drive. She had also been invited to give a talk at the district tuberculosis meeting in Salinas, Kansas, because of the excellent job she had done at the meeting the year before. Ralph had been enjoying his first year as a member of the Masons and had recently joined the Rotarians. In addition, Kate Lee and Ralph had both been asked to teach sales-marketing classes again, but had turned down the offers since they were already involved in so many other activities.[499] Hazle looked forward to hearing more about the adoption and their other endeavors when they came to Bloomington for Thanksgiving.

Hazle was also pleased to receive a letter from Frederic Morgan expressing his appreciation for their former School of Nations students. He felt especially grateful for Mallory Browne, who, at that time, held the position of European Editorial Manager for *The Christian Science Monitor* in the London office; James Penfield, who worked for the State Department in Greenland; and Bill Moreland, who was also employed by the State Department. He added, "Surely the work you initiated has an important bearing upon the service which Principia is destined to render."[500]

At Christmas time, Hazle sent a note to Davis Ewing's cousin, Adlai Stevenson II, a successful lawyer in Chicago, whom she greatly admired. She was well acquainted with his interest in establishing world peace and had often shared with him the work being done through the School of Nations program. She asked him if she had ever shown him any School of Nations folders. He responded in early January 1941: "Dear Cousin Hazle . . . I have not seen the folders for your School of Nations at Principia, though of course I have heard much about the work that is being done there. Sometime I wish you would let me see them." Learning of Adlai's desire to see a School of Nations folder, Hazle provided him with a copy of the most recent edition.[501]

Hazle attended the June 1941 commencement at Principia

College with her sister-in-law, Mrs. Rena H. Buck, the wife of her brother, Nelson. Like Hazle, Rena had graduated from the University of Chicago and had a sincere interest in the education of young people. She had already given some generous scholarships to college students in the Chicago area. Frederic Morgan, accompanied by Hazle, took Rena on a personal tour of The Principia. After their visit to the College, Hazle wrote to Frederic that she and her sister-in-law had immensely enjoyed their time at Principia. She thanked him for his hospitality and invited him and his wife, Madeline, to stop by for a visit at her home on their way to New England for the summer.[502]

Hazle especially wanted the Morgans to see the bronze statue, *Her Son* that she had purchased. Frederic knew of the statue, for she had suggested that he buy it for the College, but at the time, there were so many pressing demands on school's finances he could not buy it. Hazle had been deeply touched by the statue of the mother and son and found she could not stop thinking about it. She also desired to help the struggling young artist, Nellie V. Walker, who had created it. She finally decided to purchase it for herself. But, when she went to the gallery where she had so often admired the statue, it was no longer there. She learned that the artist had taken it. When she located the artist, she was delighted to find that it had not yet been sold. Hazle immediately purchased it and had it placed in her garden, where she often went to read and pray. She also took great pleasure in sharing the statue with her visitors.[503]

In August 1941, Hazle's mother, Lillian Brewer Buck, fell ill and passed away. Mako Matsukata, a student from Japan and a member of one of the first Japanese families to become Christian Scientists, was working at Principia and staying in Buck House that summer when he heard about Mrs. Buck's passing. He suggested to a fellow student, George Obern, that they send flowers to Mrs. Buck's Evanston, Illinois, home, as representatives of the student body.[504] They chose words of a poem written by Mary Baker Eddy, which has been set to music as hymn 30 in the *Christian Science Hymnal*, to inscribe on the card that accompanied the flowers, "And life most sweet, as heart to heart speaks kindly when we meet and part."[505] It seemed fitting that an international student would initiate the expression of compassion sent to Hazle and her family.

Confined to bed at the time of Mrs. Buck's passing, Kate Lee wrote to Hazle on August 30, "First of all I want you to know how sorry I am that we could not be with you in Wisconsin two weeks ago." She continued, "I felt you hadn't sent any . . . word because you would feel that Ralph shouldn't leave home." When Grandmother Buck's illness had become more serious, Hazle chose not to tell Ralph immediately, believing he would feel obligated to leave the pregnant Kate Lee, whose due date was near. When the couple had not heard anything from Hazle for several days, they felt certain she was caring for Grandmother Buck. Kate Lee had urged Ralph to go to the ranch to be with his mother and grandmother, but Hazle had convinced him that he should stay home with his wife. Kate Lee and Ralph derived comfort from knowing that "everyone else was available"—Ellsworth, Nelson, and their families. Desiring to provide some comfort to Hazle, Kate Lee added, "Aren't you glad that you had prevailed on her to be with you—you can feel that you did everything possible for her. She had lived a full rich life and deserved a quiet passing."[506]

Hazle felt sorrow for the loss of her mother, who had been one of the strongest supporters of Hazle's work for Principia as well as her other endeavors. But, Hazle also had the joy of being blessed by the arrival of her first granddaughter, Lucinda (Cindy) Buck Ewing. The couple had discovered that Kate Lee was pregnant shortly after they had received approval to adopt a child. Learning that they were going to have their own child, they decided not to adopt one.[507]

In retrospect, Kate Lee had been glad that Ralph had been home to support her through the difficult childbirth, and she assured Hazle that little Cindy was "worth it all." She described

Cindy to her mother-in-law as having "a beautifully round head nicely covered with brown hair, the daintiest hands—long, slender fingers." She thought that Cindy's mouth was like Ralph's—"not too small and nice full lips." She predicted that Cindy would grow up to "look a great deal like Ralph." They had named her Lucinda after Kate Lee's Grandmother Culbertson. They had used the Buck name because they thought "Lucinda Buck Ewing was most euphonious" and they would be "perpetuating two of the baby's great grandmother's names."[508]

After the events of the summer, Hazle had much to do. She helped her brothers with the distribution of their mother's belongings and went shopping for items to send to her new grandchild and her daughter-in-law. The demands of her active life gave her but few moments to dwell on the passing of her mother. On October 9, 1941, the School of Nations committee surprised her with a dinner held in her honor in St. Louis. In late November, Morgan requested her approval to send out Christmas cards to those in other countries who had contributed flags to the School of Nations, and her permission to use her name on the cards as the representative of the School of Nations and Principia.[509]

In early December, Frederic invited her to come stay at Principia in Cox Cottage for a few days so that she might get a "clearer picture of the inside work carried on . . . day to day," which would "broaden and help our work here." But Hazle declined. On December 7, 1941, five days after Morgan's invitation, the Japanese military, who had become an ally of Germany, attacked Pearl Harbor. President Franklin Roosevelt declared war on Germany and Japan on January 1, 1942, and joined forces with England and their allies, becoming one of 26 nations in the united effort to stop Hitler and his ally. Hazle hoped this would result in a quick end to the war and that the establishment of world peace would soon follow.[510]

After the attack on Pearl Harbor, Hazle sent a donation for the care of the English children on January 27 and told Frederic, "Some day, I hope that I will be sufficiently caught up so that I shall feel I can come and 'stay a week,' as you suggest." Frederic responded on February 3, thanking her for her donation and telling her of a Bloomington high school student who desired to attend Principia, "one which should receive our earnest consideration and substantial amount of assistance."[511]

The Bloomington student who desired to attend Principia was Eloise Taylor, but her widowed mother could ill-afford to send her. One of Eloise's teachers at Bloomington High School, Miss Means, had written to Frederic about her. Hazle knew Eloise and her family, and had been contacted by another teacher at Bloomington High, Miss Inman. Hazle assured Frederic that everyone she had talked to regarding Eloise had expressed "admiration and enthusiasm about her." She had read articles written by Eloise, a talented writer and the editor-in-chief of the school newspaper, *The Bloomington High School Argus*. Hazle felt that Eloise certainly deserved financial assistance to attend Principia.[512]

In early May 1942, Hazle attended the Public Affairs Conference, an event sponsored by Principia College each spring to address specific world concerns. The theme of the Conference was "All Out War for All Out Peace" and drew students from other colleges around the area, as well as those attending Principia. Hazle had been impressed by the students attending the Conference and confided to Morgan, "It was greatly encouraging to find boys and girls of college age not only able, but actually doing, much clear and constructive thinking, as was evidenced at both the round tables and during the plenary sessions on Saturday."[513]

Hazle learned from Frederic in June that Eloise had raised $950, but she still needed $325 to pay her college tuition for the first year. In addition, Eloise desired to find a job on campus that would enable her to earn at least $150 a year. Frederic suspected that Hazle had supplied at least part of the $950, but he did not say so openly. Instead, he wrote, "It was our understanding that I would let you know how the case progresses." In response, Hazle admitted to Frederic that she had done as much for Eloise as she thought she should. However, she believed that Eloise should receive additional support and suggested that the needed money could come from the scholarship fund. She assured Morgan, "When you have a chance to meet Mrs. Taylor, you will understand why I feel that both she and Eloise should be given every possible help."[514]

By August, the news that Eloise would be attending Principia that fall had spread. Mrs. Violet W. Brindley, an Editor of Bloomington's *Daily Pantagraph*, wrote to Hazle saying, "Eloise, one of the finest girls I have ever known, is going to Principia College. I think you must know it, or someone else helped her, to make this possible." She continued, "If you have, I just want to add my congratulations, because no one would be more deserving of anything done for her." Brindley explained that she had known Eloise since she was a small girl. She told Hazle that Mrs. Taylor "had been such an exceptional mother and has met many problems so cheerfully and successfully." She added that Eloise "has always wanted to go to Principia. I know something has happened to make it possible for her, and no doubt you have been of help. She is one of the best investments I could ever imagine."[515]

In addition to giving generous monetary assistance to individual students, such as Eloise Taylor, Hazle financially maintained the School of Nations program, which had benefited a number of students over the years. Acknowledging her constant support of the program, Morgan told her that she was "the one whose wisdom and generosity had made this work possible." He continued, "You have rendered a very vital contribution to Principia's progress." He commended her for doing much more than initiating the School of Nations, saying that she had always been "alert and generously ready to support any important part of Principia's program."[516]

As the war in Europe continued, Principia sponsored talks to inform the community of the war activities, which Hazle endeavored to attend when possible. One such talk was to be given by Andre Morize, on November 30, titled "The Resistance of the French People to Nazi Domination since the Fall of France." The subject of the talk alone interested her, but Morgan also offered the enticement of gathering a group to hike the trails and have an "open air picnic on the picnic grounds."[517] She responded that she would enjoy "the fragrant spiciness of the fallen leaves this season as much as the invigorating promise of new buds in the early spring." The war, however, made it difficult to secure train tickets. When she tried to make a train reservation to attend the talk, she was told that she could not be assured of getting a seat. Disappointed, she sat down and wrote a letter to Frederic, telling him that she would be unable to come.

As she was finishing the letter, she received a phone call from the agent at the Alton train station, who told her that her reservations had been confirmed. She amended her letter to Frederic, telling him, "I am delighted that this has worked out as it has. I shall hope to be able to pass on enough of what Mr. Morize tells us to make me feel that the trip was justified."[518] When she attended the talk, she did find much good information in it that she could pass on, and she enjoyed the hiking and the picnic.

While hiking on the trails, however, Hazle discovered that they had become overgrown. She knew that many young men had joined the military and were fighting the war in Europe, and Principia had barely enough workers to keep their schools running that winter.[519] She wrote to William Morgan that "both cleaning and extension of the trails is impractical for the time being," but she thought the current paths and trails should be maintained. She believed it would benefit the workers to be "able to dip into a lovely bit of woods now and then—rather than walk back and forth over the same paved roads many times a week." She added, "No matter how much lovely country we have, it does not do us much good, or give us the joy it should, unless we can get into it by comfortable, made trails." Later,

feeling guilty about her suggestion, she wrote to Frederic that she
thought she had "been too insistent about trail-maintaining at the
present time." Hearing about what she had written to Frederic,
William replied to Hazle, assuring her that he agreed that some of
the trails should be kept useable.[520]

In December 1942, Hazle had the unique opportunity to serve
as an advisor to the Public Relations Committee of the Illinois
State Normal University, by invitation of President Fairchild. Later
that month, she shared with Frederic some useful ideas for Principia
that she had gained from attending the meeting and the dinner that
followed. In a spirit of helpfulness, Hazle diligently endeavored to
find ways of supporting and improving Principia and took advantage
of the opportunities she had to be of assistance to other institutions
as well as to individuals.[521]

CHAPTER 22

SUPPORT FOR OUR TROOPS

*I*n January 1943, Hazle learned that new regulations for college students were expected to be forthcoming from the Army and Navy any day. She wondered what that would mean for Principia and other colleges. She urged Morgan to let her know about the new regulations as soon as he had any news. In the meantime, she planned to attend an upcoming talk to be given by Dr. Krishnala Shridharani entitled *Storm Over India*, which the School of Nations was sponsoring. She learned that the students had been studying the situation in India so they would be prepared to ask intelligent questions when Dr. Shridharani visited their classrooms. She expected that this approach would bring about a lively and successful interaction between the students and their visitor.[522]

Not long after Shridharani's talk, the needs of Principia and the current challenges being faced by the school administration demanded Hazle's attention and thought. She fully supported Frederic's efforts to meet those challenges. On February 26, 1943, he gave a talk to the staff and faculty in which he compared the troubles at the College with the three-pronged attack that the "armies of Hitler" had been using. The first concern, he felt, was the loss of employees for reasons other than going into the armed services. The second concern was the demoralization of the workers that caused them to feel unappreciated and their efforts fruitless. The third concern, and most alarming, was the suggestion that the school would have to close because of low enrollment. After pinpointing these challenges, he insisted, "We <u>must</u> wake up!"[523]

Addressing the problem of the loss of employees, he told the
faculty, "The only thought that should keep us at our work here
or that should lead us to go elsewhere is the thought that is clearly
God directed." And he proposed:

> If . . . we believe that special and vitally important
> opportunities for service rest upon this institution, and
> upon it alone, and that such service concerns young
> Christian Scientists in their relation to the war effort and
> the life they must live after the war—then we . . . will rise
> in the fullness of the power of demonstrated thinking,
> and will squarely meet the challenge which either
> whispers or shouts that the College cannot continue to
> operate during the war and so cannot provide the service
> which is so greatly needed. . . . If in our own hearts we are
> confident that such service is a God given idea, and . . . feel
> certain that God has placed us at Principia . . . then we will
> permit no argument or fear of uncertainty to lead us away
> from our posts.[524]

Then, taking up the challenge of demoralization among the
employees, he endeavored to awaken the faculty members to
overcome this suggestion, saying, "Let's refuse to give any power
in our thinking to signs of misunderstanding and personal sense."
He then turned his attention to the suggestions that the school
would have to operate at a greatly diminished capacity or it would
have to close for the duration of the war. He told them, "Any such
action would reflect a sad lack of creative thinking." He described
Principia as an institution seeking what it "can do to meet present
needs." He felt that they had made progress, that there would still
be young men who would attend college the following September,
and that the enrollment of young women would increase.[525]

It seemed to him that they could provide "a vital experience"
for young men preparing to enter the military. They could make
adjustments to the classes offered, provide dormitory discipline, give
guidance counseling, implement other procedures that would be

helpful, and structure their physical education program differently. He stated bluntly that the faculty needed to be fully committed to the necessary changes. He added "we must be prepared to offer a wholly new type of training, tailored to meet a wholly new situation and attuned to individual needs beyond anything Principia has yet ever undertaken in dealing with freshmen men." He believed that their cue in handling the boys preparing for armed service would come from the Army and Navy. Whenever possible, these boys would be in classes separate from the rest of the students, and most importantly, given "practical help in learning how to meet their daily problems by turning to Christian Science." He concluded that each of the staff members must make his or her "individual decisions courageously and move forward as God directs."[526]

After reading a printed copy of the talk Frederic gave to the faculty and staff, Hazle wrote a letter of encouragement to him in March, saying, it "was a clarion call that I am sure will have many courageous replies." She confided to him, "I find myself getting very eager to get back on campus, and hope that things will open up so that I can come down before too long. With so much happening and changing daily, the air of the campus must be electric."[527]

Things did open up for Hazle to be on campus for a few days and to enjoy "a glimpse of the dogwood" in late April.[528] While on campus, she inquired about the English children and was told of their continuing needs for financial support. In May, she sent a donation of $600 to help with their care. A few weeks later, she learned from Frederic that the arrival of her donation had been timely. Shortly after it had arrived, the school found it necessary to spend $500 to provide two of the English boys nursing care for several days and nights.[529]

In the following weeks after receiving this news, Hazle found herself thinking often about Principia College and all that must be happening there as the school year came to a close. She desired to attend the commencement but felt she could not be of enough help to offset the effort needed to arrange for picking her up at the train station and preparing a room for her. But Frederic assured her that they could use her help. Feeling that she could be useful, she attended the commencement assisting in whatever way was needed. She stayed a few extra days after the ceremony so that she could drive home with her friend, Mrs. Church.[530]

Returning home, she learned from the local newspaper that Illinois State University in Normal was giving aptitude tests and "squeezing" their classes. She wrote to Frederic right away to find out how Principia was handling the situation. She also told him that she had read that 21 Principians were attending the newly established Naval Course at the University. She added that she wanted "to make things pleasant for them" before she and Julia left for the ranch in mid-July.[531]

Frederic responded that Principia had not been administering aptitude tests, but they were offering accelerated courses and summer classes. He confided to Hazle that "as necessary as this process may be under war conditions, it nevertheless has its undesirable features." He felt that the accelerated courses hampered the young men from settling into college and did not allow them time to mature.[532] Hazle fully understood his concern and knew he was doing all in his power to provide the best education Principia could under the circumstances.

The changes the war brought about at the school influenced the work of the Board of Trustees. Hazle had agreed to take on the responsibilities of secretary to the Board, and soon she received the meeting minutes from the previous October, which she would be reading at their next Board meeting. The new position also required her to help Frederic plan for the meetings and arrange for the trustees' food and lodging. In preparation for their upcoming meeting, he outlined for her some changes he planned to make, which he hoped would improve their procedures and make the trustees more comfortable. He wanted to encourage the trustees to spend their free time getting to know one another, and he hoped his loosening up of the schedule would "do away with that hurried, pressed feeling which brings a burdened sense to their deliberations." He also thought it should be arranged for the trustees to meet the faculty and staff members on both campuses. He urged her to feel free to express her thoughts regarding the proposed changes. She quickly realized that being the secretary to the Board brought a whole new dimension to her work as a trustee.[533]

In addition to fulfilling her responsibilities as secretary to the Board of Trustees, Hazle planned a dinner party for the 21 Principian Navy men currently at Illinois State University. She asked Frederic to attend the party, and he accepted her invitation. She wanted this to be a special occasion for the young men, as well as the young women who accompanied them. She made arrangements to have a dinner followed by dancing at the Bloomington Country Club. The young men were encouraged to invite girlfriends from Principia to accompany them to the dinner and dance.[534]

She learned that one of the young men was Jeff Carey, the son of her fellow trustee and good friend, Archibald Carey, Sr. Because of her respect for and friendship with his father, Hazle wanted to make this an especially happy and fun event for Jeff. She suggested that he invite a couple of his friends and their girlfriends to come for the weekend, in addition to asking his own girlfriend. Jeff took her up on the offer, and Hazle arranged for Jeff's girlfriend, Beth, and the girlfriends of two of his friends to stay at her home for the weekend. Hazle also made arrangements with her fellow church members to provide accommodations for other girls who would be coming to Bloomington for the dinner and dance.[535]

On July 9, the day before the event, the girls arrived at Sunset Hill. Beth, who was from Nebraska, thought Hazle's home the most gorgeous one she had ever seen. She was most impressed with the large courtyard, that had stables on one side and garages on the other. And she openly admired the oak floors that had been polished until they glistened under the lights. That evening, Hazle had a dinner party for the six young people in her formal dining room, complete with servants attending to their every need. [536]

The next day the couples enjoyed riding around Sunset Hill on the bicycles that Julia and Hazle provided. In the evening, they attended the formal dinner and ballroom dancing at the Country Club along with Frederic Morgan. After the dance, Hazle and Julia provided a snack of cookies and milk in the kitchen with the three girls staying at Sunset Hill and their young men. When they had finished off the bottle of milk, Beth, wanting to be helpful, took the bottle to the sink to rinse it out. Just as she reached for the faucet, both Julia and Hazle cried out, "Stop! Stop!" Startled, Beth set the bottle down on the counter, wondering what she had done wrong. Hazle explained, "We have discovered that if you have finished pouring all the milk out of the bottle and then let it stand for a minute or so, at least a table spoon or more will settle at the bottom." It surprised Beth that "somebody who was giving so freely to Principia, and to all kinds of charities in Bloomington and Normal, would be so conscientious about the value of such a small thing."[537]

A few weeks after the dinner and dance, Frederic wrote to Hazle, "The dinner at the Club with the boys was a wonderful occasion for me. I enjoyed every minute of it, and I am sure you know they, too, had a glorious time." While Frederic was in Bloomington for the dinner and dance, he and Hazle talked about the tuition for Eloise and Alice Taylor for the coming year. Hazle told Frederic that she would "again offer Eloise Taylor a $500 scholarship, the same as last year." And she would "pay the full amount of tuition, room and board, and fixed fees for Alice Taylor." All she needed to know from him was how the payments were to be made.[538]

In August 1943, Hazle learned that Eloise Taylor, who had stayed out of college for one quarter, had been working in the comptroller's office. The comptroller, Eldridge Hamlin, had been so pleased with Eloise's work that he had asked her to work for him part-time throughout her college year. He explained to Hazle that Eloise had written to him that she thought she would be able to work out her financial arrangements without any further assistance and would not need the scholarship that Hazle had offered her. But her sister, Alice, did need the full amount of tuition, room and board, and other fees. Hamlin expressed his appreciation for Hazle's generosity to Eloise and Alice. He admitted that he had never met Alice, but told Hazle, "I am most enthusiastic about Eloise. She did an extraordinarily fine job in my office and we were delighted to have her and are happy that she is to be in the office at least part of the time again this year." It pleased Hazle to hear how well Eloise was doing.[539]

While the Taylor girls and others continued their education at Principia, the young men and women who had gone into the armed forces to serve their country were not forgotten. The school mailed out approximately 500 pamphlets to men and women in the different branches of the service. The pamphlets included "Information Regarding Christian Science for Servicemen" and a "List of Hospitality Committees." They had sent a letter to the Hospitality Committees and 150 copies to the Manager of Camp Welfare Activities at The Mother Church for distribution to the Christian Science Wartime Ministers.

In October, Hazle arrived the evening before the Board of Trustees gathered for their meetings and stayed at Lillian Brewer Buck House, which had been thoughtfully arranged by Frederic. She read over the minutes several times to make sure she could read them "intelligibly," and, after a night's rest and a pleasant breakfast, she felt well-prepared for the meeting. She observed that during the meeting, the trustees seemed more comfortable about expressing their ideas, which made it easier to discuss important issues. It became apparent that the trustees had been getting to know one another better during their free time.[540]

Hazle's New Year's resolution, in January 1944, was to make the trip down to the campus more often. She planned to attend, most, if not all, of the programs scheduled by the School of Nations. Her resolution had been inspired by a copy of an address given by Frederic on November 8, 1943. She wrote him a long letter in response to his address, concluding, "Such thinking and writing is an important part of the firm foundation which has made Principia possible." Her lengthy letter surprised Frederic, and he responded, "A really long letter from you is a rarity, and I can assure you that it is greatly appreciated." He had encouraged her to spend more time on the campus, and it pleased him to know that she planned to come down more often. He hoped she would stay a few days each time.[541]

Holding to her resolution, Hazle traveled to Principia to hear a talk by Sir Norman Angell on February 8, 1944. She arrived the day before Mr. Angell's talk, to speak to a class about her traveling experiences in foreign countries. Frederic, who was out of town promoting College enrollment, knew that she would be there for the talk and left her a note: "I feel that your work as Secretary to the Board makes you very much a part of this office, and those of us who work in this office appreciate that fact." He assured her if she needed anything that she should contact his secretary, Velma, and she would provide the needed help.[542]

Maintaining her commitment to attend the School of Nations programs, Hazle was there for talks at the end of February and in early March. She was grateful to have attended them both, since she found it helpful to know "what there is to meet" through prayer. She appreciated the good care that Velma had given her and sent her a "thank you" note in which she wrote that she had enjoyed the young girl, Evvy, who had taken her to the train after the talk in March. She wanted to know the name of the boy who had ridden with them, "because," she told Velma, "I liked him, and should like to remember his name." Velma responded that the young man was Walter Weiler from Glendale, California, who had graduated the previous spring. Hazle thanked Velma for the information and confided to her, "I wondered if he and Evvy were just a little especially interested in each other!" In this note to Velma, Hazle had enclosed a gift of two miniature nail files she had made, remarking, "So many of my friends use and like them now, that I have thought that I might go into business!"[543]

In early April, she attended the Public Affairs conference and wrote to Frederic how she had "enjoyed [the conference] and was greatly profited by" it. She also enclosed two of her "special invention" purse nail files for him. After receiving the nail files, Frederic playfully commented, "I am sure the little purse nail-boards will help me greatly with my disposition . . . instead of being annoyed when I'm confronted with a broken nail or hangnail, I can be grateful for your thoughtfulness." He concluded, "So, you can readily see how far reaching your own invention and act of kindness may be."[544]

As the secretary to the Board of Trustees, Hazle believed that she should attend the commencement exercises as Frederic suggested, but she felt overburdened with other demands in addition to preparing to go to the ranch that summer. Responding to Frederic, she wrote, "Many duties here make me feel that I must get back as soon as possible after commencement." After attending the ceremony, she was glad that Frederic had urged her to come. She later wrote to him, "This particular commencement will always stand out as memorable—for a number of reasons. I am grateful to have been there for it." Perhaps the commencement had been especially touching because of Principia's struggles with low enrollment and even lower faculty and staff morale—an issue that now seemed resolved. They had been able to keep the College open and the commencement ceremony denoted a successful school year.[545]

However, as the summer wore on, they all looked forward to the war ending. Frederic had stayed at Principia to get his office in order. He wrote to Hazle that "the work which [Principia] can do has never been more needed as will be the case during the years following the war." He added, "Certainly we must be big enough and spiritually alert enough to hear God's guidance and to make our plans only as He directs without the enervating influences of human opinions."[546]

Considering in retrospect the last Board of Trustees meeting for the year of 1944 held on October 19, Hazle believed that the push and hurry of earlier years had been almost entirely eliminated. The discussions of issues had been open and an important decision made. She confided to Frederic, "It almost frightens me when I think of the momentous decision we made. We shall all have to keep very close to Principle. I am grateful that I shall be on hand to see so much goodness and beauty unfold." Frederic agreed that it had been a "momentous decision," but he felt comfortable with it since they had made it after much thoughtful deliberation and with a sense of unity among the members. He assured her, "I feel sure that as we keep self entirely out of the picture and see supply as a wholly spiritual concept, we shall be given the wisdom and means necessary to carry out whatever is God's plan for Principia."[547]

In December 1944, when the notes on a loan Hazle had given Principia came due and the school did not have the funds to pay off the $77,500 owed, she graciously extended the notes for another five years. As if in response to her generosity, a few days later, the grandmother of Henry Inness (a former School of Nations student), Mrs. Lundholm sent a $550 scholarship donation to the School of Nations. Although from England, Henry and his family, including his grandmother, were living in Mexico. When Hazle had been in Mexico City three or four years earlier, she had met Mrs. Lundholm. Knowing of her situation, Hazle was deeply touched by the gift and told Frederic that it was a "remarkably fine thing for her to do."[548]

Hazle stayed true to the resolution she had made on New Years Day 1944 through the end of the year. In early December, she attended a talk given by author and journalist, Ernesto Montenegro, on Chile, which she felt was "richly worthwhile." She was also involved that month in the activity of promoting world peace through her work with the National League of Women Voters. She mailed out fliers to everyone she knew regarding the Dumbarton Oaks Conference, which had been held in August of 1944 at a mansion in Washington, D.C. to form the United Nations. Only four countries had been at the conference: the United States, Russia, the United Kingdom, and the Republic of China. It pleased her to receive many positive responses and requests from several clubs for copies to distribute to their members. But, when writing to Frederic, she confessed her amazement that so many people had not heard about the Dumbarton Oaks Proposals or Conference. Although only four countries comprised the conference, she told Frederic, "Some wise person has said, 'the way to begin is to begin!'" She also expressed how much she enjoyed the talk they had when he had taken her to the train station after Montenegro's talk.[549]

Frederic wrote December 18, 1944: "As you know, I always greatly enjoy the opportunity to talk things over with you." He believed that although the Dumbarton Oaks Conference did not achieve complete coordination of international interests, it made some real progress. He intended to talk to the head of the Social Science department about taking steps to see that the members of the Principia community understood what had been accomplished. He also shared with her, unofficially and confidentially, that the patrons of Principia had contributed over $100,000 to the Principia Fund. He believed the donation had been made as a direct result of the College making a right and concerted effort to support and encourage their students who had chosen to go into the armed services. He added that the donation was a definite sign that things were improving. Both Hazle and Frederic looked forward to the future with an expectancy of greater progress.[550]

CHAPTER 23

LIFE ON SUNSET ROAD

*H*azle had long cherished the desire to preserve a portion of the Sugar Creek area, in which her home, Sunset Hill, resided, as a park for residents and nonresidents to enjoy. She made some strides toward accomplishing this goal on December 5, 1944, when she met with a group of individuals at the Withers Library in Bloomington to discuss their interest in extending the Bloomington-Normal recreational systems, particularly the development of the Sugar Creek district. The group chose Hazle to chair the committee. One of the first things the committee did was to form a non-profit corporation so gifts of land and money could be accepted for the Sugar Creek Community Park. At that time, the project produced a moderate park system. Hazle's generous donations of land to the city of Bloomington for use as a park coincided with her deep interest in her neighborhood on Sunset Road and her surrounding community.[551]

When she received a letter from William Morgan at the end of December 1944, containing a list of the students attending Principia from her community, it surprised her to find that Eloise Taylor was not on it. She contacted him in early January to find out why. She received a quick response from William, telling her that Eloise had become a fulltime staff worker so that she could pay for her last quarter of college. Learning of Eloise's sacrifice, Hazle immediately sent the required amount to the scholarship fund, so Eloise could resume her studies that quarter.[552]

Hazle took a deep interest in young people in her community

and especially those in her own neighborhood. When she and Davis built their home, Sunset Hill, on one of the thirteen original five-acre plots in 1928, Hazle hoped they could create a neighborhood of stately homes. However, she and Davis sold their first lots in 1930, during the depression and people simply did not have the funds to build houses remotely like the home she and Davis had built, which the local residents of Bloomington called "the castle." Although disappointed that the financial state of the country dictated that more modest homes be constructed on Sunset Road, Hazle took a deep interest in her neighbors and the neighborhood. She took care to sell each piece of property to individuals whom she deemed would make good neighbors, and she welcomed each new family to the neighborhood by having them over for tea or visiting them in their homes.[553]

When the first families arrived at Sunset Road, the area was virtually undeveloped except for Sunset Hill, which had been built across the road from a cornfield. It created an ideal atmosphere for parents to raise their children. Through the years of growth and change in the area, Hazle maintained her interest in the neighborhood and knew all of her neighbors. Every Saturday morning at 10:00, when she was home in Bloomington, she went for a ride on one of her horses. On her way to the bridle path, she would visit with anyone she met. If some of the neighborhood men happened to be making repairs on Sunset Road, she would stop and express her appreciation for the work they were doing. Since it was a private road, the men had taken on the responsibility of keeping it in good repair because the city did not maintain it.[554]

Each spring, Hazle would send her gardener, Emil, around the neighborhood with boxes of plants to share with her neighbors—usually bluebells and violets, which she especially liked and grew in abundance in her own yard.[555] One neighbor remembered that when they first moved into their home in 1950, Hazle sent Emil over with two Kentucky Coffee trees and a bushel basket full of bluebells, which he planted for them.[556]

Planting trees became a neighborhood activity in the 1950s, when a disease plagued many of the fine old Dutch elm trees in the mid-west. The elms that populated Hazle's neighborhood were no exception, and many of them had to be cut down. Adults and children joined in replanting the trees in the neighborhood. For her part, Hazle supplied some of the trees. The neighborhood children learned some valuable lessons from this experience. They soon realized that it took a long time for trees to grow and understood why they had been admonished to never cut down a tree unless it was absolutely necessary. The children also learned not to judge people by the way they looked. Most of them had been somewhat afraid of Emil, a German veteran who had fought for Germany in World War II. He looked scary, and the children avoided him as much as possible. But when he worked with them planting the trees, they found him to be a kind and thoughtful person.[557]

When summer came to Sunset Road, the neighborhood children thoroughly enjoyed themselves. They played tennis at Mrs. Ewing's, rode bareback on her gentle and well-bred horses that were grazing in the pasture, and hiked up Sugar Creek from the end of the property. When the blue, red, and black berries ripened in the field northwest of Hazle's home, the children picked and ate berries until they could eat no more. All of these elements combined to make Sunset Road a special place for children. Within the bounds of their neighborhood, which Hazle had established, they lived an idyllic childhood.[558]

Hazle invited some of the older children to go horseback riding with her from time to time. Riding Eastern style, she would choose the paths they would take, often riding down Towanda Street, through a neighbor's field, and then toward Jersey Street. Those children whom she asked to go riding with her took the opportunity seriously because they knew it was serious to her. While riding, Hazle would ask each of the children, "What do you think you will do when you get older? What do you want to do?" She intended that her questioning would encourage the child to think about his or her future.[559]

After they returned to the stable, she would say to them, "Did you enjoy the ride?" The children always responded in the affirmative, and she would then tell them, "We have to brush down the horses." She said it in such a matter-of-fact way that none of the children refused to do it. They gladly brushed the horses. One day, wanting to show their appreciation to Hazle for allowing them to ride her horses, some of the children surprised her by cleaning the horses' stalls. It pleased her that they had tackled this chore on their own initiative without being asked or expected to do it.[560]

The older children in the neighborhood, through their riding experiences with her, found Hazle to be a good friend. She always took time to listen to them, and they knew that she really cared about them. Whenever or wherever she saw one of the children, she would stop and take time to talk. She would ask about his or her parents, how school was going, and if he or she had done anything helpful for anyone that day. She wanted to hear about their dreams and encouraged them to pursue their interests.

When Hazle had visitors, she did not mind if the children used the tennis court as long as they rested on the opposite side of the garden from where she was entertaining her guests. This gave the children in the neighborhood an opportunity to see some interesting people. One of the guests whom the children especially looked forward to seeing, was Adlai Stevenson, who enjoyed visiting with her when he had the time.[561]

Hazle's garden, near her house, became a favorite place for the children to play. But they avoided the garden in the early morning hours during the spring, summer, and fall months, because they knew that Hazle often read there. She appreciated that the children recognized this was a place of solace for her. She found inspiration in the quiet of the morning, reading near the statue of *Her Son*, which she had purchased in 1941. In the afternoons, the children could often be found playing in the garden. They were awed by the large bronze statue of a mother and her son and greatly admired it. The children especially enjoyed being in the garden on summer evenings, when it was aglow with the light of fireflies. Hazle did not mind the children playing in the garden; she wanted them to feel welcome at her home.[562]

When her grandchildren came to visit, Hazle made a point of inviting some similarly aged neighborhood children over to play. The large open room in the basement, which Hazle sometimes used for meetings, served as a play area where the children could romp without disturbing the adults. Hazle allowed the children to explore the rest of the basement, where they discovered a huge walk-in safe in which she kept all of her old copies of the *National Geographic*. The children spent many hours going through those old magazines. They also discovered the icebox, which Hazle continued to use, although a huge block of ice had to be brought to the house for it each day. Herman, her driver, would shave ice from it for the children's soft drinks. The laundry room, with its two big sinks and a washboard which the housekeeper used to do the laundry, was also in the basement. The children were allowed to play without interference, except at snack or lunch time, when someone would be sent down to see if they needed anything to eat or drink.[563]

Hazle had an interest in all of her neighbors, but she became an especially good friend to the Eiff family because of their shared interest in Christian Science, and they often went to church together in Hazle's limousine. Art, the oldest of the three Eiff boys, first met Hazle when he was three. When he was older, she invited him over to play with her grandchildren when they came to visit, since he was near the age of some of them. She also began inviting him to go horseback riding with her.[564]

As he matured, Art began visiting Hazle at Sunset Hill on his own without an invitation. She always greeted him warmly, inviting him into the study or the sun room where they could talk comfortably. She would serve him milk and cookies or other goodies that she had on hand. Feeling at ease with her, he could talk openly about things that he felt uncomfortable sharing with his parents. She would listen quietly, and then, she would ask questions or give encouragement.[565]

She often invited the three Eiff boys over for dinner, and they would arrive dressed like proper gentlemen and on their best behavior. Since Art was the oldest, he sat at one end of the table opposite to Hazle. The two younger boys, John and Gary, sat one on each side. Hazle knew that the boys especially liked Woodford pudding, and she often had Ruby, the cook, prepare it for their dessert. When they had finished their dinner, Hazle would ask, "Are you ready for Woodford pudding?" The boys of course responded in an eager affirmative. Shortly after, Herman (Hazle's driver and Ruby's husband) would appear, carrying the pudding on a platter into the dining room. The first time this happened, the boys wondered how Herman knew it was time to bring in the dessert. A few dinners later they discovered Hazle's secret—a buzzer hidden under the table near her chair, which could only be heard in the kitchen.[566]

Art, an unusually serious boy, often sought Hazle's counsel. Having an inquisitive mind, he asked her many questions on a variety of subjects, which she enjoyed discussing with him. When he expressed his curiosity about the house, she permitted him into rooms that other visitors did not have the opportunity to see, and he discovered some interesting features. He found that when he opened a closet door, a light would come on inside the closet. He came upon a secret passage in one of the rooms that was a combined sitting room and bedroom. Inside the bedroom closet, he discovered a door that opened into a passageway over the carriage house to the circular stairs that led to the stables. He also solved the mystery of the room from which passersby could see a window, but never a light shining from it. He learned that the staircase had been boxed in there, so no light could shine through the window.[567]

After exploring the house, Art expressed his interest in how the house was built. Hazle showed him pictures that were taken at different stages of the construction. She talked with him about how they had planned the house. His curiosity also led to the discovery that the statue in back of the garages was actually a fountain. He likewise examined the car wash in the garage, which held quite a fascination for him and the other neighborhood children. It seemed that Hazle always had new and interesting items. When she bought a bright orange Jacobsen riding lawn mower, she attracted the interest of the adults in the neighborhood as well as that of the children.[568]

Learning of Art's interest in reading, Hazle encouraged him in it and invited him to come over to her house to read some of her books. She asked him what he was currently reading so she could determine which books to choose from her collection that he would enjoy. Before long, he was reading at her house two or three times a week. Together, Hazle and Art would read in the study sitting in the black leather chairs in either corner of the room. After reading for a time, they would join Julia for a visit in the sitting room, where she had been doing needlework.[569]

One winter day, Hazle and Art were talking in the garden room, which faced north and where they could see the deep snow drifts, when he mentioned to her that he was taking accounting. She asked him, "What are you learning in accounting class?" He started telling her about double entry and other steps involved in accounting. She stopped him and said, "No, what are you *learning* in accounting?" He had to stop and really think about it. "Well," he finally said, "I am learning that there must be order. And I am learning that you have to understand the consequences of what you do." She then brought out some of her financial statements to illustrate for him what had taken place in her accounts. She explained, "What you need to know is that being organized you can see there is this much money here and there is this much money here and there is this much money there. . . . I have learned over the years that this is part of a natural cycle." By using her financial statements to illustrate what she meant, Hazle enabled Art to clearly see the need to be organized. Hazle had the ability to encourage children and adults to think more deeply.[570]

Desiring to encourage the neighborhood children to take an interest in music, theater, and art, Hazle took them to concerts, plays, and art exhibits. Through this exposure, Art developed a deep interest in music and had the opportunity to play concerts all over Europe with his high school concert band. When Hazle learned he was going to Europe, they had many conversations about it, and she told him about the world trip she and her family had taken.[571]

Hazle insisted on paying for the last trip Art made to Europe as a high school student. It was her graduation gift to him. As part of the trip, Art and his group had a tour of the United Nations complex conducted by George Bush, Sr., who was American Ambassador to the United Nations at the time. Hazle had arranged for Art's group to have a reception at the American Association for the United Nations. Prior to his departure for Europe, Hazle directed him to go to a certain hotel on the Neckar River, down from Heidelberg. She also advised him, "You want to go to Palatus. Don't take the train; take the tram. On the tram you will be above everything. If you take the train up you will miss too much." She also shared her desire for world peace with him and talked to him about the School of Nations program at Principia. He recognized that her desire for world peace had prompted her to initiate the program and that it was a labor of love for her.[572]

When traveling in Germany, Art remembered that Hazle had once asked him, "What do you think of the Germans now that they have been beaten?" He had answered that he did not know anything about them. But she had persisted, "I am sure that you have read about them. What do you think?" He had read about the war. But actually seeing the devastation and destruction caused by the war made a much greater impression on him. He found it quite disturbing and gained somewhat of an understanding of why Hazle thought it so important to establish the School of Nations to promote peace in the world.[573]

Hazle continued to encourage Art as he went through his college years. When he graduated from college in the midst of the Vietnam War and became a pilot, it greatly pleased Hazle, and she told him, "Well, you have realized part of your dream." She felt confident that he would fulfill many more dreams during his life-time.[574]

Over the years, Hazle continued her interest in the children in her neighborhood and the community. She rejoiced with them over their successes and encouraged them through their difficulties. Many of the children in her neighborhood and some from the surrounding community were like an extended family to her. She took great pleasure in having young people around her, and she generously gave to them of her time and interest. Her example and generosity meant a great deal to Art Eiff. It is certain that she also had a positive influence on the lives of some of the other children who grew up in the idyllic Sunset Road neighborhood and Sugar Creek community.

CHAPTER 24

GETTING BACK TO NORMAL

$\mathcal{E}$arly in March, 1945, the signs of spring began to appear. Sam Baker, the chairman of the School of Nations committee at the College, wrote to Hazle that the buds were swelling, although they were ice-covered at the moment. The main reason for his letter, however, was to tell her of the formation of the Institute of Asiatic Affairs in Boulder, at the University of Colorado. He enclosed a letter from the University that provided information on Asiatic affairs, which he knew would interest her. The purpose of the Institute was to "have the students formulate a unit of Asiatic history bringing out the influence of Asia on the Occident, and the interrelation of Asiatic and Western affairs." Through its student newspaper, the *Pilot*, Principia had given some publicity to the institute and intended to award a scholarship to a Principia student interested in attending the Institute that coming summer.[575]

Later in the month, Hazle received an invitation from Rebeka Dietz, a member of the School of Nations committee, to stay with her and her family in St. Louis and attend a talk to be given by Royal Gunnison, an alumnus, who had recently returned from the Philippines. Gunnison had been a student at Principia from grade school through junior college. His mother, Helena Cobb Gunnison, was serving as a member of Principia's Board of Trustees and would be arriving from Seattle to attend her son's talk. The invitation came on rather short notice because his talk had been planned for April, but he had been assigned to participate in the peace conference

235

in San Francisco during that time instead. Hazle accepted the invitation and enjoyed a few pleasant days with the Dietz family. After Hazle returned home, Rebeka sent the tentative dates for a series of lectures being sponsored by the School of Nations to be given by Dr. Alfred Gertsch in San Francisco. Hazle looked forward to hearing more about these lectures.[576]

Hazle returned to Principia in early April, 1945, to attend the Public Affairs Conference, titled "The United States: A Power for Peace." The speakers at the Conference were Erwin D. Canham, the editor of *The Christian Science Monitor*; Dr. William Y. Elliot, the co-founder of the Public Affairs Conferences; and Judge Manley O. Hudson. She later wrote to Frederic of her impressions of the Conference, telling him that she believed it was "the most important one we have had."[577]

Then, in early May, she visited Principia again and heard a talk on Mexico City given by Hubert Herring, Director of the Committee on Cultural Relations with Latin America. She had read everything she could find on the subject prior to attending the talk. But, upon hearing Herring's first-hand account, Hazle felt she had gained a much better understanding. Later in the month, Dr. Gertsch came to Bloomington, and she had the pleasure of hearing him lecture. Following the talk, he had dinner with Hazle and her family and told them of the experiences he had in San Francisco when he gave the series of lectures sponsored by the School of Nations. In mid-June, Frederic promised Hazle he would forward the many letters that had been pouring into Principia regarding the lectures Gertsch had given, which had been an obvious success.[578]

On May 8, 1945, Hazle was happy to learn of Germany's surrender, but it was not until August 15 that the Japanese conceded defeat and the war ended. A renewed hope for world peace swept America causing the government and individual citizens to turn their thoughts and efforts to regaining a more normal sense of life. The administrators of Principia expected an increase in enrollment now that the war had ended, and they purchased property for a new Upper School. Hazle heard about the purchase in September and wrote to Frederic, "Only the finest sort of straight thinking and action could have accomplished it." She had not been to Elsah since May and told him, "It has been a long time since my last visit to the campus!" She looked forward to seeing the newly acquired property when attending the Trustee meetings in October.[579]

Hazle arrived several days before the Trustee meetings began in October 1945, and stayed at the Pere Marquette Lodge in Grafton so she could visit the College campus and help prepare for the meetings. However, she had the privilege of spending the evening before the first meeting in a room at Mrs. Morgan's home, since the Trustees planned to go to St. Louis the next morning to visit the construction site of the new Upper School. When they arrived at the site, they were amazed to see that the work of clearing the land for the women's dormitory and faculty houses had already been accomplished.[580]

Later, Hazle wrote to Frederic that the meetings "were some of the most stirring and valuable" and she believed they had accomplished much. She also expressed her appreciation to him for Mrs. Morgan's hospitality in allowing her to stay at her home. It had provided her a "lovely outlook—straight into the depths of that most beautiful ravine." Frederic agreed with her about the meetings and added his hope that "such sessions can always be held with the greatest frankness."[581]

In December 1945, Hazle had the pleasure of reading in the *Principia Alumni Purpose* about a "number of alumni" who were now working for the State Department. She recognized the names of some of those individuals to be among the first School of Nations' students, including James Penfield, who had been assigned to special work with the Army and Navy; William Moreland, who was serving as the Third Secretary of the United States Legation at Baghdad, Iraq; and Fredrika Morehouse Tandler, who worked as an Information Officer covering the areas of Spain, Netherlands, and Portugal for the

State Department Information Service. These former students were
fine examples of how the School of Nations program prepared young
people to serve their country and the world.[582]

In early 1946, the School of Nations committee focused its
attention on finding ways to assist European countries in their
restoration efforts. Inspired by this idea, the committee invited
Herbert E. Rieke, of Indianapolis, a Christian Science Army
Chaplain who had been stationed in Italy, to speak at Principia on
February 22. Rieke showed films he had taken of the Holy Land
prior to his return to the United States. He then shared what he
had learned from a young man who had fought at Normandy. The
city of Caen, France, lay in ruins; only two of the great cathedrals
in the town had escaped with minor damage. The University there
desperately needed books to rebuild its library. Following Rieke's
talk, Principia, as a whole, collected nearly 200 books, which were
sent to the University Library at Caen.[583]

Desiring to take part in some of the school activities and to
prepare for the next Trustee meetings, Hazle spent a few weeks
during the last of April and the beginning of May, 1946, at Pere
Marquette Lodge. She worked on preparations for the meetings
with Evvy Shearston, of whom she had become especially fond. As
for Evvy, she appreciated having Hazle close at hand and confided
to her that she hoped to have a long visit with her outside of the
office. But Evvy's workload and Hazle's schedule prevented them
from having that pleasure.[584]

Hazle was unable to attend the commencement in June, at
which the School of Nations announced two special awards of $550
each that had been given to Carol Lyon of Elkhorn, Wisconsin, and
Marcia Marks of Newtonville, Massachusetts. The awards would
enable the two young women to study in Geneva, Switzerland,
their junior year. Sam Baker sent Hazle copies of each of the girls'
statements of purpose, which she enjoyed reading.[585]

Carol Lyon had written in part, "I feel that a year in study in

Switzerland would broaden, strengthen, and develop character. It would make demands upon my knowledge and understanding of Christian Science, upon my faith in Principia's ideals, and upon [me] as an individual." Marcia Marks had originally wanted to study in France to improve her French, but the war had made it impossible. When the war ended, she found that her reason for going abroad to study had changed and broadened. She now believed "that such an experience would be invaluable for the development of greater intellectual independence and a more international viewpoint. The first would be an entirely personal asset, but the second would become more widespread and is greatly needed by many, especially in these critical times." She felt that this experience would help her "fulfill her duties as a true citizen of the world."[586]

During the summer, weeks before school began, the number of students enrolled in the College greatly increased. Frederic soon realized there would be no rooms available for members of the board of trustees on campus when they came for the October meeting. He called on Hazle for assistance, and, as the "unofficial hostess," she made reservations for accommodations and meals at the Pere Marquette Lodge for the group.[587]

Following the October, 1946, meetings, Hazle stayed a few extra days at the College to hear a talk by Vera Micheles Dean, Chairman of the Foreign Policy Association and an authority on Russian affairs. In addition to attending the talk, Hazle went horseback riding with Ana Mary Elliott and two young men who had brought horses to school with them. Hazle had been impressed with Ana Mary's skillful horsemanship, and she began thinking about bringing her own horse, Cimon, down with her whenever she visited the campus. But when she saw the dilapidated condition of the barn, she had second thoughts.[588]

After returning home, Hazle wrote to Frederic, "I am sure you feel, as I do, that these last trustees' meetings were the most efficient and harmonious we have ever had." She also brought up the subject of the barn. She told him that, if the barn and equipment on campus were adequate, she would like to bring her horse, Cimon, with her whenever she came down. She added that she would be willing to allow Ana Mary and the two young men to take care of Cimon for her.[589]

Responding to Hazle's comments about the trustee meetings, Frederic wrote, "Surely there is good reason to believe that better protective work, more impersonal thinking, and a greater joy are finding expression in the deliberations of that grand group of people." Regarding the barn, he said that he would keep her suggestions in mind and work with Hamlin on a preliminary plan for remodeling it to present to her and the executive committee in the near future.[590]

On December 5, 1946, after attending a talk at Principia given by Dr. Travers, a distinguished Brazilian writer, Hazle wrote to Frederic, who had been too busy to attend the talk, "It was heartening to hear from Dr. Travers that Brazil was pushing forward her borders—not only to help settlers in her own country, but also to make room for the hundred thousand displaced persons of Europe who need both new hopes and new homes for the future." Frederic's absence from the talk caused her some concern. She knew that since the war ended he had taken on the responsibility of several building projects on both Principia campuses in addition to his other work. She told him, "You are much needed these days, Frederic. You are far too valuable a person to run the risk of over-working." And she added, "We all wish you would do as good a job of taking care of yourself as you have of us."[591]

The Past and the Future

CHAPTER 25

FOR THE LOVE OF HORSES

$\mathcal{W}$ orld War II had forced Hazle to abandon her desire to provide a proper riding stable on the College campus. But in early 1947, her correspondence with Frederic regarding the barn for stabling students' horses reveals the renewal of that desire. She suggested to him that they consider building a stable on the College campus instead of trying to remodel the old dilapidated barn. She had given a lot of thought to how the project could be funded and shared some of her ideas with him. She also offered to donate $40,000 to start the project. He promised to consider her proposal and forward it to the Executive Committee.[592]

Hazle's desire to have a stable on the Principia College campus evolved naturally from her many experiences with young people and horses. Over the years, she had often invited children who attended her church or lived in her neighborhood to Sunset Hill to go riding with her. Alice Taylor, Eloise's younger sister, was one of them. Alice shared Hazle's deep interest in horses and horseback riding, and she openly admired Hazle's "fine and beautiful" horses. Hazle enjoyed the company of both Alice and Eloise and had often invited them to bring their friends who were visiting from Principia to her home, not only for horseback riding, but also to play tennis or go swimming. Hazle looked forward to these visits as much as the girls did, and she always provided a delicious lunch for them. Although Alice enjoyed the other activities, she treasured "riding with Hazle on her fine horses the most."[593]

One summer, during the war years, Hazle invited Alice to

accompany her to the Thunder Mountain Ranch in Crivitz, Wisconsin, which Hazle and her brothers owned. Alice eagerly accepted the invitation. Hazle's friends, Julia Hodge and Elizabeth (Buffie) Ives, Adlai Stevenson's sister, also went with them to the ranch. Hazle and Alice went for a ride on Hazle's horses each morning. One morning, Hazle shared with Alice how she had decided to memorize all the names of the trees, flowers, and birds when she was a girl. Alice appreciated nature and learned a great deal that summer from Hazle, who pointed out different flowers and trees as they rode along the trails. Sometimes they stopped and examined the colors and shapes of the leaves, and Alice thought it amazing that Hazle could name birds just by hearing their songs as well as by seeing them.[594]

When they came back from their rides, Alice would help Hazle pick tomatoes, or corn, or some other vegetable from the garden, which the cook then prepared for their lunch while they changed clothes. After lunch, Hazle always retired to her room for a rest, allowing Alice time to explore the ranch on her own. Later in the afternoon, she and Alice went for another horseback ride or a drive in the car. Alice found the car rides almost as much fun as riding the horses.[595]

Evenings at the ranch provided a new and interesting experience for Alice, who liked being in the company of the other women. After an active day, they all gathered in the living room in front of the blazing fire that had been built in the enormous fireplace, which made the room a cozy haven. Hazle explained to Alice that she had wanted the fireplace to be as big as the one at the Old Faithful Inn in Wyoming. Several times she had rejected the architect's plans for the fireplace, telling him that she wanted it to be "Bigger, as big as Old Faithful." After her fireplace had been completed, she visited the Old Faithful Inn and realized that her fireplace *was bigger*.[596]

Hazle had arranged tables around the fireplace where she provided each of the women with reading materials for the evening.

She introduced Alice to their nightly ritual of reading and quiet contemplation, and Alice enthusiastically took her place at her own table. As the women read, they sometimes came across an item they thought might be of interest to one of the others. In such a case, they placed the item quietly on the other woman's table to be read at her convenience. Alice enjoyed reading what the other women put on her table and had fun finding things to put on theirs.[597]

The ranch gave Hazle ample opportunity to share her love of horseback riding with young people such as Alice, as well as with members of her family. Her niece Nancy, Ellsworth's daughter, first came to the ranch when she was only five. Hazle had the joy of teaching the receptive and responsive Nancy how to ride, and Nancy thought that "Aunt Hazle's well-trained and well-groomed, silky, shiny Eastern horses" were the "nicest horses of any one in the family." Nancy liked them even more than Uncle Nelson's Western horses, which he had purchased in Arizona and kept at the Ranch. Hazle, a self-taught and accomplished horsewoman, believed it important for young people to learn how to ride correctly and how to properly care for horses.[598]

The summer that Hazle's granddaughter, Cindy, turned seven, Cindy rode on the train from Russell, Kansas, to Crivitz, Wisconsin, by herself to spend some time alone with her grandmother. Her parents, Ralph and Kate Lee, planned to join her a few weeks later. One morning, when Hazle and Cindy left the stable, Cindy was riding the very tall, but gentle horse named King. Although it was a long way to the ground for her, Hazle had no fear that Cindy, who had been riding horses since she was a toddler, would fall off. As they rode along the trail, they came upon a swampy area, but Hazle was not concerned, for logs had been carefully laid close together to keep horses and riders from sinking down into the muck.[599]

Hazle started across the logs and Cindy followed. Suddenly, Hazle's horse slipped and went down. Cindy pulled King to a halt. Hazle landed on the logs with a loud thud. She managed to get up and grab hold of her horse's reins. Then she turned to Cindy and said, "You stay on your horse. It won't help to have two of us off." She found a nearby stump to stand on and remounted her horse. Cindy asked if she and her horse were okay. Hazle responded in the affirmative. As they resumed their ride, she said, "Now, Cinda, do not say anything about this. I will speak to your parents about it, at the right time. So this is just between you and me. Okay?" Cindy replied, "Yes, grandmother."[600]

Several days later, when Hazle was riding into the Crivitz train station with Cindy and her parents, she decided it was the right time to tell them about the riding incident. She said to Ralph and Kate Lee, "I want to tell you a story and I want to congratulate Cindy." Then she told them what had happened that day in the swamp and concluded, "I asked her to keep a secret, and she did. And I think she should be commended for that." Surprised by his mother's revelation, Ralph asked, "Mother, why didn't you want us to know?" Hazle answered, "Well, I was afraid you wouldn't let me go out with her just on our own anymore." What Hazle did not reveal to Cindy and her parents that day was that she had sustained a broken rib in the fall. It was not until much later, when the healing was complete, that she shared that part of the story with them.[601]

It was not only Hazle's past experiences with young people and horses that had revived her desire to provide a stable on the College campus. Recently she had become acquainted with Ana Mary Elliott, a current Principia College student in whom she recognized a natural talent for working with horses. The "enthusiastic and earnest" Ana Mary had organized a Riding Club, which Hazle had been more than glad to sponsor and support. She also approved of the plans that Ana Mary and the other club members had worked out for the stable, and she admired their determination to establish their club as a viable activity for College students.[602]

As the President of the Principia Riding Organization, Ana Mary wrote a letter to Frederic Morgan in February, 1947, which included a report of the purpose and achievements of the club and a detailed plan for the stable. She told him, "We are eager to do anything in our power to build a lasting riding organization for the campus: hammer nails, saw wood, dig holes, and level fields." The organization had acquired seven horses, one of which the club had purchased, and the others were either owned by members, on loan, or rented. They had already begun giving riding lessons to freshmen and sophomore women, who had benefited from the experience by overcoming their fear of riding horses and gaining confidence in their "own ability of intelligent expression in any experience." In addition to giving riding lessons, the club had "opened up several of the old trails and roads and explored more that [needed] opening or making."[603]

The club members had come to realize that, in order to sustain their organization they needed a "good barn" for stabling and caring for the horses and storing their equipment. They also desired to have a riding ring for "teaching advanced riding techniques." In addition, the club members believed it would be necessary to hire a regular caretaker to oversee the operation and deal with any emergency that should arise. Ana Mary concluded her report to Frederic: "Mrs. Ewing has assured the organization $700.00 for immediate use. The members of the club would be willing to work in any way for the building of a good stable."[604]

On Friday, April 25, Hazle arrived at Principia College to attend a School of Nations talk given by John Beaufort, a staff writer for *The Christian Science Monitor*. The next day, she visited with Ana Mary and was pleased to see the progress that she and the Riding Club had made in clearing the riding trails to make them useable again. Both Hazle and Ana Mary expected that Frederic and the Executive Board would approve the stables and the academic study of horsemanship, and they wanted the trails to be ready.

When Hazle heard from Frederic in May, it was not about the riding stable, but regarding a visit to Principia by her friends from

Bloomington, Dean Funk and his family, the owners of Funk's Grove, near Springfield, Illinois, where they produced maple sirup (the original spelling according to Webster). The grove and sirup business had been established in 1824 by Isaac Funk and maintained through the following generations of his family. Hazle had become a good friend of Hazel Funk Holmes, who had been given the responsibility for the business in the early1920s, and had arranged for the family timber and farmland to be protected by a trust ensuring that future generations would continue to enjoy the sirup produced there. Hazle actively supported the conservation and preservation of Funk's Grove in its natural state.[605]

She appreciated hearing about the Funk family's visit to Principia, but was sorry that Frederic did not have time to join them for dinner at Pere Marquette. She told him, "I am moved to say once again, that you are not nearly as careful about your own recreation as you are of those around you." Concluding her letter, she said, "I am sure you will keep me posted about any news in connection with the riding stable. If it can be worked out, it will be the fulfillment of a long-time dream."[606]

Hazle made her annual trip to the family-owned ranch in Crivitz, Wisconsin, in June, followed by Emil, her groomsman, and his assistant, who transported her horses to the ranch. Although some family members kept horses at the ranch all year long, Hazle preferred to keep her horses at her home when she was not at the ranch. The Thunder Mountain Ranch had originally been purchased by Hazle's father, Orlando J. Buck, in 1913. When he bought the property, it included a farm surrounded by land that had been burned over and clear-cut. When he passed away in 1919, the land still remained undeveloped. Hazle and her brothers, Nelson and Ellsworth, decided to keep the property and began developing it in the 1920s. Each of them built a home on separate but contiguous parts of the property. Believing it important to reforest the land, they had many family tree planting parties.[607]

On August 7, 1947, Hazle received a letter at the ranch from Frederic, which she anticipated would be plans for the stable. Instead, it detailed his plans for promoting Principia's Golden Anniversary. What Hazle did not know was that Frederic had sent another letter that same day which had somehow been delayed in the postal system. Consequently, it mystified her when she received a letter from him written nearly two weeks later, urging her to send the plans for the riding stable on to Mr. Gutterson as soon as possible. She wrote to Frederic explaining that she "had not received them."[608]

A few days later, the letter detailing the plans and the blueprint for the stable finally arrived. After looking them over, Hazle mailed them on to Gutterson so he would have them to present to the Executive Board in Chicago on August 29. She had found the plans to be "exceptionally clean-cut, straightforward, and attractive." She could mentally see the building, which would be on the right side of the entrance to the campus, but a good distance from the road and parallel to it. The paddocks and exercise area would be on the other side of the stables, away from the road. The blueprint included five standing stalls and two box stalls, and there would be a two-bedroom house for a groom with a growing family to occupy.[609]

Hazle wrote to Frederic praising him for the well-thought-out plans and excellent choice he had made for the site and asked if he had found a reliable person to take charge of the stable as well as a capable teacher to work with the students. She mentioned that Ana Mary's riding counselor, Roderick G. Carpenter, "is extremely eager to come to Principia," and she thought he might be willing to work with the horses until a place for him opened up in the dormitory. She assured Frederic that she was confident in Ana Mary's assessment of Carpenter's horsemanship. She concluded, "After all the years of dreaming and hoping, I am sure you know what a deep satisfaction it is to see these plans go forward. I would like to help in any way that I can."[610]

At the ranch in early September, a letter arrived from Frederic describing what had happened at the Executive Committee meeting. Gutterson had presented the plans for the stable, and the Committee had agreed that the construction costs had been estimated at a reasonable amount. However, the plans for the construction of the new Upper School campus were also on the agenda with an estimated cost of $10 million. It seemed imperative to the Executive Committee that the Upper School be moved to the new campus as soon as possible and the construction of the riding stables postponed. They put the $40,000 Hazle had donated to start the stable project into a fund which could be used for a riding stable in the future.[611]

It saddened Hazle that the fulfillment of her dream had been postponed indefinitely, but she was more concerned about how Ana Mary would take this decision. She had worked so hard to clear the trails to be used for the horsemanship classes and had been looking forward to helping run the stable. Thinking about how disappointed Ana Mary would be increased Hazle's sorrow. She put Frederic's letter aside, not knowing how she should respond to it. She needed time to think and pray over the situation.

While preparing to attend the Trustee meetings and the Golden Anniversary celebration on November 20 through 23, Hazle realized she had never responded to Frederic about the Executive Committee's decision regarding the riding stable. She wrote to him explaining, "I was greatly disappointed at first, because I thought it was all settled for this fall. But, as I reread your letter, and thought through the whole situation, I could see that the decision was a wise one—and the only one under the circumstances." She had so completely accepted the decision that she had hardly given it a thought, except for the two or three times when she received letters from Ana Mary. Hazle was grateful for the possibility of constructing the riding stable in the future, but she had "hoped the project might be worked out while [Ana Mary] was still in school." Hazle's only consolation was the thought that maybe Ana Mary would visit Principia after she had graduated and find that the riding stable had been established.[612]

After arriving home from the Golden Anniversary celebration, Hazle wrote to Frederic that it was "both notable and long-to-be remembered." She thought that, "Every detail was beautifully planned and carried through," and she added, "It was largely due to your thoughtful and expert direction." She had been glad to hear about the book, *As the Sowing*, which Edwin S. Leonard, Jr., was writing to record the early history of Principia and the School of Nations. She admitted that, "A few of the early events," which Leonard had shared at the celebration "were new, even to" her, and she looked forward to reading his book.[613]

Frederic wrote to Hazle on November 29, 1947: "Thank you for your always kindly, generous part in our meetings" and your "support of the work at Principia." Knowing how much Hazle desired to have the stable built on the College campus, he acknowledged her gracious acceptance of the decision made by the Executive Committee, and told her, "We could have no finer evidence of your unselfish love and loyalty for Principia."[614]

CHAPTER 26

A VITAL INFLUENCE

 $\mathscr{I}$ n addition to promoting the riding club and horse stable in early 1947, Hazle had been thinking about redesigning and updating the School of Nations booklet in light of the many changes that had taken place since its last revision in 1936. She received encouragement from Frederic to go forward with the project, but soon found it would take more time to accomplish than she had anticipated. Each of the committee members on both campuses had other commitments and responsibilities to manage and did not seem to have much time to devote to this work. Although disappointed that the booklet would not be completed as soon as she had hoped, she appreciated all the good work being done by the committee members.[615]

She had been especially pleased to hear from the chairman of the School of Nations in St. Louis, Robert Fisher, about the Student Model Assembly of the United Nations for Principia, which he had conducted. It had involved the participation of four other high schools in the area, and, following the Assembly, one of the participating schools asked Fisher if he would come to their school and explain how they could set up their own assembly. Fisher confided to Hazle that he believed the color provided by the School of Nations flags and costumes, which had been donated to the museum over the years, had added dramatic accents and definitely aided the success of Principia's Assembly.[616]

Thinking about the production of the booklet and the current activities of the School of Nations, Hazle reflected on how the program had evolved in the 22 years since its inception. She realized that both the College and High School had developed programs that had become increasingly more satisfying and well run by the committees. She recognized among the committee members a wealth of talent and knowledge. They always seemed to find high quality speakers to present interesting and timely lectures, sometimes from among their own members.

The list of talks scheduled for the fall of 1947, which she had received from Sam Baker, served as a good example. Frank Parker, one of the committee members, would give a talk on November 1, titled, "The Brush Sings: the Ink Dances—a Way of Understanding the Orient," which Hazle thought sounded quite intriguing. Miss Elizabeth Jenkins, another committee member, was scheduled to speak on the subject, "The Spirit of Britain," and the two students who received scholarships to go to Geneva, Switzerland, and had recently returned would be sharing their experiences at an assembly on the College campus. Sam had arranged for Hazle to have an interview with the two students, Carol Lyon and Marcia Marks, on October 26, when she planned to visit the College.[617]

At the beginning of 1948, the booklet remained in the design and revision stage, while the School of Nations committee on the College campus took advantage of an opportunity to sponsor an interesting and promising program. Four education majors from the University of Michigan, representing Japan, India, China, and Korea arrived the weekend of Saturday, January 31. The program began with the four students sharing their individual stories with Principia students on Sunday. The next day, the students conducted interactive roundtable discussions on education in the Orient. Hazle believed the program to be a unique and informative learning experience.[618] She later had an informative learning experience of her own at the Chicago Public Affairs Conference in April 1948, which prevented her from attending the last of the School of Nations' talks for the school year.[619] She did not visit Principia again until June 10, when she attended the commencement ceremonies and met with her fellow trustees.[620]

That summer, Hazle turned her attention to local matters and delayed her departure for the ranch in order to host the first meeting of independent women voters at her home on Thursday, June 24, 1948. The women came together to support a distant cousin of Hazle's former husband and her personal friend, Adlai Ewing Stevenson II, who was running for Governor of the state of Illinois. She found the meeting, which was attended by 60 women from both political parties and all walks of life, inspiring and stimulating. This diverse group of women initiated the organization of the "Stevenson for Governor—Women's Division of the Non-Partisan Independent McLean County Committee." Mrs. Gertrude Williams, the temporary chairwoman, gave an inspirational talk, and Mrs. Robert W. Morris of Chicago offered techniques and suggestions on how to organize the committee and its work. Morris also provided an explanation of the group's purpose to the local newspaper, saying, "We feel the need of honest, efficient state administration in Illinois." The women believed that the independent voters would be casting the deciding votes in the upcoming election.[621]

Following the meeting, Hazle left for the ranch, and in late July she received a letter from Frederic regarding a disease that seemed to be consuming the elm trees on the College campus. He asked if she would "be willing to be one of a committee of three to do regular metaphysical work on this problem," and told her, "This request is not made carelessly, for I assure you that the situation is one which requires very real and consecrated attention."[622] Hazle promptly responded, "Your letter about the elm trees received, and I have gone to work immediately. There is not the slightest reason why we have to accept this belief of the power of evil any more than any other." She had done prayerful work in the past for plants in her own garden and had proven that, the power of prayer brings about growth and health in vegetation.[623]

Knowing of Frederic's demanding work schedule, Hazle also

suggested that he should take some time for rest and refreshment
and invited him to come spend a few days in the "cool quietness" of
the ranch. She had found that being at the ranch always refreshed
her, and she felt certain that Frederic would find it beneficial.[624]
He responded that he would "like to come up to the ranch," but
regretted that he could not; he needed to stay at the campus.[625]

In addition to doing the metaphysical work that Frederic had
requested, Hazle gave some prayerful thought as to how she could
best promote the School of Nations and its new booklet. As a result
of her quiet listening, she began making plans to give an interview
to the Bloomington paper that would highlight the successes of
students who had been involved in the School of Nations program.

When Hazle returned to Bloomington in the fall of 1948, she
gave her support to Stevenson's campaign. After he won the election,
Hazle wrote to Frederic about the article she planned to have
printed in the Bloomington paper about the School of Nations. At
her request, Frederic had Sam Baker provide her with information
about the former School of Nations students working in the field
of Foreign Service. The list of students included Mallory Browne,
appointed Counselor of the Embassy in charge of United States
Service in London as of July 22, 1948; James Penfield, serving in
the State Department in Washington; William Moreland, who had
served as Consul in Brussels, Belgium, in Bordeaux, France, and later
in Iraq, and who was currently working on night duty dispatch for
the State Department, reporting pertinent information to Cordell
Hull,* Secretary of State; and Esther Rice (Starrett), one of the first
members to study in Paris at the Sorbonne, who now lived in Mexico
City and worked as secretary to the United States Embassy.[626]

Responding to Hazle's inquiry about the progress being made on
the School of Nations booklet, Rebeka Dietz, who was overseeing the
compilation and production of the work, reported that the manuscript

*Hull strongly supported the establishment of the United Nations and was awarded the 1945
Nobel Prize for Peace. (www.cordellhullmuseum.com/history.html-14k) June 15, 2010.

was in the process of its final draft. She hoped to have it ready by the first of the year. Since Hazle believed it important to have the updated School of Nations booklets available for anyone reading the article who might want more information about the program, she requested that the *Pantagraph* postpone printing the article.[627]

A few days before Christmas, Hazle received an elegant Christmas card from Frederic Morgan, which he sent while vacationing in Florida. She was glad to hear from him, and told him, "My earnest hope is that things will be a little easier for you from now on—and that you are making the most of the weeks of comparatively carefree sunshine."[628] Although enjoying the holiday season herself, Hazle looked forward to beginning the New Year, anticipating the completion of the School of Nations booklet.

After the first of the year arrived, Rebeka sent a draft copy of the School of Nations booklet to Miss Tolley, the Bloomington *Pantagraph* reporter who had interviewed Hazle regarding the School of Nations program, and she wrote to Hazle, "I have been greatly impressed with the quiet way in which this project has shaped campus life in all directions." Her work in compiling the information about the School of Nations had given Rebeka a unique perspective and a new vision for the booklet, which she wanted to share with Hazle. She and Hazle agreed to meet in mid-March to discuss Rebeka's new insight.[629]

Inspired by what Rebeka had shared with her during their subsequent visit, Hazle wrote to her expressing gratitude for the work she had done on the booklet and confided to her, "I am delighted that we are going to be able to be more inclusive [with this booklet] than the earlier ones have been." She added that Miss Tolley was holding up the *Pantagraph* article until she received the final draft of the booklet.[630]

Reviewing the draft of the booklet for any additional corrections that needed to be made, Frederic became more fully aware of how significant the establishment of the School of Nations had been to Principia. He wrote to Hazle on March 31, 1949, "You cannot read the very brief statement made in the booklet without realizing the vital influence which the School of Nations is having in the education of our young Principians from the years of elementary school to their final year in college." He added, "We are indeed most grateful for your wisdom and foresight in establishing this work, and for your wonderful generosity in supporting it not only financially, but with your own ideas as well."[631]

In mid-April, Hazle received the corrected draft of the School of Nations booklet and a note from Rebeka, praising her for the initiation of the School of Nations. After reading the letter and the draft, Hazle thanked Rebeka for her dedicated work and pointed out a few minor mistakes to be corrected. Responding to Rebeka's praise regarding the School of Nations, she said, "My tiny poppy-seed of an idea could not have possibly grown and prospered as it has, were it not for the fertile ground of The Principia's acceptance and development." Hazle recognized that her idea would not have accomplished much if it had not been approved by Frederic in 1925, implemented through the conscientious efforts of George Andrews, and maintained by the past and present School of Nations committees.[632]

About the time of the printing of the new School of Nations booklet, Hazle attended the wedding of her son, Nelson, who married Emily June Bode on May 3, 1949. June Bode had grown up in McLean, a town not far from Bloomington. Many members of Hazle's family came together for the happy occasion, including Kate Lee and Ralph, who acted as Nelson's best man. It delighted Hazle that Nelson and June would be making their home in Chicago, and that Nelson had found employment with the William Wrigley, Jr. gum company in the machine design department.[633]

The day after the wedding, on May 4, the long-awaited article titled "Mrs. Ewing Backs School of Nations" appeared in the *Pantagraph*. Hazle had told the reporter, Miss Tolley, "The School of Nations was a brainchild born during a trip around the world in 1924." She explained, "Every place we went, I noticed that where we were able to stop for several weeks we discovered that the people and customs did not seem so strange anymore. It was right after the war (World War I) and it seemed to me the best way to work for world peace." She added that when she had returned home from the trip, she had shared her idea with the officials at Principia College in 1925, "to make it possible for students to study nations and habits, just like they study biology or Latin." The article stated that the School of Nations' museum and library, as well as travel scholarships, were available to all students regardless of their majors. It was also noted that it would cost $300,000 to construct the School of Nations building, and that Hazle had started a fund for the project, supplying half the amount.[634]

When the article appeared in the paper, Hazle and her friend, Julia Hodge, were on their way to Carmel, California, for a month's vacation. Obviously enjoying the trip, Hazle wrote to Frederic on May 21, "At long last I have taken the San Simeon Drive all the way from San Luis Obispo to Carmel. This was my fourth attempt! Now I am eager to do it again." She added that she had received a nice note from his friend, Toni Guentner.[635]

Frederic and Toni had become quite close since his divorce from Madeline became final in December 1948, after several years of living apart. Believing for some time that Frederic had been overworking and neglecting his own needs, Hazle had often encouraged him to take some time off for himself. She was glad to hear that he was doing so, and she thought Toni was having a good influence on him. She hoped to have the pleasure of meeting her soon.[636]

In late May 1949, Hazle wrote to Mary Towle regarding the activities of Principia's International Relations Clubs.[637] There had been such a club beginning in 1937, but it had not held regular meetings. Following World War II there had been greater interest in the club, and the students had been holding regular meetings twice a month, to which they often invited one of the foreign students to come share information about his or her country and culture. They also discussed foreign and domestic problems. Mary had written to Hazle about the regional meeting of International Relations Clubs in Muncie, Illinois, on March 10 and 11.[638] Hazle was encouraged to learn that the students talked about the problems of armaments and atomic energy, and considered the need for the moral force of the United Nations to offset the over-emphasis on military strength and physical force. Hazle told Mary, "We have the United Nations. It will work if we get behind it and push." She believed it to be important for students of all ages to know about the United Nations. She hoped to be able to visit a meeting of the International Relations Club the next time she came to the College campus.[639]

Frederic wrote to Hazle on June 14, 1949, that he and Toni planned to be married on June 20 at Toni's parents' home in Highlands, North Carolina. His brother, William, and his sister-in-law, Dorinda, were to be the only others present at the ceremony. He explained, "Both of us are eager to get settled into Eliestoun and start our lives together at Principia without delay, and any appropriate wedding trip is out of the question for financial reasons, anyway." He confided that:

> The closing days of this year have not been easy ones, from certain points of view, but they are passing smoothly enough as far as Principia's official business is concerned. I want, most earnestly, to express my deep gratitude for the degree to which God's goodness has been generously expressed toward me during this past year through your loving kindness and that of my fellow Board members.[640]

On January 4, 1950, when Frederic and Toni returned to Principia after the winter holidays, he wrote to Hazle, "Your lovingly generous wedding gift played an important part in our vacation, and I know you realize that we are deeply grateful for it, and especially the depth of friendship which prompted you to send it." It is unclear what she had given them for a wedding present.[641]

A few days later, when ordering her third packet of twenty-five School of Nations booklets since the fall, Hazle told Rebeka, "As time goes on, I find more and more interest in our School of Nations project." Hazle obviously enjoyed giving out the new booklet to interested individuals in her efforts to promote the School of Nations. The process of redesigning and updating the booklet had given Rebeka, as well as Frederic and others involved in the project, a greater interest in and awareness of the vital influence that the School of Nations had on the growth and development of Principia. They had also gained a deeper appreciation for Hazle, who had initiated the program, financially supported it, and continued to promote it at home and wherever she traveled.[642]

CHAPTER 27

OF HISTORICAL SIGNIFICANCE

$\mathcal{W}$ hile doing some secretarial work for the Board of Trustees in January 1950, Hazle discovered that several School of Nations reports were missing from her file. She asked Frederic if it were possible for her to receive copies of the reports. He had his secretary, Evelyn "Evvy" Shearston, retrieve the original reports from the archives and type copies for Hazle. The replacement of the reports made Hazle increasingly aware of the importance of Principia keeping accurate historical records, which provided information, not only for her, but also for Dr. Leonard in writing the story of the first fifty years of Principia in his book, *As the Sowing*. She recalled Frederic's statement that, "Principia fifty years from now will be greatly benefited" by the information contained in [these historical records]".[643] The historical significance of the School of Nations is distinctly apparent in those records.

An article, "School of Nations Fosters World Consciousness," written in February 1950 for the *Pilot* by a student reporter, George Farve, serves as an illustration. The young reporter used the archives to gather information to write about the School of Nations. He told his readers that the School of Nations was "a multi-activity organization from which every Principian benefits, whether he is immediately aware of it or not." He recorded a brief history of the program and reported that Hazle, "a Principia parent and supporter" provided the funds to establish the program.[644]

In June 1950, for the first time in the history of the School of Nations, Hazle actively participated in the commencement ceremony, personally handing out the School of Nations scholarships. She found the experience to be so inspiring and encouraging that she later wrote to Frederic that it was nice to "be able to look into the face" of each boy and girl as she handed out the scholarship awards. In the past, she had met the recipients after they came back to school from their trips. Now, having the opportunity to meet the students before they left on their adventures, Hazle looked forward to seeing what changes had taken place in them when they returned. For the first time, she had the experience of being sought out by students after the exercises who wanted to share with her, in some detail, what he or she hoped to gain from the experience.[645]

She wrote to Frederic about talking with the students after the ceremony, and told him that her experiences with young people had given her a different view of them than some of her contemporaries seemed to have. She sometimes found herself in a group of people who bemoaned what they considered to be the fact that the young people of today were not nearly as fine as they themselves had been when young. On those occasions, Hazle would tell them about the fine boys and girls she had met at Principia and through her other activities, who "have the breadth of interest and sense of responsibility few of her generation had at their age."[646]

In the summer of 1950, it is recorded in the history of the College, and of the mid-West, that a most devastating disease was destroying the elm trees. While at the ranch in late August, Hazle received a letter from Frederic reporting that the diseased condition of the elm trees on the campus seemed to be quite serious. She had prayed about the situation in the past, and Frederic reported that, "For a considerable period of months following your work, the progress of the disease which was attacking these trees appeared blocked." But now it seemed that the disease had broken out again in a "fairly ugly form." Hazle responded immediately to his request for her "earnest metaphysical support," which she continued to give for some months.[647]

That fall, when Hazle returned from the ranch, she discovered that Mrs. Louisa L. Wright of the Chicago Council on Foreign Relations would be giving a talk titled, "The United Nations in Action," on October 24 at Principia. She had heard much positive information about Wright and had high expectations that her talk would be inspiring and interesting. After attending it, Hazle confided to Frederic that she had wondered if Wright could possibly meet her high expectations. She admitted that Wright had, and, she told Frederic, "Isn't it a heartening thing to find people of her ability and charm working for our United Nations?"[648]

On January 19, 1951, Hazle received an invitation from Douglas Swett, chairman of the School of Nations Committee, to be Principia's official representative at the Fourth United Nations Institute,* which would be held on February 13-15 in New York City near Lake Success. He told her, "Knowing of your enthusiastic interest in the United Nations and its work, and your understanding of the importance of all our support . . . We could think of no one who could represent the School of Nations better than you." The Institute had been created a few years after the establishment of the United Nations in 1945 in order to inform School administrators, educators and others about the United Nations. Although Hazle had supported the United Nations from its inception, she had never attended any of the meetings. Accepting Swett's invitation and his offer to accompany her, she suggested that some of the committee members on the St. Louis campus join them. She looked forward to reading over the detailed information that Swett promised to send about the upcoming meetings at the Institute.[649]

In early February, Hazle received the information on the Fourth United Nations Institute from Swett, who wrote that he had made their train reservations and booked rooms for them at the Commodore Hotel in New York City. But the train reservations were unsure since the GM&O railroad was on strike. The ticket

* This was the fourth meeting held in New York since 1947 and before the United Nations buildings were completed in 1952.

office had issued them blank tickets and promised to call them about which train they should board and when. The call came, and Hazle, accompanied by Douglas Swett and Jennifer Bunting of England, the Spanish teacher at the Upper School in St. Louis, set off for New York. Despite the challenging situation with the railroad strike, they enjoyed their trip.[650]

Unfortunately, the experience was marred by a telegram Hazle received from Frederic on February 15, 1951, the last day of the meetings. He told her that Marshall Brooks, a former Principia student and a World War II pilot, had been killed on February 14. Marshall's personal plane had crashed in a remote and mountainous area in California, and his body had just been found. Frederic asked Hazle to break the news to Swett, who was a friend of Brooks. When she read the telegram, her first thoughts were of Marshall Brooks's parents, whom she knew because of their dedicated support of Principia. Her heart went out to them in prayer. She felt a great sense of gratitude for their firm foundation in Christian Science and knew they would find comfort and support in their understanding of God. Then, as Frederic had requested, she told Swett of the loss of his friend. He appreciated hearing about it so soon.[651]

A few weeks after she returned home from the meetings at the Institute, Hazle wrote to Frederic thanking him for his part in having her go as the representative for Principia, and told him that, "It was an inspiring and most rewarding experience." She felt she had learned much that she could share about the United Nations with the Principia community, her friends, and her family. Frederic responded on March 2, "We need not only your enthusiasm, but your active participation in this work if it is to achieve all that both you and I expect that it will achieve." He also reported that the elm trees did not seem to be improving, but they were not growing any worse either.[652]

At the end of April 1951, Hazle received a most surprising letter from Frederic which began, "For the first time in 36 years, I am planning to be absent from Principia at commencement time." He and Toni were sailing for Amsterdam on April 27. He had met with the Executive Board of Trustees in the middle of March. They felt he needed a leave of absence and a temporary release from his responsibilities. His brother, William, would take over his work and conduct the commencement that year. Hazle had urged Frederic many times to take better care of himself and enthusiastically approved of him taking an extended vacation. Neither Frederic nor Hazle, however, recognized this compulsory vacation as a sign of things to come.[653]

That summer, Hazle took a supply of School of Nations booklets with her to the ranch, one of which she sent to Adlai Stevenson, since he had expressed an interest in seeing the new edition. In July, he wrote, "Dear Cousin Hazle . . . I have looked at the brochure on the School of Nations. The format is superb and I shall read it with interest. You were good to think of me."[654]

In November, Hazle attended the Trustee meetings and enjoyed seeing Frederic, who had returned to his work at Principia from his trip abroad rested and refreshed. Immediately following the meetings, he left for the West Coast with the main purpose of working with an architect to find ways in which they could build the School of Nations and Administration buildings most economically.[655]

While waiting to hear news from Frederic regarding the School of Nations building, Hazle enjoyed receiving a letter from Douglas Swett, whom she had come to know better while they were in New York City at the United Nations Institute meetings. He wrote that he and four students from the School of Nations had spent an evening with the Jerseyville Women's Club, who "seemed very much interested in the work of the School of Nations," and expressed their appreciation for the willingness of the students to tell them about the Principia College campus. Concluding his letter, Swett thanked Hazle for her willingness to share her experiences with the School of Nations students, and for her interest "in every individual" with whom she came in contact.[656]

At the end of December, Hazle received a letter from Frederic, telling her that the drawings for School of Nations building "will achieve economies without in any way seriously infringing on the original plans for the building," and added, "I like the new plans better than the former ones." She was also glad to hear from him about a students' forum being established in connection with the League of Women voters. She told Frederic that such an activity "does its bit toward international understanding which we must have to eliminate war."[657]

Frederic's news about the building plans gave Hazle great joy. The history of the School of Nations had revealed the significance and impact of the program. Hazle fervently believed, however, that a building to house the program would greatly enhance the education of Principia students in international understanding. In addition, the building would be a visible representation of the idea behind the School of Nations, and she hoped it would encourage the entire College community to be promoters of world peace in some way.

CHAPTER 28

POSSESS MY SOUL IN PATIENCE

$\mathcal{A}$ t the end of December, when Hazle responded to Frederic about the new plans for the School of Nations, she simply stated that the new plans should be better, "Since we are all working with Principle as our guide." But on January 2, 1952, she admitted being overwhelmed with the desire to talk with him about the building plans and told him, "I'll be eager to hear news from San Francisco as soon as you have it, and we can get together." She could hardly be blamed for her earnest interest in seeing and discussing the plans. After all, she had been waiting for the construction of the building for nearly twenty-one years. During those years, the plans had been drawn up more than once, only to be put aside because of a more urgent need at the school. She had high hopes that her dream of having a building for the School of Nations would be realized at last. But the rising cost of materials threatened to postpone their plans for construction once again. [658]

In mid-January, while waiting to hear more from Frederic about the building plans, Hazle busied herself with other activities, which included her responsibilities as secretary to the Board of Trustees. She read and returned several letters that had been forwarded to her by Evvy, Frederic's secretary. She enjoyed the friendly interactions she had with Evvy, who always added a personal note with the business letters she forwarded. In one such note, she told Hazle that she and the other office girls sent their good wishes. When returning the business letters to Evvy, Hazle told her, "Please thank the girls in the office for their good wishes and give them my best." [659]

269

Although Hazle did not hear from Frederic right away, she received a heartening letter from her good friend, Eldredge Hamlin, the Comptroller at Principia College, who reported that the architects were currently working on the library plans because of the pressing need for it to be completed. When the plans for the library were finished, they would start on the plans for the School of Nations. Knowing how long Hazle had been waiting for this project to finally go forward, he told her, "You can rest assured that the other work will proceed as rapidly as possible, and we shall keep you fully advised about them."[660]

On February 7, Hazle received a letter from Frederic reporting that the architects, Henry Gutterson and William Sturtevant, would arrive on the weekend and spend a week working on the "master plan" for the College campus. Delighted to have some news from Frederic and looking forward to discussing the plans with him after the architects left, she responded to his letter immediately. She reaffirmed her desire to meet with him to talk about the plans for the School of Nations building, as well as the other buildings, but she would not be available February 17-20 because she and Julia would be at the American Association for the United Nations Conference in Chicago. Since they had "missed the one last year," they were "especially eager to attend this one."[661]

As promised, Frederic kept Hazle informed of the progress being made on the plans, writing on February 11 that the architects had arrived and were studying the plans of the School of Nations, the School of Government, and the areas where the buildings would be erected. At that point, however, all he knew for sure was that Gertsch and Leonard, who would be teaching in the new School of Nations building, had determined the classrooms needed to be larger, which meant there would be fewer classrooms. But he felt confident this would not change the external plans of the building. The plans for the library had been completed, but there seemed to be an immense amount of work still to do before plans for the other two buildings could be finished. He confided to her that Gutterson's stay of one week "seems very short indeed, but we will do the best we can to cover all the items in that period."[662]

Hazle received another report from Frederic the first of March, in which he told her that he had received permission from the Executive Board of Trustees to instruct Gutterson to make the necessary changes to the classrooms in the School of Nations building plan, which would cost approximately $6,250. But Gutterson had been unable to complete the plans and mail them in time for the meeting. It encouraged Hazle to know that the Board members were "inspired at the thought that it may be possible to erect the School of Nations Building simultaneously with the Library." Hazle anticipated that she would soon see the plans.[663]

At the Principia Patrons' Conference on May 10, 1952, believing that the construction of the School of Nations building would soon be underway, Hazle thought it appropriate to share how she had been inspired to present the idea of the School of Nations to Principia. She told her audience that during her school years, "It seemed to me that the history of the world was made up of far too much war. As quite a young girl, I remember wishing that I could do something to bring about a more peaceful world."[664]

She explained to the Patrons that the idea for the School of Nations began to develop during the world trip that she and her family had taken in 1924 and 1925. The trip provided occasions for her to come into contact with "the thinkers, the educators, and the leaders in each of the countries." Wherever they went, she found that the people, "were so friendly, so cooperative, so generous in wishing to share . . . the good things in each of their countries" that she came home "feeling that if everyone could take such a trip . . . there would be never be any more war." A few months after they returned from their trip, she was sitting in her garden reading the Christian Science Bible Lesson when the idea for the School of Nations unfolded to her. Inspired by the idea, she wrote to Frederic Morgan, and received his approval and support. She concluded, "What we have now has all grown from that little poppy seed of an idea."[665]

As spring passed into summer, work continued on the building plans. Hazle attended the commencement ceremonies at Principia College in June, and soon after left for the ranch in Wisconsin. While at the ranch, she wrote a supportive and encouraging letter to Adlai Stevenson regarding his nomination by the Democratic Party to run for President of the United States:[666]

> I am sure you know that all the family have been deeply moved by your nomination and its promise. Remembering your earnest hesitancy about taking over the heavy burdens of such a nomination, I was heartened by finding these words while studying our Christian Science lesson a few days ago . . . – "Right motives give pinions to thought, and strength and freedom to speech and action." (*Science and Health with Key to the Scriptures* page 454, lines 19-21).[667]

> You have right motives which will give you the strength and freedom to meet the wide opportunities and great responsibilities.

> Two verses in Numbers also made me think of you and wonder if you had happened to come across them since your nomination. They are Chapter 11 verses 16 and 17.

> It is deeply heartening to know that you are turning to the Bible for inspiration and strength during these testing days.

> In spite of the fact that I am deeply sorry, on your account, that you must take over the heavy burdens of a presidential campaign, I am nevertheless profoundly grateful that . . . this highest office in our great land should seek the man (or woman), and not the man the office.[668]

She concluded her letter expressing her deep respect and affection for him, "Please know that my warmest love and heartiest good wishes are yours always." Stevenson genuinely appreciated Hazle's encouragement and support. He responded to her on August 19, 1952: "I am much heartened by your letter and [how] well you understand the months of sore trial that I have been through in seeking the right path and that there is only one place to turn for guidance."[669]

When returning home from the ranch in October, Hazle actively supported a fund drive for Principia, which Frederic hoped would bring in enough revenue to build the School of Nations, the School of Government, and the Administration buildings. She also learned that the School of Nations committee had sponsored an activity in which some young men from the Philippines had participated. The committee had been impressed by the quality of the young Filipinos, and thought they had done a "super job" in presenting points for discussion which had been highly controversial and caused them, at times, to be in sharp, but courteous disagreement. It had been a "very stimulating and thought provoking" experience for all involved. It gratified Hazle to know that the School of Nations committee continued to sponsor talks and activities that stimulated the constant flow of progressive thinking at Principia.[670]

The November Trustee meetings greatly inspired Hazle, and she wrote to Frederic: "I am still breathless from it. I'll be eager to know the reaction to the *Monitor* article about the move of the Upper and Lower Schools to the new St. Louis campus." She genuinely appreciated what this move meant to Principia, and she expressed no disappointment over the lack of progress being made on the plans for the School of Nations building. She remained unwavering in her trust that it would be built. As an indication of her conviction, she contributed Wrigley shares in the amount of $12,240 on December 30, 1952, to the School of Nations Building Fund.[671]

During the early winter months of 1953, Hazle and Julia escaped the cold weather in Bloomington and enjoyed a vacation at the South Winds Club in Lake Placid, Florida. Frederic forwarded a letter to her there, which he had received from Mrs. Elizabeth Carroll Scott's Christian Science Association praising the work of the School of Nations. The members of Scott's association wanted to award a Grant-in-Aid to a worthy student involved with the School of Nations program. In response, Hazle told Frederic, "It is gratifying to have the work of the School of Nations recognized and encouraged in this way. . . . I am deeply grateful to you and the many others on both campuses whose interest and work have contributed to the success of the School of Nations thus far." She confided to him that she sincerely wished she lived close enough to take advantage of all the talks and programs that the School of Nations provided.[672]

In late February 1953, Frederic reported to Hazle that he expected to have the School of Nations building plans by the first of March. He explained that he was endeavoring to work it out so that the School of Nations and Library could be built at the same time, as they had discussed. This plan seemed especially wise since he had learned that the price of building materials had gone up significantly and that it would cost $625,402 to construct the School Nations if built separate from the Library and Administration buildings. Including it with the other two buildings would cut the cost in half.[673]

Hazle thanked Frederic for "explaining in detail the situation about the construction of the three-building-group." Although waiting for the construction of all three buildings to begin would mean another delay, she realized that the savings on the cost made it worthwhile. She told him, "I am delighted that you have found it practical to work out the plan as we talked over the last time I was in your office." But she lamented, "Would that we could have put up the School of Nations building when I first began contributing to it."[674]

Relieved that Hazle saw the value in waiting a bit longer for the construction to begin, Frederic wrote to her, "Of course, I shall need to see you and talk some important details over with you before any action can be taken, but to know that you are so joyously ready to go ahead is good news, indeed." Before actual work could begin on the School of Nations building, though, they had to find the funds to build the ground floor of the Administration building. In spite of the delay and the need for funds, Hazle expected that Frederic would have something "interesting to report" when she returned home. [675]

On April 29, 1953, Hazle wrote to Frederic from Bloomington, "I am all eagerness for the many interesting things you will have to tell and show me." She appreciated receiving the detailed reports that he sent to her while she was away, and now that she was home, she looked forward to seeing the plans and talking with him in detail about them. But when Frederic came to discuss the building plans with her in May, it stunned Hazle to learn that the cost of building materials had once again increased.[676]

As a result of their meeting, Hazle told Frederic, "I am hoping some miracle will supply the remainder of the funds needed to build it, before costs skyrocket again. It is hard to comprehend how a building that could have been built for the $150,000, which I offered in 1931, could now cost much more than twice that amount." She had been greatly disappointed to learn that they had only $165,737.61 in the School of Nations Building Fund, and that it would take an additional $250,000 before they could even start on the foundation. She told Frederic that she wished she could "double and treble this fund right now." Although dismayed and disappointed, Hazle assured Frederic, "If the School of Nations, and the special building for it are right ideas, as they have seemed to be thus far, the way will be opened—if not, I shall have to 'possess my soul in patience' until the right time comes."[677]

WINDS OF CHANGE

CHAPTER 29

A FRIEND IN NEED

*H*azle spent the summer of 1953 at the ranch with her family, hoping to hear some encouraging news from Frederic regarding the construction of the building. But it did not come. She did receive, however, a report from the School of Nations committee regarding their upcoming programs and activities. On October 9 through 11, the School of Nations committee would be sponsoring a seminar on oriental art in Chicago. For the fall program at the College, the committee chose to focus on Egypt and Pakistan. In mid-October, students from the Middle East Institute in Washington, D.C. who came from those two countries would be visiting the College campus. The Institute had been established by George Camp Keiser and former Secretary of State, Christian Herter, in 1946, with the purpose of promoting understanding between the countries of the Middle East and the United States. In addition, the School of Nations committee had arranged for Dr. Mohannand Khlafallah, of the University of Alexandria in Egypt, to give a talk on October 16 in the Chapel, as well as a visit from Dr. Mohamed el-Bahay of Al-Azhar University. Hazle was inspired by the report and appreciated the consistently high quality of the programs and activities provided by the School of Nations committee.[678]

In late October, when Hazle arrived home from the ranch, she found a letter from Frederic awaiting her. She read the disturbing news that "building costs have advanced at an appalling rate, and union regulations and working conditions have definitely affected the type of buildings which are being constructed." Because of the

279

rising costs, he believed it necessary to completely redesign not only
the Library but the School of Nations and Administration buildings.
The situation demanded that they design "a simpler type of building
than the one originally planned, and one which can be built for a
much more reasonable figure." In addition, he would have to hire
another contractor. Hazle had cause to lament once again that the
building had not been erected in the 1930s, as first intended, but
she bore the news with patience.[679]

She responded to Frederic, thanking him for updating her on
the progress and the problems. She enclosed a newspaper clipping
titled "How Construction Trades Blackmail Contractors" from the
Milwaukee Sentinel that she had picked up in Wisconsin on her way
home from the ranch. She hoped the article would supply some
helpful information.[680]

Although the news of the rising cost of materials must have
been discouraging to Hazle, she did not dwell on it. Instead, she
addressed Frederic's concerns regarding his struggle with a personal
problem, which he had expressed in a letter to all of the Board of
Trustee members. She appreciated his openness, and told him, "It
seems to me to be far more honest and dignified for us to have the
information directly from you—than to hear gossipy and garbled
reports in round-about ways." She regretted that he was having to
deal with this personal problem in the midst of conducting a fund
drive for the St. Louis campus, and told him, "I can't help wishing
with all my heart that we could save you from it." She assured him
that she and the other trustees would be able to help, now that they
knew about it.[681]

On November 11, 1953, Frederic wrote two letters to Hazle. In
one of the letters he thanked her for the article on construction
blackmail, and explained that he had tried to find out the reason
why labor costs were so high in their area but had not received a
satisfactory answer. The other letter was of a personal nature, in
which he wrote, "Thank you most sincerely for your wonderfully

understanding letter with regard to my personal affairs." He confided that he had always felt her support for Principia during challenging times, but he especially wanted to express his gratitude for her sense of spiritual balance and unfaltering friendship that were helping him work through his personal crisis. He appreciated her calm, steady, positive ways that provided him "vital assistance in maintaining confidence in the guidance of the one divine Mind and assurance that right conditions can only be demonstrated in human experience by following divine guidance regardless of human criticism, misunderstanding, fear, or false sympathy." Frederic found Hazle to be, as she had always been, "a wonderfully true and loyal and understanding friend."[682]

When Hazle attended the Trustee meetings later in November, she stayed with Toni and Frederic at Eliestoun, their home in Elsah, which overlooked the Mississippi River. She found inspiration in being "so high above the Great River," which enabled her to remain undisturbed by the unresolved issues surrounding the excessive cost of building materials and the delay in completing the plans for the School of Nations. Hazle remained confident that these problems would be resolved, and made another substantial donation to the building fund in November.[683]

At the beginning of 1954, the Executive Board of Principia believed that Frederic's personal problems were interfering with his ability to oversee the College. William Morgan, his brother, took over as President, but Frederic was allowed to maintain his position as the Chairman of the Board of Trustees. Following his removal as President, Frederic wrote to Hazle thanking her for her donations to the School of Nations Building Fund and expressed gratitude for her unselfish and generous support of the school since its beginning. He especially wanted to thank her for being "a constant source of great satisfaction" to him during his days as President, and for "some of the happiest memories of what must always be regarded as a very constructive period in Principia's history." Hazle understood

Frederic's sorrow over being removed as the President of Principia College, and she was grateful to see that the situation had not diminished his interest in the school.[684]

When spring came, Hazle traveled to Lake Placid, Florida, and other Southern cities, which prevented her from attending the Pan American Day sponsored by the Upper School and four other schools in the area. She regretted not being there and hoped that she would have another opportunity to attend such an event in the future, for she believed that all individuals, young and old, should learn as much as possible about our Latin American neighbors "in order to understand them better."[685]

She also missed the visit that the Air Force Academy Site Selection Commission made to Principia College in March 1954. The Commission had determined four years earlier that the College was one of 29 possible sites for the Air Academy. But between 1950 and 1954, the officials at Principia had no idea that the College campus was still being considered as a candidate to become the site of the Academy. In May 1954, William Morgan received notice from the Commission that the College campus had been selected for the short list, which also included Lake Geneva, Wisconsin, and Colorado Springs, Colorado. In addition, he learned that the chambers of commerce in St. Louis and Alton were actively promoting the Elsah site. The St. Louis Chamber of Commerce President, A.P. Kaufman, had the misinformed idea that the College campus was going to be moved to the Country Campus, which was actually the new site for the Lower, Middle, and Upper Schools. William and the entire Principia community fervently opposed the idea of the College becoming "the central part of the academy."[686]

Hazle's friend, and the Comptroller for the College, Eldredge Hamlin, took on the massive task of organizing and mobilizing all Christian Scientists in a letter-writing campaign to ask President Eisenhower to spare Principia College and to locate the Academy at one of the other two sites. He also organized Principia staff members, a few students, and local volunteers in an "around-the-clock effort" to telephone, write, and telegraph thousands of Christian Scientists around the world to carry on this protest by writing directly to both President Eisenhower and the Air Force secretary, Harold Talbot.[687]

In addition to Hamlin's efforts, Principia received help from R.S. Doenges, a member of the Colorado Springs Site Committee. He became involved when he learned of Principia's situation through Jane Long Andrews, his partner's sister, who was also the wife of George Andrews and the daughter-in-law of George A. Andrews, who had been instrumental in establishing the School of Nations and had served as the first dean of the College. Doenges learned that George Andrews's brother, John Andrews, currently held the position of development director at Principia, and contacted him. John then obtained the site proposal, maps, and other information regarding the Elsah site, which he shared with Doenges, who then contacted 1,800 local property owners and businesses in the St. Louis and Alton areas to make them aware of what was happening. He and other volunteers also organized citizen meetings at schools, homes, community buildings, and the Jersey County courthouse to inform people in and around Elsah that their homes and farms could be taken under the right of eminent domain.[688]

In spite of these valiant efforts to save the Principia College campus, Secretary Talbot seemed unimpressed by the many letters and telegrams received at the White House. Later in May, he met with Principia officials and explained the position of the Air Force and what they planned to do. When the meeting concluded, the whole group walked over to the Chapel. Talbot admired the architecture of the building and then said, "This is beautiful. We can leave it, but the rest of these buildings must go." His comment must have been devastating to the Principia officials in light of all the interest, sacrifice, time, effort, and money that had gone into building up the campus.[689]

It was fortunate for the College that the newspapers focused on Principia's opposition to the Academy being built in Elsah, which provided much publicity for their cause. The promoters of the Academy in St. Louis and Alton attempted to convince Principia to stop its opposition, because they believed that having the Academy in Elsah would bring relief to the economic slump in the St. Louis and Alton areas. A few days before the final decision was made, in the midst of the disagreement, Frederic wrote to the Trustees: "Whatever may be the final outcome of this matter, I am sure we are all convinced God will protect all right ideas. Since there can be no conflict between two right ideas, there is no basis of conflict between the Air Force Academy and the needs of Principia."[690]

Refusing to give up on saving the campus from being turned into an Air Force Academy, Christian Scientists continued to write letters and send telegraphs to Talbot and Eisenhower. Then, someone remembered that Charlotte Prichard, a former staff member of Principia, had been given an appointive position by Eisenhower, a long time friend of hers and her deceased husband. William called Charlotte, who happened to be having dinner alone with Ike and Mamie that evening, and she assured him that she would seek the President's help in saving the campus. It is not known what turned the tide, but on June 24, 1954, it was decided that the Academy would be built in Colorado Springs. Having by this time returned to her home in Bloomington, Hazle received the good news and rejoiced with her friends at Principia.[691]

In mid-July, while at the ranch, Hazle received a letter from Frederic regarding a $30 contribution made by Adeline Adams for the School of Nations Fund. Adeline had written to him, "Some typing I did for our wonderful friend, Mrs. Hazle B. Ewing, has enabled me to make this contribution and her enthusiasm and inspirational ideas about this building and its purpose made me wish to give more. I hope I can." Frederic enclosed a copy of his letter to Adeline for Hazle, in which he had said, "The benefits of this work touch the lives of thousands of young people making them more intelligently aware of their brothers and sisters in other countries." Hazle appreciated knowing about Adeline's contribution and Frederic's response to her.[692]

As a Trustee, Hazle received a letter from Frederic telling of a fall he had from a ladder in early July while repairing a light fixture at Eliestoun. He had immediately called a practitioner, with whom he continued to work, but he had been out of the office for more than three weeks. His fall from the ladder had been most inopportune, since he and Toni were packing to move to St. Louis. He told the Trustees that he found he could not be of much help on the day their furniture was moved, and had spent the day at Cox Cottage. Frederic had enjoyed his stay at the Cottage, which was staffed by Christian Science nurses and provided a quiet place for students and other members of the Principia College community to work out physical problems. He confided to the Trustees, "Never before have I fully appreciated the wonderful facilities which Cox Cottage provides."[693]

Knowing that Frederic's fall and convalescence had been especially challenging because of their move to the St. Louis campus, Hazle wrote to him on August 19, 1954, "As regrettable as the fall was, we have much to be grateful for that it was not even more serious and that you are making steady progress." Since he had fallen right after the decision was made to locate the Air Academy in Colorado Springs instead of Elsah, Hazle thought that he probably did not realize the attention that the College had been receiving. She told him the newspaper coverage had given Principia publicity "far beyond anything that any of [us] could have planned or secured." She believed that although the situation had seemed to be a threat to the school, it had turned out to be a blessing instead, bringing Principia into the forefront of public thought.[694]

Hazle also expressed to Frederic her gratitude for the substantial donation that Miss Florence Bartlett had given to the School of

Nations and for the completion of the plans for the Marshall Brooks Memorial Library. She derived encouragement from this news and looked forward to the School of Nations building plans being completed as well. She recognized that Frederic had expended a great deal of effort to bring about the completion of the plans for the Library, and she invited him and Toni to come to the ranch for a few days of well-deserved vacation. But they declined since they had so much to do before the fall term began.[695]

In September, although Frederic seemed much better physically and had returned to work full time, Hazle knew that his mental anguish over being removed as President of the College still lingered. He had confided to her, "Frankly I have not been able to free myself fully of a terrible sense of hurt expressed in a number of different ways since the meeting with the Board of Trustees last November." He admitted that he had made mistakes and his personal problems had "opened the door to what took place." But he felt that the Board had acted in haste, and he seemed unable to overcome the feeling that his "career as a loyal and true Principian had been irreparably hurt by both [his] personal problems and by the action of the board." He sometimes felt overwhelmed by the "most oppressive sense of discouragement and frustration" because of what he perceived as a lack of compassion on the part of his closest associates. He believed that he had overcome his sense of resentment toward the Board, but not the disappointment. Hazle encouraged him to keep working with a practitioner, knowing that he would be freed from his feelings of frustration and disappointment and eventually be able to see the spiritual progress he had made through this experience.[696]

When she returned to Bloomington that fall, Hazle was pleased to fulfill Frederic's request that she give a short talk at the ceremony for the mounting of a plaque on the Lillian Brewer Buck House. At the ceremony, she shared with those in attendance the interest that her mother had in the prosperity of Principia, and how this building, for which her mother had supplied the funds, represented her mother's love for the College. It gave Hazle great joy to see the plaque placed on the building named in honor of her mother.[697]

Later that fall, Hazle received reports from students who had been traveling during the summer as part of the School of Nations program. Mitzi Jeanne LaBree, who had spent the summer in Europe, wrote that, she had gained "a tremendous appreciation of people with different ideas, backgrounds, and standards . . . " and an "objective love for my country, which is so strong that I can never be a passive citizen—there's too much to be done." Impressed by Miss LaBree's sentiments, Hazle saw in her a real desire to be "the best kind of American citizen," and she hoped that Miss LaBree would find a way to stimulate active participation in her own community.[698]

At the end of December, Hazle made a substantial donation of $25,356.25 to the School of Nations Building Fund. Since Frederic and William were both out of town when the donation arrived at Principia, Hamlin responded for them, admitting, "our hearts will not rest until we see that lovely building rising on the Elsah campus as a tribute to you, individually, and to what you have always stood for."[699]

Upon his return to Elsah in mid-January 1955, Frederic wrote to Hazle in appreciation of her donation to the School of Nations building: "You are certainly wonderfully generous to Principia and a true friend, and I hope with all my heart it may be possible to begin to plan for the School of Nations in the very near future." Frederic felt especially grateful to Hazle for the support of her friendship during a most trying time in his life, and he knew that she could always be depended on to support Principia in times of need. As a true friend, Hazle was genuinely glad to see Frederic once again immersed in his work. His physical disability had improved, and his feelings of hurt and frustration had been overcome. She knew that the upcoming speaking engagements he had scheduled in California would be good for him and result in increased donations for the Lower School building.[700]

CHAPTER 30

A TIME FOR CHANGE

$\mathcal{W}$illiam Morgan, as President of the College, decided in February 1955 that some changes needed to be made in the School of Nations committee and program. He was unable to make the trip to Bloomington to talk with Hazle in person, so he wrote her a detailed letter. He explained that when he had taken the position of President at the College, he had noticed "a calm and casual acceptance on the part of students" regarding the work of the School of Nations, which seemed to indicate a lack of enthusiasm or interest. He thought that there needed to be a new and more vigorous approach and proposed a change in the committee personnel, suggesting that Dr. Leonard take over as committee chairman for the School of Nations. Douglas Swett, the present chair, would stay on the committee for a year to "supply a background of understanding to the new chairman."[701]

In addition to the change in personnel, William proposed having the same number of speakers but spending less money on travel scholarships. He also planned to have a "good deal more student activity in small groups: discussion groups, informal forums, possibly study groups, involving the participation of the International Relations Club and foreign students." The committee, he told her, has already implemented part of the program and it has been "enthusiastically received."[702]

What really caught Hazle's attention, however, was the Principia Abroad program. William proposed having a group of junior and senior students go abroad with a faculty member to pursue appropriate studies for which they would earn a full college credit. She could see the advantages of this new program compared to what they had done in the past, when students studying abroad had been handicapped by losing college credits for one or more terms. In addition, the students would be involved with other Principians, which had not been the case when students participated in the Delaware Foreign Study Group at the University of Delaware to prepare for Foreign Service work.[703]

According to William's plan, students studying abroad would pay their normal tuition for a regular term at the College plus a modest travel expense. The faculty member's salary would be paid by Principia and his or her travel expenses, room, and board by the School of Nations. It had been initially thought that an Abroad would be planned for alternate years. But, a substantial bequest from Miss Florence Bartlett for the purpose of enabling Principia students to gain an understanding of foreign countries made it possible to provide one each year.[704]

On the first Abroad, which would begin in August and end in December before Christmas, the students would pursue their studies in England, and spend the last week in Paris. On the second Abroad, students would visit various parts of Europe and end their stay in London. The committee hoped to have students actually live with Christian Science families while in England and France. William concluded, "If you feel that these are good and satisfactory developments, we will proceed with the program immediately."[705]

Hazle responded to William on February 18, 1955, regarding his proposed changes: "I have read, and reread, and pondered it—and am glad to say that I do give this new plan for the School of Nations activities my whole-hearted blessing." The Principia Abroad reminded her of a similar but more limited experience she had had as a student attending the University of Chicago. She had been "deeply grateful for that broadening of [her] understanding of people and problems through [her] accepting the opportunity to have a whole quarter of study and residence in the South," at Stetson University in Florida. Her own experience convinced her that the Abroad Program would benefit students by providing them first-hand opportunities to learn what was going on in the rest of the world, which would ultimately make them better citizens in their own communities.[706]

William wrote to Hazle on March 8, 1955, that the financial aspects of the Principia Abroad plan were being worked out and an announcement of the program would be made within six months. Responding, Hazle expressed her appreciation to William for proposing the Principia Abroad program and her gratitude for the generous bequest from Florence Bartlett, which had made the Abroad possible on a yearly basis. In addition, she was thankful for the donation from Angie Cox, which provided scholarships for graduate students seeking careers with the State Department.[707]

Hazle had occasion to write William again at the end of the month confirming her interest in the Principia Abroad program and assuring him that she would be careful not to mention it to anyone except Julia, until Principia had announced it. In answer to his suggestion that the School of Government become involved in the plan, she told him, "It would be especially gratifying—in view of the many previous occasions of cooperation—if the two schools, the School of Nations and the School of Government, could join hands in this constructive and far-reaching project."[708]

Julia and Hazle enjoyed the bright and warm spring Sunday afternoon as Herman drove them down to Principia for the announcement of the Principia Abroad program the next morning, Monday, May 9. It impressed Hazle that the drive had been made significantly shorter by the completion of Route 66 further south. She realized it would now be possible for her to make the round trip in one day, which would enable her to bring a group of friends to see the campus whenever she wished.[709]

On Monday morning, before William made the announcement,

Hazle spoke to the students and faculty about her "hope for the School of Nations as a whole." When William announced the Principia Abroad program, it caused quite a stir among the students. Immediately after the disbursement of the crowd, a senior girl approached Hazle to tell her personally that she had already filled out an application for the first Abroad. A few days after Hazle had returned home, William wrote of his appreciation for her participation in the program and told her that many students had spoken to him about what she had said and "were delighted to feel that they had the opportunity of getting to know you" a little better. Hazle responded: "I thoroughly enjoyed being present, and shall long remember the enthusiastic student reaction to the announcement."[710]

An announcement of a different kind, also made in early May, gave Hazle another reason for gratitude. Her son, Nelson Ewing, had been appointed to be the new Design Director for the Elgin National Watch Company. On May 11, 1955, an article appeared in *The Daily Pantagraph* reporting Nelson's appointment and pointing out that both Nelson and his wife, June Bode Ewing, had grown up in McLean County. Friends and family members sent Hazle newspaper clippings and magazine articles from different parts of the country regarding the announcement. Hazle rejoiced with Nelson, June, and their four children, Ted, Sandra, Philip, and Davis, over the good news.[711]

Nelson's life-experience had prepared him for the position he now held in the Elgin Watch Company. He had been introduced to metal-work and design by Louise Andrews early in his education at Principia. It was Louise who "recognized that he had enough talent" to justify Hazle encouraging him to continue his study in that direction. After leaving Principia, he studied design at Cranbrook in Bloomfield Hills, Michigan, art at Washington University, and design and engineering at the Illinois Institute of Technology.[712]

After completing his formal education, Nelson studied as an apprentice under James H. Winn. Later, he organized the Silver House and designed hand-crafted jewelry. During World War II, he became the superintendent of the W.M. Wrigley Company ration machinery division. When the war came to an end, Nelson instructed disabled veterans at Hines Veterans Hospital in creative design, for which he received a commendation from the Veterans Administration. He later began working at the Elgin Watch Company as a Design Coordinator where he created an adjustable watchband, helped design a display unit, and promoted major changes in packaging. No doubt his hard work, talent, and ingenuity had ultimately brought about his promotion to Design Director.[713]

In June 1955, it meant a great deal to Hazle to attend the College commencement exercises and a surprise retirement party given in honor of her long-time friends George A. Andrews and Sam Baker. She was grateful that William had provided accommodations for Herman, her driver, since it enabled her to come and go as she needed. She had been asked by Frederic to be part of a committee assigned to determine an appropriate way to honor Mary Kimball Morgan and William Edgar Morgan as the founders of Principia. Before returning home, she met with her fellow committee members to discuss the options of having a service award dedicated to the Morgans, or a portrait made of Mrs. Morgan, or arranging a day-long celebration in honor of the founders. The committee finally settled on having a Founder's Day Celebration.[714]

When at the ranch in late June, Hazle received a copy of *As the Sowing* by Dr. Leonard, which she had requested from Principia. To her delight, the book arrived with a letter from Evvy, who was filling in for Frederic's secretary, Alice Parham, who had taken a month-long vacation. Evvy told Hazle, "It feels like old times to address a letter to you from this office." After her month filling in for Alice, Evvy planned to return to Miami, Florida, where she was employed as a first grade teacher. She confided to Hazle, "I find it awfully good to be here, and only wish I could be seeing you."[715]

On August 1, 1955, Hazle's brother, Nelson, sent a letter to William Morgan from his office in Chicago on her behalf regarding the School of Nations Building Fund. The letter pointed out that during the past two years Hazle had been faithfully adding thousands of dollars to the building fund, but the plans had not been completed. It seemed reasonable for her to ask William, "Could you let me know, sometime soon, what amount is needed—in addition to what is already on hand—before we can go ahead with the plans and actual construction of the School of Nations building?" She hoped to hear from him before Labor Day, while she was still at the ranch.[716]

William responded to the letter in late August when he returned from his summer vacation and told Hazle that Eldredge Hamlin was preparing a statement regarding how much money she had accumulated in the Building Fund. But the plans could not be completed—nor construction begin—since the School of Nations had been designed as one of three wings in a single building. The Board of Trustees would discuss the plans, however, at their annual meeting. He reminded her that "there are a good many facets that need to be considered" before "we can even start to discuss the matter with an architect—and so get actual costs." He apologized for having to put her off on a matter he knew was so important to her, and admitted, "It would be my own nature to want to go ahead rapidly and definitely on it." But he thought it would be to her advantage to wait a bit longer for the decision to be made, which he believed would result in lower construction costs. Since it seemed necessary to "wait a bit longer," Hazle wrote to William on August 28, that his suggestion was "entirely satisfactory," and added, "I'll be deeply interested in knowing the details as they develop."[717]

Although Hazle did not know when the building plans would be completed or construction on the building would begin, she made another generous donation to the School of Nations Building Fund on September 14 through Nelson Buck's office. In response, William wrote to Nelson, whom he had never met, "Our appreciation of Mrs. Ewing's many kindnesses to Principia is very great, I assure you, and we also want to thank you for the assistance you have given in many important matters."[718]

In late October, Hazle received Dr. Leonard's first report as the new chairman of the School of Nations Committee, in which he wrote, "I am particularly delighted with the way the International School of Relations Club is unfolding." The club had sent a delegate and an alternate to participate in a model United Nations assembly on the campus of Washington University on Friday, October 21, which had been televised at 9:00 p.m. that day. The club had also started charging dues so they would not have to depend upon the School of Nations fund for any large subsidy.[719]

Leonard told her about the School of Nations sponsoring a talk on the United Nations, to be given on November 14 by Jacob M. Lashly of St. Louis, a member of the United Nations Appellate Tribunal, which greatly interested her. And it gave her great satisfaction to learn that twelve students had applied for the next Principia Abroad. Leonard also reported that they would be issuing "a new up-to-date version" of the School of Nations booklet to replenish their supply. Hazle had been so focused on the building that she not given any thought to the booklet for quite some time. She was glad to know of their plan to print a new version.[720]

In November, Hazle attended the Trustee meetings expecting that the necessary decisions regarding the School of Nations building would be made in order for the plans to be completed and the construction to begin. While attending the meetings, she visited both campuses and had a thorough tour of the Marshall Brooks Memorial Library, which the administration and Trustees expected to be completed during Christmas vacation. Although other important business had been accomplished, no concrete decision was made in regard to the School of Nations building.[721]

When Hazle arrived home Monday evening after the Trustee meetings and was enjoying her dinner, a bouquet of "lovely yellow roses," arrived from Frederic. She could not imagine how he managed "to do things so instantly!" She wrote to him, "We shall enjoy them to the last golden petal!" She added that she believed the Trustee meetings had been carefully thought out and well planned. She looked forward to receiving a copy of the report from David Morey covering the closed session held by the Trustees in the Library Sunday afternoon, at which a retirement package had been presented to Frederic and the other senior officers of Principia. She hoped the action taken expressed "something of the appreciation of the Board" for the service of "Principia's senior officers." Frederic wrote to the Board of Trustees: "[A]s soon as a copy of the minutes have been received and I am able to express my thanks accurately and understandingly, I will write again. Please accept my gratitude and best wishes."[722]

On December 12, 1955, Frederic wrote to the Trustees regarding a grant from the Ford Foundation. Principia College had been selected as one of six colleges in Illinois to receive a portion of a fifty million dollar grant to be allocated to a special group of 126 colleges throughout the nation for leading the way in improving the positions and remuneration for American college professors. Hazle responded to Frederic's letter on December 20, 1955, "That was good news from the Ford Foundation and a nice tribute to what we are trying to do." She also enclosed an article about the Air Force Academy from The Daily Pantagraph, which had reminded her of how fortunate Principia had been that the Air Academy Site Selection Committee had decided on the property in Colorado Springs instead of the bluffs where Principia College stands. She believed the article, which had been widely published, to be of "special interest to all" who took part in the protective work for Principia.[723]

As 1955 drew to a close, Hazle reflected on the changes made to the School of Nations program and personnel. She believed that progress had been made in stimulating more student interest in the School of Nations, which she and William had desired. She was especially grateful for the establishment of the Abroad program. After reviewing the information Hamlin sent her regarding her School of Nations donations, she sent a contribution of $24,263.54 to the School of Nations Building Fund on December 30. The donation was an outward expression of her confidence that the plans for the School of Nations building would move forward in the near future.[724]

CHAPTER 31

GREAT JOY AND GREAT SORROW

*T*he events of 1956 would bring great joy and great sorrow into Hazle's life. At the end of April, Hazle received news from William Morgan that was a "great and complete surprise" to her. The Executive Board of the Trustees and the Faculty-Administration Honors Committee had decided to award her a Doctor of Laws Degree at the College commencement in June to acknowledge her many contributions to Principia through the School of Nations, which "has borne an increasing measure of abundant and glorious fruit." Responding to William, Hazle thanked him and the others for their generous acknowledgment of her contributions to Principia in such an "outstanding way," which she deeply appreciated. She admitted to him, "I have long wished that I might be a student at Principia," but suggested that the title of the degree was "so imposing" she wondered if she could "live up to it."[725]

Another letter from William arrived a few days later bearing the news that preliminary work was being done in preparation for developing the actual plans for the School of Nations building. He told Hazle that the plans for the building included, a good-sized fireproof museum, foreign language classrooms, history of foreign countries classrooms, a comparative literature classroom, a lecture hall that would accommodate 100 people, a language lab, and offices for the director and secretary of the School of Nations.[726] He also reported that the building funds currently amounted to $263,434.89. Nothing could have given Hazle more joy. She looked forward to the commencement weekend in June with great anticipation.[727]

In the short speech Frederic delivered in honor of Hazle on June 12, 1956, at the commencement ceremony, he said, "In 1925, a friend and patron of The Principia who had traveled widely became deeply imbued with the idea that harmony among nations and their people" could be increased by gaining a sympathetic understanding of one another. He explained that Hazle had offered to "personally encourage and financially support" a program that would promote this ideal at the College, "for she believed that the faculty and the students of a school for Christian Scientists should be especially well-informed in world affairs."[728]

The School of Nations had played the important role of preparing students to serve in the State Department and other fields of international relations for 31 years. In addition, the program had provided the opportunity for students and faculty to travel outside the United States and had contributed financial aid for foreign students to attend the school. Hazle had initiated the means by which the borders of their understanding had been extended beyond their own country and had enabled students to make valuable contributions to the world. Every member of the Principia community had been touched by the School of Nations activities in some way. Frederic believed that these reasons made it "highly appropriate" to honor her. Concluding his speech, he bestowed the honorary degree on Hazle. The clapping and cheering of an appreciative audience overwhelmed her with a great sense of joy and gratitude.[729]

The Bloomington *Pantagraph* announced in the June 15, 1956, edition of the paper, that Hazle had received "an honorary degree of Doctorate at Laws" from The Principia for her initiation of the School of Nations and its vital contribution to the education offered at the school. A second article on the same subject appeared in the paper on June 17, including a photograph, supplied by Hazle's friend, Rebeka Dietz, of Hazle receiving her degree.[730]

Weeks after the commencement ceremony, Hazle received a

note from her friend, Eldredge Hamlin, who knew how much Hazle had given to Principia in addition to initiating and supporting the School of Nations. Although he had spoken to her after the commencement, he wrote, "I want to add a further word of congratulations . . . [that] this is a well-deserved recognition."[731]

Rebeka Dietz also wrote to Hazle to tell her how happy she was to see her work for Principia officially recognized. The ceremony reminded Rebeka that Hazle had once told her that, she "really hadn't done much except to start [the idea] along and encourage its growth from time to time." Rebeka told Hazle: "I thought quite a bit about what you so modestly said about your work for The School of Nations. . . . If I may say so, that is the most wonderful type of generosity that people can exercise when giving to good causes." She added that she had often heard Frederic speak appreciatively of Hazle's selflessness in what she had done and continued to do for Principia.[732]

At the end of June, Hazle received a hand-written letter from Frederic, which began, "It would be quite impossible for me to tell you how truly grateful I am that the honorary doctorate which you had so richly earned was finally awarded by Principia earlier this month." Continuing, he added, "Because of the long, happy years when we worked closely together for Principia . . . I had hoped this honor might go to you during my years as president. . . . Please let it say also that I am deeply and truly grateful for all that you mean to Principia and for all that your friendship means to me."[733]

Hazle responded to Frederic on July 12, thanking him for his "heart-warming and generously hand-written letter." She told him, "It meant so much to me, and I shall treasure it." She, too, was grateful that they had been able to work together so harmoniously, and she expected that they would continue to do so. She added, "Please know that I deeply appreciate your writing to me as you have. The knowing that you not only approve, but had even hoped that this great honor might come to me even earlier, adds greatly to my appreciation of it."[734]

During the summer, Hazle renewed her efforts to increase the recreational area of Bloomington, and the *Pantagraph* announced on July 10, 1956: "Mrs. Hazle Buck Ewing has made the first move toward an enlarged park system for Bloomington by donating approximately 5 1/2 acres for park purposes north of her home on Towanda Avenue." She intentionally donated land that adjoined the property which had been included in the official City Plan for a 70-acre recreational area in the northeast part of the city. The recreational area included parts of the Sugar Creek and Goose Creek parkways that would surround the community from the northeast to the southwest. Hazle's donation included the stipulation, however, that she be given the legal right to use 75 feet on the west side of the property for a bridle path. The city agreed to her stipulation and expressed their sincere appreciation for her generosity and their hope that others would follow her example.[735]

Also in July, it was a great joy for Hazle to learn that, her grandson, Ted (Nelson's son), had applied for admission to Principia Upper School in the fall. Since Nelson had been a student at Principia, he was aware that all students attending the school must be currently studying and practicing Christian Science. Students going to the Upper School were required to attend Sunday school and to live a high moral standard. Although Ted had not been attending Sunday school for a couple of years, the autobiography he had sent to Principia revealed his knowledge of Principia's requirements and a sincere desire to attend the school. Nelson assured Principia officials that Ted studied the Bible and the Christian Science textbook and relied on Christian Science for healing and would soon re-enter Sunday school.[736]

On August 14, 1956, Frederic wrote Hazle about the Committee of Seventy Conference to be held in St. Louis in October. The committee had originally been formed May 21, 1953, with the purpose of making the financial needs of The Principia known to

those who could financially support the move of the Upper and
Lower Schools from the old location on Page Boulevard and Belt
Street to the new Country Campus. Frederic explained to Hazle
that the committee was inviting "people who have given generously
to Principia and who may be expected to give in larger measure as
their understanding of Principia and interest in it increases." He
asked what she thought about him inviting her acquaintance, Mrs.
Raymond Wakely.[737]

Hazle told Frederic that he should invite Mrs. Wakely to the
Conference as the owner and manager of a large and successful
business. Hazle believed "it eminently wise to broaden the list of
invitations to successful professional men and to include some of their
wives as well." She knew in some cases that the wife's financial help
was as readily available as that of her husband. Besides, she had read
that, "a considerable portion of income-bearing stocks and bonds are
owned by women in this country." She assured Frederic that Mrs.
Wakely would enjoy getting acquainted with the outstanding group
that made up the Committee of Seventy.[738]

Later in August, Hazle learned from William the encouraging
news that the plans for the School of Nations and the School of
Government buildings were being presented to the Executive
Board. He also reported that the School of Nations Building Fund
currently had $272,366.79, but the estimated cost of the building
was $30,000 above that amount. When Hazle's friend and secretary,
Adeline Adams, learned of the progress being made on the building
plans, she sent a donation to Principia saying that she would "like
to pick . . . a [class]room as her 'own,' to which to send further
contributions." Earlier contributions had been made by Hazle's
family for decorating the classrooms. Her mother, Lillian Brewer
Buck, had donated $1,000 toward decorating the English room;
Ellsworth Buck had contributed $500 for the Oriental room; and
Julia had given $100 for the French room.[739]

Additional good news came from Frederic that month, who

wrote to Hazle that the first Principia Abroad would begin on
August 22. He told her, "I feel this 'Principia Abroad' activity is an
exceedingly important step in the expression of Principia's work, and
a step for which you are primarily responsible." He confided, "I think
I should like to have you know that the inspiration of my visits with
you during the past years led to the letter which I wrote to Dr. Gertsch
two years ago," suggesting the plan that became the Principia Abroad
program. Frederic thought it best that the idea come from the Dean's
office. He asked Hazle to, "Please just let it be our secret and know
that I have full happiness in having had a part in working it out."
He concluded, "Never in my life have I known anyone more selfless,
more impersonally generous and lovingly attentive to Principia than
you have been and are. Your work stands as a monument, true to the
Principia spirit in every respect."[740]

Frederic included a copy of the letter he had written to the
students embarking on the first Principia Abroad, in which he said,
"Be 'minute men' in service of our beloved Cause, and you will
thus be able to help others appreciate the ideals of our own country
while you seek to understand and appreciate the ideals and sterling
characteristics of the people whose countries you visit." He paid
tribute to Hazle, saying, "Our hearts are filled with gratitude" for her
"God-given wisdom and foresight to establish the School of Nations.
She saw clearly the need for Principians to be alert, well-informed,
and appreciative of thinking beyond their own national borders." He
also reminded them that Hazle's ideals and generous financial support
had made The Principia Abroad possible.[741]

Soon thereafter, the good news about the School of Nations
building and the Principia Abroad was overshadowed by an
unhappy event. Hazle confided to Frederic on August 20 that her
brother, Nelson, had passed on, and "His going has left a big hole in
our family group—the first break in our generation." She requested
that he let Eldridge and William know that "Nelson has gone."
Nelson, who had not quite seemed to be himself for nearly a year,

had become seriously ill and had gone to the Evanston hospital near the end of July. He passed away in early August, leaving behind his wife, Rena Hooper Buck; three married daughters: Frances, Betty, and Caroline; and eight grandchildren, besides his siblings, Hazle and Ellsworth. This proved to be an extremely trying time for Hazle. Not only was Nelson her brother, but she had depended heavily on him for assistance in managing her finances.[742]

After graduating from the University of Chicago in 1904, Nelson had followed in his father's footsteps, going to work for the W. E. Wrigley Company. He became vice president and a director for the company in 1919, taking over the position their father held prior to his death. Nelson retired from the presidency in 1938 and the directorship in 1948. After relinquishing his positions at the Wrigley Company, he became a director of the State Bank and Trust Company, a director of the Evanston Hospital association, and an associate of Northwestern University. His employment positions provided him an acute understanding of business, on which Hazle and other family members had come to rely.[743]

When Frederic received Hazle's letter about Nelson's passing, he called her to express his sorrow for her loss. He wrote to her a few days later and told her that Nelson had "indeed guarded and guided" her "interests most thoughtfully." She appreciated Frederic's assurance that the "Wisdom and Love which [Nelson] reflected are unchanging, positive and ever-present, and will find expression through divine guidance in whatever way will best meet your needs."[744]

That summer at the ranch, Hazle had some time for uninterrupted study and prayer. She missed Nelson's presence when all the members of her family gathered for their annual visit at the ranch. But she also found a sense of peace there. She felt certain that the right answer regarding the management of her finances would become apparent.

After returning home to Bloomington, she wrote to Frederic

on October 30 of her interest in the Principia Abroad program, and thanked him for the picture of the students who had gone to Europe in August. She told him, "They are a fine looking group of which all of us can be proud." She added that she had thoroughly enjoyed the reports that Dr. Leonard, who was the faculty member traveling with the students on the Abroad, had been sending to her, especially because they "bring back vivid memories of my visits to many of the same places." She assured Frederic, "I am happy that the 'Principia Abroad' does your heart good. Your interest and approval has been an important inspiration for what has been accomplished all through the years." She also thanked him for the box of candy he had sent, which was a "nice welcome home."[745]

Although Hazle had felt great sorrow over the loss of her brother, she overcame the grief and returned to her normal activities before the end of the year. In November, her train trip to Principia for the Trustees' meetings was made quite pleasant by the company of her fellow-trustee, Helena Gunnison, with whom she talked amiably. The Trustee meetings proved fruitful, and she learned that the School of Nations plans had been completed and construction would begin in the spring. She always looked forward to spring with joyful anticipation, but never more than she did that fall.[746]

At Last

CHAPTER 32

THE REWARD OF PATIENCE

When William showed the School of Nations faculty committee the building plans and told them construction would begin in the spring, every member shared Hazle's joyful anticipation. Robert Andrews, chairman of the committee and a son of George A. Andrews, who had been instrumental in establishing the School of Nations, wrote to Hazle of their "excitement, rejoicing, and overflowing gratitude." He told her, "We recognize that this historic development marks an important step for Principia's growth–from our temporary academic structure of the past twenty-one years into buildings that will give full expression to our concept of true education." The committee appreciated her "vision and unbounded generosity that are expressed in this wonderful gift." Responding, Hazle rejoiced with the committee over the news about the building, and expressed her happiness for the success of the first Principia Abroad. She told Robert that she looked forward to hearing more about their plans for the Abroad to France in the coming fall.[747]

Hamlin also shared in Hazle's happiness about the School of Nations building, telling her, "It will be a wonderful and very fitting addition to our College campus and a real tribute to you who have been so unselfish and patient through all the years since you first instituted this project." In early December, 1956, Rebeka Dietz expressed her pleasure to Hazle regarding the good news: "I know how much you have been looking forward to this—indeed as all of us have been."[748]

Rebeka included in her letter the revised carbon copy of the text for the new School of Nations booklet which was to be "long and narrow" so that it would fit into a standard letter sized envelope. In addition, she explained that there would be illustrations of various activities sponsored by the School of Nations, including the recent World Affairs Roundtable, and the School of Nations flag collection would be the center-fold spread. Hazle enjoyed reading the text and hoped to see the completed version in the near future.[749]

On December 17, Hazle wrote to William regarding the School of Nations classrooms, explaining that she obtained a portfolio of hand-painted pictures of the "Nationality Rooms" from the University of Pittsburgh, which she forwarded to the Principia College Library. She anticipated that these pictures could be helpful when they began planning the School of Nations classrooms. She told William she especially liked the name, Nationality Room, and thought they should adopt it for the classrooms in the School of Nations building. She believed referring to the classrooms as Nationality Rooms "might inspire additional contributions on the part of some of Principia's friends, who are especially interested in some one country—either because of his own origin or admiration." She encouraged William to borrow the portfolio from the Library.[750]

When William returned to Elsah after the winter break, he wrote to Hazle, "I like the name 'Nationality Rooms' . . . and we will certainly use this title . . . I have the portfolio of pictures [from] the University of Pittsburgh . . . which I found safely cared for in our library vault." He planned to give the portfolio to the architect to look over and determine what could be done at a moderate cost in the School of Nations classrooms. Hazle expected to hear more about their ideas for the rooms before spring arrived.[751]

In February 1957, Hazle received a letter written on behalf of the members of the first Principia Abroad, which included many pleasant memories of each member who had been on the trip. They told of meeting distinguished persons, making new friends, and visiting various places. The students found it especially interesting to see the Christian Science movement in action in England and other European countries. They visited various churches, talked with two different Committees on Publication, and contacted individuals connected with *The Christian Science Monitor* staff who made the Abroad group realize "the importance of this international newspaper." They also gained a better understanding of the background of the countries they traveled through by visiting monuments and other sites of interest. Because of her own travels around the world, Hazle could relate to their experiences abroad and how their lives had been changed, and she deeply appreciated their expressions of sincere gratitude. [752]

In mid-March, as spring approached, Hazle found it possible to donate $40,000 to the building fund. William wrote to her expressing his gratitude for her "magnificent support." He told her that the architect was preparing the working drawings and figuring out the cost of the bare building first and then what the extras would cost, which would enable them to determine what to include and what to eliminate. He promised to send a copy of the plans as soon as the architect completed them, and assured her the erection of that building should start in late spring or early summer. Before the building could be erected, however, the ground had to be elevated. The School of Nations would be situated near the Library and a short distance from the Chapel. [753]

William told Hazle that they would "endeavor to do everything possible" to complete at least one of the Nationality Rooms, which she had suggested might stimulate interest and result in more donations for the other classrooms. William also shared with her that Henry Holt had expressed a desire to pay for the construction of a large central room in some building in memory of his wife. William was not sure, however, that Hazle would want a memorial room "in such a prominent place" in the School of Nations building. But she assured William that she had no objection to the auditorium in the School of Nations being used in such a manner.[754]

Hearing about Hazle's most recent and generous donation, Frederic wrote to her on March 20, 1957: "I hope you have some concept of how deep our gratitude is and what tremendous respect we have for the selflessness with which you have waited year after year to see your dream fulfilled, patiently standing aside while one after another emergency need at the college were met." He admitted that he frequently struggled with his own sense of sadness and regret that "after all our years and aspirations for the School of Nations Building, it has not been my privilege to work with you on the unfolding of plans and construction." But he assured her, "My joy in what is taking place is not in any way dimmed in that I am not your immediate partner in the unfoldment of a long anticipated idea." He was happy that he could be her "partner as a fellow trustee" and wanted her to know that she had "the unfailing measure of love and gratitude of the writer of this letter, and of your other friends at Principia."[755]

On April 2, 1957, Hazle wrote to Frederic that she could not keep from "rejoicing that at long last there is to be a School of Nations building that I shall be able to enjoy, both its construction and use." Although William had promised to send drawings of the building and its situation on the campus, she told Frederic that she wanted to see the spot where the building would stand so that she could really visualize it. She planned to stop at Elsah on her way home from Lake Placid, Florida, and hoped to see as many of her friends "as happened to be there at the time." She promised Frederic that she would telephone when her plans were more definite.[756]

Hazle, Julia, and Herman arrived at Principia near the end of April and stayed with Helen and Eldredge Hamlin for a few days. After reaching home, Hazle wrote thanking them "for taking in [her] whole touring family so cordially and comfortably." She added, "This stop-over was thoroughly rewarding, — for now each time I think of the new School of Nations Building, I can see that satisfying view of the chapel on its bluff-top green." Although Hazle had enjoyed visiting with the Hamlins, she was sorry not to have seen Frederic. When she arrived home, however, she found that he had sent another box of her favorite candy. She wrote to him, "How can you think of me and my likes so often! You must have a host of others on your list!"[757]

When Hazle attended the commencement at the Upper School in St. Louis, she had occasion to spend some time with Frederic and Toni. Enjoying their company, she invited them to come for a visit at the ranch where she would be going soon after commencement. She told Frederic, "I am sure we could enjoy the trails together." He replied, "We would love to visit Thunder Mountain Ranch some time soon, and we appreciate the invitation you have so graciously given us on several occasions. Whenever there seems to be the slightest possibility of such a visit, we shall be bold enough to advise you of the fact."[758]

Near the end of June, Frederic traveled to New England on business and wrote to Hazle that he had contacted some friends "who are in a position to be very helpful to Principia if they can get a clearer idea of just what Principia is and seeks to do." She also heard from William who told her that the plans for the School of Nations were to be presented to the Executive Board for final approval in late July. Construction on the building was projected to begin in late summer.[759]

Expecting the Executive Board's approval to begin the construction of the building in late summer, William suggested to Hazle the possibility of having a ground-breaking ceremony on July 27 or 28, when the Executive Board could be present—or they could wait until November, when the entire Board of Trustees could attend. Hazle responded: "I had tried in vain to figure out some way to be present for the mid-summer ground-breaking . . . and still have time with my family at Thunder Mountain Ranch before we have to be turning south for all the fall events." The time spent at the ranch had grown more important to Hazle with each passing year, and she told William, "My nieces and nephews and grandnieces and grandnephews (and there may even be great-grands before too long!) are so scattered during the winter that I have to make the most of the few weeks in the summer when we are all together at 'The Ranch.'" It seemed best to her, therefore, to have the ground-breaking ceremony in November.[760]

In late June, William wrote to Hazle regarding the idea of constructing a vault under the central floor of the School of Nations building instead of laying a cornerstone. The idea appealed to Hazle, and she suggested that a bronze plaque be placed right above the vault. Their recent correspondence had made Hazle aware that William had been putting in a great deal of time and effort to insure the completion of the building plans for the School of Nations in addition to attending to his other responsibilities. She told him, "If it were not that I know the great need of the School of Nations Building on the Elsah campus, I should be sorry to see you having all the details of this new college building on your hands and thoughts, in addition to your load for the Country Campus." She was glad to learn, however, that Harry Arthur, a fellow trustee and land developer, had purchased the old College property on Lackland Road in St. Louis for $210,000, which she knew would help with the construction costs at the Country Campus.[761]

Only a few days later, the School of Nations building plan came up for discussion at the Executive Board meeting, and it became apparent that "the cost of the building was nearly 50% higher" than had been planned. It seemed that there would be another delay. But, William began an immediate search for additional funds and discovered that $10,202.24 remained in the Stable Fund, which had been established by the Executive Board and Hazle several years earlier for building a stable on the College campus. Since there was no longer a plan or desire to have a stable, the money was transferred to the School of Nations Building Fund.[762]

William also met with the architect, contractor, and the president of the construction company to find practical and economical ways to reduce the building costs. His efforts paid off. They found that costs could be reduced by constructing only eight classrooms, eight offices, and one language lab instead of the originally planned ten classrooms, thirteen offices, and two language labs. They also decided that the east and west wings of the building would initially be one story and the second story would be built later. Since combining the heating and cooling systems seemed too costly, it was decided to put the heating ducts in first and add the cooling ducts at a later time.[763]

In addition to the money found in the Stable Fund and the reduction of the building costs, an unnamed estate had contributed $50,000 to Principia that could be deposited in the School of Nations Building Fund. As a result, the trustees believed that "it was reasonable to proceed and agreed" that it "would be very satisfactory to start" the construction of the building.[764]

After returning to the College from his five-day business trip in New England, Frederic wrote to Hazle of his visit with their mutual friend and a former School of Nations chairman, Sam Baker, and his wife Nancy. Frederic told her that "Sam spoke most appreciatively of you, and I am sure you would enjoy seeing them in their charming home in Camden, Maine." He also wanted Hazle to know that her acquaintance, Mrs. Wakely, had contributed $1,000 to Principia.[765]

Two days later, on July 19, Frederic wrote to Hazle, "Some very good news can be shared this morning!" Henry Holt of Indianapolis and his children authorized nearly $50,000 to pay for the construction of the auditorium in the School of Nations as a memorial to Mrs. Holt. Concluding his letter, Frederic told Hazle, "My heart will indeed be filled with gratitude when the building is actually under way." Hazle assured Frederic that she had no objection to a plaque being displayed in the auditorium expressing gratitude to the Holts for their contribution. Furthermore, she could definitely appreciate and relate to Henry Holt's "amazing patience . . . during many years" while Principia "sought to find just the right medium through which their memorial might become a permanent part of the Principia campus."[766]

William wrote to Hazle on August 19 that the excavation "is scheduled to start today." He added, "When you are here in the fall you will find the ravine filled in from the north side of the School of Nations to the north side of the Intramural Building." He assured her that the cost of the excavation would be covered by the Angie Cox estate. Hazle looked forward to seeing the "way in which the building will sit on the ground." She empathized with William's sentiments that, "This has not been too simple to work out, but the hand of God has been felt at every step of the work and planning."[767]

Writing from the Marshall Brooks Library basement on August 22, Frederic told Hazle, "Just outside and to the north, huge bulldozers are roaring their way back and forth, and carpenters are busily setting up corner frames and building panels for pouring concrete, all in preparation for the School of Nations Building." He assured her that when the trustees arrived for their November meeting, they would see that much had been accomplished in the construction of the "beautiful new building." Hazle appreciated receiving this most exciting news from Frederic. But the next day, William reported to her that the building cost had been adjusted to $473,000 instead of $450,000 that he had told her in his previous letter.[768]

Hazle did not respond to the news about the beginning of the construction or the additional money needed for the building until October 12, 1957, when she wrote to Frederic, "It has been good to have each one of your letters and communications the last few months. When I come down, I'll explain to you why I have not been writing these weeks." She told him that she was eagerly looking forward to seeing him and all of the Principia family, as well as the progress that had been made on the building.[769]

Hazle arrived at Principia for the Trustees meetings in November and had the thrill of seeing with her own eyes the actual construction of the building and how it was situated. As promised, she explained to Frederic why she had not written for the past few months. She confided to him that she had been at the Chestnut Hill Benevolent Association in Boston, endeavoring to overcome a physical problem. She had found it necessary to focus on the healing and to set aside all other interests and concerns.

As the year drew to a close on December 31, 1957, William wrote to Hazle expressing gratitude for the lovely things she had done for Principia through the years "which are now culminating in the building of this wonderful School of Nations edifice." He added that her "ideas for the School of Nations have enriched our work so greatly and have opened up opportunities for international service and international understanding to so many young people." Her dream of having a proper building for the School of Nations was coming true—a just reward for her unfaltering patience.[770]

CHAPTER 33

PRESSING ON

Although Hazle had not yet regained her former strength and health, she assured Frederic that she wanted to continue her work as the secretary for the Board of Trustees, and he trusted that she would be able to do so. However, late January 1958, Hazle again seemed to be having difficulty. Frederic called her home to confirm that she was feeling up to signing the Trustee Emeritus certificates for Hugh Prather and Percival Brooks. Her housekeeper, Ruby, told him the good news—that she was getting along nicely. When Frederic sent the certificates, he wrote in regard to her improvement, "You may be sure that your friends here will rejoice with me in this good news."[771]

Hazle signed the certificates the day she received them and wrote a letter to Frederic expressing appreciation for the special gift he had sent, saying, "yesterday afternoon came a beautiful bouquet of the golden roses that I like to associate with Principia. I thank you and Principia with all my heart—for the roses, the generous thought that sent them and the good wishes that came with them. Each one will help my continuing daily gains." She felt confident that she would be able to drive down to Principia in the "next two or three weeks" with several friends who wanted see what progress had been made on the School of Nations building.[772]

As work on the School of Nations building progressed, Hazle gained in health and strength. But she was not yet able to make the trip to Principia, so Hamlin sent her some slides of the construction work being done in which she could see one or two steel girders reaching up into the air. She appreciated Hamlin's thoughtfulness in providing the slides so she could see the progress being made, but her desire to see it in person made the winter seem much too long.

319

She bore it with patience, anticipating the completion of the School of Nations building and working steadily toward a complete physical healing so that she could make the trip to Principia in the spring. Receiving another box of candy from Frederic, who was in California in March, greatly pleased her, and she told him, "I am more impressed than ever with your thoughtfulness when I glance over your February itinerary, and realize that in the midst of it all, you remembered and took time to send us the delicious candy.[773]

In mid-April, Hazle donated $33,445.50 to the building fund. Later that month, she attended the Trustees' meetings and saw for herself how much had been done on the building, which encouraged her to think about and look forward to the dedication ceremony. She also decided to review the new School of Nations booklet and discovered an incorrect statement regarding the origin of the School of Nations museum, which she pointed out to William. He promised to check into it and see that it was corrected.[774]

During that spring, much construction work was undertaken by Principia on both campuses. Learning of Principia's need for more financial support, Hazle told William that she would loan the school $65,000. She made arrangements with her attorney, Miss Alice Bright, to send a check to Principia in that amount. When Hamlin received the check, he issued a promissory note in accordance with the agreement Hazle had made with William, and told her, "I know everyone here is sincerely and deeply grateful for this most helpful step you have taken."[775]

As the work on the exterior of the School of Nations building neared completion, Hazle turned her attention to the interior of the Nationality Rooms. She contacted William, and he met with the art department director, Jim Green, to discuss the rooms. It became apparent to them that more time was needed for planning before the decoration of the rooms could begin. They would not be able to complete the first room that summer as they had originally thought. William wrote to Hazle on May 13, 1958, seeking her approval to begin the fall quarter with the rooms finished in the "customary caliber of well-planned school rooms." He explained that Green desired to have the fall and winter to carefully study and plan how each room should be decorated. Then he would begin the work of applying the decoration to the interiors of the rooms the following summer.[776]

William telephoned Hazle a few days later to discuss the matter more fully. During their conversation, she told him that she approved of and understood Green's desire to carefully plan each of the rooms and his need for more time. She consented to allowing the rooms on the second floor to be used as classrooms in a "slightly unfinished" condition. But she expressed some concern that the work would come to a standstill. William assured her that they would take only "whatever time was absolutely required, . . . [and] work steadily toward" completing the classrooms on the first floor. He added that Jim Green would begin the work that summer in Europe, gathering ideas on how to make the rooms authentic representations of their designated countries. Hazle looked forward to hearing about his ideas when he returned.[777]

During the summer, Frank Parker wrote to William suggesting that one of the rooms be decorated to represent the Swiss and be dedicated to Dean Alfred Gertsch (who came from a Swiss family). William wrote to Hazle in support of Parker's idea. At first, Hazle had been enthusiastic about this proposal, seeing the possibility of arousing interest in completing one of the Nationality Rooms. However, she wrote to William, "For a number of years I have found that I could think things out more clearly and completely if I could 'sleep' on them—that is tuck them away in a corner of my thought for a night or two and await the result." Using this process, she had come to see that by dedicating a room to Gertsch, they would be setting an impossible precedent to continue. She pointed out to William that there were several other individuals to whom rooms could be dedicated. But there were only eight rooms. They already had funds for the English, French, Spanish, and East India rooms, and the Swiss would make five. Later, William wrote that he agreed with her that it would be wise not to dedicate the nationality rooms to specific individuals.[778]

Shortly after her discussion with William about the Nationality Rooms, Hazle left for the ranch for the summer. On June 25, she received a short letter from her son, Ralph, telling her that they had put her granddaughter, Cindy, on the plane in Kansas destined for New York City. Cindy would be visiting with their friends, the Paxtons, before leaving for Europe with their daughter, Joan, who was going to Germany. On July 1, Ralph wrote a longer letter telling Hazle that Cindy had departed for Europe, and they had been busy writing letters to the families with whom she would be staying during her trip. She would return home on August 25, her seventeenth birthday.[779]

Knowing of his mother's recent illness, Ralph told her, "Sounds like you are coming right along, being able to ride horseback. The main thing apparently—is to take it slow and easy to start. It certainly is the best way to see things and get over the rough part there at the ranch. It makes me envious. The ranch sounds beautiful." Although she knew that Ralph did not want her to concern herself about his unemployment situation, Hazle had suggested a way for him to keep the interest and principal down on their mortgage, for which he expressed sincere gratitude. She was aware that the economy in Kansas, as well as in other parts of the country, had been suffering because of the recession. But Ralph had assured her that a lot of people were out of work, and he seemed confident about starting his own business, "preferably with a partner." She trusted that he would work out a right solution.[780]

In mid-August, Hazle was especially happy to learn from William that Jim Green had sent rough sketches of some of the rooms from Paris, which she hoped to see soon. She also heard from Frederic, who told her about a generous contribution made by Mrs. Gertrude

McCalmont that would enable Principia to complete various projects. He also told her that the Dickie Construction Company had been hired as the contractor for two dormitories on the St. Louis Country Campus.[781]

Answering Frederic's letter, Hazle wrote, "I am delighted beyond measure that the Dickie Construction Company was the low bidder. . . . That fully justifies the confidence that most of us on the Board of Trustees have long held in [them]. Indeed, this company has 'served Principia loyally and well and has earned our confidence and respect." Referring to the donation made by Mrs. McCalmont, she said, "It has taken many such stories to build Principia to what it is today." Hazle hoped to visit both Principia campuses to see the progress being made as soon as possible after returning home from the ranch.[782]

On September 19, William wrote to Hazle at the ranch regarding the construction work on the School of Nations building, "We have had quite a time with labor relations . . . there has been great trouble in getting the delivery on our steel sashes," which had cost them two weeks. When the steel finally arrived, it was not all there, and another two weeks was lost before the ceiling and flooring materials could be installed. Then the grading company's machinery broke down. He had had to hire another company to finish the job. But he did have some good news. The terrazzo on the stairways and in the ceilings was going up rapidly. When the glazing was complete, the flooring would be put down. In spite of the delays, William assured Hazle that by the first day of school, September 26, the faculty would be able to use all the offices in the School of Nations building and six of the classrooms.[783]

Since the building would be in use at the beginning of the school year, William thought they should begin making plans for the dedication in November, when the trustees would be there for the ceremony. He also suggested that they invite Adlai Stevenson to give a talk at the ceremony on world problems and their possible solutions, since Stevenson had recently returned from a trip around the world. William offered to write to Stevenson, but he thought maybe Hazle would like to contact him herself. She agreed to ask Adlai about giving a speech at the dedication ceremony.[784]

As it turned out, Julia became ill and ended up in the Marinette Hospital for several weeks. Hazle wrote to Frederic on September 23, 1958, of Julia's situation, and declined his invitation to attend the Committee of Seventy meeting, since she did not know when Julia would be ready to come home. But she assured Frederic that she looked forward to reading the meeting reports, and of her desire to be able to make a "one-day" trip to Elsah to check on the progress of the School of Nations building. She also contacted William and asked him to postpone the dedication of the building, which he rescheduled for April at the time of the next Trustee meetings.[785]

As William had projected, the faculty members were moved into their offices in the School of Nations building and the classrooms on the second floor were ready to be used on September 26. He forwarded a letter of appreciation to Hazle, which he had received from the Professor of French, Ned Bradley, who wrote:

> While, I can only speak for myself, I am sure that I express the sentiments of all of us who have just finished the first week of classes in the School of Nations Building, when I say that it is a tremendous inspiration to be in it! Please convey our gratitude to Mrs. Ewing in no uncertain terms. . . . The students, too, are excited at the visible progress of the work from day to day . . . I have heard no complaints, and the spirit of pioneering which still lingered here when I came to Elsah twenty years ago seems to have been reborn in full. . . . Again, it is an inspiring thing to take this forward step together![786]

Bradley's letter gave Hazle great joy. She appreciated his expressions of gratitude as one who was among the first to have classes in the School of Nations building—the building that she had wanted to provide for the faculty and students for such a long time.

The ground-breaking ceremony took place in mid-November at the time of the Trustee meetings, which Hazle attended, having regained her health. It gave her great pleasure to see the building in use. That winter, she once again looked forward to spring, anticipating with great joy the dedication of the School of Nations building. It seemed appropriate to her to have the dedication in April when the dogwoods and red bud trees would be blooming. She expected that Julia would be well by then and able to attend the dedication with her.

CHAPTER 34

THE CULMINATION OF AN IDEA

*I*n early February1959, Hazle and William began preparing for the April dedication ceremony of the School of Nations Building. The program for the ceremony would include music provided by the school choir, Scripture readings, expressions of gratitude to the donor of the building, and an explanation of the use of the building. For her part in the dedication ceremony, Hazle began by writing down ideas that she wanted to share about the School of Nations, choosing readings from the Bible, *Science and Health with Key to the Scriptures* by Mary Baker Eddy, and an opening hymn. It was decided to hold the ceremony inside the building since the weather in April was always uncertain. She had been especially pleased that David Andrews had agreed to prepare the program for the dedication. She wanted to make a trip to Elsah before the day of the ceremony to see the progress on the building, but William had asked her to wait. Realizing that he wanted everything to be "absolutely complete" before she saw it, she complied with his request.[787]

While working on preparations, Hazle discovered an extensive article on the School of Nations building and an impressive inside spread of photographs in the current issue of the *Principia Progress*. It seemed to her that the article and pictures provided some unsought for but timely publicity for the upcoming dedication of the building.[788]

William reported to Hazle in mid-February that much progress had been made in preparing the School of Nations building for the ceremony. He told her that the first-floor classrooms were nearly ready for use, the paneling in Holt Gallery had been completed, and the elevator installed. In addition, he had received the bronze plaque with her name as the donor and showing the date she donated the money for the building as 1957, although she had offered the funds for the building many years earlier. The plaque would be placed near the south entrance on the outside of the building. Jim Green was completing the paintings of the interiors of the French and Spanish rooms, but the actual rooms would not be ready by the time of the dedication. The plan was to display the paintings where those attending the ceremony could view them. In the meantime, they would be sent to Hazle for previewing.[789]

The paintings illustrating the interiors of the French and Spanish rooms arrived at Sunset Hill in late February. After looking them over, Hazle called William and suggested some changes. During their discussion, they determined that the eight Nationality Rooms should represent Spain, France, Germany, Russia, India, Japan, Northern Africa, and South America, which Hazle believed gave "excellent coverage of the world." A steady stream of correspondence flowed between Hazle and William for the next several weeks. On March 9, he told her, "These days I seem to be becoming a very active correspondent with you, and I am enjoying it. Probably it is natural for this to be the case because we have so many things to work out just now."[790]

In the midst of the preparations, Hazle received a letter from C. Theodore Houpt, the current Chairman of the School of Nations, who had recently returned from the third Principia Abroad. He wrote to tell her about the plans for the fourth Abroad, which would be led by Frank Parker and begin in Greece, where students would be studying the beginnings of Western Civilization and Greek literature. They would also spend time in Rome to study the Roman influence on our civilization; visit Siena to gain some understanding of medieval life; and take a trip to Florence to learn about the Renaissance. Houpt concluded, "I want you as a trustee and the founder of the School of Nations to know that the program which you instituted has been an invaluable adjunct to the college curriculum."[791]

In early March, an "informal letter" to the Board of Trustees arrived from Frederic. He explained that after much prayerful thought, it had become clear to him that he should retire as chairman of the Board at the "earliest appropriate time during the present calendar year." He would present his formal resignation as the chairman of the Board at the April meeting, but if the Board members wished to defer "any formal action until the election session" of their annual meeting, he would consent to continue as chairman until that time. Hazle was sorry to receive this news. She and Frederic had worked through many challenges and opportunities together while he was the chairman and she was the secretary of the Board. Although she regretted Frederic's desire to resign from the Board, she had so many things to take care of for the dedication ceremony that she did not respond to his letter immediately.[792]

William had written regarding some revisions to the ceremony and had sent a list of items to be placed in the cornerstone box requiring her approval. She was also involved in planning the dinner that would follow the dedication, which included reserving a meeting room at Pere Marquette State Park Lodge for Houpt, who had agreed to give a talk and slide show after the dinner about the third Principia Abroad. She sent a note of thanks to him in advance for his part in making the dedication day complete. She also wrote to William, thanking him for keeping in touch and assuring him that she did not mind hearing from him often since she believed it helped them to have "a united understanding" about the dedication ceremony.[793]

On March 25, Hazle responded to Frederic regarding his retirement: "I am sorry to think that you will not be with us for our meeting after this next one—but please remember to stop in at Bloomington whenever you are anywhere near." Frederic replied that he hoped "to remain a member of the Board of Trustees for as long as my fellow members think this is desirable, but I do wish to be relieved of my post as Chairman." In regard to the School of Nations building, he told her, "My thought goes back over a long period of years during which it was my privilege to work with you in planning for the building and for the functions which it performs."[794]

A few days later, Hazle received a note from Houpt in response to her appreciation of his willingness to give a talk and slide show after the dedication dinner. He shared with her the gratitude expressed to him by students during the last Abroad and concluded, "The value of this activity, which you have made possible, is something that cannot be measured in any tangible way." Houpt was relatively new to the position of Chairman of the School of Nations Committee and did not know her well, but he had already gained a deep appreciation of Hazle's contributions to Principia and especially for the Principia Abroad program.[795]

On the last day of March, Hazle sent her "short talk" to William for his suggestions. William responded, "I think the remarks in your talk are exactly right," and added that he would include a copy of it in the cornerstone box. After receiving William's letter, Hazle called him to make final preparations for the ceremony. During their conversation, he told her of the gold-plated building key and little presentation box that he had prepared for her to present to him at the dedication. After the dedication, the key and box could be placed on the wall as a historic memento.[796]

In early April, Hazle made plans to stay with her friends, Helen and Eldredge Hamlin, the Saturday night before the ceremony. She wanted to be close by so that she could be in touch with William in case she thought of something that needed to be done. She also made reservations at Pere Marquette for Sunday night following the dedication dinner, and arranged with William for Ralph to unveil the building plaque, "since he was a Principia student at the time when the School of Nations idea began to take form." She also sent an announcement of the dedication to the *Pantagraph*, which appeared in the April 5, 1959 issue of the paper. The announcement stated that the School of Nations building was the "culmination of an idea born to [Hazle] on a world trip in 1924" and represented a small United Nations project promoting her "lifelong ambition of fostering peaceful world relations."[797]

CHAPTER 35

THESE ARE YOUR DAYS

On April 14, Frederic told Hazle, "I vividly recall your letter of many years ago in which you expressed your desire to establish the work on the School of Nations." She, too, remembered that letter well, and the cool, crisp November morning when the idea that inspired it had come to her in the garden where she had been reading her Christian Science Bible lesson. She also recalled how the plan for the program unfolded during the following months when Frederic, George Andrews, and Tom Blackwell made several trips to Bloomington to talk with her about her ideas for the School of Nations. She also appreciated the support of Bernard Maybeck, the architect, who believed that the construction of Nationality Rooms would encourage students to think in terms of the "cultural ideas and languages being studied."[798]

Frederic acknowledged her "superb patience and unselfishness in being willing to delay the construction" of her building, and added, "This is indeed your year and the days of this April meeting of our Board are indeed your days – yours as the consistently gentle, wise, and always generous and unselfish child of God, deeply, tenderly interested in her fellow man and wholly and sincerely committed to service, to the cause of Christian Science, including those wide avenues of service Principia provides." He confided that she had deeply impressed him, and told her, "I will carry with me into whatever activities that may [lay] ahead the inspiration of your example of unfailing kindness and impersonal love." A bouquet of soft yellow roses accompanied his message.[799]

A crowd began to gather in the Holt Gallery for the dedication of the School of Nations building on Sunday, April 19, 1959—a warm spring day. Only a few hours earlier, a large puddle of water had been found in the auditorium that had come from a leak in the ceiling caused by heavy rains the previous day. But at the time of the dedication, no evidence of the water remained. The ceremony began with the choir singing Hymn 203, which Hazle had selected for this occasion from the *Christian Science Hymnal*:

> O Father, may we bear each hour
>   The flag of hope and peace unfurled,
> And mirror forth Love's sacred power
>   To feed and bless a hungry world.
> We shall not falter by the way
>   If we but place our trust in Thee,
> Obeying gladly day by day
>   The living Truth that makes men free.
>
> Help us to know that all is well
>   E'en though we wander through earth's shade,
> To know that all Thy children dwell
>   Within Love's stronghold unafraid.
> Teach us to follow fearlessly
>   The way our gentle Master trod,
> 'Twill lead us safely home to Thee,
>   O loving Father-Mother, God.[800]

Following the hymn, Frederic Morgan read citations from the Bible and the writings of Mary Baker Eddy, chosen by Hazle, which closely reflected her thoughts regarding the purpose of the School of Nations:

> And it shall come to pass in the last days, that the mountain of the Lord's house shall be established in the top of the mountains, and shall be exalted above the hills; and all nations shall flow unto it. And many people shall go and

say, Come ye, and let us go up to the mountain of the Lord, . . . And he shall judge among the nations, and they shall beat their swords into plowshares, and their spears into pruning hooks: nation shall not lift up sword against nation, neither shall they learn war anymore (Isa. 2:2, 3).[801]

And many nations shall be joined to the Lord in that day, and shall be my people: and I will dwell in the midst of thee, and thou shalt know the Lord of hosts hath sent me unto thee (Zech. 2:11).[802]

And the inhabitants of one city shall go to another, saying, Let us go speedily to pray before the Lord, and to seek the Lord of hosts: I will go also. Yea, many people and strong nations shall come to seek the Lord of hosts in Jerusalem, and to pray before the Lord . . . We will go with you: for we have heard that God is with you (Zech. 8:21,22, 23).[803]

Happy are the people whose God is All-in-all, who ask only to be judged according to their works, who live to love. . . . Unlike Russia's armament, ours is not costly as men count cost, but it is rich beyond price, staunch and indestructible on land or sea; it is not curtailed in peace, surrendered in conquest, nor laid down at the feet of progress through the hands of omnipotence. And why? Because it is "on earth peace, good will toward men,"—a cover and a defence adapted to all men, all nations, all times, climes, and races, (The First Church of Christ Scientist and Miscellany, 127:4-6, 25-32, by Mary Baker Eddy, used by courtesy of The Mary Baker Eddy Collection.).[804]

Through the wholesome chastisements of Love, nations are helped onward towards justice, righteousness, and peace, which are the landmarks of prosperity. In order to apprehend more, we must practise what we already know of the Golden Rule, which is to all mankind a light emitting light (The First Church of Christ Scientist and Miscellany

282:10-15, by Mary Baker Eddy, used by courtesy of The
Mary Baker Eddy Collection).[805]

One infinite God, good, unifies men and nations;
constitutes the brotherhood of man; ends wars; fulfils the
Scripture, 'Love thy neighbor as thyself;' annihilates pagan
and Christian idolatry,—whatever is wrong in social, civil,
criminal, political, and religious codes; equalizes the sexes;
annuls the curse on man, and leaves nothing that can sin,
suffer, be punished or destroyed, (*Science and Health with
Key to the Scriptures* 340:23-29 by Mary Baker Eddy, used by
courtesy of The Mary Baker Eddy Collection).[806]

For the kingdom is the Lord's: and he is the governor among
the nations (Ps. 22:28).[807]

At the conclusion of the readings, Frederic, as the Chairman
of the Board of Trustees, expressed appreciation for Hazle and her
initiation of the School of Nations. He told the audience that
although the program had been initiated in 1925, there had been a
long delay in erecting a proper building for the program because the
country was in a depression when the College buildings were being
constructed. He explained that "Mrs. Ewing, our precious fellow
trustee and Principia's much loved friend, suggested that the funds
which she had offered for the erection of the School of Nations
building" be used for what was most needed to move the College to
the Elsah campus. In addition, she proposed that the funds could be
repaid by the Trustees "when and as they could afford to make the
repayments."[808]

By the time the school had been able to repay Hazle, twenty-
five years had elapsed and building costs had increased drastically
making it necessary for her to add substantially to her original
offer. In addition to her more than liberal contributions, the
School of Nations received a large bequest from Mrs. Gladys C.
Lovelace of Peoria and Henry Holt generously donated the money
for Holt Gallery.[809]

Introducing Hazle, Frederic said, "Mrs. Ewing has been exceedingly active in state affairs, especially matters of state parks and beautification of natural resources. In fact, she has been interested in all manner of civic projects in her section of Illinois. She is a graduate of the University of Chicago, and has always been interested in education. She is the founder and the chief contributor of the School of Nations." He told the audience that her sons, Ralph and Nelson Ewing, had been students at Principia. In addition, Hazle became a member of the Board of Trustees of Principia in 1935, a position she still held.[810]

After Frederic's introduction, Hazle began her talk: "Dr. Frederic E. Morgan, Chairman of the Board of Trustees, Dr. William E. Morgan, President, Members of the Board of Trustees, Faculty, Staff, Students and Guests—it is good to have you with us today, as we dedicate the School of Nations Building." She paused for a moment and then continued:

> Late in 1924, my husband, Davis Ewing, our older son, Ralph Nelson Ewing and I left San Francisco for a long-planned leisurely trip around the world with the Bureau of University Travel that was not to bring us home for more than a year.
>
> During all those weeks and months, we found only the greatest friendliness everywhere. This convinced me that most people . . . were friendly. We found such cordial welcome everywhere that I came home wishing that every human being, the world around, could take such a trip.
>
> As we were on our way home, with the long miles of ocean all around us, I found myself thinking that, if every world-citizen could take the same kind of trip we had taken, there would be no more war. We had found that our ideas of the good life were shared by most thinking people everywhere.

Nobody believed that war had ever really settled anything. We discovered that what every thinking person longed for was to be able to live a life of peace and security for himself and his family.

As a result of this trip, what I hoped to encourage was a study of other peoples of the world—their hopes and fears, their dreams, their accomplishments!

What sort of world citizens had their nationals become? What were their contributions to education, culture, science, world-wide well-being?

And what were our contributions?

It became clear to me that every one who goes from one country to another, in any capacity, is an unofficial and unconscious ambassador. There are schools for ambassadors. Don't we need schools for travelers, as well?

While I was searching for a name for this particular educational activity, it occurred to me to look up the definition of the word, "school." I had long been familiar with the names, "School of Law," "School of Agriculture," "School of Domestic Science," etc. My dictionary told me that the word "school" meant merely the study of law, agriculture, domestic science, etc.

The name "School of Nations,"—then would mean, the study of nations, their hopes and fears, accomplishments and failures, tragedies and victories.

Today some of our School of Nations students have responsible positions in other countries. Some are connected with the United States Foreign Service Department.

I hope you will each be able to take time to notice the sketches for the Nationality Rooms in the School of

Nations Building—in which we hope to suggest some of
the contributions made by various national cultures. We
have already had some gifts toward specific Nationality
Rooms—and hope to have others as we are ready to
decorate and furnish these rooms.[811]

She then turned to William and, handing him the key to the
building, said, "President Morgan it is my happy privilege and
pleasure to present to you, at this time, the key of the School of
Nations Building, with the hope that it may have a long life of
service in encouragement of understanding and appreciation of
the contributions made by each of the nations toward world-wide
culture and well-being." She concluded her remarks quoting from
the writings of Mary Baker Eddy: "One infinite God, good, unifies
men and nations; constitutes the brotherhood of man; ends wars;
fulfills the scripture, 'Love thy neighbor as thyself.'"[812] At the end of
her talk, Ralph unveiled the plaque on the outside of the building.[813]

William then told the crowd that, "When Mrs. Ewing became
a Principia Trustee she brought to her work . . . a clear vision of the
great need of international understanding and recognition of the
cultural, social, and economic contributions made by each of the
peoples of the world to world civilization and welfare." He explained
that the School of Nations was established as a program administered
by a faculty committee in 1927 through Hazle's encouragement
and financial support. A School of Nations committee has the
responsibility and privilege of providing speakers who expand the
understanding of the entire school regarding foreign lands; creating
a curriculum that enriches the knowledge of students about other
peoples around the world; and giving students the opportunity for
travel to other lands. He related that the School of Nations had had
such a positive influence on the entire school that by 1935 military
drill and wearing of uniforms was discontinued at the Upper School
and Junior College. In recognition of the School of Nations program,
Principia had been given flags from twenty-two different nations.[814]

In addition to its influence on the entire campus, the School of Nations program encouraged individual students to pursue graduate study that would lead them into avenues of Foreign Service, or careers in journalism, translation, and teaching, "with the hope of serving the peoples and nations of the world." As an example, one graduate, assisted by the School of Nations funds, had prepared for and passed the State Department examinations and has since served our country at Naval headquarters in China, Guam, and Greenland; and more recently in Prague, Athens, and London as Consul General.[815]

William told those in attendance about the cornerstone box that is part of the dedication of each building on the College campus. The School of Nations cornerstone box would contain: the Bible and the writings of Mary Baker Eddy with the dedication references marked in them; a copy of As the Sowing by Edwin S. Leonard, with references to the School of Nations indicated; Frederic's statement of appreciation from the Board of Trustees; and a copy of Hazle's talk. He pointed out that the School of Nations museum housed many items from around the world. The display cases in Holt Gallery would soon be used to highlight different articles from the museum. William then expressed gratitude to the Holt family for providing the auditorium in the School of Nations building, and Henry Holt, Jr., a graduate of Principia, unveiled the plaque in Holt Gallery bearing his mother's name: Vivian Small Holt.[816]

C. Theodore Houpt, the Chairman of the School of Nations Committees on the College campus, was next to speak to the crowd, and said, "It is my hope that I can convey to you some concept of what the School of Nations, whose activities are now centered in this gracious, spacious building, means to this community." He said he thought that the School of Nations largely contributes "to that 'whole' man, which is the ideal of a Principia education," by liberally educating students with an appreciation of cultures other than their own. And, as one involved in the education of the students, Houpt believed that:

> The School of Nations, through its sponsored activities, promotes largeness of thought, consideration of the achievements and problems of other nations, mastery of the means of communicating with these other peoples (through knowledge of foreign languages), appreciation of the gains they have made in their thinking and experience, gains recorded in their literatures. Thinking . . . along international cultural lines liberalizes and liberates the thought of the student who may have come from a narrowly provincial background and protects him from falling into unquestioning conformity or complacency.[817]

It seemed to Houpt that the students traveling in foreign countries provided a richer understanding between nations than could be accomplished by diplomats. He believed that, "Whatever can be done to promote it deserves support, and Mrs. Ewing has supported it in a vastly generous and practical way by founding and maintaining this School of Nations with its multiple activities," which has completed three successful Principia Abroad tours. On these trips students had the opportunity to see how people in the lands they visited lived, worked, and thought. The students also had the privilege of participating in "on-the-spot" studies of history, literature, and art. He felt that the program provided "a rich education experience for the . . . students" who took part in the program. He thanked Hazle on behalf of the School of Nations faculty and staff "for . . . one of Principia's greatest blessings, the School of Nations and its new home, this School of Nations Building." [818]

Following Houpt's speech, a student who had been a member of the 1958 Principia Abroad group, Ann Waller, talked about the "unique educational experience" the Principia Abroad program provided for students. She found that sightseeing, background reading, and attending lectures revealed the "rich heritage" of western European culture, which is the foundation of the American way of life. She believed that she had gained a "true picture of other peoples and their values." As representatives of Principia and Christian Science in foreign countries, Ann felt that students were challenged to live up to their highest sense of joy, dominion, and health. The students endeavored to keep in mind their own values and ideals while helping others to appreciate what Americans have to offer. But most importantly, they had to be constantly aware of the "characteristics and ideals of the people in the countries" they visited.[819]

Following Ann's remarks, Dr. Leonard spoke as the Dean of the College, and a former Chairman of the School of Nations, regarding what the program meant to the community as a whole. Leonard explained that the "generous provision of this splendid new classroom building" was much more than a mere convenience: "[I]t is a new dimension to the teaching situation on campus." Besides providing a place for the activities of the students and offices for teachers and staff, the building afforded a home for the museum and cases for displaying "artifacts, costumes, figurines, paintings, tapestries, and ceramics illustrative of the way of life of the various peoples of the world." He looked forward to the completion of the Nationality Rooms, which would represent nations of the world and the School of Nations' hope of promoting peace and good will.[820]

Leonard then introduced William Ward, President of the Student Council, who expressed gratitude for the new building on behalf of the students, who had previously had their classes in Radford, a wooden building, where it seemed to be either extremely warm or extremely cold, thus interfering with their ability to focus on their school-work. Ward believed the new building would enable students to do better work, telling the audience, "I am confident that we will respond to our new surroundings with increased cultural fruition." At the conclusion of Ward's remarks, the choir sang the final hymn and the audience dispersed to tour the building.[821]

That evening, Hazle was joined by her family and friends to celebrate the dedication at the Pere Marquette Lodge restaurant. Among those in attendance were Henry Holt and his family; William and Dorinda Morgan; some of Hazle's family members, including Kate Lee and Ralph Ewing; June and Nelson Ewing and their four children, Ted, Sandra, Philip, and Davis; Mrs. Nelson (Rena) Buck, and Constance and Ellsworth Buck. Hazle regretted that her granddaughter, Cindy, was unable to attend. Several friends were also there including: Julia Hodge, Adeline Adams, Melita Stodddard, Mrs. Jacob Bohrer, Mr. and Mrs. Richard Stevens, Mr. and Mrs. John Taylor, Mr. and Mrs. Fred Sauter, Mr. and Mrs. Winthrop Robinson, Mrs. Martin Hardin, Letitia Stevenson, Mr. and Mrs. Baumgarten, Mr. and Mrs. Art Eiff, Mrs. Charlotte Prichard, Mr. and Mrs. Edwin Pekette, and Mrs. Leta Guante. The members of the School of Nations Committee attending the dinner included Robert Andrews, Brook Ballard, Virginia Hall, Dorothy Hooper, Frank Parker, Douglas Swett, and C. Theodore Houpt, who was joined by his wife, Ann, by a special invitation from Hazle. The dinner was delicious, the company entertaining, and Hazle thought Houpt's talk and slide show following the dinner had been just what they needed to "top off the day."[822]

The next morning, Hazle received a note from Frederic complimenting her on her talk, which he thought was a "beautiful statement made with great dignity, ease, naturalness, and impersonality." It meant much to Hazle to receive Frederic's supportive comments and to be reminded once again of his joy over the dedication of the School of Nations building. She was happy to be considered "a wonderful friend to Principia" whose friendship he cherished "most highly." [823]

Hazle also appreciated the publicity that the *Pantagraph* gave the School of Nations on the day of the dedication through an article that included pictures of the building. And the school newspaper, the *Pilot*, provided her with several copies of the issue featuring the dedication and a picture of her in front of the plaque to share with her friends and family. Some weeks later, William presented her with a book containing photographs taken and talks given at the dedication ceremony. Ultimately, the greatest reminder of that day was the School of Nations building itself, a testament to Hazle's initiation and unselfish support of the School of Nations program.[824]

CHAPTER 36

A DREAM COME TRUE

$\mathscr{F}$ollowing the accomplishment of dedicating the School of Nations building, Hazle enjoyed the summer of 1959, part of which she spent reminiscing with Frederic about their 25 years of working together for Principia. On the bottom of her copy of the June 12 Board of Trustees' letter, Frederic had written a note expressing his gratitude for her generosity to Principia over the years. She wrote to him, "I have it in my heart to thank you for your loving appreciation of what I have been able to do for Principia through the years. It has been a most rewarding and satisfying experience. It has been a joy to work with you."[825] In response, Frederic told her:

> I do indeed hold in my heart the very happiest kind of appreciative memories in regard to the many years during which it has been my privilege to be associated with you in connection with Principia's work. My respect for the spiritual quality of unselfishness with which you live your life and for the generous and loving interest in others which results there-from has always been and will continue to be an inspiration to me.[826]

Both Hazle and Frederic knew that only part of her dream for the School of Nations had been accomplished in the construction and dedication of the building. The Nationality Rooms and Museum remained to be completed. In July 1959, Hazle loaned Principia $65,000 to begin work on the first two Nationality Rooms. Jim Green, the Director of the Principia College Art

Department, began reworking the drawings for the Spanish and French rooms in February 1960. He spent the following summer in Europe purchasing desks and chairs, sample student chairs, and light fixtures for the two Nationality Rooms, and searching for wrought iron and "old Spanish tiles" that would be used for a decorative border extending around the entire Spanish room.[827]

Hazle received the blueprints of the two rooms near the end of August, and she wrote to William, "I am very eager to see the rooms as they will be by the time I come down for the meetings." She hoped that by November there would be some progress made in at least one of the rooms. Responding to her letter, William reported that the plastering had begun and the mill work would soon arrive for the tiles in the Spanish room. But despite their expectations, not much work was accomplished on the rooms that fall.[828]

In early March 1961, when Hazle and a group of her friends visited Principia to see the Spanish and French rooms, Jim Green gave them a "personally conducted tour of the School of Nations Building." After returning home, she wrote to him: "Thank you for giving me samples of the tiles—both for the border and the floor. I have been happy to have them to show to my friends as they have come in." She added, "I have been waiting a long time to see even this much taking shape. It will be a great satisfaction when the rooms are completed—and students can have their classes surrounded by furnishings that go with the subject." She concluded:

> Please know that I appreciate greatly the importance you have had in hunting out and selecting what has gone into the rooms so far. You have done such a good job that I hope every member of the classes who meet in the rooms will absorb something of the artistry of the nation that it represents. I thank you heartily for your interest and care in selecting appropriate furnishings for each of the rooms. They should encourage appreciation of the contributions that each country has made in the art and handiwork put into their furnishings.[829]

Hazle was unable to attend the April 1961 Board of Trustees Meeting at which David Andrews was appointed to succeed William Morgan, Jr., as President of the College. But Hamlin wrote to her of the appointment. In May she received a letter from Andrews telling her, "It is with much gratitude and joy that I can tell you that the two finished Nationality Rooms have been put into use for Language Classes this week." He added, "It is our hope that you will come down soon to see the rooms actually in use. I feel confident that you will be delighted with the finished product."[830]

Making a trip to Elsah in June, Hazle had the opportunity to see the completed Spanish and French rooms, which gave her a great sense of satisfaction. During her visit, she mentioned to Andrews her desire for work to begin on the English room and perhaps the Oriental room as soon as possible. Andrews kept in close contact with Hazle during the summer and wrote to her in late September: "Ever since Summer Session,** I have wanted to share with you some of the great joy and pleasure which the Summer Session classes have derived from their work in the School of Nations Building." He told her of the many expressions of appreciation they had received about the completed rooms, and the many questions regarding the unfinished ones. He expressed his desire to begin to work with her on the unfinished rooms "whenever" she wished.[831]

By July 1962, Hazle had donated enough money to complete two more nationality rooms. In mid-August, Andrews reported that Jim Green had begun working on the preliminary sketches for the Oriental and English rooms. He also told her that the School of Nations Museum had received "a Japanese manikin clothed in ceremonial robes" from Principia's good friend, Mrs. Takai, who had worn the robes "in her position as lady in waiting to the Empress of Japan." Two museums in Japan had offered to buy the

** These are two-week courses held during the summer and attended by Principia alum and other interested Christian Scientists.

ceremonial robes, but they had been sent to the Principia instead. Hazle looked forward to seeing the picture of the manikin and robes that Andrews promised to send.[832]

In early 1963, Hazle began planning for the future of the School of Nations by sending $12,000 to Principia as the nucleus of an endowment fund. She also set aside a bequest for Principia in the event of her passing. She greatly desired to see all of the Nationality Rooms completed, but the work seemed to be progressing slowly on the English and Oriental rooms.[833]

Alice Bright, Hazle's attorney, wrote to Principia in October 1963, requesting an accounting of the donations that Hazle had made for the Nationality Rooms since 1958. Bert Clark, the treasurer for Principia, reported that the amount totaled $209,744.13. A portion of the funds, $31,500, had been allocated to the endowment fund, which needed to be increased to $100,000 in order to supply the annual amount of $4,000 for the maintenance fund.[834]

On January 10, 1964, Miss Bright and several members of Hazle's family, including Ralph and Nelson, visited Principia in Hazle's place since she was unable to make the trip. While they were there, Nelson took pictures of the English and Oriental rooms for her. They also toured the museum and discussed ideas on how to enlarge the storage space. It was thought that display cases should be installed "around the perimeter of the extensive corridor outside of and next to the present [museum] storage area," which would provide the maximum space for displaying museum items. Hazle approved of providing additional display cases for the museum in late March.[835]

In April, plans for the museum were completed, which included additional lighting for the cases that would cost between $1,200 and $1,500. Also, preliminary work was being done in preparation for creating the drawings for the remaining Nationality Rooms. Andrews wrote to Bright that he would let her know as soon as he had a clear idea of the architect's schedule.[836]

Bright and members of Hazle's family met with Andrews at Principia on June 5, 1964, to review the plans and drawings for the last four Nationality Rooms and the placement of the display cases in the museum. The estimated costs for decorating the nationality rooms and purchasing display cases would be $115,000. After seeing the sketches and learning the cost to complete the projects, Hazle gave her approval, and Bright wrote to Andrews on June 9: "Mrs. Ewing is delighted with the plans for the museum and was enthusiastic about the sketches for the Russian, Indian, and Arabic rooms." Hazle requested, however, that some changes be made to the drawing for the German room.[837]

The completion date for the interior of the building was expected to be January 1, 1965, and Bright wrote to Andrews: "Mrs. Ewing is most anxious that the work on completing the building be pushed forward as rapidly as is possible and as is consistent with the completion of the rooms in the manner heretofore discussed." Andrews responded that they looked forward to proceeding with the construction at once, and that they would work with the architect for "further refinements to the German Room."[838]

Later in June, Andrews wrote to Hazle, "I am sure you know of our great gratitude to you for making these wonderful things possible," and added, "With the additional display cases for the Museum and the completion of the Nationality Rooms, the School of Nations Building will be a full and wonderful expression of your vision for it." Hazle had long awaited the completion of this building and daily looked forward to its attainment.[839]

Eldridge Hamlin and his wife, Helen, arrived at Sunset Hill on November 20, 1964, to present a Trustee Emeritus certificate to Hazle, which had been awarded to her by the Board of Trustees in "recognition of her exceptionally loyal, able, and generous service to The Principia and its Board of Trustees beyond the usual requirements of trusteeship." She had faithfully served on the board for thirty years. The certificate read in part:[840]

> The Trustees of this Corporation by unanimous action
> have established an Emeritus recognition for those
> trustees who, upon retirement, have a record of both
> long and outstanding service. It is understood that this
> honor is awarded only after careful consideration and
> in acknowledgement of a devotion that has been of
> exceptional value to the work of The Principia.[841]

Hamlin expressed the Board's appreciation for her establishment
of the School of Nations in 1927, which has "enlarged and enriched
the vision of many young people who have participated" in its
activities. He also conveyed the Board members' desire that she
know of their gratitude for the School of Nations Museum, which
she had provided to exhibit "the rich treasures that have come to
[the College] over the years."[842]

On Sunday June 13, 1965, Hazle's family and Miss Bright
attended a ceremony at Principia to celebrate the completion of
the Nationality Rooms. Andrews read a letter that he had written
to Hazle especially for this occasion, in which he said in part:

> From the early days of the School of Nations you had
> desired to provide a building at the college which could
> serve as a center for the School of Nations program.
> Because of other even more urgent needs, you generously
> permitted your funds to be used temporarily for other
> buildings and waited patiently until, finally in 1959, the
> School of Nations Building could be dedicated. For many
> years you had dreamed of including in this building rooms
> which would portray dramatically the beauty, design and
> furnishings of cultures other than our own. . . . Each room
> has been a major project in design, in the search for just
> the right things to be included in it, and in the substantial
> cost involved. . . . Every one of the eight is an exquisite
> example of an important culture in the world society. In a

manner rarely found anywhere, they bring to us a feeling
of the way of life in these distant regions.

It is with deep gratitude that we accept these rooms as an
addition to your wonderful list of gifts to Principia.

From the early days of the School of Nations one of
its most delightful and thrilling projects had been the
development of the School of Nations Museum. . . . Your
recent decision to provide a greatly increased exhibit
area in the Museum by the addition of many new exhibit
cases makes the Museum itself a more prominent and
important center of display.

Our heartfelt thanks are always with you. We are grateful
that members of your family can be with us at this time
of rejoicing, and we send you through their kindness our
love and affectionate greetings.[843]

When the letter was later read to Hazle, the sentiments that
Andrews expressed touched her deeply.[844]

Principia's administration proposed an addition to the Museum
in late June 1965, and Bright wrote to Andrews, "Mrs. Ewing
has approved the proposed extension of the museum facilities in
accordance with the estimates given us." Ralph and Nelson were
anxious for the work on the museum to go forward as rapidly as
possible and requested an anticipated date of completion. They
hoped the work could be done in the near future "so that their
mother could see the completed Nationality Rooms and the
completed museum."[845]

Andrews wrote to Hazle in late October, 1965, "What joy we had
over the past few months watching the splendid additions being made
to the School of Nations Museum." He admitted that the work had
been slower than anticipated because of strikes and similar challenges
with the factories supplying equipment. However, the cases had been

installed and displays were being arranged. He told her, "You would be very pleased and proud, I know, with what has been accomplished as the result of your generosity and your far-reaching vision." He concluded, "You know how much love there is here for you on the campus, and what it would mean to have you visit with us."[846]

In early February 1966, the School of Nations Museum was completed, and Hazle arranged to give Principia the amount of money needed for the endowment fund to permanently maintain the scholarship program for studying abroad, provide for exchange students and teachers, and continue having visiting lecturers on the subjects of international relations and peace. Bright wrote Andrews, "It is, of course, Mrs. Ewing's hope that in the future years others may also be interested in contributing to this permanent endowment fund so as to expand the Travel-Abroad Program."[847]

Andrews wrote to Hazle regarding the endowment fund, "This is a most thrilling thing, and the wonderful contribution to start it off makes us deeply grateful for your tangible interest and support." He assured Hazle that they would use the income from the endowment fund to "help young people broaden their horizons through study and travel abroad." Through this program, Principia could continue to bring teachers and students from other lands to contribute to a greater understanding of the true brotherhood of man on the school campuses. He also believed that the lectures would broaden the knowledge of international relations and bring peace to the world. He told Hazle, "As you can see, this gift of yours opens up wonderful possibilities for our program of international understanding," and added, "It is very typical of your broad, active, and generous thought." He felt sure that her example would encourage others to make additional contributions to the fund.[848]

That spring, it became apparent that Hazle would not be making a trip to Principia, but Andrews continued to keep her informed about the School of Nations activities and the building. On November 20, 1967, he wrote, "I have just come from taking another group of visitors through the School of Nations Nationality Rooms and museum . . . we never tire of sharing these lovely things with Principia's friends." He added, "Each time that we go through the building we think of you and quietly express our gratitude for all the love you have poured into this project." He assured her, "It would please you immensely to hear the astonished and delighted comments of our visitors." And he concluded, "Our love and affection continue to be very much with you. The good you have done for Principia is having a lasting effect and will long go into the future."[849]

Aware of Hazle's desire to keep the School of Nations booklet up-to-date, Andrews sent her a copy of the new 1968 edition, saying, "I know that you and your family will enjoy seeing [it]." He also offered to send other copies, if she desired, for family members and friends. Kate Lee responded for Hazle on February 22, saying that they were "thrilled" with the School of Nations booklet and would like to have several copies to "hand out as we visit around—certainly Principia and Mother Ewing deserve widest spread information."[850]

Recalling the history of the School of Nations, Andrews wrote to Ralph and Kate Lee in March 1968, "Mrs. Ewing has been so wonderfully helpful in permitting us to use her funds for other very urgent needs over a long period of years that we really should have put a date back in the 1930s as the time that the building was to have been built." He added, "Of course, it could not have been built until the funds were released from these other projects, and in the meantime Mrs. Ewing has waited very patiently for her wonderful dream to come true."[851]

CULMINATION OF LIFE

CHAPTER 37

THE LASTING GREATNESS OF A GOOD LIFE

$\mathcal{O}$ n August 29, 1969, at the age of eighty-nine, Hazle passed away quietly in her home, Sunset Hill, where she had spent the last four years of her life in quiet seclusion. Her sons, Ralph and Nelson, and their wives had taken turns staying with her in her home. Dr. Edgar Stevenson, a local and highly respected physician, often came to visit Hazle, as a friend. He did not prescribe for nor give Hazle any medication. He had received financial assistance from Hazle to establish the Nursing School of Illinois Wesleyan University, and she had insisted that the administrative offices of the Nursing School be named after him—Stevenson Hall. Greatly appreciating what Hazle had done for him and the Nursing School, Dr. Stevenson provided assurance to the outside world that Hazle was receiving proper care.[852]

After Hazle's passing, the Bloomington newspaper, the *Pantagraph*, recounted some of her good works. An article appeared in the August 30, 1969, issue recalling that she had donated two parks to the city of Bloomington, made provision for the restoration of Miller Park Bridge, established a fund for the support and development of the park zoo, had given financial assistance for the remodeling of the former science building of the Illinois Wesleyan University for the School of Nursing (now named Stevenson Hall), assisted in the development and maintenance of Victory Hall (a home for boys), financially supported the Lucy Orme Morgan Home for Girls, and founded the School of Nations at Principia.[853]

On Sunday, August 31, another article appeared in the *Pantagraph* recording Hazle's long-time membership in the League of Women Voters and her active support of "votes for women," her work as the director of publicity for the food conservation department of the Council of National Defense during World War I, and her involvement with Girl Scouts as a troop leader for several years. The article also stated that she had been a life member of the American Association of Women, American Humane Society, American Civic Association, Art Institute of Chicago, National Audubon Society, and Staten Island Zoological Society. It went on to say she had been a member of the University of Chicago Alumni Association, the English Speaking Union, the American Red Cross, and the local and world YWCA and YMCA.[854]

On Tuesday, September 2, *The Daily Pantagraph* printed an article titled, "Feeling of Community Strong in Mrs. Ewing," which stated, "Mrs. Ewing was unique because she had a keen understanding of the responsibilities and opportunities wealth brings." She had dedicated her life to philanthropy and promoting the arts and world understanding, and "Mrs. Ewing seemed born to participate, to be interested, to be publicly and privately helpful. From her youngest days she was an activist both physically and mentally." Her interests ranged from woman's suffrage to planning miles of bridle paths along Sugar Creek. It seemed that "Mrs. Ewing so lived that none of the resentment or suspicion so often directed toward the wealthy touched her." The reporter acknowledged that although Hazle's health had forced her to withdraw from an active public life to live more privately, "her great tasks were done," and added, that, regardless of the seeming mystery of her withdrawal, "Bloomington and Normal are better places for her being here."[855]

Hazle's friends at Principia also recalled her good works, and Hamlin noted to the Board of Trustees, "All of us who have had the pleasure of knowing Mrs. Ewing will continue to be deeply grateful for her years of dedication to Principia and the many, many ways in which she contributed to its unfoldment." Hazle Buck Ewing's great tasks were done, but they would not be soon forgotten.[856]

Nearly fifty people gathered at Sunset Hill on Wednesday September 3, 1969, at 2:00 p.m., to attend the memorial service for Hazle, over which David Andrews presided. He opened the ceremony saying, "We come together to acknowledge the lasting greatness of a good life and to give grateful thanks for it. We are here to be comforted, not to mourn. As we read in the Scriptures, 'Blessed are they that mourn for they shall be comforted'" (Matthew 5:4). He then read from the *Christian Science Hymnal*, page 44:

> Come to the land of peace; From shadows come away;
> Where all the sounds of weeping cease,
>   And storms no more have sway.
> Fear hath no dwelling here; But pure repose and love
> Breathe through the bright, celestial air
>   The Spirit of the dove
> In this divine abode, Change leaves no saddening trace;
> Come, trusting heart, Come to thy God,
>   Thy holy resting place.[857]

He followed the hymn with citations, which he read from the Bible and the writings of Mary Baker Eddy. Then, speaking of Hazle, he told those gathered at her home that day:

> Virtuous woman and true philanthropist! How rightly this expresses the life of Hazle Buck Ewing. Strong, virtuous and active, Mrs. Ewing devoted the same thoughtful attention to her many civic interests as she did to her home and family, both of which she loved dearly. Those of us who have been privileged over the years to know her have recognized in her the bold imagination and fearless spirit of the pioneer, as well as the tenderness and kindly interest of the true mother thought.

More than forty years ago, when foreign travel was available only to a very few, Mrs. Ewing traveled extensively with her family. But she did not just travel. She caught a vision of the need for greater brotherhood and understanding among peoples, and she took unusual but practical steps, such as the establishment of the School of Nations at Principia, to share her ideal with hundreds of other people. Thus she has continued over many years her leadership in the cause of world understanding.

Mrs. Ewing had a deep love for all nature and the outdoors. For many years she rode horseback regularly and had an intimate knowledge of the birds, plants and animals in her environment.

Always interested in the needs and affairs of her community, she was public spirited and generous to her neighbors. Her generosity was realistic, too, often expressed in kindly homely counsel for her younger friends and in the careful management and self-discipline of her own affairs, which enabled her to save at home and thus give more bountifully to causes in which she believed.

Mrs. Ewing's influence for good was enhanced by her humility and her skill in keeping herself out of the limelight. To be in her company even for a brief period was to feel her warm and direct interest and to be infected with her idealism.

In nothing was this idealism more beautifully expressed than in her deep devotion to her church and to any activities dedicated to support of its Christian ministry. Hazle Buck Ewing has indeed lived her faith with grace and integrity. She has with great modesty been a powerful influence for good in many ways. The world is better because she walked among us. Rather than grieve at her going, we can only be grateful for all she has done and stood for.[858]

Concluding his remarks, Andrews read the following poem in honor of the "lasting greatness" of Hazle's "good life":

> "Having eyes, see ye not?"
> We have seen a life lived in nobility:
> We have seen, in this friend,
> A measure of the immeasurable,
> The serenity and the stature of being.
> Only if we have finished seeing, has a life been lost,
> Only if we forfeit to cramped human sight
> The privilege of knowing what is unalterably here,
> Is any darkened place within our range of view.
> Reopened eyes can show us quite undimmed nobility,
> The integrity of living.
> Neither our friend nor we the losers.
>
> Anonymous[859]

True to her generous and caring nature, which Andrews acknowledged in his remarks, Hazle had thoughtfully prepared for her inevitable departure from this life. She made provisions for her family, friends, and employees. Her sons, Ralph and Nelson, were to share a trust, including stock in the Thunder Mountain Ranch Company, Lake Cabin, and a substantial amount of money. Hazle had also established a life income for her friend, Adeline Adams. At Adeline's demise, what remained of her trust would revert to Principia College. The amounts awarded to her current employees depended on the length of their service in her home. Hazle's ability to manage her finances well had enabled her to leave generous bequests to those nearest and dearest to her.[860]

She left her house and property in Bloomington, which was valued at $121,500, to Illinois State University, and a $200,000 fund to maintain the house and grounds as a School of Nations museum. In December 1969, the University renamed Sunset Hill, calling it The Ewing Museum of Nations, thus honoring both Hazle and Davis, who had put a great deal of planning and supervising into the building of their home. Under that name, it was made possible for residents and guests to visit the estate. The university promoted international understanding through presenting samples of foreign culture; encouraging programs that produced collections, displays, monographs, and lectures; and sponsoring programs that provided the opportunity for cross-cultural contacts among students, faculty, and leaders in the community.[861]

Today, Hazle's former home is known as the Ewing Manor Cultural Center, and is used for a variety of cultural, educational, and social events. The courtyard and grounds provide a setting for outdoor programs, including weddings. The Japanese garden, which is now part of the grounds, was donated by Bloomington-Normal's sister city, Asahikawa, Japan. During the summer of 2000, the open air Theatre at Ewing was dedicated. The building will seat 435 and has architectural details that are in keeping with the Ewing Manor. In addition to Shakespearean performances, the "theatre is also used for cultural performances sponsored by community organizations."[862]

Throughout her life, Hazle maintained an interest in land conservation. On May 19, 1964, an article appeared in the *Pantagraph* regarding Hazle's gift of 183 acres and $25,000 for purchasing additional land to preserve Funk's Grove as a state park in Illinois. She greatly desired to preserve Funk's Grove for future generations to enjoy; it was a parcel of land on which native timber grew. At her passing she provided another bequest of 164.99 acres southwest of Funks Grove for a state park or land reserve. The land was valued at $36,600 and included a $20,000 trust for development and maintenance.[863]

Hazle had also established trust funds for Principia College in the amount of $215,000 to maintain the already established School of Nations, and she cancelled the $65,000 note on the loan the school had received from her to complete the School of Nations classrooms.

In September 1969, Andrews wrote to Ralph, "I am happy to inform you of the very substantial gift in memory of your mother which we have received from Mrs. Rena B. Robinson."[864]

In early October 1970, Bright informed Andrews that funds were being transferred to the two trusts which Hazle had set up for Principia, and told him, "Mrs. Ewing repeatedly expressed to me her desire that the income of this trust be used to further this type of activity, which she felt would help promote better understanding between people and thereby world peace."[865] Andrews believed that they were in accord with Mrs. Ewing "as to the general area of activities within which the School of Nations Program should be carried on." They had researched their records to discover "the kinds of things for which the fund had been used over the years," and outlined the program to include:

> Activities designed to promote better understanding between peoples of the world and thereby world peace, . . . [to] support the Principia Abroad, and other educational travel abroad, additions to the School of Nations Museum at Principia College, library and classroom materials dealing with international understanding, field trips to museums, lectures on foreign affairs, and loans or scholarships to foreign students attending Principia.[866]

Bright responded that their "definition of the School of Nations program is entirely acceptable and will, I am sure, carry out Mrs. Ewing's desires." Thus the work of the School of Nations, which Hazle initiated in 1925, continued.[867]

Hazle's interest in and devotion to Victory Hall, a boys' home, which she helped to establish in 1919, was not forgotten by her sons, who publicized that it was one of the places to which donations could be sent in memory of their mother. In 1965, Hazle made a generous contribution to Victory Hall, and received a letter of acknowledgement from the president of the home, who wrote, "May I tell you again what a wonderful thing you have done for Victory Hall. To think that the building is complete and entirely paid for. Truly it is a privilege and joy to know people who are so generous and feel such a sense of 'noblesse oblige.'"[868]

In 1976, a four-year consolidation program began to merge all the homes for children in Bloomington into one. The administrative office for the homes was established at 2422 East Lincoln Street in Bloomington in 1981. The Children's Foundation, a name that encompassed all the homes and an expanded program that has developed over the years to meet the needs of the community, was formed in 1988. The house that had been called Victory Hall was incorporated into the Illinois State University as a dorm for students.[869]

Much of what Hazle accomplished during her lifetime was for the benefit to others. Victory Hall and the School of Nations have had a great influence, changing the lives of countless young people. Numerous individuals, adults and children, have been impressed and inspired by her example. Ewing Manor continues as a constant reminder of Hazle's interest in her neighborhood on Sunset Road and in the community of Bloomington-Normal, Illinois. Her life consisted of more than the generous donations she made; it also included the thought, the energy, and the time she invested toward the establishment of useful institutions and to helping individuals to become active and productive citizens of the world. As one of those individuals who received aid from Hazle in a time of dire need, her cousin, Evalyn Ames, told Ralph and Kate Lee: "Probably you will never know all the kind and thoughtful things she did for many, many people."[870]

REFERENCES

Chapter 1: *THE LETTER*

[1] Hazle Buck Ewing to Frederic E. Morgan, November 7, 1925, The Principia, Archives Department, Elsah, Illinois.

[2] Personal interview: Karen Heilbrun with Lucinda Buck Ewing, February, 2006.

[3] Edwin S. Leonard, *As the Sowing* (Chicago: Lakeside Press, 1958), 40.

[4] Ibid., 87.

[5] Ibid., 104.

[6] Ibid., 99.

[7] Ibid., 114.

[8] Ibid., 115.

[9] Ibid.

[10] Frederic E. Morgan to Hazle Buck Ewing, November 10, 1925, The Principia, Archives Department, Elsah, Illinois.

[11] T. E. Blackwell to Hazle Buck Ewing, November 13, 1925, The Principia, Archives Department, Elsah, Illinois.

[12] Arthur T. Morey to Hazle Buck Ewing, November 17, 1925, The Principia, Archives Department, Elsah, Illinois.

[13] Ibid.

[14] Ibid.

[15] Frederic E. Morgan to Hazle Buck Ewing, April 28, 1926, The Principia, Archives Department, Elsah, Illinois.

[16] Ibid.

[17] Ibid.

[18] Hazle Buck Ewing to Frederic E. Morgan, May 3, 1926, The Principia, Archives Department, Elsah, Illinois.

[19] George A. Andrews to Hazle Buck Ewing, May 5, 1926, The Principia, Archives Department, Elsah, Illinois.

[20] Ibid.

[21] Ibid.

[22] Hazle Buck Ewing to George A. Andrews, June 8, 1926, The Principia, Archives Department, Elsah, Illinois.

[23] Hazle Buck Ewing to Frederic E. Morgan, June 8, 1926, The Principia, Archives Department, Elsah, Illinois.

[24] George A. Andrews to Hazle Buck Ewing, September 17, 1926, The Principia, Archives Department, Elsah, Illinois.

[25] Ibid.

[26] Hazle Buck Ewing to George A. Andrews, December 19, 1926, The Principia, Archives Department, Elsah, Illinois.

[27] George A. Andrews to Hazle Buck Ewing, December 27, 1926, The Principia, Archives Department, Elsah, Illinois.

Chapter 2: WORLDS AND WORLDS OF PEOPLE

[28] "Davis Ewing Concrete Co. Has Splendid Plant Here," *Pantagraph*, March 24, 1923.

[29] Davis Ewing, *Around the World with a Camera*, Vol. 1 Chap. 1:1, an unpublished journal used by permission of Lucinda Buck Ewing, granddaughter of Davis Ewing.

[30] Ibid., 14.

[31] Hazle Buck Ewing, journal of world trip, September 6, 1924, used by permission of Lucinda Buck Ewing, granddaughter of Hazle Buck Ewing.

[32] Ibid., September 8, 1924.

[33] Ibid.

[34] Ibid.

[35] Ibid.

[36] Ibid.

[37] Ibid., September 11, 1924.
[38] Ibid., September 9, 1924.
[39] Ibid., September 21, 1924.
[40] Ibid.
[41] Ibid., September 23, 1924.
[42] "Miss Julia Hodge, Civic Leader, Dies," *Pantagraph*, Bloomington, Illinois, February 12, 1966.
[43] Hazle Buck Ewing to Julia Fairfax Hodge, September 23, 1924, a letter used by permission of Lucinda Buck Ewing, granddaughter of Hazle Buck Ewing.
[44] Ibid., September 23, 1924.
[45] Ibid.
[46] Ibid., September 26, 1924.
[47] Ibid., September 27, 1924.
[48] Ibid., September 29, 1924.
[49] Ibid., September 28, 1924.
[50] Hazle Buck Ewing to Julia Fairfax Hodge October 1, 1924, a letter used by permission of Lucinda Buck Ewing, granddaughter of Hazle Buck Ewing.
[51] Ibid., October 1, 1924.
[52] Ibid.
[53] Ibid.
[54] Hazle Buck Ewing to Julia Fairfax Hodge, October 2, 1924, a letter used by permission of Lucinda Buck Ewing, granddaughter of Hazle Buck Ewing.
[55] Ibid., October 1, 1924.
[56] Davis Ewing, *Around the World with a Camera*, Vol. 1, Chap. 2:38, an unpublished journal used by permission of Lucinda Buck Ewing, granddaughter of Davis Ewing.
[57] Hazle Buck Ewing to Julia Fairfax Hodge, October 6, 1924, a letter used by permission of Lucinda Buck Ewing, granddaughter of Hazle Buck Ewing.
[58] Ibid.
[59] Ibid., October 10, 1924.
[60] Davis Ewing, *Around the World with a Camera*, Vol. 2, Chap. 2:56-57, an unpublished journal used by permission of Lucinda Buck Ewing, granddaughter of Davis Ewing.
[61] Hazle Buck Ewing to Julia Fairfax Hodge, October 24, 1924, a letter used by permission of Lucinda Buck Ewing, granddaughter of Hazle Buck Ewing.
[62] Ibid.
[63] Ibid.
[64] Ibid.

Chapter 3: PLACES OF MYSTERY AND MAJESTY

[65] Hazle Buck Ewing to Julia Fairfax Hodge, November 7, 1924, a letter used by permission of Lucinda Buck Ewing, granddaughter of Hazle Buck Ewing.
[66] Davis Ewing, *Around the World with a Camera*, Vol. 2, Chap. 4:102-10, an unpublished journal used by permission of Lucinda Buck Ewing, granddaughter of Davis Ewing.
[67] Ibid., Vol. 3, Chap. 1:23-30.
[68] Ibid., Vol. 3, Chap. 2:34.
[69] Ibid., Vol. 3, Chap. 2:40-60.
[70] Ibid., Vol. 3, Chap. 2:61.
[71] Ibid., Vol. 3, Chap. 3:60-72.
[72] Ibid., Vol. 3, Chap. 3:72-73.
[73] Ibid., Vol. 3, Chap. 3:74-87.
[74] Hazle Buck Ewing to Julia Fairfax Hodge, December 22, 1924, a letter used by permission of Lucinda Buck Ewing, granddaughter of Hazle Buck Ewing.
[75] Davis Ewing, *Around the World with a Camera*, Vol. 4, Chap. 1:1-8, an unpublished journal used by permission of Lucinda Buck Ewing, granddaughter of Davis Ewing.
[76] Ibid., Vol. 4, Chap. 1:12-14.

[77] Ibid., Vol. 4, Chap. 1:15-30.

[78] Ibid., Vol. 4, Chap. 2:43-53.

[79] Ibid., Vol. 4, Chap. 3:57- 65.

[80] Ibid., Vol. 4, Chap. 3:66-71.

[81] Ibid., Vol. 4, Chap. 3:78.

[82] Hazle Buck Ewing to Julia Fairfax Hodge, January 19, 1925, a letter used by permission of Lucinda Buck Ewing, granddaughter of Hazle Buck Ewing.

[83] Ibid.

[84] Ibid.

[85] Ibid.

[86] Ibid.

[87] Davis Ewing, *Around the World with a Camera*, Vol. 4, Chap. 4:96-99, 108, an unpublished journal used by permission of Lucinda Buck Ewing, granddaughter of Davis Ewing.

[88] Hazle Buck Ewing to Julia Fairfax Hodge, February 4, 1925, a letter used by permission of Lucinda Buck Ewing, granddaughter of Hazle Buck Ewing.

[89] Davis Ewing, *Around the World with a Camera*, Vol. 4, Chap. 4:109-110, an unpublished journal used by permission of Lucinda Buck Ewing, granddaughter of Davis Ewing.

[90] Ibid., Vol. 5, Chap. 1:3-5.

[91] Ibid., Vol. 5, Chap. 1:6-10, 21.

[92] Ibid., Vol. 5, Chap. 1: 24-32.

[93] Ibid., Vol. 5, Chap. 1:39.

[94] Ibid., Vol. 5, Chap. 1:57-62.

[95] Hazle Buck Ewing to Julia Fairfax Hodge, March 8, 1925, a letter used by permission of Lucinda Buck Ewing, granddaughter of Hazle Buck Ewing.

[96] Ibid.

[97] Ibid.

[98] Davis Ewing, *Around the World with a Camera*, Vol. 5, Chap. 1:65, an unpublished journal used by permission of Lucinda Buck Ewing, granddaughter of Davis Ewing.

Chapter 4: MEMORIES FROM AN ANCIENT LAND

[99] Davis Ewing, *Around the World with a Camera*, Vol. 5, Chap. 2:82-84, an unpublished journal used by permission of Lucinda Buck Ewing, granddaughter of Davis Ewing.

[100] http://biblicalproductions_german_emperor.htp, March 26, 2007.

[101] Davis Ewing, *Around the World with a Camera*, Vol. 5, Chap. 2:84, an unpublished journal used by permission of Lucinda Buck Ewing, granddaughter of Davis Ewing.

[102] Ibid., 87.

[103] Ibid., 86.

[104] Ibid., 88-89.

[105] Ibid., 91.

[106] Ibid., 93.

[107] Ibid., 97.

[108] Ibid., 98-101.

[109] Ibid., 102-104.

[110] Ibid., 106-109.

[111] Ibid., 113-117.

[112] Ibid., 120-123.

[113] Ibid., 123-124.

[114] Ibid., Vol. 6, Chap. 1:9.

[115] Ibid., 4-12.

[116] Ibid., 11-12.

[117] http://www.istanbulinfolink.com/the_city/monuments/land_walls.htm, March 7, 2007.

[118] http://www.boun.edu.tr/about/history.html. March 7, 2007.

[119] Davis Ewing, *Around the World with a Camera*, Vol. 6, Chap.1:15-22, an unpublished journal used by permission of Lucinda Buck Ewing, granddaughter of Davis Ewing.

[120] Ibid., Vol. 6, Chap. 2:25-28.
[121] Ibid., 29-36.
[122] Ibid., 30-48.

Chapter 5: CLOSER AND CLOSER TO HOME

[123] Davis Ewing, *Around the World with a Camera*, Vol. 6, Chap. 2:51, 58, an unpublished journal used by permission of Lucinda Buck Ewing, granddaughter of Davis Ewing.
http://www.mnsu.edu/emuseum/archeology/sites/europe/pompeii.htm, March 27, 2007.
[124] Davis Ewing, *Around the World with a Camera*, Vol. 6, Chap. 2:54, 55, an unpublished journal used by permission of Lucinda Buck Ewing, granddaughter of Davis Ewing.
[125] Gabriella Di Cagno, *Michelangelo* (Minneapolis: The Oliver Press, Inc., 2008), 36, 37.
[126] Davis Ewing, *Around the World with a Camera*, Vol. 6, Chap. 2:59-72, an unpublished journal used by permission of Lucinda Buck Ewing, granddaughter of Davis Ewing.
[127] Lauro Martines, *Fire in the City: Savonarola and the Struggle for the Soul of Renaissance Florence* (New York, New York: Oxford University Press, Inc., 2006), 275-276.
[128] Hazle Buck Ewing to Julia Fairfax Hodge, June 8, 1925, a letter used by permission of Lucinda Buck Ewing, granddaughter of Hazle Buck Ewing.
[129] Hazle Buck Ewing to Julia Fairfax Hodge, June 17, 1925, a letter used by permission of Lucinda Buck Ewing, granddaughter of Hazle Buck Ewing.
[130] Ibid.
[131] Ibid.
[132] Davis Ewing, *Around the World with a Camera*, Vol. 7, Chap. 1:13, 14, an unpublished journal used by permission of Lucinda Buck Ewing, granddaughter of Davis Ewing.
[133] Ibid., Vol. 7, Chap. 2:16-18.
[134] Ibid., 20-30.
[135] Ibid., 30, 31.
[136] Hazle Buck Ewing to Julia Fairfax Hodge, July 24, 1925, a letter used by permission of Lucinda Buck Ewing, granddaughter of Hazle Buck Ewing.
[137] Davis Ewing, *Around the World with a Camera*, Vol. 7, Chap. 2:32, an unpublished journal used by permission of Lucinda Buck Ewing, granddaughter of Davis Ewing.
[138] Ibid., Vol. 7, Chap. 2:46-61.
[139] Hazle Buck Ewing to Julia Fairfax Hodge, August 13, 1925, a letter used by permission of Lucinda Buck Ewing, granddaughter of Hazle Buck Ewing.
[140] Ibid.
[141] Ibid.
[142] Ibid.
[143] Hazle Buck Ewing to Julia Fairfax Hodge, an undated letter from Chester, England, used by permission of Lucinda Buck Ewing, granddaughter of Hazle Buck Ewing.
[144] Hazle Buck Ewing to Julia Fairfax Hodge, September 1, 1925, a letter used by permission of Lucinda Buck Ewing, granddaughter of Hazle Buck Ewing.
[145] Ibid., September 7, 1925.
[146] Ibid., September 8, 1925.
[147] "Mr. and Mrs. Davis Ewing Back from Year's Trip Around World; Not one Storm on Three Oceans," *The Daily Bulletin*, Normal, Illinois, September 18, 1925.
[148] Ibid.
[149] Ibid.

Chapter 6: FROM A GIRL

[150] "Orlando J. Buck," *Historical Encyclopedia of Illinois*, 787-788.
[151] Ibid.
[152] Ibid.
[153] Personal interview: Karen Heilbrun with Alice Taylor Reed, May, 2005, 5.
[154] "Orlando J. Buck", *Historical Encyclopedia of Illinois*,787-788.

[155] Ibid.

[156] Ibid.

[157] Personal interview: Karen Heilbrun with Alice Taylor Reed, May, 2005, 4.

[158] "Women's Basketball," *The Cap and Gown*, (Chicago: University of Chicago Press, 1901) 233.

[159] Ibid.

[160] "The Dramatic Club," *The Cap and Gown*, (Chicago: University of Chicago Press, 1902) 89.

[161] Ibid., 90.

[162] Ibid., 90.

[163] Mary Baker Eddy, "Message of the Pastor Emeritus," *The Christian Science Journal*, June 4, 1899, Vol. 17, 226.

[164] "Buck-Ewing" in an unidentified newspaper article (possibly the Bloomington/Normal *Pantagraph* or *Bulletin*), 1907, in possession of Lucinda Buck Ewing, granddaughter of Hazle Buck and Davis Ewing.

Chapter 7: THE RIGHTS OF WOMEN

[165] Brenda Stalcup, ed., *Woman's Suffrage* (San Diego, California: Greenhaven Press, 2000), 73.

[166] Ibid.

[167] Doris Stevens, Carol O'Hare, eds., *Jailed for Freedom: American Women Win the Vote*, (Troutdale, Oregon: NewSage Press, 1995), 38.

[168] Brenda Stalcup, ed., *Woman's Suffrage* (San Diego, California: Greenhaven Press, 2000), 33.

[169] Ibid., 34.

[170] Ibid., 35, 36.

[171] Sally H. Bunch to Hazle Buck Ewing, May 21, 1915, Illinois State University, Milner Library Archives, Normal, Illinois.

[172] Ibid.

[173] Lucy Burns to Hazle Buck Ewing, June 5, 1915, Illinois State University, Milner Library Archives, Normal, Illinois.

[174] Ibid.

[175] Ibid.

[176] Gertrude Lynde Crocker to Hazle Buck Ewing, June 15, 1915, Illinois State University, Milner Library Archives, Normal, Illinois.

[177] Alice Paul to Hazle Buck Ewing, November 25, 1915, Illinois State University, Milner Library Archives, Normal, Illinois.

[178] Ibid.

[179] Ibid.

[180] Dora Lewis to Hazle Buck Ewing, January 10, 1916, Illinois State University, Milner Library Archives, Normal, Illinois.

[181] Mabel Sippy to Hazle Buck Ewing, Spring 1915, Illinois State University, Milner Library Archives, Normal, Illinois.

[182] Ibid.

[183] Congressional Union to Hazle Buck Ewing, Spring 1915, Illinois State University, Milner Library Archives, Normal, Illinois.

[184] Wm. Elza Williams, House of Representatives, Committee on The Judiciary, to Hazle Buck Ewing, March 23, 1916, Illinois State University, Milner Library Archives, Normal, Illinois.

[185] Mellie to Hazle Buck Ewing, April 12, 1916, Illinois State University, Milner Library Archives, Normal, Illinois.

[186] "A Letter to the Editor from Mrs. Davis Ewing," *Pantagraph*, Bloomington, Illinois, May 11, 1916.

[187] Ibid.

[188] Virginia Arnold, Chairman of Convention Luncheon, Women's Party Convention (Congressional Union for Woman Suffrage) to Hazle Buck Ewing, May 27, 1916, Illinois State University, Milner Library Archives, Normal, Illinois.

[189] Robert A. Crowlers to Hazle Buck Ewing, September 7, 1916, Illinois State University, Milner Library Archives, Normal, Illinois.

[190] Alva Belmont, National Woman's Party, to Hazle Buck Ewing, September 13, 1916, Illinois State University, Milner Library Archives, Normal, Illinois.

[191] Jessie Hardy McKaye, National Woman's Party, to Hazle Buck Ewing, September 14, 1916, Illinois State University, Milner Library Archives, Normal, Illinois.
[192] Ibid.

Chapter 8: THE CONFLICT WITHIN

[193] E. E. Donnelly to Hazle Buck Ewing, September 16, 1916, Illinois State University, Milner Library Archives, Normal, Illinois.
[194] Ibid.
[195] Hazle Buck Ewing to E. E. Donnelly, September, 1916, Illinois State University, Milner Library Archives, Normal, Illinois.
[196] E. E. Donnelly to Hazle Buck Ewing, September 23, 1916, Illinois State University, Milner Library Archives, Normal, Illinois.
[197] Mrs. Gilson Gardner, National Woman's Party, to Hazle Buck Ewing, September 26, 1916, Illinois State University, Milner Library Archives, Normal, Illinois.
[198] Alva Belmont to Hazle Buck Ewing, October 2, 1916, Illinois State University, Milner Library Archives.
[199] E. E. Donnelly to Hazle Buck Ewing, October 10, 1916, Illinois State University, Milner Library, Archives, Normal, Illinois.
[200] Sara Feltman to Hazle Buck Ewing, October 10, 1916, Illinois State University, Milner Library Archives, Normal, Illinois.
[201] Hazle Buck Ewing to E. E. Donnelly, October, 1916, Illinois State University, Milner Library Archives, Normal, Illinois.
[202] Mabel Sippy to Hazle Buck Ewing, November 14, 1916, Illinois State University, Milner Library Archives, Normal, Illinois.
[203] Ibid., November 23, 1916.
[204] Hazle Buck Ewing, "Federal Suffrage Law," *The Daily Pantagraph*, November 27, 1916, 4, Bloomington, Illinois.
[205] Ibid.
[206] Ibid.
[207] "Delegation of Suffragists Calls on Congressman, Who States His Attitude," *The Daily Pantagraph*, November 28, 1916, Bloomington, Illinois.
[208] Ibid.
[209] Ibid.
[210] Hazle Buck Ewing to *Pantagraph* reporter, November 28, 1916, Illinois State University, Milner Library Archives, Normal, Illinois.
[211] Agnes E. Ryan to Hazle Buck Ewing, December 8, 1916, Illinois State University, Milner Library Archives, Normal, Illinois.

Chapter 9: SWEET VICTORY

[212] Elizabeth L. Kind to Hazle Buck Ewing, February 9, 1917, Illinois State University, Milner Library Archives, Normal, Illinois.
[213] Doris Stevens, O'Hare, Carol, ed., *Jailed for Freedom: American Women Win the Vote*, (Troutdale, Oregon: NewSage Press, 1995), 67-68.
[214] Ibid.,79-82.
[215] Ibid., 82-83.
[216] Ibid., 91.
[217] Treasurer National Woman's Party, August 20, 1917, Illinois State University, Milner Library Archives, Normal, Illinois.
[218] Ibid.
[219] Doris Stevens, O'Hare, Carol, ed., *Jailed for Freedom: American Women Win the Vote*, (Troutdale, Oregon: NewSage Press, 1995), 95, 101.
[220] Margaret Whittemore to Hazle Buck Ewing, September 25, 1917, Illinois State University, Milner Library Archives, Normal, Illinois.
[221] Lucy Ewing to Hazle Buck Ewing, October 1917, Illinois State University, Milner Library Archives, Normal, Illinois.

[222] Margaret Whittemore to Hazle Buck Ewing, September 25, 1917, Illinois State University, Milner Library Archives, Normal, Illinois.

[223] *The Daily Pantagraph*, October 8, 1917, 3.

[224] Margaret Whittemore to Hazle Buck Ewing, October 9, 1917, Illinois State University, Milner Library Archives, Normal, Illinois.

[225] Alice Paul to Suffragists, October 16, 1917, Illinois State University, Milner Library Archives, Normal, Illinois.

[226] Secretary of Herbert Hoover to Hazle Buck Ewing, October 29, 1917, Illinois State University, Milner Library, Normal, Illinois.

[227] Lucy Burns to Hazle Buck Ewing, November 9, 1917, Illinois State University, Milner Library Archives, Normal, Illinois.

[228] Doris Stevens, O'Hare, Carol, ed., *Jailed for Freedom: American Women Win the Vote*, (Troutdale, Oregon: NewSage Press, 1995), 129-130.

[229] Ibid., 131.

[230] Anne Martin to Hazle Buck Ewing, December 24, 1917, Illinois State University, Milner Library Archives, Normal, Illinois.

[231] Ann Martin to Hazle Buck Ewing, December 27, 1917, Illinois State University, Milner Library Archives, Normal, Illinois.

[232] John A. Sterling to Hazle Buck Ewing, January 9, 1918, Illinois State University, Milner Library Archives, Normal, Illinois.

[233] Doris Stevens, O'Hare, Carol, ed., *Jailed for Freedom: American Women Win the Vote*, (Troutdale, Oregon: NewSage Press, 1995), 137.

[234] Lawrence Y. Sherman to Hazle Buck Ewing, May 13, 1918, Illinois State University, Milner Library Archives, Normal, Illinois.

[235] Doris Stevens, O'Hare, Carol, ed., *Jailed for Freedom: American Women Win the Vote*, (Troutdale, Oregon: NewSage Press, 1995), 143.

[236] Ibid., 144.

[237] Ella J. Abeel to Hazle Buck Ewing, August 29, 1918, Illinois State University, Milner Library Archives, Normal, Illinois.

[238] Dora Lewis to Suffragist, September 5, 1918, Illinois State University, Milner Library Archives, Normal, Illinois.

[239] Doris Stevens, O'Hare, Carol, ed., *Jailed for Freedom: American Women Win the Vote*, (Troutdale, Oregon: NewSage Press, 1995), 146-147.

[240] Ibid., 149,152.

[241] Ibid., 157.

[242] Ibid., 161.

[243] Mable Vernon to Hazle Buck Ewing, February 28, 1919, Illinois State University, Milner Library Archives, Normal, Illinois.

[244] Doris Stevens, O'Hare, Carol, ed., *Jailed for Freedom: American Women Win the Vote*, (Troutdale, Oregon: NewSage Press, 1995), 174-176.

[245] Ibid., 174-176.

Chapter 10: A HOME FOR THE BOYS

[246] Gertrude Williams, "The Story of Victory Hall," *Home Town in the Corn Belt: A Source History of Bloomington, Illinois, 1900-1950*, vol. V (Bloomington, Illinois, 1950), 184.

[247] Ibid.

[248] Meeting Minutes of the Board of Directors of Victory Hall, February 5, 1919, Children's Foundation Archives, Bloomington, Illinois.

[249] Ibid, February 26, 1919.

[250] Ibid., March 17, 1919.

[251] Ibid., April 4 and 14, 1919.

[252] Gertrude Williams, "The Story of Victory Hall," *Home Town in the Corn Belt: A Source History of Bloomington, Illinois, 1900-1950*, Vol. V (Bloomington, Illinois, 1950), 185.

[253] Ibid.

[254] Meeting Minutes of the Board of Directors of Victory Hall, May 7, 1919, Children's Foundation Archives, Bloomington, Illinois.
[255] Ibid., May 16 and 23, 1919.
[256] Ibid., May 26, 1919.
[257] Ibid.
[258] Ibid., June 9, 1919.
[259] Gertrude Williams, "The Story of Victory Hall," *Home Town in the Corn Belt: A Source History of Bloomington, Illinois*, 1900-1950, vol. V (Bloomington, Illinois, 1950), 185.
[260] Meeting Minutes of the Board of Directors of Victory Hall, June 9, 1919, Children's Foundation Archives, Bloomington, Illinois.
[261] Ibid., June 9, 1919.
[262] Ibid., July 14, 1919.
[263] Ibid.
[264] Ibid., September 8, 1919.
[265] Ibid.
[266] Ibid., September 25, 1919.
[267] Ibid.
[268] Ibid., October 13, 1919.
[269] Ibid.
[270] Ibid., November 10, 1919.
[271] Ibid.
[272] Ibid.
[273] Ibid., December 8, 1919.
[274] Ibid.
[275] Ibid.
[276] Ibid.

Chapter 11: A PROMISING YEAR

[277] Meeting Minutes of the Board of Directors of Victory Hall, January 12, 1920, Children's Foundation Archives, Bloomington, Illinois.
[278] Ibid.
[279] Ibid.
[280] Ibid.
[281] Meeting Minutes of the Board of Directors of Victory Hall, February 9, 1920, Children's Foundation Archives, Bloomington, Illinois.
[282] Ibid.
[283] Meeting Minutes of the Board of Directors of Victory Hall, March 8, 1920, Children's Foundation Archives, Bloomington, Illinois.
[284] Ibid.
[285] Gertrude Williams, "The Story of Victory Hall," *Home Town in the Corn Belt: A Source History of Bloomington, Illinois, 1900-1950*, vol. V (Bloomington, Illinois, 1950), 182.
[286] Meeting Minutes of the Board of Directors of Victory Hall, April 12, 1920, Children's Foundation Archives, Bloomington, Illinois.
[287] Ibid.
[288] Ibid., May 10, 1920.
[289] "Open Campaign for Boys Home," *The Daily Pantagraph*, June 5, 1920, Bloomington, Illinois.
[290] Ibid.
[291] Meeting Minutes of the Board of Directors of Victory Hall, June 14, 1920, Children's Foundation Archives, Bloomington, Illinois.
[292] Ibid.
[293] Ibid., August 9, 1920.
[294] Ibid.
[295] Ibid., September 13, 1920.
[296] Ibid., October 11, 1920.

[297] Ibid., November 9, 1920.
[298] Ibid., December 13, 1920.
[299] Ibid., January 10, 1921.
[300] Ibid., January 31, 1921.

Chapter 12: BOYS OF HER OWN

[301] Personal Telephone Interview: Karen Heilbrun with Lucinda Buck Ewing, December 2, 2006.
[302] Ibid.
[303] Ibid.
[304] Nora Hasslinger to Hazle Buck Ewing, March 11, 1921, a letter used by permission of Lucinda Buck Ewing, granddaughter of Hazle Buck Ewing.
[305] Order of the Court, Bloomington, Illinois, August 19, 1921, Ewing Manor Archives, Bloomington, Illinois
[306] Ralph Nelson Ewing to Hazle Buck Ewing, May 6, 1921; Ralph Nelson Ewing to Hazle Buck Ewing, November 21, 1921, a letter used by permission of Lucinda Buck Ewing, granddaughter of Hazle Buck Ewing.
[307] "Mrs. Ewing Head of Victory Hall," The Daily Pantagraph, January 23, 1923.
[308] Ralph Nelson Ewing to Hazle Buck Ewing, October 28, 1922, a letter used by permission of Lucinda Buck Ewing, granddaughter of Hazle Buck Ewing.
[309] "Victory Hall to Get $3,800 Of Proceeds From Welfare Drive," The Daily Pantagraph, December 9, 1922.
[310] "Mrs. Ewing Head of Victory Hall," The Daily Pantagraph, January 23, 1923.
[311] "Victory Hall to Get $3,800 Of Proceeds From Welfare Drive," The Daily Pantagraph, December 9, 1922.
[312] Ralph Nelson Ewing to Hazle Buck Ewing, February 8, 1923, a letter used by permission of Lucinda Buck Ewing, granddaughter of Hazle Buck Ewing.
[313] Ibid., February 11, 1923.
[314] "Mrs. Ewing Head of Victory Hall," The Daily Pantagraph, January 23, 1923.
[315] Ralph Nelson Ewing to Hazle Buck Ewing, March 18, 1923, a letter used by permission of Lucinda Buck Ewing, granddaughter of Hazle Buck Ewing.
[316] Ibid., Undated letter 1923.
[317] Ibid., July 2, 1923.
[318] Ibid., Undated post-Christmas letter.

Chapter 13: THE MEETING

[319] Hazle Buck Ewing to Frederic E. Morgan, January 8, 1927, The Principia, Archives Department, Elsah, Illinois.
[320] George A. Andrews to Hazle Buck Ewing, January 26, 1927, The Principia, Archives Department, Elsah, Illinois.
[321] George A. Andrews, "Proposal for Proceeding with International Education at Principia." January 31, 1927, The Principia, Archives Department, Elsah, Illinois.
[322] Frederic E. Morgan to Hazle Buck Ewing, February 1, 1927, The Principia, Archives Department, Elsah, Illinois.
[323] Ibid.
[324] Ibid., February 7, 1927.
[325] George A. Andrews to Hazle Buck Ewing, February 6, 1927, The Principia, Archives Department, Elsah, Illinois.
[326] Hazle Buck Ewing to George A. Andrews, February 9, 1927, The Principia, Archives Department, Elsah, Illinois.
[327] George A. Andrews to Hazle Buck Ewing, May 27, 1927, The Principia, Archives Department, Elsah, Illinois.
[328] Ibid.
[329] Ibid.
[330] Ibid.
[331] Ibid.
[332] Iolani Ingalls, "How the Individual Can Help Promote a Better Understanding," May, 1927, The Principia, Archives Department, Elsah, Illinois.

[333] George A. Andrews, "Recommendations for Proceeding with the School of Nations Project in The Principia," May 27, 1927, The Principia, Archives Department, Elsah, Illinois.

Chapter 14: THE ANNOUNCEMENT
[334] George A. Andrews, "School of Nations Fund Scholarship," June 1, 1927, The Principia, Archives Department, Elsah, Illinois.
[335] Ibid.
[336] George A. Andrews to Hazle Buck Ewing, June 7, 1927, The Principia, Archives Department, Elsah, Illinois.
[337] Frederic E. Morgan to Hazle Buck Ewing, June 12, 1927, The Principia, Archives Department, Elsah, Illinois.
[338] George A. Andrews to Hazle Buck Ewing, June 7, 1927, The Principia, Archives Department, Elsah, Illinois.
[339] Hazle Buck Ewing to Frederic E. Morgan, August 17, 1927, The Principia, Archives Department, Elsah, Illinois.
[340] Edwin S. Leonard, As the Sowing (Chicago: Lakeside Press, 1958), 150.
[341] George A. Andrews to Hazle Buck Ewing, October 19, 1927; The Principia, Archives Department, Elsah, Illinois.
[342] Ibid., October 24, 1927.
[343] Ibid., November 5, 1927.
[344] Ibid., November 23, 1927.
[345] George A. Andrews to Hazle Buck Ewing, November 14, 1927, The Principia, Archives Department, Elsah, Illinois.
[346] Ibid.
[347] Ibid.
[348] Ibid.
[349] Frederic E. Morgan to Hazle Buck Ewing, December 22, 1927, The Principia, Archives Department, Elsah, Illinois.

Chapter 15: BUILDING A FIRM FOUNDATION
[350] Davis Ewing to Frederic E. Morgan, January 12, 1928, The Principia, Archives Department, Elsah, Illinois.
[351] Ibid., January 18, 1928.
[352] Author unknown to Hazle Buck Ewing, January 12, 1928, The Principia, Archives Department, Elsah, Illinois.
[353] Gertrude Foster Brown to Hazle Buck Ewing, February 14, 1928, Illinois State University, Milner Library Archives, Bloomington, Illinois.
[354] Gwen Edwards and Jeanne Wroan, "A Brief History of Ewing Manor," Sunset Road: History and Memories (Bloomington: Gwen Edwards and Jeanne Wroan, 2003), 6.
[355] "Davis Ewing's Home Finished," Pantagraph, September 26, 1929.
[356] Hazle Buck Ewing to Frederic E. Morgan, April 3, 1928, The Principia, Archives Department, Elsah, Illinois.
[357] Gertrude Foster Brown to Hazle Buck Ewing, April 24, 1928, Illinois State University Archives, Milner Library Archives, Bloomington, Illinois.
[358] George A. Andrews to Hazle Buck Ewing, May 29, 1928, The Principia, Archives Department, Elsah, Illinois.
[359] Frederic E. Morgan to Hazle Buck Ewing, May 30, 1928, The Principia, Archives Department, Elsah, Illinois.
[360] Ibid., June 7, 1928.
[361] George A. Andrews to Hazle Buck Ewing, October 20, 1928, The Principia, Archives Department, Elsah, Illinois.
[362] Ibid.
[363] Ralph Nelson Ewing to Hazle Buck Ewing, November 15, 1928, used by permission of Lucinda Buck Ewing, granddaughter of Hazle Buck Ewing.
[364] Ibid., December 11, 1928.

³⁶⁵ Ibid., December, 1928.
³⁶⁶ George A. Andrews to Hazle Buck Ewing, January 1, 1929, The Principia, Archives Department, Elsah, Illinois.
³⁶⁷ Hazle Buck Ewing to George A. Andrews, January 1, 1929, The Principia, Archives Department, Elsah, Illinois.
³⁶⁸ Hazle Buck Ewing to George A. Andrews, January 5, 1929, The Principia, Archives Department, Elsah, Illinois.
³⁶⁹ Ibid., January 5, 1929.
³⁷⁰ George A. Andrews to Hazle Buck Ewing, February 8, 1929, The Principia, Archives Department, Elsah, Illinois.
³⁷¹ Hazle Buck Ewing to George A. Andrews, February 13, 1929, The Principia, Archives Department, Elsah, Illinois.
³⁷² George A. Andrews to Hazle Buck Ewing, February 14, 1929, The Principia, Archives Department, Elsah, Illinois.
³⁷³ Ralph Nelson Ewing to Hazle Buck Ewing, January 15, 1929, used by permission of Lucinda Buck Ewing, granddaughter of Hazle Buck Ewing.
³⁷⁴ Ibid., February 8, 1929.
³⁷⁵ Ibid., February 28, 1929.
³⁷⁶ George A. Andrews to Hazle Buck Ewing, March 5, 1929, The Principia, Archives Department, Elsah, Illinois.
³⁷⁷ Ibid., April 18, 1929.
³⁷⁸ Ibid., June 10, 1929.
³⁷⁹ Ibid., June 27, 1929.
³⁸⁰ Ralph Nelson Ewing to Hazle Buck Ewing, July 12, 1929, used by permission of Lucinda Buck Ewing, granddaughter of Hazle Buck Ewing.
³⁸¹ Ibid., July 15, 1929.
³⁸² George A. Andrews to Hazle Buck Ewing, September 11, 1929, The Principia, Archives Department, Elsah, Illinois.
³⁸³ Gwen Edwards and Jeanne Wroan, "A Brief History of Ewing Manor," *Sunset Road: History and Memories* (Bloomington: Gwen Edwards and Jeanne Wroan, 2003), 61.

Chapter 16: THE UNEXPECTED

³⁸⁴ Frederic E. Morgan to Hazle Buck Ewing, October 22, 1929, The Principia, Archives Department, Elsah, Illinois.
³⁸⁵ Hazle Buck Ewing to Frederic E. Morgan, November 14, 1929, The Principia, Archives Department, Elsah, Illinois.
³⁸⁶ Frederic E. Morgan to Hazle Buck Ewing, November 11, 1929, The Principia, Archives Department, Elsah, Illinois.
³⁸⁷ Hazle Buck Ewing to Frederic E. Morgan, November 14, 1929, The Principia, Archives Department, Elsah, Illinois.
³⁸⁸ Frederic E. Morgan to Hazle Buck Ewing, November 18, 1929, The Principia, Archives Department, Elsah, Illinois.
³⁸⁹ Frederic E. Morgan to Arthur T. Morey, November 26, 1929, The Principia, Archives Department, Elsah, Illinois.
³⁹⁰ Frederic E. Morgan to Hazle Buck and Davis Ewing, November 26, 1929, The Principia, Archives Department, Elsah, Illinois.
³⁹¹ A. J. Hannah to Hazle Buck Ewing, December 4, 1929, The Principia, Archives Department, Elsah, Illinois.
³⁹² Hazle Buck Ewing to George A. Andrews, March 24, 1930, The Principia, Archives Department, Elsah, Illinois.
³⁹³ Ibid., August 17, 1930.
³⁹⁴ George A. Andrews to Hazle Buck Ewing, September 22, 1930, The Principia, Archives Department, Elsah, Illinois.
³⁹⁵ Ibid.

[396] Ibid., November 17, 1930.

[397] Edwin S. Leonard, *As the Sowing* (Chicago: Lakeside Press, 1958), 141.

[398] Frederic E. Morgan to Hazle Buck Ewing, December 11, 1930, The Principia, Archives Department, Elsah, Illinois.

[399] Ibid.

[400] Hazle Buck Ewing to George A. Andrews, January 16, 1931, The Principia, Archives Department, Elsah, Illinois.

[401] Frederic E. Morgan to Hazle Buck Ewing, January 19, 1931, The Principia, Archives Department, Elsah, Illinois.

[402] George A. Andrews to Hazle Buck Ewing, January 21, 1931, The Principia, Archives Department, Elsah, Illinois.

[403] Hazle Buck Ewing to George A. Andrews, May 11, 1931, The Principia, Archives Department, Elsah, Illinois.

[404] Hazle Buck Ewing to Dorinda Morgan, May, 1931 (Friday), The Principia, Archives Department, Elsah, Illinois.

[405] Report of Opening Ceremony, September, 1931, The Principia, Archives Department, Elsah, Illinois.

[406] Ibid.

[407] George A. Andrews to Hazle Buck Ewing, September 9, 1931, The Principia, Archives Department, Elsah, Illinois.

[408] Ibid., September 29, 1931.

[409] Hazle Buck Ewing to George A. Andrews, October 12, 1931, The Principia, Archives Department, Elsah, Illinois.

[410] George A. Andrews to Hazle Buck Ewing, October 16, 1931, The Principia, Archives Department, Elsah, Illinois.

[411] Ibid., October 26, 1931.

[412] Frederic E. Morgan to Hazle Buck Ewing, October 29, 1931, The Principia, Archives Department, Elsah, Illinois.

[413] George A. Andrews to Frederic E. Morgan, November 3, 1931, The Principia, Archives Department, Elsah, Illinois.

[414] Ibid.

[415] Personal telephone interview: Karen Heilbrun with Lucinda Buck Ewing, December 2, 2006, page 3.

[416] George A. Andrews to Hazle Buck Ewing, November 5, 1931, The Principia, Archives Department, Elsah, Illinois.

[417] George A. Andrews to Hazle Buck Ewing, December 7, 1931, The Principia, Archives Department, Elsah, Illinois.

[418] Hazle Buck Ewing to Frederic E. Morgan, December 19, 1931, The Principia, Archives Department, Elsah, Illinois.

Chapter 17: RISING ABOVE DISAPPOINTMENT

[419] Frederic E. Morgan to Hazle Buck Ewing, December 22, 1931, The Principia, Archives Department, Elsah, Illinois.

[420] Hazle Buck Ewing to George A. Andrews, January 1, 1932; George A. Andrews to Hazle Buck Ewing, January 2, 1932, The Principia, Archives Department, Elsah, Illinois.

[421] M.H.S. (secretary to George A. Andrews), to Hazle Buck Ewing, February 10, 1932, The Principia, Archives Department, Elsah, Illinois.

[422] Hazle Buck Ewing to William E.Morgan, February 18, 1932, The Principia, Archives Department, Elsah, Illinois.

[423] Hazle Buck Ewing to George A. Andrews, February 20, 1932, The Principia, Archives Department, Elsah, Illinois.

[424] Ibid.

[425] Ibid.

[426] George A. Andrews to Hazle Buck Ewing, February 25, 1932, The Principia, Archives Department, Elsah, Illinois.

[427] Arthur T. Morey to Thomas E.Blackwell, May 28, 1932, The Principia, Archives Department, Elsah, Illinois.

[428] E.B. Brindley, "School of Nations Is Unique Educational Project at Principia College for Fostering World Peace," *Pantagraph*, June 12, 1932.

[429] Ibid.

[430] Ibid.

[431] George A. Andrews to Hazle Buck Ewing, June 17, 1932, The Principia, Archives Department, Elsah, Illinois.

[432] Ibid., June 21, 1932.

[433] Ibid.

[434] Ibid., October 10, 1932.

[435] Hazle Buck Ewing to William E. Morgan, Jr., October 28, 1932, The Principia, Archives Department, Elsah, Illinois.

[436] Hazle Buck Ewing to Mr. Morgan, January 8, 1933, The Principia, Archives Department, Elsah, Illinois.

[437] Ibid.

[438] Virginia Ruf to Hazle Buck Ewing, January 10, 1933, The Principia, Archives Department, Elsah, Illinois.

[439] George A. Andrews to Hazle Buck Ewing, April 7, 1933, The Principia, Archives Department, Elsah, Illinois.

[440] Ibid.

[441] Arthur T. Morey to Hazle Buck Ewing, September 25, 1933; Hazle Buck Ewing to Arthur T. Morey, September 28, 1933; Frederic E. Morgan to Hazle Buck Ewing, October 2, 1933, The Principia, Archives Department, Elsah, Illinois.

[442] Frederic E. Morgan to Hazle Buck Ewing, December 21, 1933, The Principia, Archives Department, Elsah, Illinois.

[443] Ibid.

Chapter 18: THE TRUSTEE

[444] Frederic E. Morgan to Hazle Buck Ewing, January 19, 1934, The Principia, Archives Department, Elsah, Illinois.

[445] Ibid.

[446] Hazle Buck Ewing to Frederic E Morgan, February 26, 1934; Frederick Morgan to Hazle Buck Ewing, February 27, 1934, The Principia, Archives Department, Elsah, Illinois.

[447] Frederic E. Morgan to Hazle Buck Ewing, June 16, 1934, The Principia, Archives Department, Elsah, Illinois.

[448] Hazle Buck Ewing to Frederic E. Morgan, October 1934, The Principia, Archives Department, Elsah, Illinois.

[449] Ibid.

[450] Hazle Buck Ewing to Frederic E. Morgan, November 8, 1934; Frederic E. Morgan to Hazle Buck Ewing, November 9, 1934.

[451] Hazle Buck Ewing to Frederic E. Morgan, November 14, 1934, The Principia, Archives Department, Elsah, Illinois.

[452] Frederic E. Morgan to Hazle Buck Ewing, November 16, 1934, The Principia, Archives Department, Elsah, Illinois.

[453] Ibid.

[454] Ibid.

[455] Hazle Buck Ewing to Frederic E. Morgan, December 20, 1934, The Principia, Archives Department, Elsah, Illinois.

[456] Ibid., January 15, 1935.

[457] Frederic E. Morgan to Hazle Buck Ewing, January 28, 1935, The Principia, Archives Department, Elsah, Illinois.

[458] George A. Andrews to Hazle Buck Ewing, February 14, 1935, The Principia, Archives Department, Elsah, Illinois.

[459] Ibid.

[460] Mary Kimball Morgan to Principia Alumni and former Students, February 28, 1935, The Principia, Archives Department, Elsah, Illinois.

[461] Frederic E. Morgan to Hazle Buck Ewing, May 23, 1936, The Principia, Archives Department, Elsah, Illinois.

[462] Arthur T. Morey to Hazle Buck Ewing and Kathryn C. Davis, June 8, 1935, The Principia, Archives Department, Elsah, Illinois.

[463] Frederic E. Morgan to Hazle Buck Ewing, November 7, 1935, The Principia, Archives Department, Elsah, Illinois.

Chapter 19: MATTERS OF THE HEART

[464] George T. Nickerson, Cranbrook School, Lone Pine Road, Bloomfield Hills, Michigan to Hazle Buck Ewing, February 12, 1936; Hazle Buck Ewing (at 1258 Hillcrest Avenue, Pasadena, CA) to Frederic E. Morgan, March 16, 1937, The Principia, Archives Department, Elsah, Illinois.

[465] Ralph Nelson Ewing to Hazle Buck Ewing, March 24, 1936, a letter used by permission of Lucinda Buck Ewing, granddaughter of Hazle Buck Ewing.

[466] Personal telephone interview: Karen Heilbrun with Lucinda Buck Ewing, July 18, 2005, page 7.

[467] Ralph Nelson Ewing to Hazle Buck Ewing, November 16, 1936, a letter used by permission of Lucinda Buck Ewing, granddaughter of Hazle Buck Ewing.

[468] "Santa turns Cupid," The Flying Horse, Vol. 2, Num. 5, (a paper put out by the Stix, Baer, and Fuller Company.)

[469] "Ralph Ewing takes Bride," The Democratic Globe, an undated article in the St. Louis newspaper.

[470] Hazle Buck Ewing to Frederic E. Morgan, September 8, 1937, The Principia, Archives Department, Elsah, Illinois.

[471] Frederic E. Morgan to Hazle Buck Ewing, September 8, 1937, The Principia, Archives Department, Elsah, Illinois.

[472] Hazle Buck Ewing to Frederic E. Morgan, September 9, 1936, The Principia, Archives Department, Elsah, Illinois.

[473] Hazle Buck Ewing to Frederic E. Morgan, September 10, 1937, The Principia, Archives Department, Elsah, Illinois.

[474] Frederic E. Morgan to Hazle Buck Ewing, September 15, 1937, The Principia, Archives Department, Elsah, Illinois.

[475] Ibid.

[476] Ibid.

[477] Ibid.

[478] Ibid.

Chapter 20: VARIED INTERESTS

[479] Frederic E. Morgan to Hazle Buck Ewing, December 4, 1937, The Principia, Archives Department, Elsah, Illinois.

[480] Hazle Buck Ewing to Frederic E. Morgan, December 8, 1937, The Principia, Archives Department, Elsah, Illinois.

[481] Frederic E. Morgan to Hazle Buck Ewing, December 15, 1937, The Principia, Archives Department, Elsah, Illinois.

[482] Hazle Buck Ewing to William E. Morgan, Jr., July 25, 1938, The Principia, Archives Department, Elsah, Illinois.

[483] Ibid.

[484] Frederic E. Morgan to Hazle Buck Ewing, June 18, 1938, The Principia, Archives Department, Elsah, Illinois.

[485] Hazle Buck Ewing to Frederic E. Morgan, July 27, 1938; Frederic E. Morgan to Hazle Buck Ewing, July 28, 1938, The Principia, Archives Department, Elsah, Illinois.

[486] Nelson Ewing to Frederic E. Morgan, July 21, 1938; Frederic E. Morgan to Nelson Ewing, August 1, 1938; Frederic E. Morgan to Hazle Buck Ewing, August 1, 1938, The Principia, Archives Department, Elsah, Illinois.

[487] William E. Morgan, Jr. to Hazle Buck Ewing, October 27, 1938, The Principia, Archives Department, Elsah, Illinois.

[488] Hazle Buck Ewing, "Scenic, Historic Illinois Calls," *Motor News*, 28, No. 10 (October 1938), 6,7.

[489] Frederic E. Morgan to Hazle Buck Ewing, December 20, 1938, The Principia, Archives Department, Elsah, Illinois.

[490] William E. Morgan, Jr. to Hazle Buck Ewing, February 8, 1939, The Principia, Archives Department, Elsah, Illinois.

[491] Hazle Buck Ewing to William E. Morgan, Jr., May 31, 1939; Don Laughlin to William E. Morgan Jr., June 1, 1939, The Principia, Archives Department, Elsah, Illinois.

[492] Frederic E. Morgan to Albert C. Mann, June 27, 1939, The Principia, Archives Department, Elsah, Illinois.

[493] Hazle Buck Ewing to Frederic E. Morgan, October 10, 1939, The Principia, Archives Department, Elsah, Illinois.

[494] Frederic E. Morgan to Hazle Buck Ewing, December 21, 1939, The Principia, Archives Department, Elsah, Illinois.

Chapter 21: A SPIRIT OF HELPFULNESS

[495] Frederic E. Morgan to Hazle Buck Ewing, August 29, 1940, The Principia, Archives Department, Elsah, Illinois.

[496] Sam N. Baker to Hazle Buck Ewing, June 3, 1940, The Principia, Archives Department, Elsah, Illinois.

[497] Hazle Buck Ewing to Frederic E. Morgan, September 3, 1940, The Principia, Archives Department, Elsah, Illinois. Winston S. Churchill, "The Miracle of Dunkirk," *Reader's Digest: Illustrated Story of World War II* (The Reader's Digest Association, Inc., Pleasantville, NY, 1969) 112, 114.

[498] Hazle Buck Ewing to Frederic E. Morgan, September 3, 1940, The Principia, Archives Department, Elsah, Illinois.

[499] Ralph Nelson Ewing to Nelson Buck, October 6, 1940, a letter used by permission of Lucinda Buck Ewing, granddaughter of Hazle Buck Ewing.

[500] Frederic E. Morgan to Hazle Buck Ewing, November 20, 1940, The Principia, Archives Department, Elsah, Illinois.

[501] Adlai Stevenson to Hazle Buck Ewing, January 11, 1941, McLean County Historical Museum, Bloomington, Illinois.

[502] Hazle Buck Ewing to Frederic E. Morgan, May 29, 1941, The Principia, Archives Department, Elsah, Illinois.

[503] Ibid., July 7, 1941.

[504] Frederic E. Morgan to Hazle Buck Ewing, August 19, 1941, The Principia, Archives Department, Elsah, Illinois.

[505] Mary Baker Eddy, "Love," *Miscellaneous Writings 1883-1896* and *Poems*, (Boston: The Christian Science Publishing Society, used by courtesy of The Mary Baker Eddy Collection), 388 and 7.

[506] Kate Lee Ewing to Hazle Buck Ewing, August 30, 1941, a letter used by permission of Lucinda Buck Ewing, granddaughter of Hazle Buck Ewing.

[507] Ibid.

[508] Ibid.

[509] Interoffice Correspondence from Eldridge Hamlin, October 8, 1941; Frederick E. Morgan to Hazle Buck Ewing, November 22, 1941, The Principia, Archives Department, Elsah, Illinois.

[510] Frederic E. Morgan to Hazle Buck Ewing, December 2, 1941, The Principia, Archives Department, Elsah, Illinois.

[511] Hazle Buck Ewing to Frederic E. Morgan, January 27, 1942; Frederic E. Morgan to Hazle Buck Ewing, February 3, 1942, The Principia, Archives Department, Elsah, Illinois.

[512] Frederic E. Morgan to Hazle Buck Ewing, February 3, 1942; Hazle Buck Ewing to Frederic E. Morgan, February 19, 1942, The Principia, Archives Department, Elsah, Illinois.

[513] Hazle Buck Ewing to Frederic E. Morgan, May 6, 1942, The Principia, Archives Department, Elsah, Illinois.

[514] Frederic E. Morgan to Hazle Buck Ewing, June 11, 1942; Hazle Buck Ewing to Frederic E. Morgan, July 2, 1942, The Principia, Archives Department, Elsah, Illinois.

[515] W. Violet Brindley, editor of the *The Daily Pantagraph* to Hazle Buck Ewing, August 28, 1942, The Principia, Archives Department, Elsah, Illinois.

[516] Frederic E. Morgan to Hazle Buck Ewing, June, 1942, The Principia, Archives Department, Elsah, Illinois.

[517] Ibid., November 18, 1942.

[518] Hazle Buck Ewing to Frederic E. Morgan, November 24, 1942, The Principia, Archives Department, Elsah, Illinois.

[519] William E. Morgan, Jr. to Hazle Buck Ewing, December 2, 1942, The Principia, Archives Department, Elsah, Illinois.

[520] Hazle Buck Ewing to William E. Morgan Jr., December 9, 1942; Hazle Buck Ewing to Frederic E. Morgan, December 16, 1942; William E. Morgan, Jr. to Hazle Buck Ewing, December 17, 1942, The Principia, Archives Department, Elsah, Illinois.

[521] Hazle Buck Ewing to Frederic E. Morgan, December 16, 1942, The Principia, Archives Department, Elsah, Illinois.

Chapter 22: SUPPORT FOR OUR TROOPS

[522] Hazle Buck Ewing to Frederic E. Morgan, January 4, 1943; Frederic E. Morgan to Hazle Buck Ewing, January 6, 1943; Cavour Truesdale to Hazle Buck Ewing, January 16, 1943, The Principia, Archives Department, Elsah, Illinois.

[523] Frederic E. Morgan, "Paper read before the College Faculty on February 26, 1943," The Principia, Archives Department, Elsah, Illinois.

[524] Ibid.

[525] Ibid.

[526] Ibid.

[527] Hazle Buck Ewing to Frederic Morgan, March 24, 1943, The Principia, Archives Department, Elsah, Illinois.

[528] Ibid., April 28, 1943.

[529] Frederic E. Morgan to Hazle Buck Ewing, May 20, 1943, The Principia, Archives Department, Elsah, Illinois.

[530] Hazle Buck Ewing to Frederic Morgan, June 18, 1943; Frederic E. Morgan to Hazle Buck Ewing, June 21, 1943, The Principia, Archives Department, Elsah, Illinois.

[531] Hazle Buck Ewing to Frederic E. Morgan, June 18, 1943, The Principia, Archives Department, Elsah, Illinois.

[532] Frederic E. Morgan to Hazle Buck Ewing, June 21, 1943, The Principia, Archives Department, Elsah, Illinois.

[533] Ibid., June 23.

[534] Personal telephone interview: Karen Heilbrun with Jeff and Beth Carey, May 31, 2005.

[535] Ibid.

[536] Ibid.

[537] Ibid.

[538] Frederic E. Morgan to the Principia Comptroller and Corresponding Secretary, July 23, 1943, The Principia, Archives Department, Elsah, Illinois.

[539] Eldridge Hamlin to Hazle Buck Ewing, August 13, 1943, The Principia, Archives Department, Elsah, Illinois.

[540] Hazle Buck Ewing to Frederic E. Morgan, October 11, 1943; Frederic E. Morgan to Hazle Buck Ewing, November 5, 1943, The Principia, Archives Department, Elsah, Illinois., Elsah, Illinois.

[541] Hazle Buck Ewing to Frederic E. Morgan, January 12, 1944; Frederic E. Morgan to Hazle Buck Ewing, January 24, 1944, The Principia, Archives Department, Elsah, Illinois.

[542] Frederic E. Morgan to Hazle Buck Ewing, February 2, 1944, The Principia, Archives Department, Elsah, Illinois.

[543] Hazle Buck Ewing to Frederic E. Morgan, received on March 17, 1944; Hazle Buck Ewing to Velma, March 15, 1944; Velma to Hazle Buck Ewing, March 18, 1944; Hazle Buck Ewing to Velma, March 22, 1944, The Principia, Archives Department, Elsah, Illinois.

[544] Hazle Buck Ewing to Frederic E. Morgan, received April 26, 1944; Frederic E. Morgan to Hazle Buck Ewing, April 26, 1944, The Principia, Archives Department, Elsah, Illinois.

[545] Hazle Buck Ewing to Frederic E. Morgan, May 24, 1944; Hazle Buck Ewing to Frederic E. Morgan, May 29, 1944, The Principia, Archives Department, Elsah, Illinois.
[546] Frederic E. Morgan to Hazle Buck Ewing, August 17, 1944, The Principia, Archives Department, Elsah, Illinois.
[547] Hazle Buck Ewing to Frederic E. Morgan, October 26, 1944; Frederic E. Morgan to Hazle Buck Ewing, October 28, 1944, The Principia, Archives Department, Elsah, Illinois.
[548] Hazle Buck Ewing to Frederic E. Morgan, December 7, 1944, The Principia, Archives Department, Elsah, Illinois.
[549] Ibid.
[550] Frederic E. Morgan to Hazle Buck Ewing, December 18,1944, The Principia, Archives Department, Elsah, Illinois.

Chapter 23: LIFE AT SUNSET ROAD

[551] "Sugar Creek Park Committee Chosen," *Pantagraph*, December 5, 1944, 3.
[552] William E. Morgan, Jr. to Hazle Buck Ewing, December 28, 1944; Hazle Buck Ewing to William E. Morgan, Jr., January 5, 1945; William E. Morgan, Jr. to Hazle Buck Ewing, January 10, 1945, The Principia, Archives Department, Elsah, Illinois.
[553] Gwen Edwards and Jeanne Wroan, *Sunset Road: History and Memories*, (Bloomington: Gwen Edwards and Jeanne Wroan, 2003), 29.
[554] Personal interview: Karen Heilbrun with Art Eiff, June 9, 2005 in Bloomington, 3.
[555] Ibid., 9, 18.
[556] Gwen Edwards and Jeanne Wroan, *Sunset Road: History and Memories*, (Bloomington: Gwen Edwards and Jeanne Wroan, 2003), 42.
[557] Personal interview: Karen Heilbrun with Art Eiff, June 9, 2005 in Bloomington, 3, 9, 18.
[558] Ibid., 1, 8.
[559] Ibid., 1, 2, 9, 12
[560] Ibid., 1, 2, 9, 12, 13.
[561] Ibid., 9, 11.
[562] Ibid., 3.
[563] Ibid., 6.
[564] Ibid., 2.
[565] Ibid., 4.
[566] Ibid.
[567] Ibid., 5, 6.
[568] Ibid., 15.
[569] Ibid., 5, 6.
[570] Ibid., 7,8.
[571] Ibid., 5, 6.
[572] Ibid., 7, 16, 17.
[573] Ibid., 9.
[574] Ibid., 16.

Chapter 24: GETTING BACK TO NORMAL

[575] Sam N. Baker to Hazle Buck Ewing, March 6, 1945, The Principia, Archives Department, Elsah, Illinois.
[576] Lee McCandless to Hazle Buck Ewing, March 16, 1945; Rebeka A.P. Dietz to Hazle Buck Ewing, March 31, 1945, The Principia, Archives Department, Elsah, Illinois.
[577] Hazle Buck Ewing to Frederic E. Morgan, April 11, 1945, The Principia, Archives Department, Elsah, Illinois.
[578] Hazle Buck Ewing to Frederic E. Morgan, May 15, 1945; Frederic E. Morgan to Hazle Buck Ewing, June 15, 1945, The Principia, Archives Department, Elsah, Illinois.
[579] Hazle Buck Ewing to Frederic E. Morgan, September 26, 1945, The Principia, Archives Department, Elsah, Illinois.
[580] Frederic E. Morgan to Hazle Buck Ewing, October 8, 1945; Hazle Buck Ewing to Frederic E. Morgan, October 28, 1945, The Principia, Archives Department, Elsah, Illinois.

[581] Hazle Buck Ewing to Frederic E. Morgan, October 28, 1945; Frederic E. Morgan to Hazle Buck Ewing, November 2, 1945, The Principia, Archives Department, Elsah, Illinois.
[582] *Principia Alumni Purpose*, December 1945, page 14, The Principia, Archives Department, Elsah, Illinois.
[583] Sam N. Baker to Hazle Buck Ewing, February 5, 1946, The Principia, Archives Department, Elsah, Illinois.
[584] Evelyn R. Shearston to Hazle Buck Ewing, May 1, 1946, The Principia, Archives Department, Elsah, Illinois.
[585] Sam N. Baker to Hazle Buck Ewing, June 1, 1946, The Principia, Archives Department, Elsah, Illinois.
[586] Ibid.
[587] Frederick E. Morgan to Hazle Buck Ewing, July 12, 1946, The Principia, Archives Department, Elsah, Illinois.
[588] Hazle Buck Ewing to Frederic E. Morgan, November 5, 1946; Frederic E. Morgan to Hazle Buck Ewing, November 6, 1946, The Principia, Archives Department, Elsah, Illinois.
[589] Ibid.
[590] Ibid.
[591] Hazle Buck Ewing to Frederic E. Morgan, December 9, 1946, The Principia, Archives Department, Elsah, Illinois.

Chapter 25: FOR THE LOVE OF HORSES
[592] Frederic E. Morgan to Eldridge Hamlin, February 11, 1947, The Principia, Archives Department, Elsah, Illinois.
[593] Personal telephone interview: Karen Heilbrun with Alice Taylor Reed, May 2005, 3.
[594] Ibid., 5.
[595] Ibid., 5, 6.
[596] Ibid., 6.
[597] Ibid., 5.
[598] Personal telephone interview: Karen Heilbrun with Nancy Ranson, March 28, 2006, 4.
[599] Personal telephone interview: Karen Heilbrun with Lucinda Buck Ewing, July 18, 2005, 5.
[600] Ibid., 5.
[601] Ibid.
[602] *1947 Sheaf*, 49; Ana Mary Elliott to Frederic E. Morgan, February 10 1947; The Principia, Archives Department, Elsah, Illinois.
[603] Ana Mary Elliott to Frederic E. Morgan, February 10, 1947, The Principia, Archives Department, Elsah, Illinois.
[604] Ibid.
[605] www.funksmaplesirup.com/-9k, August 11, 2007.
[606] Hazle Buck Ewing to Frederic E. Morgan, May 22, 1947, The Principia, Archives Department, Elsah, Illinois.
[607] Personal telephone interview: Karen Heilbrun with Lucinda Buck Ewing, July 18, 2005, 1. Personal interview: Karen Heilbrun with Nancy Ranson, March 28, 2006, 4.
[608] Frederic E. Morgan to Hazle Buck Ewing, August 7, 1947; Frederic E. Morgan, to Hazle Buck Ewing, August 18, 1947, The Principia, Archives Department, Elsah, Illinois.
[609] Frederic E. Morgan to Hazle Buck Ewing, August 7, 1947, The Principia, Archives Department, Elsah, Illinois.
[610] Hazle Buck Ewing to Frederic E. Morgan, August 22, 1947, The Principia, Archives Department, Elsah, Illinois.
[611] Frederic E. Morgan to Hazle Buck Ewing, September 3, 1947, The Principia, Archives Department, Elsah, Illinois.
[612] Hazle Buck Ewing to Frederic E. Morgan, November 17, 1947, The Principia, Archives Department, Elsah, Illinois.
[613] Ibid., November 26, 1947.
[614] Frederic E. Morgan to Hazle Buck Ewing, November 29, 1947, The Principia, Archives Department, Elsah, Illinois.

Chapter 26: A VITAL INFLUENCE

[615] Frederic E. Morgan to Sam N. Baker, February 10, 1947, The Principia, Archives Department, Elsah, Illinois.

[616] Robert Fisher, Chairman of the School of Nations at St. Louis campus, to Hazle Buck Ewing, February 10, 1947, The Principia, Archives Department, Elsah, Illinois.

[617] Sam N. Baker to Hazle Buck Ewing, October 7, 1947, The Principia, Archives Department, Elsah, Illinois.

[618] Ibid., January 22, 1948.

[619] Hazle Buck Ewing to Frederic E. Morgan, February 28, 1948, The Principia, Archives Department, Elsah, Illinois.

[620] Lee McCandless to Hazle Buck Ewing, June 2, 1948, The Principia, Archives Department, Elsah, Illinois.

[621] "Independent Unit for Stevenson: Non Partisan Group States Aim, Purpose," *Pantagraph*, June 26, 1948, 6.

[622] Frederic E. Morgan to Hazle Buck Ewing, July 23, 1948, The Principia, Archives Department, Elsah, Illinois.

[623] Hazle Buck Ewing to Frederic E. Morgan, July 29, 1948 (date letter received by Morgan), The Principia, Archives Department, Elsah, Illinois.

[624] Ibid.

[625] Frederic E. Morgan to Hazle Buck Ewing, July 29, 1948, The Principia, Archives Department, Elsah, Illinois.

[626] Sam N. Baker to Hazle Buck Ewing, November 29, 1948; Frederic E. Morgan to Sam N. Baker, memorandum prior to November 29, 1948, attached to letter from Sam Baker to Hazle Buck Ewing, The Principia, Archives Department, Elsah, Illinois.

[627] Sam N. Baker to Hale Buck Ewing, December 13, 1948, The Principia, Archives Department, Elsah, Illinois.

[628] Hazle Buck Ewing to Frederic E. Morgan, December 18, 1948, The Principia, Archives Department, Elsah, Illinois.

[629] Rebeka Dietz to Hazle Buck Ewing, February 22, 1949, The Principia, Archives Department, Elsah, Illinois.

[630] Hazle Buck Ewing to Rebeka Dietz, March 21, 1949, The Principia, Archives Department, Elsah, Illinois.

[631] Fredric E. Morgan to Hazle Buck Ewing, March 31, 1949, The Principia, Archives Department, Elsah, Illinois.

[632] Hazle Buck Ewing to Rebeka Dietz, April 18, 1949, The Principia, Archives Department, Elsah, Illinois.

[633] *Pantagraph*, undated article; Ewing Manor Archives, Bloomington, Illinois.

[634] "Mrs. Ewing Backs School of Nations," *Pantagraph*, May 4, 1949.

[635] Hazle Buck Ewing to Frederic E. Morgan, May 28, 1949, The Principia, Archives Department, Elsah, Illinois.

[636] Ibid.

[637] Hazle Buck Ewing to Mary Towle, May 31, 1949, The Principia, Archives Department, Elsah, Illinois.

[638] Lillian S. Parker, Secretary, Carnegie Endowment for International Peace, 405 West 117th Street, New York to Mary Towle, The Principia, Archives Department, Elsah, Illinois.

[639] Hazle Buck Ewing to Mary Towle, May 31, 1949, The Principia, Archives Department, Elsah, Illinois.

[640] Frederic E. Moran to Hazle Buck Ewing, June 14, 1949, The Principia, Archives Department, Elsah, Illinois.

[641] Ibid., January 4, 1950.

[642] Hazle Buck Ewing to Rebeka Dietz, January 6 and January 9, 1950, The Principia, Archives Department, Elsah, Illinois.

Chapter 27: OF HISTORICAL SIGNIFICANCE

[643] Frederic E. Morgan to Hazle Buck Ewing, January 20, 1950; Hazle Buck Ewing to Frederic E. Morgan, January 19, 1950, The Principia, Archives Department, Elsah, Illinois.

[644] George Farve, "School of Nation Fosters World Consciousness," *The Pilot*, February 15, 1950, The Principia, Archives Department, Elsah, Illinois.

[645] Hazle Buck Ewing to Frederic E. Morgan, June 20, 1950, The Principia, Archives Department, Elsah, Illinois.

[646] Ibid.

[647] Frederic E. Morgan, to Hazle Buck Ewing, August 29, 1950, The Principia, Archives Department, Elsah, Illinois.

[648] School of Nations Committee to Hazle Buck Ewing, October 16, 1950; Hazle Buck Ewing to Frederic E. Morgan, October 30, 1950, The Principia, Archives Department, Elsah, Illinois.

[649] Douglas Swett to Hazle Buck Ewing, January 19, 1951, The Principia, Archives Department, Elsah, Illinois.

[650] Ibid., February 6, 1951; Mary Louise Moseley, Transportation Supervisor, GM&O Railroad, February 6, 1951, The Principia, Archives Department, Elsah, Illinois.

[651] Frederic E. Morgan to Hazle Buck Ewing at the Commodore Hotel in New York City, New York, February 15, 1951, The Principia, Archives Department, Elsah, Illinois.

[652] Hazle Buck Ewing to Frederic E. Morgan, February 28, 1951; Frederic E. Morgan to Hazle Buck Ewing, March 2, 1951, The Principia, Archives Department, Elsah, Illinois.

[653] Frederic E. Morgan to Hazle Buck Ewing, April 5, 1951; Hazle Buck Ewing to Frederic E. Morgan, February 28, 1951; Hazle Buck Ewing to Frederic E. Morgan, March 30, 1951, The Principia, Archives Department, Elsah, Illinois.

[654] Adlai E. Stevenson II to Hazle Buck Ewing, July 14, 1951, McLean Historical Museum, Bloomington, Illinois.

[655] Hazle Buck Ewing to Frederic E. Morgan, October 18, 1951; Frederic E. Morgan to Hazle Buck Ewing, November 23, 1951, The Principia, Archives Department, Elsah, Illinois.

[656] Douglas Swett to Hazle Buck Ewing, December 7, 1951, The Principia, Archives Department, Elsah, Illinois.

[657] Frederic E. Morgan to Hazle Buck Ewing, December 21, 1951, The Principia, Archives Department, Elsah, Illinois.

Chapter 28: POSSESS MY SOUL IN PATIENCE

[658] Hazle Buck Ewing to Frederic E. Morgan, December 31, 1951, The Principia, Archives Department, Elsah, Illinois. Hazle Buck Ewing to Frederic E. Morgan, January 2, 1952, The Principia, Archives Department, Elsah, Illinois.

[659] Evelyn Shearston to Hazle Buck Ewing, January 16, 1952; Hazle Buck Ewing to Evelyn Shearston, January 22, 1952, The Principia, Archives Department, Elsah, Illinois.

[660] Eldredge Hamlin to Hazle Buck Ewing, January 24, 1952, The Principia, Archives Department, Elsah, Illinois.

[661] Frederic E. Morgan to Hazle Buck Ewing, February 7, 1952; Hazle Buck Ewing to Frederic E. Morgan, February 9, 1952, The Principia, Archives Department, Elsah, Illinois.

[662] Frederic E. Morgan to Hazle Buck Ewing, February 11, 1952, The Principia, Archives Department, Elsah, Illinois.

[663] Ibid., March 3, 1952.

[664] Hazle Buck Ewing, talk given at Patrons' Conference, May 10, 1952, The Principia, Archives Department, Elsah, Illinois.[682] Ibid.

[665] Hazle Buck Ewing to Frederic E. Morgan, June 2, 1952; Frederic E. Morgan to Hazle Buck Ewing, June 5, 1952, The Principia, Archives Department, Elsah, Illinois.

[666] Hazle Buck Ewing to Honorable Adlai E. Stevenson, The Executive Mansion, Springfield, Illinois, August 13, 1952; William McC. Blair Jr., Administrative Assistant, Office of the Governor, Springfield, Adlai E. Stevenson, Governor to Hazle Buck Ewing, May 26, 1952, McLean County Museum of History, Bloomington, Illinois.

[667] Mary Baker Eddy, Science and Health with Key to the Scriptures, (Boston: The First Church of Christ, Scientist, used by courtesy of The Mary Baker Eddy Collection.), 454.

[668] Hazle Buck Ewing to Honorable Adlai E. Stevenson, August 13, 1952, McLean County Museum of History, Bloomington, Illinois.

[669] Hazle Buck Ewing to Honorable Adlai E. Stevenson, August 13, 1952; Adlai E. Stevenson to Hazle Buck Ewing, August 19, 1952; McLean County Museum of History, Bloomington, Illinois.

[670] School of Nations Committee to Hazle Buck Ewing, November 5, 1952, The Principia, Archives Department, Elsah, Illinois.

[671] Hazle Buck Ewing to Frederic E. and Toni Morgan, November 24, 1952, The Principia, Archives Department, Elsah, Illinois.

[672] Frederic E. Morgan to Hazle Buck Ewing, February 3, 1953; Hazle Buck Ewing to Frederic E. Morgan February 7, 1953, The Principia, Archives Department, Elsah, Illinois.

[673] Frederic E. Morgan to Hazle Buck Ewing, February 3, 1953, The Principia, Archives Department, Elsah, Illinois.

[674] Hazle Buck Ewing to Frederic E. Morgan, March 13, 1953, The Principia, Archives Department, Elsah, Illinois.

[675] Hazle Buck Ewing to Frederic E. Morgan, March 31, 1953, The Principia, Archives Department, Elsah, Illinois.

[676] Ibid., April 29, 1953.

[677] Ibid., May 23, 1953.

Chapter 29: A FRIEND IN NEED

[678] School of Nations Committee Meeting Minutes, September 25, 1953; School of Nations Committee Minutes, October 1, 1953; School of Nations Committee Minutes submitted by Iolani Ingalls, Secretary, October, 1953, The Principia, Archives Department, Elsah, Illinois. http://wwmideasti:about-mideast-institute October 5, 2007.

[679] Frederic E. Morgan to Hazle Buck Ewing, October 10, 1953, The Principia, Archives Department, Elsah, Illinois.

[680] Hazle Buck Ewing to Frederic E. Morgan, November 7, 1953, The Principia, Archives Department, Elsah, Illinois.

[681] Ibid.

[682] Frederic E. Morgan to Hazle Buck Ewing, November 11, 1953 (there are 2 letters with this date), The Principia, Archives Department, Elsah, Illinois.

[683] Hazle Buck Ewing to Toni Morgan, November 28, 1953; Nelson L. Buck to Illinois Philanthropic and Educational Foundation, December 14, 1953; John Fawsthorne of the Illinois Philanthropic and Educational Foundation, December 28, 1953, The Principia, Archives Department, Elsah, Illinois.

[684] William E. Morgan, Jr. to Hazle Buck Ewing, January 9, 1954; Frederic E. Morgan to Hazle Buck Ewing, January 21, 1954, The Principia, Archives Department, Elsah, Illinois.

[685] Hazle Buck Ewing to Lois Gartner, April 8, 1954, The Principia, Archives Department, Elsah, Illinois.

[686] "Campus Eviction Averted," *Principia Purpose*, Spring 2004, p. 16, The Principia, Archives Department, Elsah, Illinois.

[687] Ibid., 17.

[688] Ibid.

[689] Ibid., 18.

[690] Ibid.

[691] Ibid.

[692] Mrs. Arthur (Adeline) Adams to Frederic E. Morgan, July 14, 1954; Frederic E. Morgan to Mrs. Arthur (Adeline) Adams; Frederic E. Morgan to Hazle Buck Ewing, July 21, 1954, The Principia, Archives Department, Elsah, Illinois.

[693] Frederic E. Morgan to Trustees of the Principia Corporation, July 21, 1954, The Principia, Archives Department, Elsah, Illinois.

[694] Hazle Buck Ewing to Frederic E. Morgan, August 19, 1954, The Principia, Archives Department, Elsah, Illinois.

[695] Ibid.

[696] Frederic E. Morgan to Hazle Buck Ewing, September 10, 1954, The Principia, Archives Department, Elsah, Illinois.

[697] Ibid., October 22, 1954.

[698] Mitzi Jeanne LaBree to Douglas Swett, School of Nations, October 10, 1954, The Principia, Archives Department, Elsah, Illinois.

[699] Eldredge Hamlin to Hazle Buck Ewing, December 30, 1954; John K. Andrews, Assistant Treasurer, to Hazle Buck Ewing, January 25, 1955, The Principia, Archives Department, Elsah, Illinois.

[700] Frederic E. Morgan to Hazle Buck Ewing, January 20, 1955; Frederic E. Morgan to Hazle Buck Ewing, January 22, 1955; Frederic E. Morgan to Hazle Buck Ewing, January 12, 1955, The Principia, Archives Department, Elsah, Illinois.

Chapter 30: A TIME FOR CHANGE

701 William E. Morgan, Jr. to Hazle Buck Ewing, February 10, 1955, The Principia, Archives Department, Elsah, Illinois.

702 Ibid.

703 Ibid.

704 Ibid.

705 Ibid.

706 Hazle Buck Ewing to William E. Morgan, Jr., February 18, 1955, The Principia, Archives Department, Elsah, Illinois.

707 William E. Morgan, Jr. to Hazle Buck Ewing, March 8, 1955, The Principia, Archives Department, Elsah, Illinois.

708 Hazle Buck Ewing to William E. Morgan, Jr., March 31, 1955, The Principia, Archives Department, Elsah, Illinois.

709 Ibid., April 26, 1955; May 14, 1955.

710 William E. Morgan, Jr. to Hazle Buck Ewing, April 21, 1955; William E. Morgan, Jr. to Hazle Buck Ewing, May 13, 1955; Hazle Buck Ewing to William E. Morgan, Jr., May 14, 1955, The Principia, Archives Department, Elsah, Illinois.

711 "Nelson Ewing Heads Elgin Design Force," The Daily Pantagraph, May 11, 1955, 21.

712 Ibid.

713 Ibid.

714 William E. Morgan, Jr. to Hazle Buck Ewing, April 12, 1955; Hazle Buck Ewing to William E. Morgan, Jr., April 26, 1955; Hazle Buck Ewing to William E. Morgan, Jr., June 30, 1955, The Principia, Archives Department, Elsah, Illinois.

715 Evelyn Shearston to Hazle Buck Ewing, July 12, 1955, The Principia, Archives Department, Elsah, Illinois.

716 Hazle Buck Ewing to William E. Morgan, Jr., August 1, 1955, The Principia, Archives Department, Elsah, Illinois.

717 William E. Morgan, Jr. to Hazle Buck Ewing, August 24, 1955; Hazle Buck Ewing to William E. Morgan, Jr., August 28, 1955, The Principia, Archives Department, Elsah, Illinois.

718 William E. Morgan, Jr. to Frederic E. Morgan, September 1, 1955; William E. Morgan, Jr. to Nelson Buck, September 19, 1955, The Principia, Archives Department, Elsah, Illinois.

719 Edwin S. Leonard to Hazle Buck Ewing, October 31, 1955, The Principia, Archives Department, Elsah, Illinois.

720 Ibid.

721 Frederic E. Morgan to Hazle Buck Ewing, November 2, 1955; Hazle Buck Ewing to Frederic E. Morgan, November 10, 1955; The Principia, Archives Department, Elsah, Illinois.

722 Hazle Buck Ewing to Frederic E. Morgan, November 22, 1955; Frederic E. Morgan to Hazle Buck Ewing, December 2, 1955, The Principia, Archives Department, Elsah, Illinois.

723 The Principia Corporation to Members of the Board of Trustees, December 15, 1955; Hazle Buck Ewing to Frederic E. Morgan, December 20, 1955, The Principia, Archives Department, Elsah, Illinois.

724 Eldredge Hamlin to Hazle Buck Ewing, December 30, 1955, The Principia, Archives Department, Elsah, Illinois.

Chapter 31: GREAT JOY AND GREAT SORROW

725 William E. Morgan, Jr. to Hazle Buck Ewing, May 3, 1956; Hazle Buck Ewing to William E. Morgan, Jr., May 8, 1956, The Principia, Archives Department, Elsah, Illinois.

726 William E. Morgan, Jr. to Hazle Buck Ewing, May 7, 1956, The Principia, Archives Department, Elsah, Illinois.

727 Ibid.

[728] Frederic E. Morgan, "Presentation of Hazle Buck Ewing for (Hon.) Doctor of Laws," June 12, 1956, The Principia, Archives Department, Elsah, Illinois.

[729] Ibid.

[730] "Principia Patroness Ewing Receives Honorary Doctorate," *Pantagraph*, June 15, 1956, 2; "Gets Honorary Degree," *Pantagraph*, June 17, 1956, 2.

[731] Eldredge Hamlin to Hazle Buck Ewing, June 18, 1956, The Principia, Archives Department, Elsah, Illinois.

[732] Hazle Buck Ewing to Rebeka Dietz, June 21, 1956; Rebeka Dietz to Hazle Buck Ewing, June 26, 1956, The Principia, Archives Department, Elsah, Illinois.

[733] Frederic E. Morgan to Hazle Buck Ewing, June 27, 1956, The Principia, Archives Department, Elsah, Illinois.

[734] Hazle Buck Ewing to Frederic Morgan, July 12, 1956, The Principia, Archives Department, Elsah, Illinois.

[735] "Mrs. Ewing Gives Park Plan a Boost," *Pantagraph*, July 10, 1956, 4; "Council Accepts Gift of Land from Mrs. Ewing," *Pantagraph*, July 10, 1956, 12.

[736] Carey Browne, Secretary of Admissions, to Nelson Ewing, July 23, 1956, The Principia, Archives Department, Elsah, Illinois.

[737] Frederic E. Morgan to Hazle Buck Ewing, August 14, 1956, The Principia, Archives Department, Elsah, Illinois.

[738] Hazle Buck Ewing to Frederic E. Morgan, August 21, 1956, The Principia, Archives Department, Elsah, Illinois.

[739] William E. Morgan, Jr. to Hazle Buck Ewing, August 15, 1956, The Principia, Archives Department, Elsah, Illinois.

[740] Frederic E. Morgan to Hazle Buck Ewing, August 20, 1956, The Principia, Archives Department, Elsah, Illinois. Evanston, Illinois newspaper clipping, August 9, 1956.

[741] Frederic E. Morgan to "All Members of the Principia Abroad," August 17, 1956, The Principia, Archives Department, Elsah, Illinois.

[742] Hazle Buck Ewing to Frederic E. Morgan, August 21, 1956, The Principia, Archives Department, Elsah, Illinois.

[743] Evanston, Illinois newspaper clipping, August 9, 1956.

[744] Frederic E. Morgan to Hazle Buck Ewing, August 28, 1956, The Principia, Archives Department, Elsah, Illinois.

[745] Hazle Buck Ewing to Frederic E. Morgan, October 30, 1956, The Principia, Archives Department, Elsah, Illinois.

[746] Robert A. Andrews to Hazle Buck Ewing, November 23, 1956, The Principia, Archives Department, Elsah, Illinois.

Chapter 32: THE REWARD FOR PATIENCE

[747] Robert A. Andrews to Hazle Buck Ewing, November 23, 1956, The Principia, Archives Department, Elsah, Illinois.

[748] Eldredge Hamlin to Hazle Buck Ewing, November 27, 1956; Rebeka Dietz to Hazle Buck Ewing, December 6, 1956, The Principia, Archives Department, Elsah, Illinois.

[749] Rebeka Dietz to Hazle Buck Ewing, December 6, 1956, The Principia, Archives Department, Elsah, Illinois.

[750] Hazle Buck Ewing to William E. Morgan, Jr., December 17, 1956, The Principia, Archives Department, Elsah, Illinois.

[751] William E. Morgan, Jr. to Hazle Buck Ewing, January 9, 1957, The Principia, Archives Department, Elsah, Illinois.

[752] The Members of Principia Abroad 1956 to Hazle Buck Ewing, February 22, 1957, The Principia, Archives Department, Elsah, Illinois.

[753] William E. Morgan, Jr. to Hazle Buck Ewing, March 18, 1957, The Principia, Archives Department, Elsah, Illinois.

[754] Ibid.

[755] Frederic E. Morgan to Hazle Buck Ewing, March 20, 1957, The Principia, Archives Department, Elsah, Illinois.

[756] Hazle Buck Ewing to Frederic E. Morgan, April 2, 1957, The Principia, Archives Department, Elsah, Illinois.

[757] Hazle Buck Ewing to Helen and Eldredge Hamlin, April 27, 1957; Hazle Buck Ewing to Frederic E. Morgan, April 27, 1957, The Principia, Archives Department, Elsah, Illinois.

[758] Hazle Buck Ewing to Frederic E. Morgan, June11, 1957; Frederic E. Morgan to Hazle Buck Ewing, June 19, 1957, The Principia, Archives Department, Elsah, Illinois.

[759] Frederic E. Morgan to Hazle Buck Ewing, May 10, 1957; Hazle Buck Ewing to Eldredge Hamlin, May 17, 1957; Hazle Buck Ewing to Frederic E. Morgan, June 11, 1957, Frederic E. Morgan to Hazle Buck Ewing, June 19, 1957, The Principia, Archives Department, Elsah, Illinois.

[760] William E. Morgan, Jr. to Hazle Buck Ewing, June 24, 1957; Hazle Buck Ewing to William E. Morgan, Jr., June 29, 1957, The Principia, Archives Department, Elsah, Illinois.

[761] The Principia Corporation to Members of the Board of Trustees, June 26, 1957; Hazle Buck Ewing to William E. Morgan, Jr., June 29, 1957, The Principia, Archives Department, Elsah, Illinois.

[762] William E. Morgan, Jr. to Eldredge Hamlin, July 31, 1957; William E. Morgan, Jr. to Hazle Buck Ewing, August 19, 1957, The Principia, Archives Department, Elsah, Illinois.

[763] Ibid.

[764] William E. Morgan, Jr. to Hazle Buck Ewing, August 19, 1957, The Principia, Archives Department, Elsah, Illinois.

[765] Frederic E. Morgan to Hazle Buck Ewing, July 17, 1957, The Principia, Archives Department, Elsah, Illinois.

[766] Ibid., July 19, 1957.

[767] William E. Morgan, Jr. to Hazle Buck Ewing, August 19, 1957, The Principia, Archives Department, Elsah, Illinois.

[768] Frederic E. Morgan to Hazle Buck Ewing, August 22, 1957; William E. Morgan, Jr. to Hazle Buck Ewing, August 23, 1957, The Principia, Archives Department, Elsah, Illinois.

[769] Hazle Buck Ewing to Frederic E. Morgan, October 12, 1957, The Principia, Archives Department, Elsah, Illinois.

[770] William E. Morgan, Jr. to Hazle Buck Ewing, December 31, 1957, The Principia, Archives Department, Elsah, Illinois.

Chapter 33: PRESSING ON

[771] Hazle Buck Ewing to Frederic E. Morgan, October 12, 1957; Frederic E. Morgan to Hazle Buck Ewing, January 24, 1958, The Principia, Archives Department, Elsah, Illinois.

[772] Hazle Buck Ewing to Frederic E. Morgan, January 25, 1958, The Principia, Archives Department, Elsah, Illinois.

[773] Ibid., March 4, 1958.

[774] Eldredge Hamlin to Hazle Buck Ewing, March 17, 1958; Hazle Buck Ewing to Eldredge Hamlin, April 17, 1958; William E. Morgan, Jr. to Hazle Buck Ewing, May 7, 1958, The Principia, Archives Department, Elsah, Illinois.

[775] Eldredge Hamlin to Hazle Buck Ewing, May 12, 1958, The Principia, Archives Department, Elsah, Illinois.

[776] William E. Morgan, Jr. to Hazle Buck Ewing, May 13, 1958, The Principia, Archives Department, Elsah, Illinois.

[777] Ibid., May 27, 1958.

[778] Ibid., June 23, 1958; Hazle Buck Ewing to William E. Morgan, Jr., June 30, 1958, The Principia, Archives Department, Elsah, Illinois.

[779] Ralph Nelson Ewing to Hazle Buck Ewing, June 25, 1958, and July 1, 1958, Ewing Manor Archives, Bloomington, Illinois.

[780] Ralph Nelson Ewing to Hazle Buck Ewing, July 1, 1958, Ewing Manor Archives, Bloomington, Illinois.

[781] Hazle Buck Ewing to William E. Morgan, Jr., August 12, 1958; Hazle Buck Ewing to Frederic E. Morgan, September 8, 1958, The Principia, Archives Department, Elsah, Illinois.

[782] Hazle Buck Ewing to Frederic E. Morgan, September 8, 1958, The Principia, Archives Department, Elsah, Illinois.

[783] William E. Morgan, Jr. to Hazle Buck Ewing, September 19, 1958, The Principia, Archives Department, Elsah, Illinois.

[784] Ibid.

[785] Hazle Buck Ewing to Frederic E. Morgan, September 23, 1958; William E. Morgan, Jr. to Hazle Buck Ewing, October 14, 1958, The Principia, Archives Department, Elsah, Illinois.

[786] Ned Bradley to William E. Morgan, Jr., October 6, 1958; The Principia, Archives Department, Elsah, Illinois.

Chapter 34: THE CULMINATION OF AN IDEA

[787] William E. Morgan, Jr. to Hazle Buck Ewing, February 18, 1959, The Principia, Archives Department, Elsah, Illinois.

[788] Hazle Buck Ewing to William E. Morgan, Jr., February 9, 1959; Hazle Buck Ewing to William E. Morgan, Jr., February 13, 1959, The Principia, Archives Department, Elsah, Illinois.

[789] William E. Morgan, Jr. to Hazle Buck Ewing, February 18, 1959, The Principia, Archives Department, Elsah, Illinois.

[790] Hazle Buck Ewing to William E. Morgan, Jr., March 9, 1959, The Principia, Archives Department, Elsah, Illinois.

[791] C. Theodore Houpt to Hazle Buck Ewing, March 6, 1959, The Principia, Archives Department, Elsah, Illinois.

[792] Frederic E. Morgan to Hazle Buck Ewing, March 9, 1959, The Principia, Archives Department, Elsah, Illinois.

[793] William E. Morgan, Jr. to Hazle Buck Ewing, March 16, 1959; Hazle Buck Ewing to C. Theodore Houpt, March 24, 1959; Hazle Buck Ewing to William E. Morgan, Jr., March 25, 1959, The Principia, Archives Department, Elsah, Illinois.

[794] Hazle Buck Ewing to Frederic E. Morgan, March 25, 1959; Frederic E. Morgan to Hazle Buck Ewing, April 1, 1959, The Principia, Archives Department, Elsah, Illinois.

[795] C. Theodore Houpt to Hazle Buck Ewing, March 30, 1959, The Principia, Archives Department, Elsah, Illinois.

[796] William E. Morgan, Jr. to Hazle Buck Ewing, April 2, 1959, The Principia, Archives Department, Elsah, Illinois.

[797] Ibid., April 4, 1959; Hazle Buck Ewing to William E. Morgan, Jr., April 7, 1959, The Principia, Archives Department, Elsah, Illinois. "Principia Dedication," *Pantagraph*, April 5, 1959, 26.

Chapter 35: THESE ARE YOUR DAYS

[798] Frederic E. Morgan to Hazle Buck Ewing, April 14, 1959, The Principia, Archives Department, Elsah, Illinois.

[799] Ibid.

[800] Lewie Prittie Castellain, untitled hymn, *Christian Science Hymnal*, ©1932, renewed 1960, The Mary Baker Eddy Collection, 203.

[801] King James Version of the Bible, Isaiah 2:2, 3.

[802] Ibid., Zechariah 2:11.

[803] Ibid., Zechariah 8:21, 22, 23.

[804] Mary Baker Eddy, *The First Church of Christ Scientist and Miscellany* (Boston: The First Church of Christ, Scientist, used by courtesy of The Mary Baker Eddy Collection), 127.

[805] Ibid., 282.

[806] Mary Baker Eddy, *Science and Health with Key to the Scripture* (Boston: The First Church of Christ, Scientist, used by courtesy of The Mary Baker Eddy Collection), 340.

[807] King James Version of the Bible, Psalms 22:28.

[808] Frederic Evan Morgan, Chairman of Board of Trustees, The Principia, "School of Nations Building Dedication – April 19, 1959," The Principia, Archives Department, Elsah, Illinois.

[809] Ibid.

[810] Frederic E. Morgan, "Mrs. Hazle Buck Ewing, School of Nations Dedication, April 19, 1959," The Principia, Archives Department, Elsah, Illinois.

[811] Hazle Buck Ewing, "School of Nations Dedication, April 19, 1959," The Principia, Archives Department, Elsah, Illinois.

[812] Mary Baker Eddy, *Science and Health with Key to the Scriptures*, (Boston: The First Church of Christ, Scientist, used by courtesy of The Mary Baker Eddy Collection, 1934), 340.

[813] Hazle Buck Ewing, "Remarks at the School of Nations Dedication, April 19, 1959," The Principia, Archives Department, Elsah, Illinois.

[814] William E. Morgan, Jr., "Remarks at the School of Nations Building Dedication, April 19, 1959," The Principia, Archives Department, Elsah, Illinois.

[815] Ibid.

[816] Ibid.

[817] C. Theodore Houpt, "Remarks at the School of Nations Building Dedication, April 19, 1959," The Principia, Archives Department, Elsah, Illinois.

[818] Ibid.

[819] Frances Ann Waller, "Member of 1958 Principia Abroad Group, Remarks at the School of Nations Building Dedication, April 19, 1959," Elsah, Illinois.

[820] Edwin S. Leonard, Jr., "Remarks at the School of Nations Dedication, April 19, 1959," The Principia, Archives Department, Elsah, Illinois.

[821] Edwin S. Leonard, Jr., "Remarks at the School of Nations Dedication, April 19, 1959;" William Ward, President of the Student Council of The Principia College, "Remarks at the school of Nations Dedication, April 19, 1959;" Dedication Program, School of Nations Building, April 19, 1959, The Principia, Archives Department, Elsah, Illinois.

[822] Hazle Buck Ewing to William E. Morgan, Jr., April 7, 1959, Inter Office Memo, "List of School of Nations Committee," April 14, 1959, The Principia, Archives Department, Elsah, Illinois.

[823] Frederic E. Morgan to Hazle Buck Ewing, April 20, 1959, The Principia, Archives Department, Elsah, Illinois.

[824] "Principia To Dedicate Ewing Gift Building," *Pantagraph*, 19 April, 1959; Hazle Buck Ewing to William E. Morgan, Jr., May 1, 1959, The Principia, Archives Department, Elsah, Illinois.

Chapter 36: A Dream Come True

[825] Hazle Buck Ewing to Frederic E. Morgan, July 1959, The Principia, Archives Department, Elsah, Illinois.

[826] Frederic E. Morgan to Hazle Buck Ewing, July 29, 2959, The Principia, Archives Department, Elsah, Illinois.

[827] Eldredge Hamlin to Hazle Buck Ewing, September 4, 1959; William E. Morgan, Jr. to Hazle Buck Ewing, December 9, 1959; Hamlin to Hazle Buck Ewing, December 11, 1959; William E. Morgan, Jr. to Hazle Buck Ewing, February 23, 1960; William E. Morgan, Jr. to Hazle Buck Ewing, August 8 and 10, 1960, The Principia, Archives Department, Elsah, Illinois.

[828] Hazle Buck Ewing to William E. Morgan, Jr., August 21, 1960; William E. Morgan, Jr. to Hazle Buck Ewing, September 8, 1960, The Principia, Archives Department, Elsah, Illinois.

[829] Hazle Buck Ewing to James Green, March 6, 1961, The Principia, Archives Department, Elsah, Illinois.

[830] David K. Andrews to Hazle Buck Ewing, May 8, 1961, The Principia, Archives Department, Elsah, Illinois.

[831] Hazle Buck Ewing to Eldredge Hamlin, June 9, 1961; David K. Andrews to Hazle Buck Ewing, September 18, 1961, The Principia, Archives Department, Elsah, Illinois.

[832] David K. Andrews to Hazle Buck Ewing, August 17, 1962, The Principia, Archives Department, Elsah, Illinois.

[833] Interoffice letter from Eldredge Hamlin to Bert Clark, March 5, 1963, The Principia, Archives Department, Elsah, Illinois.

[834] Bert Clark to Alice Bright, November 12, 1963, The Principia, Archives Department, Elsah, Illinois.

[835] Eldredge Hamlin to Hazle Buck Ewing, January 14, 1964; David K. Andrews to Hazle Buck Ewing, January 14, 1964, The Principia, Archives Department, Elsah, Illinois.

[836] David K. Andrews to Alice Bright, April 9, 1964; Alice Bright to David K. Andrews, April 28, 1964, The Principia, Archives Department.

[837] Cyrus A. Bunting, "School of Nations Building: Decorating Project," June 5, 1964; Alice Bright to David K. Andrews, June 9, 1964, The Principia, Archives Department, Elsah.

[838] Alice Bright to David K. Andrews, June 9, 1964; David K. Andrews to Alice Bright, June 16, 1964, The Principia, Archives Department, Elsah, Illinois.

[839] David K. Andrews to Hazle Buck Ewing, June 17, 1964, The Principia, Archives Department, Elsah, Illinois.

[840] Eldredge Hamlin to Hazle Buck Ewing, November 19, 1964, The Principia, Archives Department, Elsah, Illinois.

[841] Emeritus Certificate made out to Hazle Buck Ewing, November 14, 1964, Principia College, Elsah, Illinois.

[842] Eldredge Hamlin to Hazle Buck Ewing, November 19, 1964; Eldredge Hamlin, "A Bulletin to the Board of Trustee Members," November 20, 1964, The Principia, Archives Department, Elsah, Illinois.

[843] David K. Andrews to Hazle Buck Ewing, June 8, 1965, The Principia, Archives Department, Elsah, Illinois.

[844] June Bode Ewing to Helen Hamlin, June 17, 1965, The Principia, Archives Department, Elsah, Illinois.

[845] Alice Bright to David K. Andrews, June 17, 1965, The Principia, Archives Department, Elsah, Illinois.

[846] David K. Andrews to Hazle Buck Ewing, October 27, 1965, The Principia, Archives Department, Elsah, Illinois.

[847] Alice Bright to David K. Andrews, February 4, 1966, The Principia, Archives Department, Elsah, Illinois.

[848] David K. Andrews to Hazle Buck Ewing, February 7, 1966, The Principia, Archives Department, Elsah, Illinois.

[849] Ibid., November 20, 1967.

[850] David K. Andrews to Hazle Buck Ewing, January 3, 1968, The Principia, Archives Department, Elsah, Illinois.

[851] David K. Andrews to Kate Lee Ewing, March 4, 1968, The Principia, Archives Department, Elsah, Illinois.

Chapter 37: THE LASTING GREATNESS OF A GOOD LIFE

[852] Personal Interview: Karen Heilbrun with Lucinda Buck Ewing, July 18, 2005; Lloyd M. Bertholf, President, Illinois Wesleyan University, Bloomington, Illinois to Hazle Buck Ewing, May 30, 1963; Hazle Buck Ewing to IllinoisWesleyan University, Bloomington, Illinois, August 23, 1963, Illinois Wesleyan University Archives, Bloomington, Illinois; Kate Lee Ewing to David K. Andrews, February 22, 1968, The Principia, Archives Department, Elsah, Illinois.

[853] "Mrs. Hazle B. Ewing, Philanthropist, Dies," Pantagraph, August 30, 1969, A-2.

[854] "Service Wednesday for Mrs. Hazle B. Ewing," Pantagraph, August 31, 1969, A-3.

[855] "Feeling of Community Strong in Mrs. Ewing," The Daily Pantagraph, September 2, 1969.

[856] Eldredge Hamlin to the Members of the Board of Trustees, September 2, 1969, The Principia, Archives Department, Elsah, Illinois.

[857] Felicia D. Hemans, untitled hymn, Christian Science Hymnal, ©1932, The Mary Baker Eddy Collection, 44.

[858] David K. Andrews, "Service for Hazle B. Ewing," September 3, 1969, The Principia, Archives Department, Elsah, Illinois.

[859] Ibid., 2.

[860] "Ewing Bequests Top $1 Million," Pantagraph, September 6, 1969.

[861] "The Ewing Museum of Nations," The Illinois State University Foundation, Bloomington, Illinois.

[862] "Ewing Manor Cultural Center," Foundation of Illinois State University, Bloomington, Illinois.

[863] "Funk's Grove State Park Plan Gains New Impetus," Pantagraph, (May 19, 1964); "Ewing Bequests Top $1 Million," Pantagraph, September 6, 1969.

[864] David K. Andrews to Ralph Nelson Ewing, September 30, 1969; The Principia, Archives Department, Elsah, Illinois. "Ewing Bequests Top $1 Million," Pantagraph, September 6, 1969.

[865] Alice Bright to David K. Andrews, October 8, 1970, The Principia, Archives Department, Elsah, Illinois.

[866] David K. Andrews to Alice Bright, October 19, 1970, The Principia, Archives Department, Elsah, Illinois.

[867] Alice Bright to David K. Andrews, November 2, 1970; Documentation of meeting held November 30, 1970, at office of Sidley and Austin; Henry Holt to Thomas M. Anderson, Trust Officer, First National Bank of Chicago, Illinois; Henry Holt to Alice Bright, December 4, 1970, The Principia, Archives Department, Elsah, Illinois.

[868] President of Victory Hall Board of Directors, "Centennial Edition," Reaching Out: A Quarterly Publication of the Children's Foundation, Spring 1989.

[869] "Foundation Marks 110 Years," Pantagraph, July 19, 1999, 5.

[870] Evalyn Ames to Kate Lee Ewing, April 24, 1971, letter used by permission of Lucinda Buck Ewing, granddaughter of Hazle Buck Ewing.

INDEX

Ordering Information

To order additional copies of
Hazle Buck Ewing: Promoter of Peace on Earth
and Goodwill toward Men you may:

Email orders:
  orders.shimmeringswan@gmail.com

Postal order:
  Shimmering Swan Creations
  P.O. Box 778
  Aurora, OR 97002-0778, USA.

  Telephone: 503-678-1886

There will be an additional cost for shipping and handling.